Business Forecasting

Business Forecasting

Elmer C. Bratt

Professor of Economics
Lehigh University

1958

McGRAW-HILL BOOK COMPANY, INC.

New York

Toronto

London

Preface

Increasing interest in forecasting highlights the need for a convenient guide to forecasting practices and achievements. This book is intended to provide such a guide.

New conceptions of the management function in private business have accentuated the importance of forecasting. For example, decisions depend more and more on expected sales, whose figures depend on the use of sales budgets, which are in turn based on sales forecasting. Management also applies this method in using cash budgets from which forecasts are made to economize cash funds.

The Federal government has made increasing use of forecasting, especially since the enactment of the Employment Act of 1946, and has given the business community helpful guidance and coordination.

In reality, forecasting is inevitable. Good business decisions are related to future expectations, and any looking to the future means that a forecast is involved, even though conclusions may be based only on past and present information. Using a quick appraisal of the past as an offhand guide means that forecasts are made but not carefully developed.

Improvement in forecasting techniques represents greater care in formulating assumptions and greater attention to the detailed development of their implications, frequently in quantitative form. After all is said and done, the casual forecast may sometimes come closer to the mark than one carefully developed; but on the average we can expect the latter to be more accurate. A check on the adequacy of forecasts points to this conclusion. The evaluation of forecasts is discussed in the final chapter.

A forecast is frequently said to rest on the judgment of the forecaster. His judgment counts most in the assumptions he makes and in the improvisations he uses to show the future conditions the assumptions predispose. Appropriate assumptions that are carefully developed produce the most promising forecasts. The assumptions which can usefully be made vary with the type of forecast required. For this reason separate consideration is given to a number of different forecasts in the text; for example, the distinction between growth and short-term forecasting is illustrated.

I have presented actual forecasts when I thought they would help the reader. Methods can often be most effectively visualized when they are illustrated. In cases of growth, the reader may find that the forecasts stretch into the future. Since I take responsibility for the assumptions made, I believe that they have a reasonable degree of reliability, but it is probable that all forecasts will be improved by the reader's bringing into play current information.

Methodology is of prime importance in forecasting, and I have been concerned about it at every step. Methods used, however, depend upon the assumptions employed, and such methods are most readily grasped when illustrated by the actual forecast. I have been conscious of the reader's need to understand why one particular method has been used; if important alternative methods exist I have tried to explain why they have not been used. Although I have not found it desirable to develop methods in great detail, an attempt has been made to clarify the advantages of those procedures which seem most useful and suitable at the present level of our understanding. This book does not present a handbook of the details of minute mechanics for a limited set of methods.

Cases which describe current business practices dramatize the present uses of forecasting, and I have used them extensively. In studying these cases the reader can trace the assumptions and methods employed and see the ways in which forecasting analysis is applied. Most of the cases are concerned with sales rather than more general forecasting, but they graphically illustrate the direct business application of forecasting.

In writing this book I have used an outline which covers the major areas of business forecasting. These include growth of total industry and individual industries, short-term movements of total industry and individual industries, company sales, and several miscellaneous processes. Two chapters describe those economic indicators which are essential in carrying out forecasting procedures.

In checking the adequacy of forecasts, recent advances in weather analysis have been of great benefit. I have analyzed at some length the performance level of business forecasting as it relates to the new emphasis on the need for it. Since any appraisal of forecasts must be objective to be of value, I have been guided by the fact that the reader's needs will not be fulfilled by efforts to defend or deprecate current practices.

I am grateful for the assistance of so many persons that detailed acknowledgment is impractical. I do wish to give specific thanks to several individuals who read and commented on particular sections of the book. These include Professors Carl L. Moore, Eli Schwartz, John H. Urban, and S. George Walters of Lehigh University; and Dr. Harlow D. Osborne of the National Income Division of the Department of Commerce. My wife contributed by rendering a measure of constant and generous assistance during the various stages of the book's development.

Elmer C. Bratt

Contents

PREFACE   v

CHAPTER 1. The Forecasting Problem   1

2. Measurement of Total Expenditures   8

3. Forecasting the Growth of Total Industry   29

4. Forecasting the Growth of Major Expenditure Divisions   65

5. Forecasting Growth in Particular Industries   94

6. Indicators of Business Conditions   133

7. Short-term Forecasting of Aggregate Industry   157

8. The Commodity Price Forecast   198

9. Short-term Forecasting of Individual Industries   218

10. The Sales Forecast: Methods and Uses   237

11. The Sales Forecast: Company Practices   260

12. Forecasting Various Economic Processes   288

13. Checking the Adequacy of Forecasts   311

BIBLIOGRAPHY   349

INDEX   359

CHAPTER 1

The Forecasting Problem

Forecasts are indispensable in planning. All decisions involve planning, whether it be implicit or explicit. In earlier times relatively more decisions were made extemporaneously as problems arose. Extemporaneous decisions, in common with decisions made with more care, involve future action. They are satisfactory to the extent that future conditions are immediately obvious to the decision makers. Generally, future conditions are not immediately obvious, and to an increasing extent, therefore, explicit forecasts are made.

Forecasts are statements of expected future conditions; definitive statements of what will actually happen are patently impossible. Expectations depend upon the assumptions made. If the assumptions are plausible, the forecast has a better chance of being useful. As shown in the following chapters, much of the work on forecasting analysis in recent years has proceeded from careful statements of the assumptions to be employed. When the underlying assumptions are spelled out in some detail, the plausibility of forecasts can be more readily judged.

In order to make quantitative forecasts, mechanical methods must be formulated for drawing reliable conclusions from established assumptions. Methodology varies in accordance with the assumptions, the available information, and the ingenuity of the forecaster. Primary attention throughout this book is given to techniques employed in forecasting.

Forecasting assumptions and techniques vary with the kind of planning needed. The rapid strides made in planning in recent years are largely responsible for the increasing attention given to business forecasting. Decisions have become increasingly varied, so that diverse types of planning are required. Major needs for business forecasting can be identified, however, with two broad types of planning: for requirements growing out of short-term and out of long-term changes in demand. Short-term changes in demand are the more pressing, and major attention has been given to them.

1

Increasing interest is being displayed in long-term forecasting because it provides a rational basis for planning commitments for durable goods. The future requirement for durable goods must be estimated from expected demand for their services. Long-term forecasts develop a type of average expectation under stated assumptions. Such an expectation may be said to represent the growth potentiality. In modern forecasting the assumptions made are usually closely related to conditions of full employment or some approach thereto.

LONG-TERM FORECASTING BY GOVERNMENT

Forecasts of the demand for services of durable goods are needed by public bodies and by private business. Public bodies frequently must make decisions regarding various types of installations, notably, waterworks and other public utilities, roads, and streets. These decisions may be reflected in budget estimates, and certainly the administration is going to be held accountable if the expenditure for installations falls substantially short of demand or grossly exceeds it. Frequently, makeshift adjustments from year to year produce quite unsatisfactory results in the absence of careful estimates of long-term requirements. The wrong-size power plant or pipeline, for instance, may prove expensive in future years.

Public responsibility to conserve natural resources calls for some understanding of the need for resources in the future as established by future demand for them. Therefore an intelligent resource policy must rest partly on forecasts of the demand. It was with this thought in mind that the President's Materials Policy Commission in 1952 made forecasts of various raw-material needs to 1975.[1]

Knowledge of the requirements for growth will lend substantial reassurance in the practice of fiscal policy. Current action to curtail or expand public construction can be most intelligently taken in the light of potential needs. If the needs are envisioned to be so great that no conceivable speeding up in depression would exhaust them, curtailment of public construction in prosperity would be called for only to the extent that new inflationary pressures should be avoided. If, on the other hand, forecasting indicates that potential needs are limited, care would be required to avoid exhausting useful projects in prosperity. The cost of delaying public works is clarified by forecasting.

An understanding of the expected demand for durable goods of various sorts gives public bodies a basis upon which to encourage private

---

[1] See *Resources for Freedom* (Washington: President's Materials Policy Commission, June, 1952), frequently called the "Paley Report." Forecasting material is scattered through the five volumes of the report.

industry to sight on workable goals, and thus enables them to provide leadership rather than blindly follow evanescent indications of current markets in the private economy. Frequently, private industry needs all the encouragement it can get in order to visualize the future in true perspective. The functions of government are generally accepted to include at least some degree of responsibility with regard to industrial leadership, as is surely indicated by the Employment Act of 1946.

Public bodies also frequently need forecasts of the demand for durable equipment and structures in order to provide more judicious control, although it must be admitted that even now many public bodies fail to recognize this need. For instance, in the late thirties the Interstate Commerce Commission reached unfavorable decisions regarding the value of many junior railroad securities by looking to the low level of railroad traffic of the thirties and ruling against giving any consideration to expected future levels of traffic. Railroad stocks thus declared worthless failed to give the owners the equity that true potentialities would frequently have accorded them.[2]

LONG-TERM FORECASTING BY PRIVATE BUSINESS

When orders are placed on the books, it is a costly mistake to have too much or too little capacity. With too much capacity, operations must proceed at uneconomically low rates. If capacity is too limited, some orders cannot be filled, and a very high rate of operation increases the per-unit cost. Of course, no businessman can expect to attain a capacity which is precisely commensurate with his order books at all times. What he can rationally hope for is a capacity which will satisfy most of the demand when times are good and which will not be bankrupting, because of idle plants, in less prosperous periods. To achieve these conditions he must know something about the long-term demand for his products. Satisfactory knowledge of long-term demand would lead him to point his capacity at levels which would not fall far short of peak demands and which would be out of relation to current demand only in depressed conditions arising from a temporary restriction in ordering.

As troublesome as the problem of too much or too little aggregate capacity is the problem of its distribution. If capacity is specialized and not readily convertible to different kinds of products, the appropriate level of aggregate capacity may become unprofitable because it is concentrated in the wrong products. A knowledge of the growth po-

[2] The Interstate Commerce Commission's decisions were founded on the absolute priority rule and on the major emphasis placed on earnings of the recent past. The cases are widely discussed in the literature. See, for instance, Harry G. Guthman and Herbert E. Dougall, *Corporate Financial Policy* (Englewood Cliffs, N.J.: Prentice-Hall, Inc., 1955).

tentialities of various types of products will help keep the distribution of capacity adjusted to the distribution of demand. If a company attains a better comprehension than its competitors of the growth potentiality of aggregate demand and of the distribution of the demand, the company's competitive position will be substantially enhanced.

Knowledge of growth potentialities will help keep down the cost of capacity, for such knowledge will make it possible to adopt the expedient of allocating increased expenditures to expansion in periods when costs are relatively low. In contrast, when current demand is relied upon as an indicator of expansion needs, capital building tends to be concentrated in periods when current demand and costs are relatively high. In addition, companies which take advantage of low costs when demand is low will be contributing significantly to the stabilization of the economy, for one of the principal deficiencies in demand during depressed periods is inadequate expenditure on capital building.

Improved knowledge of growth potentialities should be of some aid in developing sound labor relations. Labor will hold management in greater respect if convinced that management has an enlightened understanding of the growth of demand. Industrial objectives can be more intelligently stated. Added capital building in depressed periods will expand employment in trying times. If competitive positions are improved, labor demands ordinarily can be more readily met.

The above comments relate to the advantages which might be gained from accurate growth forecasting. No assumptions are made regarding the adequacy of past forecasting and the degree of accuracy which may be expected in the future. These questions are given detailed consideration in later parts of this book. The need for growth forecasting is so great that its use will be rewarding unless complete inaccuracy is to be expected.

SHORT-TERM FORECASTING BY GOVERNMENT

There is a great need not only for forecasting long-term potentialities but also for forecasting near-future developments. In short-term forecasting, as contrasted with long-term, indications of *actual* future levels are sought rather than an *average* expectation. In facing the immediate future, we must look toward the actual level of activity expected even though it may appear to be quite transitory.

Much attention has been given to the need for short-term forecasting by public bodies in carrying out fiscal and monetary policy. Control action must look not to the present and the past but to the future in which its effects will be felt. Costly mistakes may be made if control action is taken solely on the basis of present levels of activity. For instance, in the fall of 1954, many persons called for positive inflationary action to assure adequate levels of activity in 1955;[3] such action would have resulted in serious harm since activity rose to high levels without the introduction of inflationary measures.

Even if the policy were not to guide current changes in economic activity, some knowledge of the short-term trend would be helpful. We can at least hope that government will not be a major interference, as would happen, for instance, if large deficits occurred in peak prosperity or large surpluses occurred in deep depression. Even without planned control, any government wishes to avoid action which would appear foolish in retrospect. Forecasting is required because action taken today will influence business activity tomorrow regardless of conscious intent.

In addition to actions implementing fiscal policy and monetary control, intelligent debt management is partially dependent upon near-future business conditions. The rates to be charged on government securities should take into consideration the tightness of the money market shortly after flotation, when the market must absorb a substantial portion of the securities. Again, the success of efforts to shift the proportion of outstanding debt in long- or short-term securities will be dependent to a large extent on the level of business conditions which follows the decision. Either short-term or long-term flotations may be chosen, within limits; a decision in favor of one or the other may create increasing pressure to take the opposite course in the near future. Long-term issues can be more advantageously chosen if the near future is expected to bring high levels of activity.

Alongside long-term forecasting, short-term public forecasts are needed to aid and influence private business. Public bodies can afford to give much more attention than private business to changes in the aggregate economic situation. Sales forecasting by business must be sighted narrowly on conditions in particular markets, but forecasts of changes in conditions in the broader economy would often be very helpful to the individual businessman. Without the forecasting studies made by public research bodies, forecasts of the broad market would be unavailable to many companies. The forecasts may provide reassurance at critical times and may circumvent some of the dangers of false hopes when the overall prospects are poor, for the markets in individual industries are closely related to the conditions in total industry. Particularly, aggregate forecasts may guide companies in following a sounder inventory policy, one which is less subject to rapid reversal.

[3] See, for instance, Arthur R. Upgren, "Policies for Economic Expansion," *Michigan Business Review*, 7:34–37, 1955.

SHORT-TERM FORECASTING BY PRIVATE BUSINESS

In most types of private business a knowledge of near-future conditions is essential to the development of an effective inventory policy. Today's decisions determine tomorrow's inventories. If tomorrow's sales are implicitly assumed to equal those prevailing today and inventory levels have been appropriate and about constant, production schedules should remain unchanged. The outcome, however, would be unfortunate if the level of sales were to change greatly: a rapid increase in sales would result in an undesirable runoff in inventories, and a rapid decrease in sales would result in an undesirable inventory accumulation.

It is clear that production schedules should be geared to expected, rather than to actual, sales. There are many striking illustrations of the unhappy outcome which may result from uncritically anticipating a continuation of prevailing conditions. For example, in 1937 and again in 1949 many textile companies were faced with the necessity for a rapid curtailment of operations when retailers made drastic reductions in their inventories.[4] It is possibly even more serious to assume that a continuation of such rapid curtailment is needed or that inventory accumulation, once begun, should be continued with rising sales. An understanding of near-future prospects would make it possible to avoid some of the rapid vacillations which often occur in production scheduling.

The most important decisions on inventory levels are dependent upon expected sales. Nevertheless, there are times when expected price changes must be given independent consideration. For instance, if prices are expected to rise, as is likely with expanding sales, some businessmen will try to take advantage of the rise by earlier buying. Although such decisions frequently become self-defeating, they do represent a use to which forecasts are sometimes put. For the past thirty-five years most businessmen have resisted the temptation to rely heavily on expected price changes in formulating buying policies. Typically, businessmen will frankly tell you that they buy to service sales, not to speculate on price changes.

More important for businessmen is the need to know the future level of sales in setting their own administered prices. The raising of prices is avoided when near-future markets are not expected to be strong, and the lowering of prices is avoided when costs or sales levels are likely

---

[4] See, for instance, Robert P. Ulin, "1950 Production: More Sustained than in 1949," *Textile World*, February, 1950. The executives of many of the large textile companies, on their own testimony, "fly by the seats of their pants." In January, 1938, several officials in the industry assured the writer that, in spite of strenuous efforts to get operating schedules into line the preceding fall, inventories built up at their plants.

to rise materially. Future market conditions are thus of major importance in setting administered prices.

Many companies find it advantageous to set sales targets for the purposes of establishing controls and providing incentives. But sales targets will accomplish no such purposes unless they are realistically geared to the sales levels which will eventuate. If the targets are too low, they will be too easily met to provide any incentive or control, and if too high, they will be discouraging. A sales target may be of little value and even detrimental if not geared approximately to future sales levels.

The amount of cash required depends upon the level of operations and the level of sales, so that an intelligent financial plan necessitates forecasting. Some advance notice is usually needed to obtain additional funds on the best terms or to limit the funds held idle. It is to be noted that production scheduling poorly geared to prospective sales levels will complicate financial planning. If undesired inventory accumulation is induced, cash requirements will be unduly increased; if inventories are unintentionally run off, idle cash will be increased at the expense of inventories.

The most effective time to start expansion projects is at the beginning of a long rise in sales. Short-term forecasting cannot be expected to be of substantial aid in predicting the length of the rise, but it should help to spot the time when sales will begin to rise.

Short-term forecasting is needed in budget making. A budget set for the following year will be much more useful if geared to sales levels which will eventuate rather than merely to current sales levels. A budget distributed according to current sales levels may establish policy as to lines of emphasis, but will obviously require successive adjustments if sales levels change. The effectiveness of such successive adjustment is limited because a changed level of sales is likely to necessitate a relative shift in cost and expenditure distributions.

Sales and cash budgets have experienced increasing development through the use of sales forecasts. This has led to revolutionary developments in management controls, as explained in Chapter 11.

FORECASTING NEED AND FORECASTING ABILITY

The main purpose of this book is to describe forecasting methods and to appraise the rational bases on which they are founded. Forecasting work can be placed in true perspective only by an appraisal of the adequacy of its results. That the need for forecasting has led to many ingenious efforts to produce forecasts is well known. These efforts have not been wholly successful. An appraisal is made in the final chapter.

CHAPTER 2

Measurement of Total Expenditures

The two following chapters are concerned with forecasting the growth of total industry and major types of expenditures which add up to the total. To facilitate the analysis we present here a brief statement on the standard measurements. These are measurements of "final" expenditure in the sense that the product counted is not resold in the year, or other time period, to which the measurement refers. Included are expenditures made by consumers for goods and services for personal use, expenditures by business for investments which increase total assets, and expenditures made by government which may be considered to be consumed in the combined interest of the total residents of the country. Summing the expenditures in these classifications provides an effective measure of total expenditure.

The development of a comprehensive measure involves many detailed problems, most of which are too technical to be analyzed here.[1] These relate principally to the procedures employed to obtain figures which will add up to a consistent total. In the over-all procedural pattern, receipts from final sales are balanced against the distributed use of the funds obtained, as illustrated in Table 2–1. The complexity of the economy is so great that some special adjustments are made to market figures, but the adjustments are of relatively minor importance.[2]

The total-expenditure figure most frequently employed follows the above description and is called "gross national product." Its movement

[1] The data generally used are the estimates made by the Department of Commerce. They are reported currently on annual and quarterly bases. The technicalities of developing the estimates are discussed in a basebook supplement; the most recent was issued in 1954. See *National Income: A Supplement to the Survey of Current Business* (Washington: U.S. Department of Commerce, 1954). Yearly data are brought up to date in the July issue of the *Survey of Current Business*. A new issue of the supplement probably will appear in 1958 or 1959 and can be expected to include revisions which will change previously reported figures to a minor extent.

[2] Most important are imputations for services which do not flow through the business economy. For instance, nearly $20 billion of gross rent for owner-occupied houses is included in the gross-national-product estimate for 1955.

8

TABLE 2–1

INCOME AND PRODUCT ACCOUNT, 1955

(In billions of dollars)

Employee compensation	223.0	Personal consumption expenditures	254.4
Unincorporated enterprise income.	39.2	Gross private domestic investment.	60.6
Rental income of persons	10.2	Government purchases of goods and	
Corporate profits	40.7	services	77.1
Personal interest income from private sources	10.9	Net foreign investment	−0.4
Business transfer payments	1.3		
Indirect business taxes	32.7		
Capital-consumption allowances	31.6		
Total	389.8		
Less: subsidies minus current surplus of government enterprises	0.2		
Statistical discrepancy	2.1		
Gross national product	391.7	Gross national product	391.7

SOURCE: *Survey of Current Business*, July, 1957.

is shown in Chart 2–1. Product and expenditure, used in this sense, are the same because final sales represent the ultimate output, or product, of the economy. The total is called "gross" because it includes expenditures made to replace durable capital. Net product can be estimated by subtracting the amount of expenditures for capital replacement, but the difference between new and replacement expenditure is vague.[3] To the extent that investment does no more than keep capital intact it represents a replacement rather than an increase in assets. Except for capital replacement, gross national product is composed of net expenditures.

Notably, so-called "intermediate expenditures" are omitted. These represent production expenditures made in the process of preparing the product for market. For instance, automobile manufacturers usually buy some component parts from other manufacturers. These become an integral part of the assembled automobile, and only the consumer's expenditure for the completed automobile is included in gross national product.

Furthermore, there are many expenditures made in the economy which are unrelated to buying the product of the current period. A major example is the sale of already existing assets. Sale of an old house or of a stock certificate involves expenditure which is unrelated to current

[3] The best available estimate of replacement is derived from capital-consumption allowances set up by operating accounting systems, adjusted to a minimum extent by the Department of Commerce to conform to established concepts. Principally, the adjustment makes allowance for capital outlays charged to current expense.

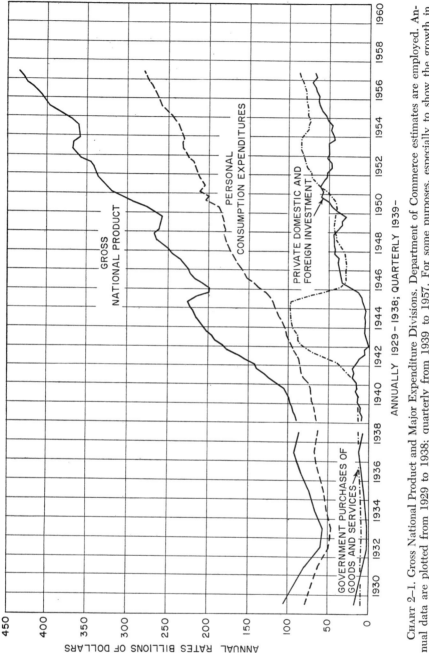

CHART 2–1. Gross National Product and Major Expenditure Divisions. Department of Commerce estimates are employed. Annual data are plotted from 1929 to 1938; quarterly from 1939 to 1957. For some purposes, especially to show the growth in physical output, constant dollar figures are preferable. The *Federal Reserve Chart Book* shows a chart on that basis. SOURCE: *Federal Reserve Chart Book on Financial and Business Statistics* (Wash.: Board of Governors, Federal Reserve System, 1957).

10

activity. Only the cost of making such sales is properly included in gross national product.

Government transfer and interest payments are not reflected in gross national product because they are not payments for product. Transfer payments represent benefits paid from social security funds and direct relief. Government interest payments do not represent economic return from current use of capital, as in the private economy, but mainly service payments on the war debt. Although government transfer and interest payments are not considered part of gross national product, measurements are supplied and are considered to be a part of disposable income, as noted below.

Data representing gross national product and income payments are usually those developed by the Department of Commerce. No other series are kept up to date quarterly and annually. The Commerce data are extensively reproduced in various publications, and minor disparities frequently appear because the data are published before the most recent revisions are released. Improved information leads to periodic revisions for some time after the data first become available. Less frequently, conceptual changes lead to revisions.

The advantage of data on gross national product and the distributed use of funds, as shown in Table 2–1, is that they provide measurements of the total expenditure and income which support any given level of business activity. The totals break down into component parts of total activity, and each part is counted only once. Other than for income and product aggregates, double counting of certain types of activity, notably in readily recorded basic industry, has been troublesome in measuring total economic activity.

CONTRASTING COMPANY INCOME STATEMENTS

Table 2–1 is similar to the familiar company income statement. Sales may appear on the right-hand side of the company statement, as they do in the much more inclusive expenditure aggregates shown in Table 2–1. Allocation of funds made available by sales of the private company may be shown on the left-hand side, just as they are in the inclusive income and product account. The income and product account represents a consolidation of the income and product of all private companies and other economic activity which can be put on the same *pro forma* basis, with all duplications eliminated.

The purposes of the company income statement and the income and product account are not the same, however. The company income statement is principally concerned with deriving an estimate of profit achieved. In the income and product account, profit is just one of the allocations to income. The income and product account shows the various types of expenditure which provide funds and the allocation of the funds to various types of income and non-income charges. Capital consumption allowances are the most important type of non-income charges. The company income accounts show similar distributions, although payments made to other companies cancel out in the national income and product account.

PERSONAL CONSUMPTION EXPENDITURES

In forecasting analysis the various expenditure and income streams are useful in getting a line on changes expected to occur in economic activity. Background on each type of expenditure and income is helpful.

Personal consumption accounts for about 65 per cent of total expenditures, as indicated in Table 2–1. The percentage is somewhat higher in less prosperous times because most consumer expenditures are more stable than other expenditure streams, and thus they become relatively more important when the total level of expenditure recedes.

Personal consumption expenditures are divided into durable goods, nondurable goods, and services. Durable goods, comprising automobiles, household appliances, and furniture, account for less than a sixth of the total and experience more variation than the other types of consumer expenditure. Nondurable commodities, such as food, clothing, and gasoline, represent about half of the total. Services, such as medical care, rent, and public transportation, represent more than a third. Expenditures for services, on the whole, are very stable. Recently they have shown no decline in recessions, partly because of lagging price increases which have continued to occur during recessions. As included in the product measurement of the Department of Commerce, expenditure for new houses is considered investment rather than personal consumption.

Certain imputed expenditures are added to several categories of market expenditure to bring the categories to a level more representative of actual consumption. An estimate is made of the cost which would be incurred if food produced and consumed on farms and food furnished free in the military service and to domestic servants and nurses had to be purchased. Rent is imputed for owner-occupied houses to bring the total house-rent aggregate up to a more representative level. Free service furnished by banks and other financial institutions is put on an estimated cost basis so that the actual wages and other income received in these institutions can be appropriately allocated.[4]

---

[4] The interest income received by financial institutions is allocated to individuals receiving free service; only interest income accruing to individuals can be included as personal income.

From figures which are available it is possible to reconstitute income and product accounts so that imputed items are eliminated. It is sometimes advisable to do so, because questions of particular interest in forecasting relate to changes taking place in market transactions.

Illegal expenditures are not included in the Department of Commerce figures, even though they may sometimes amount to a considerable sum, as was true of alcoholic-beverage expenditures in the prohibition era. The Twentieth Century Fund found it desirable to estimate these expenditures in order to get a more representative picture.[5] The Department of Commerce does take care to include legal betting expenditures; pari-mutuel receipts of nearly $400 million are included for 1955.

Nonprofit corporations, such as religious organizations, social and athletic clubs, labor organizations, private schools and hospitals, and charitable and welfare organizations, are consolidated with individuals by the Department of Commerce in estimating personal income and expenditures. This means that individual payments to these institutions are not included when duplicative of included wage and other payments made by nonprofit corporations; in effect, the consumer is looked on as paying directly the outlays of these corporations.

Furthermore, when individuals hire others as domestic servants, the wages paid are included in consumer expenditures. The total wages paid by households and nonprofit corporations included in consumption expenditures in 1955 came to more than $12 billion. This does not represent a serious distortion, for, in general, one would wish to say that consumers paid these wages or provided funds which paid them. One should not forget, however, that the wages paid are in turn largely spent, by the consumers receiving them, on goods and services included in consumption expenditures. The picture would be clarified somewhat if nonprofit institutions could be treated separately.

GROSS PRIVATE DOMESTIC INVESTMENT

The second expenditure category shown in Table 2–1 is gross private domestic investment. It includes private expenditures for producers' durable equipment, for residential building and all other construction, and for changes in business inventories.

Private purchases of producers' durable equipment are estimated at $24 billion in 1955. Some of the items included are business furniture, hand tools, engines, tractors, electrical and mechanical machinery, commercial passenger cars, trucks, aircraft, railroad equipment, ships, and

---

[5] Alcoholic-beverage expenditures are estimated at $2 billion in 1929. See J. Frederic Dewhurst and Associates, *America's Needs and Resources: A New Survey* (New York: The Twentieth Century Fund, Inc., 1955), pp. 965 ff. No estimate has been made for sales of bootleg liquor in recent years.

boats. The estimates are by type of equipment and not by type of industry purchasing the equipment. It is generally believed that the current high level of equipment purchases is related to rapid technological improvement and arises partly from a rapid rate of obsolescence. Government purchases of durable equipment are included in government purchases of goods rather than in investment.

Private residential building includes expenditures for new dwelling units, for additions to, and alterations of, existing units, and expenditures for nonhousekeeping units (transient hotels, motor courts, tourist cabins, vacation cottages, and dormitories). In 1955 residential building came to more than $17 billion and was greater than all other private construction. Private housing is included in investment, whether it is initiated by a contractor or by an individual building for himself. Public housing is included in government expenditures for goods.

Other private construction includes industrial and commercial building; social and recreational types, comprising religious, educational, and medical facilities; public-utility building; farm construction; petroleum and natural gas well drilling; and a small miscellaneous group comprising such nonstructural items as parks and playgrounds, sewer and water systems, roads, and bridges. Expenditures for construction generally are planned well into the future and usually react less quickly to changes in total business activity than expenditures for equipment. Long lead times are the rule, and construction under way may have been planned years before. Public construction is included under government purchases of goods.

Repair and maintenance of construction is expensed and is not included as a part of investment. Being treated as a cost rather than as final product, it is not counted in gross national product. However, it is one kind of expense which may play a vital part in total activity, for it can be speeded up or delayed to a substantial extent when expedient. Measurements of repair and maintenance are very poor at the present time and, in practice, may not always be well segregated from measurements of new construction expenditure. Officially expenditures on repair and maintenance have been estimated at more than $15 billion in 1955 and nearly $17 billion in 1956, but these may well be underestimates.[6]

A widely used measure of plant and equipment expenditures is derived from a quarterly survey conducted cooperatively by the Department of Commerce and the Securities and Exchange Commission.[7] These expenditures are classified by manufacturing, mining, railroad, other

[6] *Construction Review,* October, 1957, p. 6.

[7] The data are reported currently in the *Survey of Current Business* and in current releases on business-capital expenditures by the Securities and Exchange Commission.

transportation, public utilities, and commercial and other industries. The survey has not made available equipment expenditures separate from construction. The survey is not as inclusive as the construction- and equipment-expenditure components of gross national product. Omitted are expenditures by farmers, professionals, and institutions, all of residential housing, petroleum and natural gas well drilling, and capital expenditures charged to current expense (notably, hand tools). In spite of the differences in content, the survey provides a useful series because of the industry breakdown made. Also, for short-term forecasting, the survey of business-investment plans made in connection with the collection of these data is of major importance.[8]

Change in business inventories is the final component of gross domestic investment. It is highly variable, for inventory stocks rise and fall rapidly to accommodate to current conditions. To a significant extent inventory movements are related to changes in the sales the inventory services. If sales increase 10 per cent, this may mean a need for an increase of about 10 per cent in inventory stock, whereas if they increase only 5 per cent, the need may be for an increase of about 5 per cent in inventory stock. The increase in inventories is only half as much in the second case. When sales decrease, inventory stock may be pared, representing a decrease in inventory investment. In fact, inventory investment is so variable that its decrease accounts for a large part of the decline in gross national product in minor recessions.

The level of most nonfarm business inventories (stocks) is currently reported by the Department of Commerce [9] in connection with an industry survey. Manufacturing, wholesale, and retail groups are shown separately. The manufacturing group is broken down into purchased materials, goods-in-process, and finished goods, a very useful classification for forecasting, because differing implications regarding intended and unintended inventory increases can be drawn for these categories. Further breakdowns within manufacturing, retail, and wholesale trades are provided and are helpful in locating the points at which inventory change is occurring.

Change in business inventories as an investment component of gross national product is stated in current prices by the Department of Commerce. For nonfarm inventory investment, which must be taken from change in value of inventory stocks, a special adjustment is required. The problem is most complex when inventories are carried on company books in accordance with the common rule of cost-or-market-whichever-is-lower. When prices are rising, an item will typically be charged out

[8] This survey, as well as one made by the McGraw-Hill Department of Economics, is discussed more fully in Chap. 6.

[9] Reported in the *Survey of Current Business* and in mimeographed releases entitled *Industry Survey*.

of inventory stock at a price less than is current, and items will be added to the inventory stock at current prices. The increase in inventory stock will reflect differences in the prices at which inventories are added to and withdrawn from inventory stock as well as reflect any physical change which may have occurred in the amount of inventory in stock. What is desired is change in physical stock of inventory valued at current prices. Adjustment to put inventory change on that basis is achieved by index numbers showing the change in price valuation of inventories in stock. We do not need to go into the technicalities of making that adjustment. It is called "inventory valuation adjustment" and typically indicates that change in inventories at current prices is less than shown by the increase in dollar value of inventory stocks when prices are rising. In watching changes in the value of inventory stocks carried by the *Industry Survey* this fact must be kept in mind.

Farm inventories are computed on the basis of physical change in inventory stock and thus do not require the application of an inventory valuation adjustment. Estimates of farm inventories are very poor, however, because of the paucity of information on the current stocks of farm products held on farms. Also, the movement of farm inventories is not clearly related to other business inventories. For these reasons, change in nonfarm business inventories, which are more dependent on business prospects, is a better business indicator than change in total business inventories.

GOVERNMENT PURCHASES OF GOODS AND SERVICES

The government-expenditure component of gross national product comprises payment of wages and salaries and purchases from business and from abroad. In 1955 about 44 per cent was paid in wages and salaries and about 56 per cent in goods purchased. The total government spending was much greater than the $77 billion paid for these purposes; by the amount of $16 billion in transfer payments and $5 billion in net interest payments. Only product expenditures may be included as a part of the gross national product.

Of the $43 billion purchased from business and abroad in 1955, $12 billion was spent for construction. This is included as government expenditure rather than as investment in the Department of Commerce product account. Construction by the government is paid for out of taxes and not out of savings as in private investment. A change in concepts and statistical procedures would be required to handle durable government installations as investment.[10] The government also buys producers' equipment, but no estimate of the amount is available.

[10] Harlow D. Osborne, of the Department of Commerce, points out that the conceptual problem might not be too difficult in the case of construction, but that

In 1955 the Federal government accounted for over 60 per cent of government purchases of goods and services, with state and local governments accounting for less than 40 per cent. This is a marked shift from the situation existing before the Great Depression. In 1929 the Federal government accounted for only about 15 per cent. The change is principally due to the growth of national-security expenditures by the Federal government. These represented more than half of the total of all government expenditures for goods and services in 1955.

The recognition of the movement of government expenditures is particularly important because these expenditures are motivated by factors substantially different from the governing factors in the private economy. Furthermore, fiscal-policy planning may involve deliberate attempts to generate inverse expenditure movements.

In figuring the amount of Federal expenditures for goods and services, the relatively small amount of surplus goods sold by the government is subtracted. Such sales amounted to $0.4 billion in 1955. The addition to the civilian supply of goods reduces demand for business output.

NET FOREIGN INVESTMENT

The final subdivision shown in Table 2–1 is net foreign investment. It reflects our market with the rest of the world. Compared with most countries, it is indeed relatively small. There is another difference. A predominant influence in our relations with the rest of the world is our foreign-aid contribution. This amounted to $4.5 billion in 1955, which is added to the $−0.4 billion shown in Table 2–1 to develop an export surplus of more than $4 billion; foreign aid is added to foreign purchases to make the accounts balance, as the accounts are now set up.[11] Adjustment of the export surplus is necessary to obtain a figure for net foreign investment; aid and gifts reduce the amount of our increase in ownership.

For many purposes the export surplus is more important than net foreign investment, since it gives a better picture of the balance between the goods and services we are sending abroad and receiving from abroad. For this purpose an even more desirable figure is the export surplus of goods and services, with net investment income subtracted. Each of the figures is important for particular purposes. Net foreign

---

many producer durables bought by the government, such as aircraft carriers, are unlike private investment.

[11] Additionally, $0.2 billion of net personal remittances to foreign countries is added in as part of personal consumption expenditures. Allowing for this and subtracting $2.7 billion net earnings received on United States investment abroad, a net export of $1.5 billion on goods and services is developed.

investment plus foreign aid and personal remittances equals the export surplus; subtracting net investment income received from abroad, we obtain the export surplus on goods and services.

CORRECTION FOR PRICE CHANGES

For total gross national product and each of the expenditure divisions, comparable price indices are computed. By dividing these price indices into the current dollar totals in each time period, a reasonable approximation of physical changes is represented. Currently the physical changes are expressed in terms of 1954 dollars. So expressed, gross national product rises from the prewar level less than half as much as shown in Chart 2–1.

The corrected result is very useful, for it provides an approximation of changes in product abstracted from price changes. The price deflation is not perfect, because estimated price changes are not wholly accurate. Part of the change in product is a change in quality, and available information on prices does not fully reflect this change. Over the short period, figures on deflated product tend toward overstatement, because recorded prices usually understate short-term price changes. Part of price adjustment is represented by premiums, discounts, extras, and other factors which do not always get recorded in market-price figures. However, short-term adjustments missed in market prices tend to average out in the long run, and deflated figures are most useful in long-run forecasting.

In the short term, actual dollar-value changes are as important as deflated figures. As pointed out in Chapter 7, it is most useful to make initial short-term projections of actual dollar-value figures.

PERSONAL INCOME

Product expenditures provide funds for income and non-income charges, as shown on the left-hand side of Table 2–1. Employee compensation, consisting of wages and salaries and supplements thereto (principally, employer contributions for social insurance and private pension funds), represents 60 per cent of the total.

Income of unincorporated enterprises represents around 10 per cent and is composed of profits and wages of management in noncorporate business; about three-fourths is earned by general business and professional enterprises and the rest by farmers. Corporate profits account for another 10 per cent in a prosperous period but for considerably less in a depression. They were negative in 1932 and 1933. At the present time about half of corporate profits is absorbed by income taxes, about a fourth by dividends, and a fourth by undistributed profits. The aggregates shown for income of unincorporated enterprises and corporate profits may poorly reflect changing conditions when there is a shifting balance between companies achieving a profit and those experiencing a loss. Separate information on profitable and unprofitable companies would be helpful.

Rental income represents a property return received by persons. Rent received by companies is not included because it is a company receipt rather than personal income; individuals are affected by the extent to which such rent payments influence profit levels. Interest received by persons is another income allocation. Interest received by business, like rent, does not become an income allocation. Its influence on national income is reflected in the profits made by the companies receiving it. These two types of property income amount to about 5 per cent of total product.

The income included in Table 2–1 is national income because it is entirely the allocation of product expenditures. Persons do not currently receive all of it, notably, undistributed corporate profits; and they receive income not related to product transactions, including government interest and transfer payments. The actual income received is given primary consideration in forecasting; it is considered later in the chapter.

NON-INCOME CHARGES

The principal non-income charges are indirect business taxes and capital-consumption allowances. Each absorbs about a twelfth of the total funds provided by product expenditures. Since capital-consumption charges do not vary a great deal, even with fluctuations in business activity, they represent an important part of gross savings. Replacements are not made with as great regularity. Business transfer payments, such as corporate gifts and bad debts, create disposable income, but they are classified as non-income charges for they are not in payment for productive activity.

As shown in Table 2–1, the income and non-income charges so far noted nearly equal gross national product. Subsidies minus profits of government enterprises is a small remaining allocation. Subsidies add to income payments, but they do not add to product; as funds furnished rather than funds earned in the market, they must be subtracted to get a balance with the product figure. Profits of government enterprises are called "current surplus of government enterprises" and are similar to the profit allocation of private companies. Putting these two unlike items in one undistributed allocation is awkward, but the difference between profit and subsidy is not always clear in government enterprises. For instance, payments by the Post Office for air-mail contracts included for a time an element of subsidy.

The expenditure figures shown in Table 2–1 are estimated separately from the allocations which they are balanced against. The difference between the estimates in 1955 is an understatement of $2.1 billion for income and non-income charges or an overstatement for expenditures— whichever way one wishes to view it. The difference is labeled "statistical discrepancy." If the estimates are independent, regardless of how thorough they may be, a discrepancy between them is likely to be found in so comprehensive a task.

SAVING AND INVESTMENT PROCESS AS REFLECTED IN THE PRODUCT ACCOUNTS

Certain parts of income payments are destined for use in investment expenditures. This is important in forecasting because failure of adjustment between saving and planned investment is a highly disturbing factor in the economy. Unfortunately, a direct measurement cannot be taken from income and product accounts, for these accounts measure what has happened rather than what is anticipated. As a matter of past history, saving must come to the amount spent for investment, for saving is equal to the increase in our assets. Although measurements of disturbing differences between savings and planned investment are not available, some clues can be developed from information on income accounts by segregating savings. Information of this sort is not significant in long-term forecasting, but it is useful in short-term forecasting.

The parts of income payments destined for investment expenditures in 1955 can be identified as follows (stated in billions of dollars):

Personal savings	15.7
Undistributed corporate profits	9.9
Capital-consumption allowances	31.6
Federal government surplus	3.6
State and local government deficit	−1.0
Corporate inventory valuation adjustment	−1.7
Plus understatement *	2.1
Gross investment	60.2
Less net foreign investment	−0.4
Gross private domestic investment	60.6

* This is called "statistical discrepancy" in the literature and is accounted for by the fact that income and product figures are derived from different sources.

It will be seen that personal savings represent only about a fourth of the total, a fact overlooked when change in total savings is assumed to depend principally on action of individuals. Furthermore, savings of unincorporated enterprises are included with the personal-savings figure.[12] A substantial part of personal savings is contractual, such as life insurance premiums, and therefore little open to shifting decisions. Variation in noncontractual savings does occur, however, and it is not always correlated with changing investment decisions. For instance, when individuals lay more aside because of partial saturation in important lines of consumer durables, there is no assurance that businessmen will plan to increase investment outlays and thus absorb the additional savings in expenditures. The timing of expanded investment in the automobile industry in 1956 with shrinking automobile demand, for instance, would seem to be an exceptional case.

Undistributed profits are coordinated with investment expenditure in many cases, but not universally. The extent to which undistributed profits are promptly spent on investment varies from one time to another, depending on the level of investment expenditures, the difficulty of obtaining funds on the market, and the possibility of tax penalties under the laws of a particular time. Near a downturn an increased proportion of earnings is frequently paid out in dividends as the need for investment expenditure declines; similarly, the earning proportion paid in dividends may shrink when investment expenditures are rising rapidly in expansion.

Replacement expenditures sometimes exceed and sometimes fall short of capital-consumption allowances. In a depressed period, when the outlook is uncertain, the spending of such allowances is frequently delayed, whereas in early expansion, replacement expenditures may substantially exceed current allowances made available.

The degree to which government surpluses are timed with investment expenditures depends on the fiscal policy followed. Government expenditures might be held down in prosperity when investment expenditures are high. Government expenditures relative to government receipts might be held high in depression when private investment is low in order to produce deficits to cancel the effect of large planned savings in the private economy.

Neither inventory valuation adjustment nor the statistical discrepancy affect the actual balance between savings and investment. The inventory investment recorded on the books of companies is adjusted for inventory valuation in order to get a truer picture of the product change occurring, necessitating a similar adjustment in the allocation of funds. The "understatement," known as a statistical discrepancy in the literature, merely records the amount of difference in independent estimates of product expenditures and of total allocation of funds.

[12] This point is developed more fully below, in the section on relation between disposable income and personal-consumption expenditure.

RELATION BETWEEN GROWTH AND INVESTMENT

There is some relation, probably reasonably stable, between the average investment needed and the increase in product required to attain the growth the economy can sustain. It is true that capital requirements for increasing product vary greatly among industries. In public utilities a relatively large amount of capital is required to increase sales of product, but a relatively small amount is required in many service industries. Barring a major shift in industry distribution, there is some plausibility in the idea that the ratio of investment required relative to increase in gross national product is in the order of 1.5.[13] The figure is very rough because the value of capital stock in the economy has been very crudely estimated. Investment required to produce a dollar of product is probably less today than in the twenties because long-lived construction has not grown as fast as short-lived equipment.

If gross national product is growing at about 3 per cent a year, as indicated in the following chapter, and if 1.5 times as much investment is required, net investment needs are 4.5 per cent of gross national product. In addition, of course, there are needs for capital replacement which probably are at least as great as for net investment.[14]

RELATION BETWEEN GROSS NATIONAL PRODUCT AND DISPOSABLE INCOME

Various levels of aggregation are possible in summarizing income or product. Net national product which does not include replacement financed by capital-consumption allowances would be important if we could be confident that capital-consumption allowances fairly represent replacement needs and if actual replacement moved closely with replacement needs. National income, which shows the total amount earned in the market, has its uses, but we find it less helpful than a product figure in forecasting; in fact, it is logical to think of deriving anticipations of the amount earned in the market from the sales we expect to be effected. Personal income, including all income which is received,

---

[13] The ratio could be expressed in various ways. Since government investment is not included as part of the numerator in the 1.5 ratio, it may be felt that the purchase of government services should be omitted from the denominator. (The purchase of product by the government should not be omitted, for such product is produced with private capital.) If adjustment is made to eliminate government services, the ratio at the present time would be increased from 1.5 to 1.65. One might argue that if government workers were shifted to private industry, more capital would be necessary.

[14] Some quantitative information on manufacturing investment stock is found in D. G. Wooden and R. C. Wasson, "Manufacturing Investment since 1929," *Survey of Current Business,* November, 1956.

whether or not it is derived from making product, is useful. Disposable income which represents personal income minus taxes is even more useful because it is our best measure of what people have to spend.

There is an accounting relation between disposable income and gross national product, as shown by the following figures for 1955 (in billions of dollars):

Gross national product..........................		391.7
Less:		
Personal taxes........................	35.7	
Capital-consumption allowances.......	31.6	
Indirect business taxes...............	32.9	
Corporate-profits taxes..............	21.5	
Surpluses of government enterprises....	*	
Undistributed corporate profits........	9.9	
Contributions for social insurance......	11.0	
Inventory valuation adjustment.......	−1.7	
Statistical discrepancy..............	2.1	143.0
		248.7
Plus:		
Government subsidies...............	0.2 *	
Government interest................	5.2	
Government transfer payments........	16.1	21.5
Equals: disposable personal income...............		270.2

* Surpluses of government enterprises should be subtracted, but they are not available separately from government subsidies so the difference is added as subsidies. Some government charges are not traditionally called taxes so, instead of the label taxes which we employ, the phrase "and nontax" payments or liability is frequently added.

The first seven subtractions in the tabulation are fund allocations which are unavailable for individual spending. The eighth, inventory valuation adjustment, is an accounting correction to provide a closer approximation to product figures. The statistical discrepancy represents an unallocated amount by which the statistical estimation on the product side exceeds that on the income side of the account; it could not be a source of funds for individual spending, but may be an overstatement of spending.

Government interest and transfer payments obviously provide funds for individual use but are not derived in making product.[15] They therefore must be added to develop disposable income. In like manner government subsidies do not add to product, at least in an accounting distribution of past figures, but they do add to the funds put into the economy.

[15] The government interest figures given represent the net interest paid by the government to individuals, the amount received by the government having been subtracted. The gross amount paid in 1955 was $8.0 billion.

RELATION BETWEEN DISPOSABLE INCOME AND PERSONAL CONSUMPTION EXPENDITURES

Of the $270.2 billion of disposable income in 1955, $254.4 billion was spent on personal-consumption expenditures and $15.8 billion, or about 6 per cent, was saved. In the long run, there may be some stability in the proportion saved, and we make some use of that idea in the forecast of personal-consumption expenditures in Chapter 4. Personal saving provides part of the funds available for investment, as noted above.

A difficulty one must face in the use of figures on disposable income, personal consumption expenditures, and personal savings arises from the fact that nonprofit corporations, such as private hospitals and universities, are grouped with persons in organizing the accounts. Any dividends or interest received by nonprofit corporations become a part of personal income and any part of such receipts not spent becomes a part of personal savings. The arrangement is made for convenience— to avoid undue complications in setting up the accounts. The trouble is that we do not know how much distortion results. Nonprofit corporations are assumed to be relatively unimportant, but their importance may be increasing.

Savings of unincorporated businesses are also included in the personal account. There is some doubt regarding our ability to segregate unincorporated businesses; a farmer or a small merchant may make no differentiation even in his own mind between his personal and his business accounts. But an undetermined amount of savings of unincorporated businesses is handled on a business rather than on a personal basis. Some unincorporated businesses retain earnings for the specific purpose of making business-investment expenditures.[16]

THE FEDERAL RESERVE INDEX OF INDUSTRIAL PRODUCTION

The Federal Reserve Index of Industrial Production is a more limited but highly useful aggregation.[17] The Index covers only manufacturing and mining, which represent in the general magnitude of a third of total product in the United States. It is much more important than the proportion indicates in representing economic change because of the high sensitivity of manufacturing industry to shifting prospects. Partly for that reason and partly because the data on the Index are

---

[16] The amount of internal funds used for durable investment by unincorporated business and nonprofit corporations can be estimated from Securities and Exchange Commission figures. At times the amount has been substantial.

[17] Figures on this Index can be found in almost any compilation of economic data. The most recent thorough revision was made in 1953. A description will be found in the December, 1953, issue of the *Federal Reserve Bulletin*.

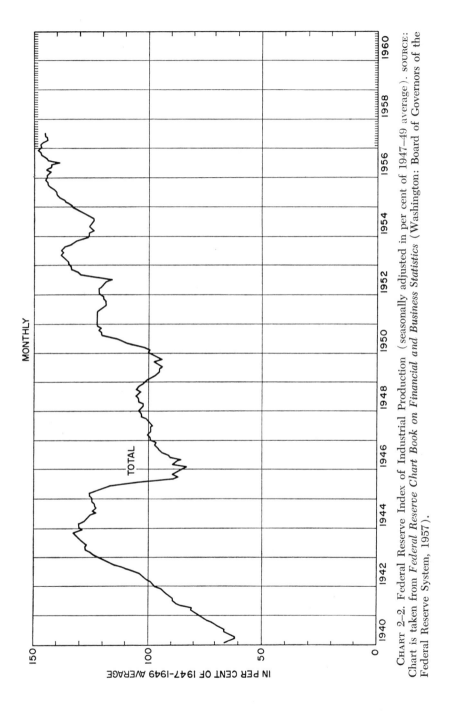

MONTHLY

IN PER CENT OF 1947-1949 AVERAGE

TOTAL

CHART 2–2. Federal Reserve Index of Industrial Production (seasonally adjusted in per cent of 1947–49 average). SOURCE: Chart is taken from *Federal Reserve Chart Book on Financial and Business Statistics* (Washington: Board of Governors of the Federal Reserve System, 1957).

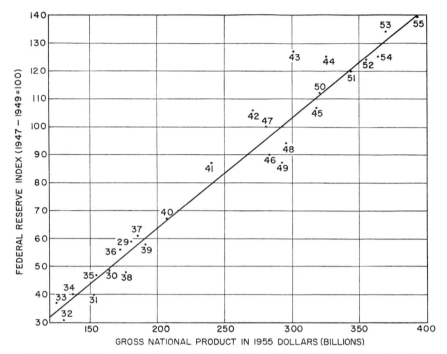

CHART 2–3. Industrial Production Related to Gross National Product in 1955 Dollars. The relationship is between the Federal Reserve index of industrial production, in per cent of 1947–49 average, and gross national product, in 1955 dollars. The equation of the regression line shown is $Y_c = -15.52 + 0.395 X$, where Y_c is estimated industrial production in per cent of 1947–49. X is gross national product in billions of 1955 dollars; the equation was derived from the 1929 to 1955 period with the years 1942, 1943, and 1944 eliminated in the computation. The reason for omitting those years is that, owing to the war, industrial production was abnormally high in relation to gross national product; these years would distort the growth relationship.

available monthly, it is frequently more useful in evaluating current conditions than income and product figures. The omission of sluggish parts of the economy focuses attention on changes which are occurring.

The Federal Reserve Index is a weighted combination of physical production series, and therefore the difficulties of allowing for price change in measurements of product and income are avoided.[18] No price index

[18] In many areas of relatively complicated manufacture the counting or measuring of physical product is impossible, and adjusted manhour data are utilized to represent output; leather products and aircraft parts are cases in point. Four per cent of the annual index and 45 per cent of the monthly index are based on manhour data. The monthly figures derived from manhour data are subjected to extrapolations of adjustment factors for productivity (output per manhour) change drawn smoothly through the year. Much controversy has arisen from the use of these adjustment factors because they introduce a hypothetical, as contrasted to currently measured, monthly change.

is on a basis precisely comparable with the Index of Industrial Production, but the Bureau of Labor Statistics Index of Wholesale Prices usually provides a satisfactory comparison.[19]

The Federal Reserve Index can be broken down into parts by using the weight factors by which the combined Index was obtained. A weakness of these factors is that they do not represent proportions of final product as do the expenditure divisions of gross national product.

In spite of important differences noted in this brief description, the long-term movement of the Federal Reserve Index is quite comparable to that of deflated gross national product, as indicated in Chart 2–3. Most of the points cluster closely about the line of relationship. The most important exceptions are the war years during which industrial production was disproportionately high because of industrial product required for war purposes. If gross national product rises to approximately $525 billion in 1965, as indicated in the following chapter, a contrasting advance in the Federal Reserve Index of Industrial Production will be to 193 (in per cent of the 1947–49 level). This is an increase of nearly 35 per cent in constant dollars from 1955 for gross national product and an increase of nearly 40 per cent for industrial production.

MEASUREMENT OF THE LABOR FORCE AND EMPLOYMENT

In the analysis of growth in the following chapter, gross national product is compared with employment. Census figures provide current estimates of labor force, employment, and unemployment.[20] The labor force includes those persons fourteen years of age and over who were (1) at work, (2) not at work but had a job, (3) unemployed and looking for work, (4) waiting to be called back to a job from which they had been laid off, (5) waiting to be called to a new job which was scheduled to start within thirty days, or (6) not looking for work because of temporary illness or because they believed that no job was available in their line of work.[21] Those in categories (1) and (2) are listed as em-

[19] This price index is currently available in all of the standard sources. For further discussion see Chap. 6.

[20] These figures are reported in *Current Population Reports: Labor Force*, published by the Census Bureau from the blow-up of a sample of about 35,000 households in 330 areas (expanded to this level in May, 1956), in which a contrast is made with Bureau of Labor Statistics estimates of employees in nonagricultural establishments. The latter figures are smaller than the census figures on employed in nonagricultural industries because of major differences in inclusiveness, such as coverage of the self-employed and other factors. The data are available in most reports of economic data.

[21] Those who were working without pay for fifteen hours or more on a family farm or in a family business are included in (1). The reasons for being temporarily not at work under (2) are: vacation, illness, industrial dispute, bad weather, and

ployed, and those in (3), (4), (5), and (6) as unemployed. Prior to 1957, persons whose layoffs were for definite periods of less than thirty days [part of those in (4)] and persons who were waiting to be called to a new job scheduled to start within thirty days [all of those in (5)] were classified as employed. The effect of the redefinition is to reduce the estimate of employment by about 200,000 to 300,000 persons and to increase the estimate of unemployment by an equal amount.

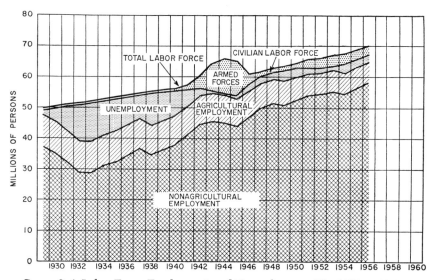

CHART 2–4. Labor Force, Employment, and Unemployment. The 1929-to-1939 estimates are those made by the Bureau of Labor Statistics, and the 1940-to-1957 are those made by the Bureau of the Census. SOURCE: Chart is taken from *Federal Reserve Chart Book on Financial and Business Statistics* (Washington: Board of Governors of the Federal Reserve System, 1957).

The estimate of employment is broken down into persons in the armed services, in agriculture, and in nonagricultural industries. Workers are also classified as to sex and weekly hours of work. Comparison is made with the noninstitutional population fourteen years of age and over; in September, 1957, about 121 million persons were so covered, and about 50 million of these were not in the labor force. Of the 71 million in the labor force, 6.5 million were working in agriculture and 59 million in nonagricultural industries; 2.5 million were unemployed, and slightly less than 3 million were in the armed services.[22]

---

various other reasons for taking time off. Persons attending school in the survey week are not included under (5).

[22] The sample is taken monthly, covering the week containing the twelfth of the month. Prior to July, 1955, the week containing the eighth was covered.

CHAPTER 3

Forecasting the Growth of Total Industry

Growth forecasting is related to the average expectation in the future. It is aimed far enough into the future to make temporary variations in demand a minor consideration; interest is focused on the general movement of demand. The forecast needed for the distant future is the average level which may be expected over a period of years, as outlined in Chapter 1.

Variation in demand is thus generally ignored in growth forecasting. Emphasis can be placed on supply conditions, especially in forecasting total industry. Natural resources, the labor force, and capital installations are the pertinent supply considerations. The simplest method is to center attention on one of these factors and relate the others to it; the method now generally employed places the labor force in the central position.[1] The labor force is the most readily predictable factor. Some background is available in considering the natural resources and capital used by labor, and therefore these factors can be visualized in relation to the labor force.

Conditions of full employment have come to be understood as that level of business activity which draws the labor force into a satisfactory level of employment. Hence, full-employment conditions are widely used to indicate the growth level at any particular time. It is important to recognize that there is considerable vagueness in this concept, although, at the same time, it does provide a basis for obtaining an approximate indication of growth levels in total industry. Full employment is used to mean a manageable employment of the "normal" labor force.

The normality of the labor force rests on habits and institutions which place individuals in the labor market in peacetime conditions. The

---

[1] One reason for this is, no doubt, the great social importance attached to the employment of labor. The reasons given in the text relate to the utility of the method in forecasting rather than to the historical reasons for the development of the method.

29

underlying habits and institutions usually change slowly if at all, so that at most times a satisfactory projection can be obtained for as much as twenty or twenty-five years by developing a constant or slowly changing rate at which age groups and other population groups participate in the labor force. The problem of developing participation rates is considered more fully below. Urgent demand in time of war leads to an above-normal labor force, so that projection from past participation rates would be unsatisfactory under these conditions; in World War II, for instance, an abnormal increase of 7 million occurred in the labor force.

The employing of absolutely all of those in the labor force at any given time is impracticable because of various kinds of "frictions" resulting from such factors as changing employment, seasonal slack periods for various industries, and illness which keeps employees away from work. The part of the labor force not employed for these and other similar reasons is called a "labor float," and is subtracted from the labor force to get the so-called full-employment figure.

Increased levels of full employment are assumed to imply increased use of natural resources and capital. Generally, the error thought to arise from this assumption is not disturbing. It is thought that the very broad distribution of products at full-employment levels would not change greatly in, say, twenty years. The same broad distribution of products would involve unpredictable shifts in the per-employee use of capital and raw materials only to the extent that uneven technological change occurred. As we shall see later, it is necessary to recognize movement of labor from farms to industry and the parallel shifting product distribution.

The level of activity at full employment is often considered to represent the growth or secular-trend level of total industry. Whether it is sound to assume that growth proceeds along so high a level is open to question. Past experience shows that considerable variation occurs in demand over short periods of time. Peacetime prosperity does not often lead to significant abnormal increases in the labor force. Under the best peacetime conditions, then, full-employment levels of activity are not greatly exceeded, and under less favorable conditions, activity falls below full-employment levels. The full-employment level would seem to be too high for the best representation of growth or secular trend.

Even though full-employment levels may be too high to provide a reasonable picture of growth or secular-trend levels, they may adequately portray the slope. The rate at which aggregate growth is proceeding can be developed analytically at full employment more effectively than at somewhat lower levels. A trend line can be mathematically fitted most readily at lower levels which give consideration to recurrent retreat from full employment, but the analytical development is to be preferred. Analytical development of aggregate growth is available at full-employment levels because an analysis can be made of the growth from the labor available as distinct from changes in efficiency in the use of labor when part of the labor force is unemployed. The methods presented later in the chapter employ this analytical device.

After changes in full-employment levels are developed, it is not difficult to convert them to lower, more conservative levels. To the extent that the fitted secular trends of the past fall short of full-employment levels, the representation of the growth level may be reduced. Projection into the future can be made at the same slope as that shown by full-employment levels, but as a continuation of the lower, fitted secular trend. In an analytical sense, what is implied by this procedure is a larger labor float. The average departure from complete employment of the labor force is greater than at full-employment levels. The idea that growth lies at the fitted-trend level is more realistic, in that employment has not been continuously at full-employment levels during the growth which occurred in the past.

EARLIER CONCEPTS ON GROWTH FORECASTING

The forecasting framework summarized above is of recent origin. Earlier ideas are not now thought to throw much light on growth forecasting, but they should be recognized as providing a basis for contrast even if no other value is attributed to them. Consideration of discarded methods may foster a desirable degree of humility, especially in view of the considerable looseness existing in our currently accepted methods.

The "law of growth" as developed by Raymond Pearl gained wide currency in the twenties.[2] Pearl's law is represented by a symmetrical logistic curve mathematically fitted to past data. The symmetrical logistic has the shape of a stretched-out S when plotted on arithmetic paper, starting with a phase of slow growth and evolving into rapid growth, first accelerating arithmetically and then slowing down until growth becomes barely perceptible, as shown in Chart 3–1. Pearl applied his law principally to human populations, describing the population growth of every country of the world for which data were available as well as the growth of other biological phenomena under suitably restricted conditions. The logistic curve proved to be a surprisingly good fit, with but few exceptions. The exceptions could always be identified with fundamental changes in the condition of available resources, and thus could be held to mark a new cycle of growth; the resulting movement

[2] See Raymond Pearl, *The Biology of Population Growth* (New York: Alfred A. Knopf, Inc., 1925).

could be described by one fitted logistic followed by another, the new one beginning at the point where the fundamental change occurred. The skeptic might note that this neat explanation of exceptions illustrates

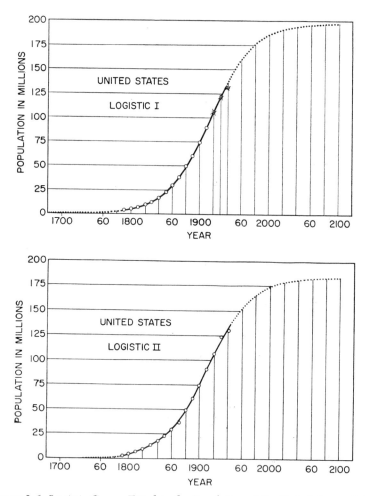

CHART 3–1. Logistic Curves Fitted to the Population of the United States. I. Fitted to 1790 to 1910. II. Fitted to 1790 to 1940. SOURCE: Reproduced with permission, from Raymond Pearl, Lowell J. Reed, and Joseph F. Kish, "The Logistic Curve and the Census Count of 1940," *Science*, 92:486–488, 1940.

an ingenuity found in many forecasting schemes, for it is common practice in forecasting to provide facile explanations of exceptions. However, Pearl's explanation follows naturally from the logic of his method.

Pearl was so convincing in his presentation of the law of growth as applied to human populations that very soon the method was being adapted to describe growth in various forms of economic activity.[3] As applied to the growth of a given product, the fitted trend could be rationalized as describing, successively, stages of experimentation, exploitation, and finally stability or saturation in the market for any product. In the almost universal application made at the time, the fit of the curve to existing data was startlingly close in general, as it had been when related to human populations.

The logistic curve as a description of growth came to be widely discussed, and certain logical and mathematical difficulties came to light. However, it is fair to say that the deficiencies discovered did not add up to a particularly damning indictment.[4] What did ultimately lead to a general discarding of the method was the discovery that the *projections* made from the fitted curves appeared to describe the future poorly, as revealed with the passage of time. The resulting projections appeared particularly bad in the thirties because of the long and deep depression. The method was adaptable to a study of growth only, and it should have been clear that projections would lie far above actual conditions in a serious depression; but it is fair to say that there had been no universal acceptance of the idea that growth is independent and distinct from other types of economic movement.

It did become clear, however, that fitting the logistic curve to different periods of data provided disconcertingly unlike projections into the future. This was true even though each fitting might appear to be an equally accurate description of the past period to which it was related. This discovery greatly reduced confidence in any method which depended for its results upon projection from a curve fitted to past data.[5]

---

[3] See, for instance, W. W. Hay, "Study of the Nature of Demand Would Obviate Many Mistakes of Management," *Annalist*, May 22, 1931.

[4] Of some importance is the fact that the sum of logistics is not a logistic. If the growth of the total country is a logistic, the growth of the cities and other divisional parts is not properly conceived to be logistic in type. In the early applications, not only the population of the total country but also that of the cities was fitted by logistic curves. Perhaps it should be noted that, in actual application, only highly empirical methods are available for fitting the logistic curve. See N. O. Johnson's "Notes" in the *Journal of the American Statistical Association*, 30:717, 31:731, for a description of a similar curve which may be fitted more simply.

[5] It is true that part of the difficulty arose from carelessness in the choice of data series as well as from the disturbing differences resulting from fitting to different periods of time. At best, it is a difficult matter to develop a series which lends itself to a description of growth in a given area, and frequently no attention whatever was given to this problem. As an illustration, it may be noted that although pig-iron production very poorly describes the growth of the steel industry, largely because of the increasing substitution of scrap in the steel-making process, many studies of the steel industry used pig-iron production to describe its growth. See the author's "How Can the Growth of the Steel Industry Be Measured?" *Iron Age,* vol. 136, Nov. 14, 1935.

Because the logistic trend is a particularly intractable type of curve, slight shifts in the slope of movement in various parts of the fitted period result in major differences in the projection obtained.

The critical concept in Pearl's law of growth is the pressing of demand against available resources. This is well illustrated by his experiment with the multiplication of fruit flies confined to the space limitations of a glass jar.[6] Fly-population readings at successive dates, as the flies pushed against the available capacity of the jar, provided an excellent fitting for the logistic curve.

We have noted above that the modern conception of growth for total industry is dependent upon the growth in available resources, demand adjustment being assumed to average out to some fairly stable reduction from the activity which supply conditions would support. The fundamental conceptions of growth involved in the two methods are in marked contrast.[7] Demand for, or absorption of, resources is taken to be a passive factor as regards growth of total industry in the modern conception, whereas in Pearl's law of growth it is the active factor, with adjustment being made up to the limits of available resources. Only when the final phase of slow, stable growth is reached is there a substantial correspondence of fundamental conceptions.[8]

Pearl's law of growth is more closely related to the Malthusian law, with which it has been frequently contrasted.[9] Pearl hotly denied that he was merely restating the Malthusian law. He was, in fact, establishing a basis for projecting population growth which is not the point in the Malthusian law. The fundamental concept that relates population growth to the exploitation of resources is, however, similar to the position held in Pearl's later stages of growth, when there is an implied contrast of geometric progression in relation to population pressure and arithmetic progression in relation to resources.

It is also easy to draw comparisons between Pearl's law of growth

[6] Raymond Pearl, *The Rate of Living: Being an Account of Some Experimental Studies on the Biology of Life Duration* (New York: Alfred A. Knopf, Inc., 1928).

[7] It is only fair to say that originally Pearl's law was developed to apply to human populations, whereas the resources involved in total industry include natural resources and capital. Pearl's method assumes these latter resources to be approximately fixed while population catches up. Such reasoning, however, does not apply to the universal application of the law of growth.

[8] The logistic curve better fits the conditions of growth in a consumer durable-goods industry than those in total industry. The growth of consumer durable goods represents a progressive exploitation of the market until a saturation of relatively universal use is achieved. It is not surprising, therefore, that the application of the law of growth to these industries was widely heralded in the twenties.

[9] See *The Nation's Food Supply* (Philadelphia: W. B. Saunders Company, 1920) for Pearl's basic statement that no pressure on the food supply should be expected in the United States in the foreseeable future.

and the Ricardian iron law of wages. Like the Malthusian law, the Ricardian law provides no technique of projection; Ricardo, like Malthus, was interested in pointing up relations between different economic forces, principally as a basis for establishing policy. Ricardo's conclusion that the workingman's standard of living can scarcely be increased may not be implied in Pearl's law until a stable level is attained. The fundamental conception that population grows to the limits of available resources is common to all three laws when applied to the later stages of growth. But it is not rewarding to generalize grandly on when the later stages of industrial growth will be reached.

Another variant related to policy formation but not to techniques of projection is the Keynesian theory of secular stagnation. This is a rationalization growing out of the depressed condition of the thirties, more than a century after Malthus and Ricardo stated their laws. Growth is seen to depend on demand conditions, as in the early stages of Pearl's law of growth. The fundamental conception of the Keynesian theory, however, is almost precisely the opposite of that involved in the Malthusian and Ricardian laws. The Keynesian theory does not hold that the population or the standard of living is significantly limited by available resources; rather, the growth of total industry is limited by growth in population and growth in the standard of living. The basic conception in the Keynesian theory is inadequacy of demand. Growth is not limited by the expansion of available resources according to this theory, for demand is thought not to rise fast enough to keep up with the resources which are available. In the early stages of population growth Pearl's law relies upon growth in demand, for supply conditions are considered to be far more than adequate.

Pearl's demand growth is expressed by his law of growth, so that it leads to a forecast of growth. The Keynesian theory states that the growth of demand depends upon policies which are adopted by the government, implying that the growth which will result from natural forces is essentially unpredictable. If the inadequacy-of-demand limitation is withdrawn, there would be no objection to the use of the modern methods of forecasting the growth of total industry. In fact, analyses which point to the danger that demand will be too limited are frequently accompanied by a projection of full-employment potential along the lines outlined in this chapter.[10]

[10] See Gerhard Colm and Marilyn Young, *The American Economy in 1960*, Planning Pamphlet 81 (Washington: National Planning Association, 1952). Alternative models which could produce full employment are presented, but in each case the increase is "beyond the level reached by a projection of present attitudes and policies" (p. 43). An adjusted model is then presented to show the need for government controls to provide full employment.

GROWTH RELATED TO LABOR FORCE, WORKING WEEK, AND PRODUCTIVITY

Centering attention on the labor force, analysis of the growth of total industry can be reduced to a relatively simple technique. Measures are developed to show the number of persons employed, the number of hours they work, and the total output produced.[11] The method is to point to a growth forecast of total output produced. By dividing output produced by manhours worked (number of persons employed times the average hours worked), a measure called productivity is obtained. Projections of persons employed, hours of work, and productivity may be multiplied together to obtain a projection of total output produced. In essence, this is the method now employed in forecasting the growth of total industry, and it represents the essential technique described in this chapter.

Adjustments in detail are necessary to provide effective procedures, and these are discussed below. Although the indicated factors are measurable, the measurements which can be obtained are not as precise as one would wish. Limitation of the measurements adds to the haziness of the forecast, although this limitation is sometimes exaggerated. Presumably, the errors are generally in the same direction and tend to be somewhat similar in amount year after year, so that the trend slope may not be too greatly influenced.

A method which assumes raw materials and capital as well as labor to be independent factors no doubt would be preferable, but effective measurements of raw material and of capital employed are not available. Furthermore, relatively complicated techniques are necessary to show the combination of raw material, capital, and labor in producing the output of total industry. Perhaps, satisfactory data and techniques may be developed, but little can be done along this line now.

The methods now employed combine the influence of changes in raw materials, capital, and labor efficiency as the "productivity" measurement. In terms of pure logic we have a frightening concept, and it is important to be aware of the several unrelated forces which are involved. Experience indicates that, in spite of the bundle of unrelated forces incorporated, measurements of the long-period movement of productivity in total industry follow a substantially stable path. Our reliance on the productivity measurement in forecasting is largely founded on that fact.

[11] A product concept in the national income and product framework is ordinarily employed to represent output produced. See description of such a measure in Chap. 2.

The various factors influencing the productivity measurement can be grouped under four headings:

1. Change in the effectiveness of a manhour because of changes in labor quality; character of the labor force, fatigue, and interest of the employee
2. Changes in efficiency growing out of changes in the type and quality of raw materials available
3. Changes in efficiency growing out of the use of capital, revised plant layout, and management decisions in general
4. Change in the composition of the output

1. The contribution made by a manhour of labor does not remain constant. It will rise if the quality of labor improves. Possibly, all workers do a better job as time passes merely because they are better trained and have a better understanding of what they are doing, but there is no evidence that this is so. In like manner, better health, better diets, and improved living conditions may be bringing about a steady increase in the quality of work, but again there is no satisfactory evidence. It is reasonable to believe that the more interest an employee has in his job, the better his work is, but there is no assurance that there has been a general increase in the interest with which work is done. We can be sure that shorter hours of work have improved manhour output at least to some extent by reducing fatigue, but reliable quantitative measurements are not available.

2. We know that shortage or reduced quality of raw materials will hamper efficiency. Over the long run, shortage of raw materials probably has produced little or no crippling effect, for when old sources have dried up, new ones, synthetic or otherwise, have been discovered. Frequently the new synthetic materials have actually increased efficiency.

3. We know that a man with a machine can usually produce much more than he can without one. Even when allowance is made for the cost of the machine (depreciation), there is usually a large net saving. Rapid rise in the number and quality of machines is presumptive evidence of rising productivity. In some cases, improved plant layout has been equally important; a good layout can be of substantial aid in developing a consistent flow of work. Also, management can improve efficiency in various other ways: by locating plants effectively in relation to supplies of material and product demand; by developing efficient controls; by generating confidence that every effort is being made to provide a good product and good labor conditions; by helping workers feel pride in their work; and by taking advantage of profitable oppor-

tunities. It is hard to say how much general-management factors count in rising productivity, and their effect is to some extent interwoven with the influence of improved mechanization.

4. Change in the distribution of product may bring a change in the total-industry productivity measure, since the gross output per worker is far greater in some industries than in others. The point may be clarified by a simple arithmetic illustration. Suppose that gross output per worker is $2 per hour in one industry and $6 in another. If all workers were in these two industries, with the same number of workers in each, the average output per manhour would be $4. If, however, there were three times as many workers in the second industry as in the first, the average output per manhour would be $5. This assumes that no change in productivity occurs in either industry; other simple arithmetic illustrations will convince the reader that redistribution may be influential whatever the changes in productivity. The distribution change assumed above is extreme, but redistribution has been influential. The automobile industry, for instance, has a high dollar output per worker, and the number of workers has increased substantially over the years; in contrast, agriculture has a low dollar output per worker, and the number of workers has decreased. The relative increase in mechanized industries has been a factor in increasing the measurement of productivity obtained for total industry. Measurements of the effect of increasing proportions of nonfarm product are summarized below.

FORECAST OF PRODUCTIVITY

Chart 3–2 shows a secular trend fitted to the productivity of total industry. The projection of this trend has been widely employed, but, as we shall see, it represents a relatively low forecast. Substantial stability of the general trend during reasonably prosperous conditions of the past is impressive. The assumption that trend projection is warranted merely because a good fit has been obtained with past data is dangerous, however, and should be replaced or modified when conflicting evidence is at hand. We would like to have as good a secular-trend fit as possible, but we must look searchingly behind the trend fitting and consider the probable movement of causal factors.

Causal factors can be employed only to modify secular-trend projections, for measurements are not available to show the influence of each causal factor. Our attention should, therefore, be first directed at development of the productivity trend. Ordinarily, the trend is fitted to productivity changes in the private, or nongovernment, part of the economy, as is done to obtain the picture shown in Chart 3–2. The reason is that there is no effective way of measuring productivity changes arising in government product.[12]

The idea involved in fitted trends is that short variations are averaged out. A long enough period to accomplish this ideally is seldom avail-

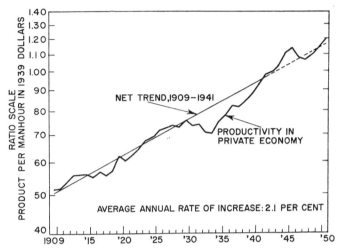

CHART 3–2. Constant-Dollar Gross Private Product per Manhour in the United States (Trend of Productivity in the Private Economy). The equation of the fitted trend line is $\log Y_c = 1.6245 + 0.0023X + 0.0089t$, with Y_c representing estimated gross private product per manhour in 1939 dollars, X representing the ratio of civilian employment to the civilian labor force, and t representing time in years from the 1925 origin. SOURCE: Taken, with permission, from John W. Kendrick, "National Productivity and Its Long-term Projection," in *Long-range Economic Projection*, vol. XVI in National Bureau of Economic Research, *Studies in Income and Wealth* (Princeton: Princeton University Press, 1954).

able. Therefore, it is advantageous to correct for the influence of variation in any way possible. Some variation in productivity does occur over the business cycle, as shown by Chart 3–2. This variation is related to the ratio of employment to the labor force; productivity falls in depres-

[12] Government product is represented by purchased services; the goods purchased from business reflect productivity changes in the private economy. Government services are paid in salaries and wages; in 1955 they amounted to about $34 billion. Dividing the amount paid by manhours of government work performed would give merely an hourly-wage-rate figure, unsatisfactory as a measurement of productivity.

It is a mistake to assume that the difficulty in measuring government product relates to its character as services. A substantial part of private product also represents services. Generally, private services sold to consumers represent jobs done, not just so many hours of work. Dividing the amount received for jobs done by hours of work expended may reflect changes in productivity.

Productivity must be measured by changes in *physical* output per labor input, and therefore deflated product figures must be used. Deflated product figures are obtained by dividing current-dollar-product figures by appropriate price indices.

sion. In the trend line shown on Chart 3–2, adjustment has been made in order to average out some of the short-term variation in productivity. The trend line has been mechanically raised to the level at which it would lie if employment were always at 96.5 per cent of the labor force; in other words, if a constant 3.5 per cent unemployment were assumed to exist. The level of the productivity trend is thus raised slightly above the level given by a simple time trend, but its slope is altered only to the extent that times of prosperity and depression are not well distributed over the period studied.

The trend line is fitted on the assumption that productivity has grown at a constant geometric rate. The justification is largely empirical. When plotted on ratio paper, as in Chart 3–2, the productivity line is straighter than when plotted on arithmetic paper. The assumption of a constant geometric rate is also logical in that the increase occurring in productivity at any particular time is in proportion to the rising level of existing resources, and hence the increase is properly considered to be geometric rather than arithmetic. The secular-trend increase shown in Chart 3–2 can be expressed as 2.1 per cent a year; that is a reasonable representation of the average rate of growth which productivity has shown in the past. What information there is indicates that when measurements are pushed back to the beginning of the century, the full-period secular trend of productivity shows approximately the same rate of increase.[13]

We turn now to a consideration of those causal factors which appear to be of major importance: changes in the distribution of product, reduction in fatigue, and improved mechanization. As noted above, a consideration of these factors, if only on a crude qualitative basis, is very important, for there is always danger that the slope of a secular trend may be shifting. An examination of the possible causes for such shifting is good insurance against inadvertent oversight.

The increasing proportion of total product accounted for by the nonfarm sector has been responsible for a significant part of the growth in productivity occurring in the past. Agriculture represented about 40 per cent of the total manhours worked in the private economy fifty years ago, and less than 15 per cent in the mid-fifties. Each manhour in the farm sector produces only about a third as much as in the nonfarm sector. Hence a disproportionate increase in the nonfarm sector results in a greater increase in product than in manhours. The influence of this shift is shown in Chart 3–3. It accounts for about a tenth of the average secular-trend increase in productivity appearing in Chart 3–2. Therefore, a continuation of the past growth in productivity implies that a

[13] The productivity figures shown in Table 3–5 indicate a higher yearly average rate of increase from 1900 to 1910 than from 1910 to 1950. The early estimates are very crude.

large shift from farm to nonfarm product will continue. Is it reasonable to assume that this will happen?

Perhaps the most effective way to see the picture is to analyze the change which has been occurring in harvested acres per agricultural worker.[14] The figure rose from 35.0 to 46.8 acres in the decade 1940 to 1950, and it has continued to rise. The potential of increased farm size

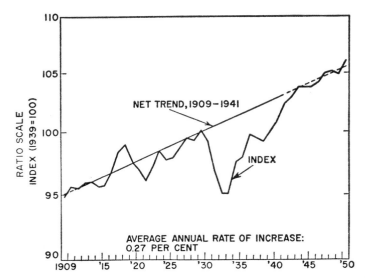

CHART 3–3. Effect on Productivity in Private Economy of Farm-to-nonfarm Shift in Manhours. The equation of the fitted trend line is log $Y_c = 1.8985 + 0.0010X + 0.0011t$, with Y_c representing estimated index, in per cent of 1939, of ratio of productivity computed with variable manhour weights to productivity computed with constant manhour weights, X representing ratio of civilian employment to civilian labor force, and t representing time in years from the 1925 origin. SOURCE: Taken, with permission, from John W. Kendrick, "National Productivity and Its Long-term Projection," in *Long-range Economic Projection*, vol. XVI in National Bureau of Economic Research, *Studies in Income and Wealth* (Princeton: Princeton University Press, 1954).

is founded on increased use of farm machinery and increased industrialization of the South, where most of the small-scale and relatively unprofitable farms are located. Increases along these lines may be projected at least until 1965. The Twentieth Century Fund book referred to in footnote 14 projects the rise in acres per worker to 56 in 1960.

An important shift in distribution of product takes place over the business cycle, with highly mechanized industries accounting for an increased part of the total product in prosperity. Over a virtually unbroken long period of prosperity, such as occurred in the twenties and such as

[14] See J. Frederic Dewhurst and Associates, *America's Needs and Resources: A New Survey* (New York: The Twentieth Century Fund, Inc., 1955), pp. 809–810, from which the information presented here was taken.

has occurred recently, productivity remains at a higher level than at secular growth if variation in output will be as descriptive of the future as it was of the past.

The reason is that rapid increase in the quotient obtained by dividing total private product by manhours employed, under the conditions now prevailing, is partly the result of shift in product distribution to more mechanized industries, in which the output per worker is relatively high. The expansion in capital formation and other types of durable goods recently has outstripped expansion in other sectors of the economy. This is at least partly a temporary influence. If the distribution begins to shift toward the less mechanized industries, the opposite distortion will be obtained. Allowance must therefore be made for temporary shifts in product distribution.

The influence on fatigue of reduced hours is difficult to appraise. The effect certainly varies a great deal in various types of occupation. With the advent of more mechanical processes and less dependence on human guidance for mechanical operations, it may be that the effects are becoming less important. Also, after some point, the reduction in fatigue resulting from the shortening of hours will be at a rapidly diminishing rate. Whether this point has been reached with the shortened hours now prevailing it is hard to say. No doubt the irregular decline in hours of work occurring in the past will continue. The safest assumption would appear to be that decline in hours will reduce fatigue to a diminishing extent.

The high rate of capital formation occurring in the postwar period augurs well for a continuation of the favorable influence exerted on productivity by improving mechanization. It would appear that generally the new capital is more productive than the old, whether it represents replacement or extension. Not only is the potential of installed machinery being increased, but improvements in plant layout, better coordination between various stages in the production process, and mechanization of raw-material flow, as well as many other factors popularly known as automation, are leading to rising productivity. New technological discoveries in World War I were thought to have led to the minor fillip which occurred in productivity after the war, and it is often stated that an analogous situation is occurring in the forties and fifties.

This reasoning might be held to imply that the influence of mechanization is about to become retarding, since the influence of World War II must be about spent by now. On the other hand, many persons hold that current increases in productivity are largely fostered by the vast increase occurring in research expenditure. Although subject to considerable qualification as to what should be classified as research, the figures show a yearly research expenditure in the order of $6 billion currently, as compared with less than $0.5 billion before World War II.[15] Even after allowing for the difference in price levels, a striking increase is involved. There is no doubt some lag between research and its application in improved mechanization; therefore, since acceleration in the rate of expenditure has occurred recently, an accelerated rate of improvement in productivity might be expected in near-future years. The reasoning involved is vague, however, and it would be a mistake to draw precise conclusions.

For one thing, the purpose of research expenditures frequently is not related to mechanization. For instance, they may be directed to the development of a more salable product, although not necessarily an improved one. Even when directed at improved mechanization, the achievements may be disappointing. On net, though, it is reasonable to believe that the rate of mechanization has been speeded up to a significant extent.

We may expect productivity to continue to increase somewhat more rapidly than the rate shown by the long-period secular trend. As developed later in the chapter, we assume productivity growth to continue at the 1950–55 rate of 2.3 per cent a year for the total economy, including government services. The long-period secular trend has been at nearly 2 per cent on a comparable basis. (The 2.1 per cent trend indicated in Chart 3–2 is higher because it is for the private economy only and is adjusted to correct for short-period variation.) At the end of the chapter a contrast is made with widely publicized forecasts, and our projection is found to fall at a median position. Those who project more growth in productivity than has occurred in recent years are anticipating accelerated achievement from improved mechanization. As indicated above, shift to nonfarm product and reduced fatigue can be expected to do no more than maintain their past influence.

FORECAST OF THE LABOR FORCE

It is axiomatic that population projections are most essential in forecasting the labor force. The labor force is drawn from the working-age groups in the population. If the labor-force forecast is made for a period of fifteen years or less, as shown in the examples in this book, dependence can be placed on survival of the existing population in the country plus net immigration.

We must start with a population forecast, or at least with an estimate of the survival of the present population. If the labor force is to be

---

[15] *Science and Engineering in American Industry,* National Science Foundation, NSF 56–16, 1956; *Scientific Research and Development in American Industry,* Bureau of Labor Statistics Bulletin 1148, 1953. Early estimates must be pieced together from various source materials.

forecast further than fifteen years into the future, attention must be given to fertility rates as well as to mortality and migration. The greatest mistakes in population forecasting have been made in projecting fertility rates. In the thirties, pronounced declines in births were accepted to represent secular change. The demographers explained the decline by the growing pattern of family limitation and other factors, most importantly, the movement from farm to city, where the economic disadvantage of having children apparently kept the birth rate low.

At first, the rapid rise in birth rates after World War II was explained as a catching-up process, following delay in marriage in the Great Depression and augmented by wartime separations. The high birth level has continued past the middle fifties. The "cold war" arising from heightened international tension has been a contributing factor. Continued prosperity has made it easier to plan for larger families. Possibly, some change has occurred in the institutional patterns with the rising popularity of early marriage and with social adaptation to families of three children rather than one or two. But these are not adequate reasons for assuming that the present high level of birth rates will continue. A more conservative position is that current birth rates are somewhat high, just as those in the thirties were low. This leads to population forecasts far above those made by demographers in the prewar and early postwar periods, but somewhat less than obtained by projecting a continuation of the current birth rate indefinitely into the future. Since attention in this section is limited to a forecast of the labor force to 1965, no forecast of the birth rate is required.

In projecting the survival of the present population of working-age groups, it is essential to study "cohorts" (survivals by age groups) separately, because a shift is occurring in the age distribution, with a resulting drift in the over-all survival rate. Table 3–1 shows the Census Bureau's age-group projection to 1965. Mortality for the late forties was overestimated because of the advent of the new "wonder drugs." However, changes actually occurring in the late forties projected into the early fifties were not in substantial error.[16] In Table 3–1 these decreases in mortality are projected to continue to 1960, after which the mortality rates are assumed to remain constant at the projected 1955–60 level.[17]

The volume of net immigration into the United States is small and unlikely to produce a major error unless the laws controlling immigration

---

[16] See p. 4 of the reference cited for Table 3–1.

[17] It will be noted that only one mortality level is projected. In fact, the Census Bureau has discontinued entirely the projection of "high," "low," and "medium" population levels. These projections may have represented plausible differences in statistical assumptions, but they did not represent probable range of movement, and the present tendency to throw emphasis on the logical implications of the assumptions is a wholesome one. For discussion of a new mortality assumption now being formulated by the Census Bureau, see Chap. 12.

TABLE 3–1

PROJECTED POPULATION IN WORKING-AGE GROUPS FOR 1960 AND 1965

(In millions)

Age group	1955	1960	1965
14–19 years...........	13.58	16.15	21.86
20–24 years...........	10.77	11.28	13.46
25–34 years...........	24.14	22.67	22.26
35–44 years...........	22.81	23.96	24.12
45–54 years...........	18.90	20.86	22.08
55–64 years...........	14.53	15.63	17.04
65 years and over......	14.13	15.80	17.37
Total.............	118.85	126.34	138.19

SOURCE: "Revised Projections of the Population of the United States, by Age and Sex: 1960 to 1975," *Current Population Reports*, ser. P-25, no. 123, Oct. 20, 1955. Rounding errors account for differences between column sums and totals given.

are changed. The net number of immigrants arriving from 1950 to 1955 was 1.4 million, and this is the number assumed to arrive from 1955 to 1960. For 1960 to 1965, the assumption is 1.2 million. The age-sex distribution of the immigrants is based on several recent postwar years.

Table 3–2 shows labor-force projections. These depend on the participation rates given in Table 3–3. The participation rates for males are expected to decline for ages above 65. The participation rates for females are expected to decline under age 20 and to rise for all other ages. In making these projections the assumption is that the 1950–55 changes in participation rates will continue.

The projection does not differ a great deal from that shown in the second panel of Chart 3–4. The longer-period growth shown in the first panel of the chart is less steep. Results quite similar to those shown in Table 3–2 are obtained by making projections from other plausible assumptions.[18]

It will be noted that, in spite of the difference in movement in the various groups, the over-all participation rate declines by only one-tenth

[18] These assumptions are: (1) average annual rates of change in participation rates from 1920 to the average of April, 1954, 1955, and 1956 will continue (on the assumption that 1920 and the mid-fifties represent similar population conditions); (2) the assumption stated in the text; (3) the projection of men 14 to 24 and women 14 to 34 on the basis of (1) and the projection stated in the text for other age groups; and (4) continuation of the flat 1955 labor-force participation rates to 1975. See p. 5 of the reference cited for Table 3–2.

Business Forecasting

TABLE 3–2

LABOR-FORCE PROJECTIONS, 1960 AND 1965

(In millions)

Age group	1955	1960	1965
14–19 years	5.37	6.05	7.53
20–24 years	7.29	7.62	9.04
25–34 years	15.73	14.98	14.90
35–44 years	15.65	16.79	17.26
45–54 years	13.04	14.99	16.46
55–64 years	8.52	9.60	10.90
65 years and over	3.31	3.36	3.36
Total	68.90	73.37	79.44

SOURCE: "Projections of the Labor Force in the United States, 1955 to 1975," *Current Population Reports*, ser. P-50, no. 69, October, 1956. The Census Bureau labels the projection shown here "projection II." It assumes that the average annual rates of change in participation rates from 1950 to 1955 will be maintained. Rounding errors account for differences between column sums and totals given.

TABLE 3–3

LABOR-FORCE PARTICIPATION RATES, 1955–1965

(In per cent of population at given age)

Age group	1955			1960			1965		
	Total	Male	Female	Total	Male	Female	Total	Male	Female
14–19 years	39.5	49.0	29.7	37.5	46.0	28.7	34.4	43.7	28.2
20–24 years	67.7	89.5	45.8	67.6	88.2	46.5	67.2	87.0	46.9
25–34 years	65.2	96.5	34.8	66.1	96.8	35.8	66.9	97.0	36.8
35–44 years	68.6	96.9	41.4	70.1	97.3	44.0	71.6	97.7	46.5
45–54 years	69.0	95.1	43.5	71.9	95.7	49.2	74.5	96.2	54.2
55–64 years	58.6	86.4	32.2	61.4	87.4	37.5	64.0	88.4	41.9
65 years and over	23.4	38.5	10.3	21.3	33.4	11.1	19.3	28.9	11.9
Total	58.0	82.3	34.5	58.1	80.7	36.5	57.9	78.7	38.2

SOURCE: "Projections of the Labor Force in the United States, 1955 to 1975," *Current Population Reports*, ser. P-50, no. 69, October, 1956, and other material covered in the tables.

of a percentage point from 1955 to 1965. For the other assumptions noted in footnote 18 the decline is somewhat greater, although the labor-force totals remain in the same order of magnitude.[19]

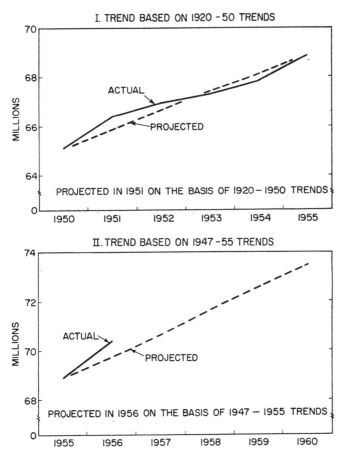

CHART 3–4. Secular-trend Projections of the Labor Force. I. Trend Based on 1920–50 Trends. II. Trend Based on 1947–55 Trends. Trend lines shown were obtained by fitting to the periods stated in the two panels of the chart. SOURCE: Supplied by the Bureau of Labor Statistics, Department of Labor.

The chief uncertainty in this forecast is the rapidity with which female-participation rates will rise. The rise has been quite rapid in recent years. It is possible that women will join the labor force more rapidly than projected, but the fact that a large part of the new women

[19] For assumption (1) the labor-force projection is 79.2 million in 1965, with an over-all participation rate of 57.7 per cent; for assumption (3), 78.3 million, with 57.1 per cent; for assumption (4), 77.4 million, with 56.5 per cent.

workers take part-time work should not be overlooked.[20] Obviously, the impact of added part-time workers is less than that of full-time workers.

There is evidence of considerable geographical variation in female-participation rates. The suggestion has been offered that a better understanding of the probable movements of these rates might be obtained if a careful analysis were made of geographical differences.[21]

The simple techniques of projection employed are frankly not based on causal forces, but available information on the factors responsible for changes in participation rates is too vague to warrant more sophisticated assumptions. For instance, we cannot quantify the influence of the increasing relative importance of nonagricultural industry, the establishment of social security and pension programs, or the rising importance of white-collar occupations.

FORECAST OF WORKING HOURS

Hours of work have declined steadily, if irregularly, over the past hundred years, as shown by Table 3–4. The average decline of four hours per decade in this century represents a strong secular trend toward more leisure time. The techniques by which the Twentieth Century Fund computes the figures results in counting paid vacations as reduced hours. The trend toward increased vacation time is reducing hours of work in this sense, and has been taken into consideration in the forecast. Since the hours of work are somewhat higher in agriculture than in industry generally, a continued shift out of agriculture also makes for a slightly lower forecast.

Failure of hours to decline in the first half of the fifties is related to the generally high level of activity. The two years 1950 and 1954 marked slight recessions, and a decline in hours occurred. The depressed periods were too slight, however, for reduced hours to become customary.

Overtime is generally charged only for time over 40 hours, and management has little inducement to reduce hours below that level; labor is reluctant to take a reduction in weekly pay. A somewhat longer de-

[20] The percentage of married, widowed, and divorced women in the labor force has grown markedly since before the war. See A. J. Jaffe and C. D. Stewart, *Manpower Resources and Utilization* (New York: John Wiley & Sons, Inc., 1951), p. 172. The difficulty seems to be that new cultural patterns of work are being established, and the shift is hard to follow by mechanical rules such as those used by the Census Bureau in making the projections described. Of course, the change has been going on for a long time, although somewhat more rapidly in recent decades. Only about 5 per cent of the married women were in the working force in 1890, compared with about 16 per cent in 1940, but the figure had shot up to 22 per cent in 1949.

[21] Harold Wool, "Long-term Projections of the Labor Force," in *Long-range Economic Projection,* vol. XVI in National Bureau of Economic Research Conference on Research in Income and Wealth, *Studies in Income and Wealth* (Princeton, N.J.: Princeton University Press, 1954), p. 62.

TABLE 3–4

DECLINE IN WORKING HOURS: TOTAL PRIVATE INDUSTRY

Year	Weekly working hours	Decade declines
1850	69.8	
1860	68.0	−1.8
1870	65.4	−2.6
1880	64.0	−1.4
1890	61.9	−2.1
1900	60.2	−1.7
1910	55.1	−5.1
1920	49.7	−5.4
1930	45.9	−3.8
1940	44.0	−1.9
1950	40.0	−4.0
1955	40.4	
1960	39.0	−1.0
1965	37.5	−2.9

SOURCE: J. Frederic Dewhurst and Associates, *America's Needs and Resources: A New Survey* (New York: The Twentieth Century Fund, Inc., 1955), p. 1073. The figures are weighted averages of all private industry, including agriculture. Paid vacations are counted as reductions in average working hours. The 1955 figure is our preliminary estimate, and the 1960 and 1965 figures are our projections.

pression would probably introduce shorter hours, which might come to be expected.

About a fourth of the projected decline represents the combined effects of longer paid vacations and the shift out of agriculture. The other three-fourths represents a general drift to shorter hours, but much of the decline might not occur if only extremely mild recessions should prevail. Some secular declines could be expected even without more extended recessions, as, for instance, have been occurring recently among retail workers. Generally, however, there is little current evidence of secular decline in hours of work in the recent past.

ASSUMPTIONS ON THE LABOR FLOAT

The projection in Table 3–5 is made on the basis of 96 per cent employment of the labor force. The assumption of overfull employment is thus avoided. The 4 per cent labor float corresponds closely with actual experience in 1956. For the seven years 1950 to 1956, civilian unemployment averaged 3.7 per cent of the civilian labor force and for the

TABLE 3–5

PROJECTION OF THE GROWTH OF GROSS NATIONAL PRODUCT [a]

(All dollar figures in 1955 prices)

Year	(1) Labor force [b] (millions)	(2) Employment (millions)	(3) Hours per week [c]	(4) Manhours per year [d] (billions)	(5) Gross National Product ($ billions)	(6) Productivity [e] (dollars)
1900	29.2	26.7	60.2	83.6	82.2	0.98
1910	36.0	34.0	55.1	97.4	121.5	1.24
1920	41.7	39.7	49.7	102.6	132.8	1.29
1930	49.3	45.8	45.9	109.7	163.8	1.49
1940	54.7	47.9	44.0	109.6	208.1	1.90
1950	64.6	61.5	40.0	127.9	320.7	2.51
1955	68.9	66.2	40.4	139.1	390.9	2.81
1960	73.4	70.5	39.0	143.0	450.5	3.15
1965	79.4	76.2	37.5	148.6	524.6	3.53

[a] The principal sources of the estimates are the Department of Commerce and J. F. Dewhurst and Associates, *America's Needs and Resources: A New Survey* (New York: The Twentieth Century Fund, Inc., 1955). The projections, of course, are ours.

[b] Labor-force and employment figures include the armed forces.

[c] The hours-per-week series is as developed in Dewhurst and Associates, *op. cit.*, p. 1073. Paid vacations are considered equivalent as a reduction in average weekly hours. Thus, one week of paid vacation amounts to a reduction of about 0.8 hours per week at the present time.

[d] Col. (2) times col. (3) times 52.

[e] Col. (5) divided by col. (4). The projections for 1960 and 1965 are at the geometric rate between 1950 and 1955, 2.3 per cent per year.

ten-year period 1946 to 1955, 3.8 per cent, but these were exceptionally prosperous periods.

The projection could have been made at the level of the full labor force, but the implications of such an impractical level should be avoided. Employing the same mechanical method, the slope would not have been appreciably altered by using labor-force figures. In practice, 100 per cent employment of the labor force at all times would modify the structure of the labor market more markedly than the mechanical example might indicate.

There is no question about the existence of a labor float arising from such factors as voluntary quits, discharges, business failures, mechanical failures, shifting demand, and seasonal variation. Precisely what the level of the float is cannot be determined either by theory or by empirical investigation at the present time. Measures of the separate influences causing the float are not available. Usually, subtraction of the labor float is not intended to lower the growth line far enough to account for the drag which may be produced by depressions like those experienced in the past. The slope of the trend might not be substantially altered if depression conditions were explicitly introduced, for the indicated growth is developed from past experience in depressions. The level of the trend computed at so-called full-employment levels is near our best efforts rather than our poorest.

FORECAST OF THE GROWTH OF TOTAL INDUSTRY

In Table 3–5 we project gross national product to 1960 and 1965 by multiplying labor force minus 4 per cent labor float by working hours and productivity. The labor force and working-hour forecasts have been discussed above. It should be noted that the working-hour figures represent estimates for the private economy only, for there are no compiled figures on working hours in the government. Probably, working hours in the government are similar to the average for private industry, and a fair representation of the total economy is obtained.

The rise in productivity shown in the table is at an average geometric rate of 1.9 per cent a year from 1900 to 1955. If allowance is made for the effect of substantial departure from full employment and comparison is limited to the private economy, a figure of 2.1 per cent is obtained, as summarized above (see Chart 3–2).

We have assumed a somewhat higher productivity rise in the near future because of the rapid capital advancement now occurring. The productivity rise from 1950 to 1955 shown in Table 3–5 is approximately 2.3 per cent a year. This rate of advance has been assumed to 1960 and 1965. The productivity figures thus developed in the last column of the table are multiplied by the projected total manhours per year to obtain the projected gross national product in 1955 dollars; the figures shown for gross national product represent an increase of more than 15 per cent from 1955 to 1960 and more than 34 per cent to 1965.

Table 3–5 shows the projection of total product, including both private and government. There are weaknesses involved in so aggregative a procedure,[22] but there are also advantages. If growth depends upon the

[22] With different distributions of the total, there will be differences in the growth of productivity and possibly in the decline of working hours. With our present knowledge, however, the weighting of different distributions of the total would require the use of poor data and might be as complicating as helpful. For a discussion of the advantages of using interrelations between a substantial number of sectors in making projections, see Marvin Hoffenberg, "Prices, Productivity, and Factor Return Assumptions in Long-range Economic Projections," in *Proceedings of the Business and Economic Statistics Section, American Statistical Association,*

ability of the total economy to produce, there is something to be said for starting with the movement of the grand total. That is why we examine the movement of the total in this chapter before proceeding to an analysis of the growth of separate divisions and industries. In developing the growth of the parts, growth of the total is usually employed as one of the explanatory factors. Furthermore, separate assumptions regarding the growth of government product cannot be effectively made without knowledge of the growth of total industry, a fact developed in the following chapter.

The compelling reason why most analysts have considered government product separately in projecting total product is that government does not lend itself logically to the use of a productivity figure. The government "product" is merely the total amount paid government workers. Their services are not sold on the market, so that when we divide the total paid to them by the hours they work, we obtain no more than an hourly wage payment. Private product is sold in the market, and thus it has a better claim to be called "product"; when deflated by market-price changes, physical product is roughly represented; divided by the hours worked, the change in product produced in an hour's work is obtained.

Tables 3–6 and 3–7, developed by the author, show a projection with private and government product considered separately. The methods used in developing Table 3–6 are the same as those used in over-all Table 3–5. We have assumed the growth in productivity of private product for 1955 to 1960 and to 1965 to be 2.3 per cent a year, equal to the assumed growth of total product in Table 3–5. Unless the productivity of government services is assumed to increase equally, a slightly reduced increase in productivity is implied.

In Table 3–7 no attempt is made to estimate change in productivity of government services, but a projection of the amount paid for government services has been obtained by making guesses on the amount of government employment and the amount paid per worker. Such projections lack the firm foundation of acceptable assumptions. In estimating the number of government employees, a major difficulty is uncertainty about the effect of increasing defense mechanization. It should be noted that a smaller number of government workers would probably increase the proportion of highly paid workers, thus increasing the average wage rate. For 1960 we have taken the Dewhurst estimate of 10.5 million government workers,[23] and have projected to 1965 by the same amount

---

Washington, 1957, pp. 16–19. For an illustration of forecasting the total by summing the forecasts of major expenditure divisions, see Bonnar Brown and M. Janet Hansen, *Production Trends in the United States through 1975* (Menlo Park, Calif.: Stanford Research Institute, 1957).

[23] Dewhurst and Associates, *op. cit.,* p. 45.

TABLE 3–6

PROJECTION OF THE GROWTH OF GROSS PRIVATE PRODUCT [a]
(All dollar figures in 1955 prices)

Year	(1) Employed private workers [b] (millions)	(2) Hours per week [c]	(3) Manhours per year [d] (billions)	(4) Gross private product ($ billions)	(5) Gross private product per manhour [e] (dollars)
1910	32.1	55.1	92.0	99.3	1.08
1920	36.8	49.7	95.1	118.7	1.25
1930	42.4	45.9	101.2	152.7	1.51
1940	43.3	44.0	99.1	189.5	1.91
1950	54.0	40.0	112.3	294.7	2.64
1955	56.3	40.4	118.3	356.8	3.02
1960	60.0	39.0	121.7	411.3	3.38
1965	65.2	37.5	127.1	480.4	3.78

[a] The principal sources are the Department of Commerce, J. F. Dewhurst and Associates, *America's Needs and Resources: A New Survey* (New York: The Twentieth Century Fund, Inc., 1955), and John W. Kendrick, "National Productivity and Its Longterm Projection," in *Long-range Economic Projection*, vol. XVI in *Studies in Income and Wealth* (Princeton, N.J.: Princeton University Press, 1954). The projections, of course, are ours.

[b] The 1960 and 1965 projections are obtained by subtracting the assumptions on government workers shown in Table 3–7.

[c] These are the same as in Table 3–5 because figures for government workers are unavailable.

[d] Col. (1) times col. (2) times 52.

[e] Col. (4) divided by col. (3). The projections for 1960 and 1965 are at the geometric rate of 2.3 per cent, as used in Table 3–5. The rate between 1950 and 1955 in this table is 2.7 per cent. If the projection had been at that rate, the productivity figure for 1965 would be about $3.95, and the figure for gross private product about $500 billion. The difference is largely accounted for by the relatively small increase in private workers from 1950 to 1955, as compared with the increase in total employment shown in Table 3–5.

of increase as from 1955 to 1960. The $3,500 per government worker used in the computations for 1960 and 1965 is approximately equal to the 1956 rate.

When the projections for government and private products are added together, the figure for 1960 is only slightly under the gross-national-product projection shown in Table 3–5, but the 1965 gross-national-product projection is about 1 per cent less. Although we cannot expect to make a projection of this kind within 1 per cent, the difference ob-

Table 3-7

Sum of Separately Projected Government and Private Gross Product

(All dollar figures in 1955 prices)

Year	Employed government workers including armed services (millions)	Gross government product ($ billions)	Gross product per government worker (dollars)	Gross private product from Table 3–6 ($ billions)	Total gross product ($ billions)
1930	3.4	10.5	3,088	152.7	163.2
1940	4.7	18.5	3,936	189.5	208.0
1950	7.7	25.8	3,351	294.7	320.5
1955	10.0	33.9	3,390	356.8	390.7
1960	10.5	36.8	3,500	411.3	448.1
1965	11.0	38.5	3,500	480.4	518.9

source: Department of Commerce and Table 3–6. The projections, of course, are ours.

tained by the two methods should not be ignored. The three major assumptions leading to the difference are:

1. Assumed division of workers between government and private industry

2. The amount earned per government worker

3. The percentage increase assumed in productivity (2.3 per cent a year in private industry and virtually zero in government)

The first two of these assumptions may well be more important in practice than the third, but it helps little to vary the assumptions made regarding number and wages of government employees. As to the third assumption, the discrepancy in gross-national-product projections would be eliminated if a productivity increase in private industry of 2.4 per cent instead of 2.3 per cent were assumed for 1955 to 1965. On the other hand the $519 billion projected in Table 3–7 may be about as easily defended as the $525 billion in Table 3–5. The former figure would be obtained in the over-all projection if productivity were assumed to increase by the historic rate of 2.1 per cent from 1960 to 1965, leaving the projection at 2.3 per cent from 1955 to 1960. Such a slower rate might occur after 1960 if depressions became somewhat more severe or if the rate of technological development should slow down. We shall use the $525 billion figure in this book, but hold it to indicate no more than an approximate range.[24]

[24] Especially for students interested in probing into methodology, note may be taken of the fact that generally we have projected from the *actual* level in 1955 instead of from the trend level, because we have felt that there is no effective way

The results we have achieved may be compared with direct secular-trend projections of gross national product, as shown in Chart 3–5. It will be seen that when the abnormally low levels of the thirties and abnormally high levels of the early forties are ignored in the fitting, as in the trend labeled (2), the results differ only to a limited extent from those more tediously obtained above. In the first place, the trend as shown in that fitting lies below the actual level in 1955 nearly as much as below our estimate for 1960.[25] Our methods used above implicitly assume the 1955 actual level to be the trend level. The difference between our projection and the indication of the secular trend is slightly greater in 1965 because we have assumed some speeding up of productivity increases (instead of projecting the historic productivity trend).

We believe that the secular-trend projection is inferior because it does not bring to light shifting influences making for growth, such as change in working hours, shifts in product distribution from agriculture to general industry, and speeding up of technological change. Our techniques do not provide precise methods of evaluating these changes, but they force explicit recognition and require the making of judgments about them. The secular-trend procedure does not provide a precise method of locating the difference between actual and secular-growth levels, as can be seen by contrasting the two trends drawn on Chart 3–5. The one discussed above eliminates from consideration the actual levels for the fifteen-year period 1931–1945. On reflection it is clear that shutting out what actually happened in that period will produce a trend closer to the actual levels in the mid-fifties than number (1) on the chart, which takes the actual activity in the fifteen-year period at face value. But it is not clear that the method develops the appropriate deviation of the growth level from actual levels. The growth level being experienced in the present period is difficult to rationalize, and we employ the common current practice of starting with an actual level; in our case the actual level used is 1955, above the earlier cyclical low and below the later cyclical peak.

Another method, somewhat like a secular-trend line but inferior to it, is drawing a line through past cyclical peaks. The difficulty in doing this effectively is that some cyclical peaks are relatively higher than others. The trend slope obtained therefore is questionable. The important objective is to obtain a good estimate of the slope. Adjustment of trend level is readily made once the right slope is found.

---

at the present time to draw a clear distinction between trend and actual 1955 levels for any of the magnitudes involved. Attention is particularly called, however, to the assumption in the Dewhurst book that the productivity projection is on a line parallel to but above the trend. See Dewhurst and Associates, *ibid.*, p. 43. There is further discussion of this topic in the text.

[25] The trend is $17.8 billion in 1955 prices below the actual level in 1955 and $19.2 billion below our projection for 1960.

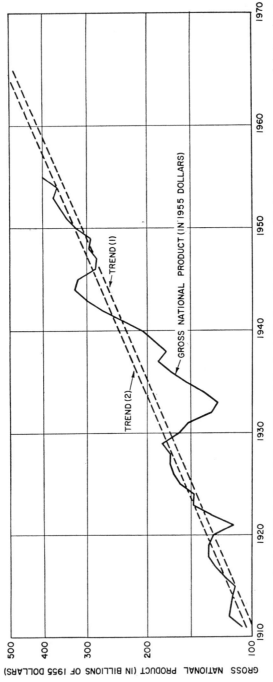

CHART 3-5. Secular-trend Projection of Gross National Product. Each of the trends is fitted to the nine 5-year averages 1913 to 1953. Trend (1) is fitted to the nine 5-year averages 1913 to 1953; the equation is log $Y_c = 2.2736 + 0.06303\,X$, where Y_c is the estimated gross national product in 1955 dollars, and X is time in 5-year units with a 1933 origin. Trend (2) is fitted to 5-year averages for the same period, except that the 1933, 1938, and 1943 averages are not used in the fitting; the equation is log $Y_c = 2.0426 + 0.06300\,X$, where Y_c is the estimated gross national product in 1955 dollars, and X is time in 5-year units with a 1913 origin.

56

CONTRAST WITH OTHER PROJECTIONS

The major projection presented above contrasts with other well-known projections as follows (gross national product stated in billions of 1955 dollars):

Projection	1960		1965	
	Product	Per cent difference	Product	Per cent difference
Our projection...............	450.5	0	524.6	0
Dewhurst *.................	417.0	−7.4		
Joint Committee †..........	...	...	545.0	+3.9
Stanford Research Institute ‡.	447.7	−1.6	532.6	+1.5
Fortune §..................	472.0	+4.8	570.7	+8.8

* J. Frederic Dewhurst and Associates, *America's Needs and Resources: A New Survey* (New York: The Twentieth Century Fund, Inc., 1955).

† Joint Congressional Committee on the Economic Report, *Potential Economic Growth of the United States during the Next Decade*, 83d Cong., 2d Sess., 1954.

‡ Bonnar Brown and M. Janet Hansen, *Production Trends in the United States through 1975* (Menlo Park, Calif.: Stanford Research Institute, 1957). Gross product is built up separately for 13 expenditure divisions. No decline in weekly hours is assumed from 1955 to 1975.

§ Gilbert Burck and Sanford S. Parker, "Another Big Decade for Capital Goods," *Fortune*, December, 1956.

The variation in forecasts for 1960 and 1965 is interesting but not as revealing as the different rates of growth indicated:

Projection	Geometric yearly percentage rate of growth implied	
	1955–1960	1955–1965
Our projection...............	2.9	3.0
Dewhurst....................	1.3	
Joint Committee..............	...	3.4
Stanford Research Institute.....	2.8	3.2
Fortune......................	3.6	3.8

The differences in rates of growth are largely due to varying assumptions about the increase in productivity, although some differences do appear in assumptions about labor time (all figures are in geometric percentage rates of growth per year):

Projection	1955–1960		1955–1965	
	Total manhours	Productivity	Total manhours	Productivity
Our projection.............	+0.6	+2.3	+0.7	+2.3
Dewhurst.................	−0.7	+2.1		
Joint Committee...........	...	...	+0.6	+2.9
Stanford Research Institute..	+1.1	+1.6	+1.3	+1.8
Fortune...................	+1.0	+3.0	+1.0	+3.0

The differences in assumptions regarding productivity relate to the expected effect of stepped-up mechanization. The differences appearing in assumed increases in total manhours relate largely to different assumptions regarding reduction in weekly hours. The Joint Committee projection assumes almost exactly the same increase in workers as our projection, but visualizes weekly hours as dropping to 36.2 in 1965 instead of to 37.5, as in our projection. The Dewhurst manhours projection is negative from 1955 to 1960 [26] because of a sharp decline in weekly hours from 40.4 to 37.5, and because employment was conceived to grow by only 2.8 million persons although a figure over 4 million now appears more probable. The Stanford Research Institute forecast assumes no decline to occur in weekly hours.

Except for the low Dewhurst forecast in 1960, these forecasts probably would give approximately the same answers in most applications. If the applications require great precision, a very careful analysis must be made, and it is necessary to realize that large risks are involved. The inference should not be drawn that the forecasts presented here provide a probable range. However, lower forecasts would imply a tapering off of productivity or drastic cuts in the workweek, and higher forecasts would imply unprecedented rises in productivity, no decline in the workweek, or a stepped-up participation of females in the labor force.

[26] The 1955 figures were not available when the Dewhurst forecast was made, and the projections were from 1950 or 1952. From 1950 to 1960 the total-manhours projection rises 0.5 per cent a year. We have used the 1955 to 1960 comparison to make the forecast comparable with the others.

THE SECULAR TREND OF PRICES

The reader will note that all the above analysis relates to the projection of physical product. The projection of price has been ignored for two principal reasons: (1) analyses of the factors responsible for secular change in prices have not led to a generally accepted technique for projecting that movement; and (2) secular change in prices, unlike rise in physical product, cannot be looked on as an objective or aim.

Few analysts have attempted to provide a secular-trend projection of prices, for the determining factors are generally thought to be largely the result of arbitrary decisions made by those in control of the monetary system. Also, long swings in prices are vastly changed by the advent of war. Some efforts to develop uniformities on the basis of which a projection can be made are reviewed below, but their use in this connection is so recent that the methods evolved have not met the test of wide criticism.

In the era of twenty-five years ago, when mechanical projection of secular trends was the recognized method of growth forecasting, little use was made of trend projection to forecast prices. Prices were thought to move in a long cycle but were usually not believed to follow a consistent longer trend.

The long-term trend of prices is of major importance, as we shall note below, but it is commonly considered important in a negative way. Either inflationary or deflationary prices of any substantial extent are accepted as bad, although some analysts argue for a slowly rising price level and others for a slowly falling one. Still others argue that the ideal situation is achieved when average prices neither rise nor fall. In all of these cases, the movement of general prices is not thought to be an objective of inherent importance; rather, it is viewed as a means for providing a more desirable physical-production goal, in terms either of achieving a higher level or of avoiding variation in production, or as a means for providing a more desirable distribution of product from an ethical standpoint. Rise in physical production is, of course, considered to be an appropriate objective for its own sake.

. Turning now to the importance of the future level of prices, the influence of the price movement on physical output should be emphasized. As often noted, the past level of output would scarcely have been the same with a different movement of prices. Hence, we cannot expect the future level of physical product to be unrelated to the price movement. Some analysts have gone so far as to contend that physical-production projections should be made only on the assumption that price changes will be similar in the future. This position seems a bit extreme in so far as secular trends are concerned, for the trends are conceived to represent the result obtained when short-period movements are averaged out. It is scarcely necessary to assume that the short-period variations would be precisely duplicated from one time to another. The general drift of prices is another matter. When the trend of prices is gently upward, incentives to produce may be somewhat increased, so that growth in physical production might be significantly encouraged. The opposite situation develops with declining prices. Certainly a real weakness in the technique of projecting physical product outlined above is that no allowance is made for the difference in outcome to be expected with different price movements. An allowance of this sort would be possible if a reliable forecast of the secular movement of prices were available, as noted below.

A forecast of the secular trend of prices is also important because of its relation to financial commitments. Notably in the case of capital formation, the future price level is of first importance in deciding what financial arrangements are most desirable. With rising prices the enterprising firm may gain by bond flotation because, on the average, property purchased will gain in value while the commitment is for a fixed amount. In similar circumstances the investor will usually gain by purchasing stocks, for his equity will tend to increase in relation to the increase in prices. Many institutional investors have shifted to investment in stocks in recent years, partly because secular increases in prices were anticipated.

Rex F. Daly has developed the most promising procedure for forecasting the secular trend of prices, and we employ it with slight modifications in the forecast presented here.[27] Daly's principal assumptions are that the quantity theory is essentially a tool for long-run appraisals, that the amount of means of payment is more nearly a result than an independent cause of change in the price level, that the government will be at least partly effective in its countercyclical measures to maintain full employment, and that there will be no wartime conditions or long periods of semimobilization of sufficient magnitude to produce continued inflationary pressure of substantial extent. We adopt these assumptions although we do not assume that the defense effort will drop much, if at all, below present levels. The general price level appears to have followed a rising secular trend since the 1880s, and this trend is projected into the future in Chart 3–6.[28] It is clear that over the long period, total money in the

---

[27] Rex F. Daly, "Some Considerations in Appraising the Long-run Prospects for Agriculture," in *Studies in Income and Wealth*, vol. XVI. Also see Daly's more recent price projections in "The Long-run Demand for Farm Products," *Agricultural Economics Research*, July, 1956.

[28] The secular trend of a price index is a particularly vulnerable measure, in that the long-period price index is obtained by splicing together separate indices weighted by the importance of the commodities in each subperiod. However, some-

economic system has risen more rapidly than quantity output of goods and services.[29] We assume, however, that means of payment will ultimately adapt to the need for them, so we would expect money in use to continue to rise proportionately more rapidly than the physical volume of trade, as similarly occurred in the past. Under these circumstances,

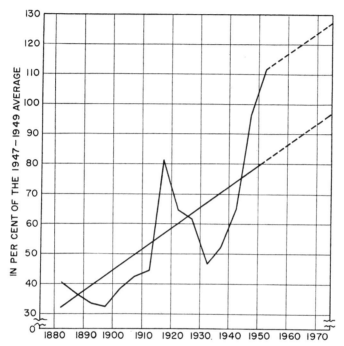

CHART 3–6. Secular Trend of the Wholesale Price Index. The equation of the computed trend line is $Y_c = 56.53 + 3.491\ X$, with Y_c representing estimated price index in per cent of the 1947–49 average, and X representing time in 5-year units with a 1918 origin. The trend line starting at the 1953 average point is merely a line parallel to the computed trend line lying at a lower level. SOURCE: The price data are from the Bureau of Labor Statistics Index of Wholesale Prices, with splicing to early series by the Bureau of Labor Statistics.

something like the price projection shown in Chart 3–6 would eventuate if the quantity theory were assumed to describe the long-term movement.

In the price projection shown in Chart 3–6 no assumption is made as to a price deflationary movement in the near future. Therefore, the price trend is projected from the level of the early fifties. Since the postwar rise has been substantial, the price level of the early fifties was con-

---

what the same trend, as shown in Chart 3–6, is found when various different indices of prices are employed.

[29] See Daly's charts indicating this and his discussion of the reasons for it in *Studies in Income and Wealth*, vol. XVI, pp. 139–140.

siderably above the level of trend fitted to past data. The trend projection is made from the level of the early fifties, but at the slope established by the fitted trend.

The secular trend of prices should also be checked against the relation between rising wage rates and rising productivity. If relatively prosperous levels of business activity continue, strong wage pressures are likely under our present institutional arrangements. Under these circumstances, the trend projected in Chart 3–6 is not implausible. However, the approximate trend shown is by no means implied. The relation between rises in wage rates, productivity, and physical product might be employed as the central technique in forecasting the secular trend of prices, but essential assumptions would have to be made regarding the relations to expect between these trends. Any method so far developed for making such assumptions is too subjective to warrant consideration.

Since we assume that there will be no protracted deflationary periods, the rising price movement will not be effectively offset by declines. If a war were to break out, the price rise certainly would be accelerated, but our assumption is that a war will not occur. In this connection, the secular trend shown on Chart 3–6 might be criticized, in that the general slope developed in the past arose principally from the price movement during wars and after wars. The peak in the 1870s is a post-Civil War development, and the two price highs in the twentieth century follow World Wars I and II. It might be asked: Does not a continuation of a trend so produced assume the occurrence of other wars?

As noted, no substantial deflation is expected in the future and therefore no major retreat from the present price level is in the picture. Since a continuation of the past trend is consistent with the rise which has been occurring in the quantity output of goods and services and in the supply of money (as emphasized above), it is a general movement logically consistent with an extension of the trend in the quantity output of goods and services. In a realistic sense, this means that a price rise has been built into the system much as otherwise might have arisen as the result of war. The extrapolation of the trend is not the method emphasized in the earlier part of this chapter for forecasting growth in physical product, but such an extrapolation was found to provide results reasonably consistent with the method recommended.

If a secular-trend projection of prices is to be made, the question might be asked: Why did we not project the trend of value product to begin with? With our present knowledge, it is preferable to consider physical product and price separately, for we are better able to visualize the responsible forces in each than in an undifferentiated value product. For some purposes it may be desirable to put the forecast in the form of the secular trend of value product. We do not multiply the two forecasts to show this result, for we feel, in view of the uncertainties in the price forecast, that the resulting value-product figure might well be more improbable than the segregated physical-product projection. However, the forecast of the secular trend of prices, being consistent with past relationships, should not be considered an unreasonable statement of the price movement implied by our forecast of growth in physical product.

The degree of artificiality introduced into the problem by considering price and physical product separately must not be ignored. Our initial data on physical product are derived from totaled figures on the market value of goods and services. To reduce the data to a physical basis, the values had to be divided by price indices. Although this was done with some care, the result is necessarily an imperfect estimate. The time may come when a better-integrated forecast of value product can be derived, but it is not useful to attempt to anticipate that time by employing present inadequate tools to make a joint forecast in one step.

LENGTH OF GROWTH FORECAST NEEDED

The growth forecast is needed both for the perspective gained with some understanding of the total level of activity to be expected and for estimating the amounts of various types of durable goods which will be needed. Illustrations of what the perspective of future total growth can contribute to our understanding are almost endless. The knowledge of change to be expected in standards of living helps us to perceive many sorts of readjustments which will take place in our way of living. Standards of leisure, education, and public spending, for instance, will be vitally affected. Planning for such adjustments will help us make them more smoothly. The length of forecast required to attain the desired perspective depends upon how rapidly the standards of living are rising and upon the kinds of problems envisaged. When the rise is very slow, adjustments may be made effectively enough without explicit allowance for the amount of change. When change in living standards is very rapid, a forecast of ten to twenty years may be required to dramatize the decided change to which adjustment must be made.

As noted in Chapter 1, public bodies are concerned not only with the life of man-made durable goods but also with the rate at which natural resources are being exhausted. For the latter it is not easy to estimate in general the length of forecast needed. For each resource the problem turns on the rapidity of exhaustion and the apparent prospect for developing substitutes.

For the building of durable plant and equipment, theoretically, we should know the needs for the product for as long as the new facility will last. In many cases the forecast theoretically required would be so long as to be impractical, e.g., in the case of dams and water-front developments. The most pressing need, however, is to estimate the usefulness of the facilities for limited periods into the future, say twenty or thirty years. The loss sustained because of lack of understanding of the use to be made of any structure beyond thirty years into the future is not likely to be great.

The need for over-all growth forecasts in understanding the requirements for durable goods of all kinds arises because a prime determinant of requirements for any particular kind of durable goods is the total level of activity in support of which it will be required.

Private industry is constantly faced with decisions about the amount and kind of capital expansion which is desirable. The building of facilities which cannot be used is to be avoided, but failure to build needed facilities may be equally costly. Logically, a forecast is needed for the full period the installed facility can be expected to last. In actual practice, resort is frequently had to such devices as charging for the facility over relatively short payout periods. Although such procedures may aid in maintaining solvency, in the absence of any knowledge of needs over the period the facilities will last, they in no way obviate the problem. Profits will be influenced just as much, if too much or too little equipment is built, as if no accounting hedge had been employed to provide some assurance that the principal expended can be recouped within a limited time.

Even though adequate forecasts for the full life of the facility cannot be made, it will be very helpful to extend the period for which an approximation of requirements is estimated. As indicated above, the importance of such knowledge dwindles rapidly for the latter years of the life of a highly durable facility. Necessary adjustments can frequently be made, possibly by slightly earlier retirements of old equipment or, in the opposite situation, by making new additions earlier than at first expected. Precise estimates cannot be made of depreciation or obsolescence in any case.

Many of the forecasts presented in this book are for shorter than the most desirable periods, as are most of those now in use in business. As we become better acquainted with the techniques available and improve them, longer forecasts may become less hazardous.

CHAPTER 4

Forecasting the Growth of Major Expenditure Divisions

Growth in various parts of the economy cannot be represented by growth in the total economy, although growth in every part is obviously dependent upon the growth occurring in the total economy. One industry may grow very rapidly while another grows very slowly or declines, even though they are both related to total growth. Consideration should be given to growth in the various parts of the economy so that the growth arising in the total economy may be better understood. Furthermore, we are generally interested in specific areas of growth.

As a first step, we consider in this chapter growth in the major expenditure divisions. This provides a broad background for visualizing the directions in which growth is to be expected. It also provides a first step in getting down to more specific growth. In most individual industries the relation to particular expenditure divisions is better than to aggregate gross national product.

The major expenditure divisions separately considered are those employed by the Department of Commerce. A ready reference to known measurements is thus available. Recent studies have most commonly been made with these groupings so that comparisons can be readily applied to current changes and to past relations.

RESIDENTIAL BUILDING

Before considering actual forecasting procedures, it is well to note the influences which will be responsible for growth in residential building. The most important influence is growth in number of households, if we define a household, in accordance with the usual practice, as a unit of one or more persons occupying separate living quarters. Households thus give us a housekeeping inventory comprising houses, apartments, groups of rooms, and even, in some cases, single rooms. The increase in households, when buttressed with other indicators, measures new housing demand. It must be immediately recognized, however, that the other indicators are by no means unimportant.

1. There are what is known as "quasi households," representing those persons living in institutions, hotels, and large rooming houses. In 1930 the population in quasi households amounted to 2.5 per cent of the nonfarm-household population and rose to 4.5 per cent in 1950. It would appear, therefore, that centering attention on households which exclude the quasi household facilities will understate growth requirements.

2. In the World War II period increase in the supply of housing was far under the demand level, and considerable "doubling up" occurred, i.e., families lived together in the same household to an abnormal extent. While "undoubling" was taking place in recent years, the growth of households proceeded with unusual rapidity. Little further undoubling remains to be effected.

3. However, "the number of social units forming households has great potential flexibility. This point may be illustrated by reference to 1950 data. Given the marital and age composition of the United States nonfarm population in 1950, it is possible to arrive at a potential maximum for that year of at least 57 million households as against an actual number of only 37.4 million, or half again as large." [1] The most important part of this potential of roughly 20 million is covered by single, widowed, divorced, or separated persons who are eighteen or older and living with relatives. Single-person households rose from 7.7 per cent of the total in 1930 to 7.9 per cent in 1940 and to 9.1 per cent in 1950. These figures represent the effect of a substantial tendency for single adults in younger age groups to establish a household, either individually or in small groups, and for older single persons to maintain or establish households. Almost a fourth of all occupied nonfarm dwelling units were absorbed in 1950 by other than husband-wife households. There is a definite probability that this proportion will expand still further.

4. The size of new houses built for middle-income families is increasing because families are becoming larger and because living standards are rising. The value of new housing will thus advance more rapidly than is indicated by increases in *number* of households.

5. Large expenditure for additions and alterations to old houses is a similar factor; it is also generated by rising living standards and the trend to larger families. It is just as truly a new-demand factor as increase

---

[1] Leo Grebler, David M. Blank, and Louis Winnick, *Capital Formation in Residential Real Estate: Trends and Prospects* (Princeton, N.J.: Princeton University Press, 1956), p. 80.

in the size of houses built for middle-income families, although it may not relate to work done on houses made for additional households.

6. Housing supply has partly come from conversion of large old houses. Relatively few such structures remain available for further conversion. Since the construction cost of conversion is ordinarily less than is required to provide equal facilities by new building, fewer conversions will result in an increase in the value of housing demand.[2]

7. A substantial increase has been occurring recently in what may be called nonhousekeeping residential facilities. These cover tourist cabins, motor courts, transient hotels, and dormitories. Such living quarters are not included among households as defined above, and it is not feasible to estimate their number. The number would be of limited significance anyway, for the type of facilities involved varies widely. The best procedure is to analyze such facilities in terms of dollar expenditure involved. Indications are that expenditures of this type are likely to show significant increases.

Consideration must be given to demand for replacement as well as to new housing demand. Replacement of housing, unlike most types of capital goods, would appear not to be closely related to age. It is important therefore to consider carefully the various factors which will result in demolition:

1. Demolition occurs in the razing of blighted areas and of other substandard units in urban-renewal projects. The work has grown because of governmental policy and has generally won public approval.

2. The road-building program will result in substantial demolition of houses through condemnation procedures or otherwise.

3. Relative oversupply may result in demolition in areas from which emigration has been substantial. Such demolition is likely to occur somewhat later than supply is added by the emigrants in their new abode. Demolition when residential neighborhoods change to commercial or industrial districts produces a similar result.

4. There are disaster losses arising from fire, windstorm, etc. Most of such losses lead either to replacement or to the occupancy of an idle house.

5. In a realistic sense, few houses ever "wear out." They may become uninhabitable because of neglect. Neglect is likely to result from slack housing demand in a particular area, from obsolescence requiring a

---

[2] In the value figures, conversions ordinarily are shown as a part of additions and alterations. A direct division of the value of new houses by the number of new households would thus assume that conversions added costlessly to housing supply, which is of course in error. Increased cost in servicing an aging housing stock may in the future make up for the slowing in additions and alterations produced by less conversions.

major program of rehabilitation, from failure to make current repairs and reasonable maintenance expenditures, or for other reasons. If incomes are high, replacement or rehabilitation expenditures are greatly increased. Regular replacement or rehabilitation of old houses is thus most significantly influenced by the level of income.

It seems probable that, all of these factors considered, demolition is likely to increase in near future years, and thus add to the growth in gross new housing demand.

Change in housing costs will influence to a greater or less degree all of the above factors bearing on new housing. So little is known about probable long-term changes in housing costs that it may as well be assumed that such costs will move in direct proportion to the consumer price index.

In summary, visualized from the point of view of the long term, new housing demand will depend principally upon growth in the number of families, the number of single adults forming households, increase in size and quality of housing, growth in nonhousekeeping residential facilities, expenditures for additions and alterations and for rehabilitation of obsolete houses, and replacements forced by demolitions.

Twentieth Century Fund Method.[3] Various ingenious approaches have been taken in projecting residential construction. The method employed by the Twentieth Century Fund in the monumental work *America's Needs and Resources* is a useful illustration. The change in construction is made to depend upon a forecast of house rent, including both actual and imputed rent. The house-rent figure is $20.2 billion in 1950, and it is projected to $24.7 billion in 1960, representing a very slight decline in percentage of projected total consumption expenditures (from 10.4 to 10.2). The projection of rent is made by relating it to total disposable income and studying the trend of rent as a per cent of total consumption expenditures.

The house-rent figure is estimated to represent 8.5 per cent of the value of housing stock. Housing-stock values are derived by dividing house-rent figures by 0.085. Housing stock is thus estimated to come to $238 billion in 1950 and $291 billion in 1960. The increase of $53 billion divided by 10 provides an estimate of $5.3 billion new-owner demand per year.

To obtain estimates of replacement, the Bureau of Internal Revenue's allowable depreciation rate of 2.5 per cent is employed. For 1960, 2.5 per cent of $291 billion is $7.3 billion.[4] Total housing demand in 1960 is

---

[3] J. Frederic Dewhurst and Associates, *America's Needs and Resources: A New Survey* (New York: The Twentieth Century Fund, Inc., 1955), pp. 196–231, 1004, 1008, 1012–1015. Both farm and nonfarm housing are included in these estimates.

[4] We have carried too few decimal places in these illustrations, and therefore our rounding of decimal places is artificial.

therefore estimated (in billions of 1950 dollars) at 12.6, the sum of 5.3 plus 7.3.

National Planning Association Method.[5] The number of new nonfarm dwelling units projected for 1960 is 864,000. This figure is obtained by taking a tenth of the projected total demand for 1950–60. The demand is visualized as made up of three parts—to provide for new families, to bring the vacancy ratio up to 4 per cent, and to make replacements:

Demand factor	Millions of units
New families	5.0
Establish 4% vacancy ratio	1.0
Replacements	2.64
Total	8.64

The replacements are made up of 1.4 million units thought to "wear out" by 1960; 400,000 to compensate for disaster and demolition losses; 300,000 to compensate for removal of temporary war housing; and 540,000 to replace a fifth of the 2.7 million houses estimated by the Housing and Home Finance Agency to be in a dilapidated condition.[6]

In making dollar-expenditure projections it is possible to be more inclusive. The 864,000 new nonfarm dwelling units are assumed to cost $7.5 billion and, in addition, allowance is made for expenditures for farm houses, nonhousekeeping units, and additions and alterations, as follows:

Demand factor	Billions of 1951 dollars
New nonfarm dwelling units	7.5
New farm dwelling units	0.7
Additions and alterations	1.0
Nonhousekeeping units	0.2
Total	9.4

Grebler, Blank, and Winnick Study.[7] Although the authors take the sound position that to provide a numerical forecast of the volume of capital formation in residential real estate would involve tasks beyond the scope of the study of one sector of the economy, such as specific assumptions on changes in nonfarm population and gross national product, they throw more light on the outlook for residential housing than does

[5] Gerhard Colm and Marilyn Young, *The American Economy in 1960*, Planning Pamphlet 81 (Washington: National Planning Association, 1952), pp. 127–129. The work is based primarily on the Housing and Home Finance Agency pamphlet "How Big Is the Housing Job?"

[6] Actual need is assumed to be larger, but it is felt that additional policy measures would be required to meet this need.

[7] Leo Grebler, David M. Blank, and Louis Winnick, *op. cit.*

any other study to date. They arrive at the conclusion that demolitions "seem to reach proportions calling for a large volume of new construction over and above the long-term rate of net household formation." Thus,[8]

If withdrawals from housing supply of 300,000 dwelling units per year are added to an annual average net nonfarm household formation in the neighborhood of 1,000,000 for the period 1950 to 1975, close to the median estimate derived from the projections of the Bureau of the Census, the average number of new dwelling units that would equal these two potential sources of demand far exceeds any historical record for a similar period.

The annual average of a million new nonfarm households a year depends partly on the median Census Bureau population projection and partly on decline in the average number of persons per household. The number declined every decade, from 4.36 persons in 1900 to 3.44 persons in 1950.[9] An assumed average of about 3.2 persons for the period 1950–75 would imply 25 million added households at the Census Bureau's median estimate. As a matter of fact, the average persons per household may come closer to 3.0, which would imply about 30 million households, or an average of 1.2 million per year. The reasons for expecting a continued decline in number of persons per household are: [10]

. . . continued urbanization; the likely further decrease in age at time of marriage; the adoption of culture patterns dominant among white natives by sons and daughters of immigrants; the increase in longevity coupled with the desire of older persons to maintain their own households; social security and pension programs which make it increasingly possible for retired persons to do so; the tendency for single adults in younger age groups to establish a household either individually or in small groups; and, perhaps as the most important force permitting an increasingly larger number of households from a given population, a rise in real per capita income.

Furthermore, increases in the housing inventory considered broadly are not limited to the provision of primary housekeeping facilities for new households. With advancing income levels, an increasing number of households are demanding supplementary seasonal dwelling units— summer or vacation cottages. Vacant seasonal dwelling units almost doubled, from slightly over a half million, between the 1940 and 1950 censuses.

The decline in real expenditure per new dwelling unit may be arrested

---

[8] *Ibid.*, p. 322. The Census Bureau's projections, modified by the authors of the study, together with number of nonfarm households, at various assumed numbers of persons per household, are given on p. 269.

[9] *Ibid.*, p. 82. Quasi households are included in totals employed to develop these averages.

[10] *Ibid.*, p. 268.

or reversed. The most important factor which will operate to reduce real capital per dwelling unit is continued population shift to the South and West where climatic conditions make less elaborate housing acceptable. Working in the opposite direction are rapid increases in the number of children in their teens, increasing installation of expensive types of equipment, and a trend toward more bathrooms and a finished recreation room, and other factors. On balance, it is felt that the odds are in favor of a further decline in real capital per dwelling unit, but with the rate of decline slowing down substantially.

The proportion of expenditures for additions and alterations is thought likely to increase in the future, as it did in the past. There will be a larger housing stock of increasing average age. The income elasticity for additions and alterations is greater than for new houses, and therefore rising income will exert a major influence. Progressive removal of rent control will lead to greater expenditure in tenant-occupied dwellings.

Turning to withdrawals from the housing supply, demolitions are likely to increase because of stricter enforcement of local safety and sanitary laws, because of the expansion of highway construction through built-up urban areas, and because of government aids to urban redevelopment. Internal nonfarm migration may, for the first time, lead to substantial demolitions because slower growth or decline in the old developed areas may create pockets of vacancies in areas of emigration. Sustained rise in real income and a more even income distribution may cause consumers to abandon the least desirable housing facilities. However, the migration and immigration of less priviliged persons may absorb such facilities in the future as they have in the past. Advancing age of the housing stock may produce a higher rate of demolitions, but there is little historical or logical evidence to support the conclusion.

The analysis is enriched by studies of average change from one long cycle to the next, long cycles being a well-known characteristic of residential housing. No direct method of forecasting is developed by making such contrasts, however; notably, no effort is made to project long cycles into the future.

The forecasts in this study are more qualitative than quantitative, but they may be as useful as quantitative forecasts at the present stage of our knowledge, or even more useful. The coverage given is not readily available in quantitative form at the present time. On the basis of the evidence presented, we project 1.2 million new units per year to 1965 as a plausible forecast to employ in integrating the forecasts of major expenditure divisions later in the chapter.[10a]

[10a] See the author's "Prospects for Growth in the Housing Industry," *Commercial and Financial Chronicle,* vol. 187, June 5, 1958.

OTHER PRIVATE CONSTRUCTION AND PRODUCER EQUIPMENT

Construction includes many diverse areas, for instance, railway lines, office buildings, churches, steel furnaces, hospitals, and electric power plants. Equipment is equally varied, ranging from a machine tool or a tractor to a ship or a locomotive. Construction, as distinct from equipment, refers to immobile structures and to facilities which become integral parts of them and which are essential to their use for any general purpose. We shall not attempt at all times to distinguish between construction and equipment, for in many ways the forecasting problems they present are common to both. The principal difference for our purpose is that construction is usually the more durable. Each type of construction and equipment represents a durable stock which is employed to produce goods or services. This characteristic is our chief concern in forecasting.

Durable private capital—covering both construction and equipment—is needed to the extent that there will exist a future demand for the product it will produce. Theoretically, then, the capital forecast should be derived from the product forecast. Although this is a simple, straightforward concept, several qualifications are essential. It may not well describe the way businessmen decide to make an investment, although to an increasing extent decisions are formed by looking at expected future demand. In some cases, especially in small businesses, the period envisaged is so short that the method might be better characterized as a decision founded on current demand. Even in business organizations which go through rather elaborate forecasting analysis, forecasts of the far future are likely to be qualified by the level of current demand at the time of the forecast.

Of course, it is true that failure to visualize future demand clearly makes the demand for capital variable rather than primarily reducing or raising it. If future demand is underestimated, capacity may appear insufficient in a following prosperity, leading to a high rate of capital expansion. If such an expansion is excessive in the light of long-term capital demand, a period of very limited capital formation will follow, and such a cycle may continue to repeat itself. Capital expansion has been highly variable in the past, although this is partly the outgrowth of wars.

Wide variations reduce the growth level and thus cut down on the future level of product demand, for periods of low capital formation generate deficient demand which cannot be entirely compensated for at prosperity peaks. The forecasting practice will modify at least to some minor extent the actual need for capital.

We have been referring to a total capital stock sufficient to provide a required level of product. If attention is directed to more detailed expenditures, part of the total stock may be found to comprise unadaptable capacity which would be excessive in relation to a demand which may be shrinking. The extent of such ineffective capacity may vary from time to time, especially with an inconstant rate of development in new industries, so that some uncertainty about the level of capacity needed is introduced. Somewhat similarly, shifting distribution of demand will change the level of capacity needed, for the capacity required to produce a product of given value varies greatly among industries.

To maintain a satisfactory level of capacity, it is necessary not only to make additions in accordance with growing demands for the product it is used to make but to replace parts which wear out or become obsolete. A fairly common procedure assumes that capital possesses a given life and that yearly replacements are required in accordance with that life. No very reliable information is available as to what that length of life actually is. At the present time much of the demand for capital is for modernization and is founded on obsolescence rather than on exhaustion.

Another method assumes that depreciation and obsolescence are represented by accounting capital-consumption allowances and that future replacement can be projected by allowing for changes taking place in the age and life expectancy of capital stock. A difficulty is that present capital-consumption allowances probably do not represent depreciation and obsolescence very effectively. This is true partly because accounting procedures setting them up are oriented to take advantage of permissive depreciation allowances for income tax purposes. It is sometimes possible to make rational adjustments which would appear to bring the accounting figures closer to realistic depreciation levels, but truly satisfactory levels have not been achieved.

An additional difficulty is represented by price changes, especially if these have been great for capital installed, because dollar consumption allowances are dependent upon original costs. Adjustments to eliminate differences in price level represented in the value of capital stock require much information not readily available and have not been entirely satisfactory.

With rapid technological advancement, obsolescence is speeded up, and needs for replacement increase. Replacements may be required more rapidly than indicated by the length-of-life actuarial procedure.

Attention is often given to the level of interest rates as an important factor determining demand for capital, but it is doubtful that it should be emphasized in connection with long-term forecasting. If interest rates should reach permanently high levels, the cost of capital would be influenced accordingly, but the demand for it relative to other goods might not be affected. Labor substitution, where technically feasible, might be no less desirable in a high-interest-rate economy, for wage rates might also be proportionately high in any extended period.

Twentieth Century Fund Method.[11] The forecast of durable private investment is obtained by projecting a logarithmic straight-line trend of the percentage durable private capital is of gross private product.[12] The trend value for 1960 is 11.0 per cent; multiplying by projected gross private product, a forecast of $47.6 billion in 1955 prices is obtained. Variation about the trend line is very large, but, omitting the period from 1931 to 1946, it is not so large as to make a trend passing through the series appear implausible. However, similar trends drawn separately through the construction and plant subdivisions show much greater fluctuation about their trend lines, and hence less plausible fits. The fit to the postwar period for total durable capital is, in fact, founded on a large positive deviation for equipment and a large negative deviation for construction; it is generalized that the proportionate importance of construction and equipment may have permanently shifted.[13]

The 11.0 per cent developed for 1960 is slightly higher than for any previous period for which estimates are available. This is argued to be credible because of notable new technological developments, probable government encouragement, and population growth greater than in recent decades.

National Planning Association Method.[14] The 1960 forecast of durable private capital investment is made on the assumption that it will represent 9.5 per cent of gross private product. The actual figure from 1919 to 1951 is 10.2 per cent, and from 1929 to 1951 is 9.1 per cent. Both figures are considered to have disadvantages, so the figure of 9.5 per cent is chosen. Checked against past and projected relations, this is held to be reasonable.[15]

---

[11] Dewhurst and Associates, *op. cit.*, pp. 481–486.

[12] Gross private product is gross national product minus government purchases of services. Machinery and Allied Products Institute series and trends, fitted to the 1910 to 1930 period, are employed; they are reproduced in a chart on p. 481 of *America's Needs and Resources.* Capital charged to current expense is excluded in the MAPI study.

[13] Dewhurst and Associates, *op. cit.*, p. 482.

[14] Gerhard Colm and Marilyn Young, *op. cit.*, pp. 121–127.

[15] A check is made to determine how much investment stock should grow in order to provide for a 3 per cent growth in gross private product. From studies of the Machinery and Allied Products Institute (*Capital Goods Review*, no. 4, November, 1950, and no. 22, May, 1955), an estimate of 1.55 times as much capital stock as gross private product is developed. If gross private product grows by 3 per cent per year and stock has to keep 1.55 times as big, stock will have to grow by 3 times 1.55, or 4.65 per cent of gross private product. New investment will have to be 4.65 per cent of gross private product. But even if the stock-to-product ratio is approximately correct, there remains the difficulty of estimating capital replacement

An adjusted model is set up using the assumption that durable private capital investment will be 10.5 instead of 9.5 per cent of gross private product. Possible reasons for the higher figure are suggested: capital stock may have to be higher than shown by past relationships to a year's output because some stand-by facilities may be built in the defense program, and automation may be raising the rate of obsolescence. At the present time, five years after this study was made, it seems clear that heavy reliance placed on the 1919–51 period gives too much weight to the Great Depression. It will be noted that even the adjusted-model percentage is lower than the 11.0 per cent projection employed in the Twentieth Century Fund study.

Machinery and Allied Products Institute Method.[16] The stock of equipment is projected to rise 4 per cent per year from 1960 to 1965 and the plant stock 3 per cent. The rate for equipment has been substantially higher in the postwar period to date than shown in these projections, and the rate for plant has been somewhat lower. Since equipment expenditures are much greater than plant expenditures, the combined expenditure is projected to grow at about 3.7 per cent per year. Replacement expenditures are expected to grow at approximately the same rate. They were only about a third of total plant and equipment expenditures in the immediate postwar period, but they have risen to constitute approximately two-thirds and are expected to remain at about that level from 1960 to 1965. More attention is given here to dividing the expenditure between replacements and additions than in the other studies reviewed, and replacements are estimated to represent a larger precentage of the total.

The 3.7 per cent growth is about the same as shown by the Twentieth Century Fund study from 1950 to 1960. The types of equipment included in these estimates are not the same as in the *Fortune* study reviewed below since a more limited area is represented, but when adjustment is made for arithmetic differences, the order of magnitude is not materially different.[17]

The Fortune Studies.[18] In 1954 durable private investment was projected at slightly less than 10 per cent of gross national product, but sights on future prospects for investment had risen by 1956, so that the projection was increased to around 11 per cent.[19] The percentage held

---

and no adequate basis for doing it, so estimates along these lines are presented as purely illustrative.

[16] *Capital Goods Review*, nos. 22 and 24, May, 1955, and November, 1955.

[17] See footnotes 19 and 20.

[18] Gilbert Burck and Sanford S. Parker, "Another Big Decade for Capital Goods," *Fortune*, December, 1956. See also a series of four articles in the September to December issues of 1954.

[19] Even though expressed in terms of gross national product instead of gross private product, these percentages are roughly comparable to those given in the

between 10 and 11 for the most part from 1947 to 1956, reaching 10.8 in 1956. The projection is at 11.3 per cent in 1960 and at 10.6 per cent in 1965. The capital-goods industry is thought not to be "gorging itself on its market prematurely."

A key factor in reaching this conclusion is the capital-output ratio, i.e., the ratio of capital stock to yearly gross national product. This figure is estimated to have declined steadily from early in the Great Depression to the end of World War II, from well over 2 to about 1.5. The principal reason for the decline is the increasing proportion of relatively short-lived equipment in the total stock. Equipment investment was running at about the same level as nonresidential construction in the twenties, but recently it has been 50 per cent greater. Equipment investment is not expected to rise further relative to construction investment, and therefore the capital-output ratio is expected to stabilize at about its present level. Gross national product is projected to rise 4 per cent per year, and with a constant capital-output ratio, new durable private investment would also grow at that rate.[20]

It should be clear from the discussion of the two preceding studies that the capital-output ratio is useful only in estimating the amount of

---

studies reviewed above. *Fortune* employs the Department of Commerce estimates of investment; the Twentieth Century Fund and the National Planning Association rely principally on Machinery and Allied Products Institute data in the forecasts outlined above. There are some substantial differences in the investment numerator and government services are omitted in the denominator when gross private product is employed as the base in the Twentieth Century Fund study. The Twentieth Century Fund converted the 11.0 per cent projected to 1960 into the form of private productive facilities (excluding residential and institutional investment) over gross national product and obtained 11.4 per cent as the result. But in doing so, capital outlays charged to current expense were used as estimated in the 1951 edition of the Department of Commerce's *National Income Supplement* (MAPI had omitted entirely capital charged to current expense), and these have since been revised to a much lower level; the revised series is a component part of the series used by *Fortune*. The revision in the series depicting capital charged to current expense is enough to account for the difference between the 11.0 and the 11.4 per cent. Most of the conceptual differences and revisions could be adjusted for statistically to provide a more precise comparison.

[20] The percentage of new investment to be added to capital stock will equal the growth rate of gross national product multiplied by the capital-output ratio. This is 4 times 1.52 for 1960, or 6.08 per cent of $483 billion, or $29.4 billion. Replacement investment is projected at $25.2 billion, making total new durable private investment $54.6 billion (all in 1956 prices).

In a letter dated January 16, 1957, Sanford S. Parker stated: "The figures on stock of capital goods were derived basically from similar figures published by the Machinery and Allied Products Institute. Their figures, in turn, were calculated from data on the purchases of the various products and survival curves (not depreciation curves). We modified their figures to include institutional construction (excluding religious construction). The stock data cover only privately held plant and equipment. However, we use total GNP, including government product, as an output measure mainly for presentation purposes. By including government product, we introduce some error in the capital-output ratio but this did not distort the picture appreciably."

capital investment to be added to capital stock; replacement investment must be estimated by some other method. Replacement investment is projected to rise 40 per cent from 1956 to 1965, at approximately the same rate as investment made to add to capital stock. The method employed in estimating replacement investment is described in the 1954 *Fortune* articles. Survival curves are built up based on length of life permissible for establishing capital-consumption allowances for income tax purposes (as estimated by the Internal Revenue Service).

The projected levels of durable capital investment are somewhat higher than those made by the National Planning Association and the Twentieth Century Fund at earlier dates because gross national product is projected to rise at a rate of 4 per cent per year, substantially higher than the rate used in these earlier studies. The estimate for 1960 is $54.6 billion out of a projected gross national product of $483 billion (both in 1956 prices), or 11.3 per cent. The estimate for 1965 is $62 billion out of a projected gross national product of $585 billion, or 10.6 per cent. These capital projections were checked against surveys of business plans, conducted by *Fortune,* and separate estimates for other types of investment. The producers of capital goods estimated the market at $65 billion in 1965, and the estimate of the buyers of capital goods was $59 billion. The two figures average at the $62 billion projected.

Adding together estimates for major divisions of capital investment, the total for 1965 again comes to $62 billion. Of this, $38.5 billion is seen going to equipment and $23.5 billion to construction, a proportional distribution about equivalent to that existing in recent years. Capital investment in some industries, however, is expected to rise more rapidly than in others. The electrical industry is expected to increase its investment expenditure by more than 80 per cent from 1956 to 1965, but the metalworking industries are expected to show an increase of only about 15 per cent. Such differences, though, are due to a considerable extent to the relatively low or high levels of capital expansion in 1956 and thus do not represent unmixed secular-trend changes.

To improve perspective, the 1954 articles attempt two new kinds of measurements. An attempt is made to distribute capital expenditures, especially for equipment, according to purchasing industries in order to show more clearly the relation between capital growth and the uses to which it is put. Another attempt is made to segregate the part of capital expenditures accounted for by the "new technology." This is estimated to amount to 18 per cent in 1929 and to have risen to 25 per cent in 1947 and to 33 per cent in 1954. To the extent that such a measure is effective, some indication is given of changing rates of obsolescence. It also lends substance to the belief that a dynamic market exists.

It should be noted that all of these forecasts project durable-capital formation at substantially higher than present or past levels. Compared with approximately $40 billion expenditure in 1955 dollars from 1950 to 1955, for instance, most forecasts for 1960 are about $50 billion. The reason is that all of the methods assume that expenditure of this kind will represent approximately a constant percentage of gross national product in the long run, and that gross national product will be much higher in 1960.[21]

INVENTORY INVESTMENT

Stocks of goods are essential to orderly production and distribution. In the long-run problem we can ignore any speculative accumulation because inventories are not expected to be held indefinitely for that purpose. To service sales, inventory stock can be contrasted with a pipeline. As sales rise, some increase in the size or length of the pipeline is to be expected. The simplest concept indicates an inventory need in proportion to sales. As noted below, some factors tend to increase this proportion and others tend to reduce it. The statistical data, unsatisfactory as they are, do not clearly indicate that a significant change has occurred in the secular movement of the ratio of inventory stock to sales.

There are factors which will tend to change the inventory stock required for a given level of sales. The greater the number of companies which handle or process a product on its way to the consumer the higher will be the level of stocks required relative to final sales. Changes do occur in the number of companies involved, but no general rise or fall is indicated.

The establishment of a new company would increase total inventories even though total sales did not increase, for the new company must have a minimum inventory. The development of new products has a

---

[21] An idea potentially as useful as the ones outlined in this section is to project investment per employee, visualizing capital requirements as the amount necessary for a given labor force under the technical conditions existing. The present capital stock divided by the labor force can be considered representative of capital requirements with unchanged technical conditions. To allow for capital required for changed technical conditions, past increases in productivity are compared with increases in capital investment per worker. The trouble is that there are no firm figures on capital stock. A start in developing illustrative figures can be gotten by referring to Dewhurst and Associates, *op. cit.,* pp. 911–912.

Investment requirements are better correlated with manufacturing production than with gross national product, so that the reader may well wonder why we do not use that relationship. The difficulty is that the forecast of manufacturing production is a considerable additional problem. The method employed in this book is to correlate with gross national product. See Chart 2–3. If the reader is interested in the relationship to manufacturing production, he may find an illustrative correlation in the author's "Short- and Long-term Capital Requirements," *Journal of Finance,* 7:128–137, May, 1952.

similar effect because minimums are essential for each type of inventory. The rapid expansion of defense production in 1950–51 resulted in a spurt in inventory accumulation, but thereafter a leveling occurred so that the inventory stock–sales ratio was changed only temporarily. No clear evidence is available to show that the formation of new companies and the development of new products occasion permanent changes in the level of inventories required in relation to sales.

An increasing standardization of products induces the opposite effect: sales can be serviced with smaller inventories. But again there is no evidence that any important decline in the long-term need for inventories results.

Inventories play a larger part in the production and distribution of goods than in the selling of services. A redistribution between goods and services might change inventory requirements. Consumer expenditure may be growing less rapidly for goods than for services, but the rapidly growing services, such as the medical, utilize goods to an increasing extent.

Since great reliance is placed on the inventory stock–sales ratio in projecting the need for inventories, factors tending to produce secular shifts should be watched carefully. Although broad qualitative judgments do not appear to indicate that secular changes are occurring in this ratio, new evidence could modify the picture.

National Planning Association Method.[22] Forecast for 1960 is made by projecting the ratio of inventory stock to gross national product. It will be remembered that gross national product is a measure of final expenditure, or final sales. The stock of manufacturing and trade inventories is thought to be generally in balance with sales at the end of 1951. Gross national product is projected to rise at a rate of 3 per cent per year, and inventory stock must rise at the same rate to keep constant the ratio of inventory stock to gross national product. The stock of manufacturing and trade inventories at the end of 1951 was reported at $70 billion. At 3 per cent per year that stock would reach $89 billion by the end of 1959. Inventory investment in 1960 would be 3 per cent of that stock (to maintain the 3 per cent growth in inventory stock), or $2.7 billion.

Nonfarm trade inventories other than in manufacturing and trade (in construction, services, and mining) are poorly measured. They are estimated to have risen 6.6 per cent as much as manufacturing and trade inventories from 1939 to 1951. Adding that percentage to the 1960 estimate of increase in manufacturing and trade inventory produces a figure of $2.9 billion for total nonfarm inventory investment. Since farm

[22] Colm and Young, *op. cit.*, pp. 129–130.

business inventories showed no increase from 1928 to 1951, they are projected not to increase in 1960 and thus add nothing to the estimated $2.9 billion inventory investment.

This estimate, made by the National Planning Association in 1952, may be checked against the actual inventory investment (change in inventories adjusted for inventory valuation) since that date. For the five years 1952 to 1956 the average was $2.6 billion, with farm business inventory investment accounting for only $0.1 billion. Since very large inventory investment occurred in 1950 and 1951, the average is raised to more than $4 billion by including the seven years 1950 to 1957. Taking the ten years 1947 to 1956, the average is $2.9 billion; farm business-inventory investment accounts for less than $0.1 billion of this amount.

A recent measurement of the long-period increase in manufacturing inventory stocks, put on a real dollar basis, comes to slightly less than 3 per cent per year.[23] Perhaps we should add that recent projections of gross national product are at a rate somewhat higher than 3 per cent. If available information continues to indicate that inventories are growing at 3 per cent or slightly less, it may be found that the ratio of inventory stock to final sales is declining slightly.

GOVERNMENT EXPENDITURE

State and Local Expenditures. State and local government expenditures will be considered first because a clearer basis for projection can be developed for them than for Federal expenditures. We shall argue that the growth line for state and local government expenditures should represent an approximately constant percentage of gross national product. These expenditures were a little less than 7 per cent[24] in both 1929 and 1955. Fluctuations were substantial between the two dates, but the fluctuations do not appear to pertain principally to secular-growth conditions. The percentage rose to well over 10 in the depressed thirties. It fell to well under 4, because of the pinches produced by the war, in the early forties. After the war the percentage rose steadily.

The defense of belief in some stability in proportionate state and local

[23] D. G. Wooden and R. C. Wasson, "Manufacturing Investment since 1929," *Survey of Current Business,* November, 1956, p. 14. The increase from 1928 to 1955, in 1947 prices, is from $17.3 billion to $37.2 billion, or at a geometric rate of 2.8 per cent per year.

[24] In this statement, expenditures additional to the purchase of goods and services —transfer payments and net interest paid—are ignored. The transfer payments and net interest paid represent an additional 1.2 per cent of gross national product in 1955 (they of course are not included in the gross-national-product total). For the purposes of this analysis, Federal grants-in-aid are not included in state and local expenditures. If included, the total state and local expenditure for goods and services in 1955 is 7.7 per cent.

government expenditures arises from (1) the fact that many of these expenditures, e.g., schools, roads, golf courses, etc., bear a close relation to the size of the population and the standard of living; (2) potential revenue is distinctly limited by the somewhat inflexible taxation sources available, and borrowing must bear a reasonable relation to available revenue. Increased construction expenditures for such things as schools and roads were delayed in the early postwar period by difficulties of expanding revenue in adaptation to the higher price level, because the urgency of need was not at first fully realized and because of shortage of materials.

More than half of the postwar increases in expenditure have been for construction; such increases are likely to be extended further, although partly by expansion in Federal grants-in-aid (which we have allocated to Federal expenditures). However, the states and local communities have come to depend to a greater extent on income, wage, or sales taxes, which are more flexible than most of the earlier tax sources. We think therefore that state and local government expenditures will approximate a secular level 7.5 per cent of gross national product in the early sixties, an increase from nearly 7 per cent in 1955. Rapid expansion of this area is likely to continue and movement above the relative level of the late twenties may be explained by augmented needs and improved financing ability.

Federal Expenditures. The visualizing of the secular growth level of Federal government expenditures is complicated by the fact that the total is composed of several parts which move differently. First, there are the expenditures of the standard government departments which advance slowly along a rather stable line. Second, there are expenditures for nonmilitary construction which advance a bit more rapidly and show a little more variation. Third, there are transfer payments which have been increasing with great rapidity but which may not move so rapidly in the future. Fourth, there are national security expenditures which have fluctuated wildly with the threat or advent of war and which have reached new high peacetime levels. And fifth, there are interest payments which have increased to much higher levels as an aftermath of the war.

Expenditures of the first two types, if we include grants-in-aid to the states in Federal government expenditures, came to somewhere near 2 per cent of gross national product in 1929 and fluctuated between 2 and somewhat more than 3 per cent in the postwar period. In the thirties the percentages were higher and in the war lower, but these periods do not reflect secular-growth conditions. With relatively high public construction, including grants to the states, projection at 3 per cent in the early sixties seems a reasonable guess.

Transfer payments by the Federal government came to less than 1.5 per cent of gross national product before the war but have risen from 2.6 per cent in 1952 to 3.2 in 1955. They were relatively much higher immediately after the war because of veterans' allowances, aid, and bonuses, but these do not reflect secular change. We can extrapolate from the 3.2 per cent in the mid-fifties. If we guess that the continued expansion of social security will be relatively minor, we can project a 3.5 per cent secular level for the early sixties.[25]

National security expenditures are completely unpredictable, depending on defense buildup or the advent of war. They dropped to less than 6 per cent of gross national product in 1947, rose to more than 14 per cent in 1952 and 1953, and then dropped to scarcely more than 10 per cent at the end of 1955. With little prospect for international agreement or an end to turmoil, a guess of 12 per cent for the early sixties seems to be as good as any.

Government interest payments of course are principally the outgrowth of debt financing of the war. These payments have risen since the war because interest rates have risen and in spite of the fact that the level of the debt has increased only moderately. The rise in interest payments has been much less than that in gross national product, however, and the percentage has declined almost steadily from 2.0 in 1946 to 1.2 in 1955.[26] We project interest payments of $6 billion in 1960 because of probable high interest rates and because of large borrowings projected by state and local governments. The $6 billion would come to 1.3 per cent of gross national product. About 80 per cent would be Federal government interest, or approximately 1 per cent of gross national product.

Adding the percentages developed we obtain the following results:

State and local governments:
   Product expenditures.................... 7.5
   Transfer and net interest payments...... 1.2
Federal government:
   Standard government departments
     and nonmilitary construction.......... 3.0
   National security..................... 12.0
   Transfer payments..................... 3.5
   Net interest payments................. 1.0
     Total............................ 28.2

[25] Since government transfer payments are not a part of gross national product, the statements in this paragraph do not, of course, refer to an integral part of a total as most of the other percentage comparisons to gross national product in this chapter might be thought to do. Gross national product, nevertheless, provides a convenient base with which these expenditures may be compared.

[26] These percentages reflect net interest payments, i.e., interest paid by the government less interest received by the government. Since interest payments of the

Twentieth Century Fund Study.[27] The method involves a functional classification of all government expenditures and projection of each category by analysis of conditions to which it is related. Total government expenditures are obtained by summing the separate projections made for each expenditure category. Although explicit reference is not made to what proportion expenditures are of gross national product, it is interesting that the 1960 projection represents about 28 per cent of the projections employed for gross national product. The expenditure distribution differs from our estimates to a greater extent, with Federal security expenditures at 10 instead of 12 per cent.

The dollar level of the estimates would be substantially below ours, even if converted to measurement in 1955 dollars. It is impossible to say how much of the difference is due to the fact that gross national product in 1960 is visualized at 29 per cent above 1950, as compared with 41 per cent for our estimate. In other words, the extent to which the estimates depend on a percentage relationship to total expenditures in the economy is not clearly indicated.

The categories in the functional distribution are shown in Table 4–1. The defense-expenditure projection assumes 3.5 million armed forces, costing $23 billion, and recurring expenditure for military equipment of about $10 billion. Under foreign aid, it is assumed that economic assistance would be approved only to the extent of 1950 expenditures but military assistance would be granted more freely. Police protection, fire fighting, and correction services (civilian public safety) are projected principally in proportion to population growth. Federal expenditure for education is projected on the declining trend of potential ex-servicemen trainees. State and local education expenditures are projected on expected increase in the student body.

Expenditures for public welfare and veterans' pensions are analyzed in terms of aid to the aged, veterans' pensions and bonuses, aid to dependent children and the blind, general and work relief, institutional care, and other welfare programs. The method may be indicated in major cases as follows. Aid to the aged is projected to a reduced level on the assumption that the Old Age and Survivors Insurance Program will assume an increasing part of the burden of providing economic security in old age. Veterans' pensions are projected to rise because of the rise in the military establishment after World War II. Aid to dependent children is expected to rise in proportion to the increased number of children under twenty. Social insurance is projected on the basis of rise

---

government are not an integral part of gross national product as now constructed, the comment made in footnote 25 also applies here.

[27] Dewhurst and Associates, *op. cit.*, pp. 577–662, 1050–1063.

TABLE 4–1

FUNCTIONAL DISTRIBUTION OF GOVERNMENT EXPENDITURES
As Developed in the Twentieth Century Fund Study
(In billions of 1950 dollars)

Category	1950	1960 projection
Defense...	$12.6	$ 33.4
International affairs........................	4.6	3.6
Civilian public safety......................	1.5	1.7
Federal education *.........................	3.1	1.5
State and local education.................	7.2	10.9
Public welfare and veterans' pensions..........	5.5	5.7
Social insurance............................	7.3	12.3
Health and community facilities..............	5.5	6.2
Highways....................................	4.2	5.8
Other transportation.......................	1.6	2.0
Agriculture and natural resources............	4.4	6.2
Postal service..............................	2.2	3.1
Federal interest †.........................	5.8	6.4
State and local interest †...................	.6	1.3
Other ‡.....................................	2.9	3.9
Total....................................	$69.0	$104.0

* Chiefly educational benefits to veterans.

† The interest rates given here are gross payments as distinct from the figures quoted earlier in this section, which are net of interest received by the governments.

‡ Liquor stores, regulation and promotion of business and labor, and general administrative responsibilities of the government.

SOURCE: J. Frederic Dewhurst and Associates, *America's Needs and Resources: A New Survey* (New York: The Twentieth Century Fund, Inc., 1955), pp. 577–662. Summary table is on pp. 657–658.

in the labor force, expanded income per employee, and the addition of a few programs thought to be in prospect.

Health and community facilities are analyzed in terms of public health, hospitals, sanitation and water supply, recreation, local electric and gas utilities, and housing and community development. Most of these expenditures are projected in accordance with constant dollar trends. Hospital service is projected on the basis of population growth. Public housing and community redevelopment is taken at the same dollar level as in 1950.

Highway expenditure is projected on the volume of highway-user revenue, assuming no change in rates (gasoline taxes, for instance). The new highway program established by the Federal Highway and Highway Revenue Acts of 1956 makes this projection out of date. New user taxes mark up the rates on which the Twentieth Century Fund study was based approximately 15 per cent. Expenditures under the Highway Act will be running at $3 billion a year by the mid-sixties. The $3 billion cannot be considered entirely a net gain, however, for the Act will out-date some programs, particularly toll roads. The National Industrial Conference Board projects $7.5 to $8 billion in 1956 dollars of total highway expenditure program by the mid-sixties.[28] About half of this higher projection (in comparison with Table 4–1) is due to a rise in prices from 1950 to 1956. Price deflated, the program visualized by the National Industrial Conference Board is higher than that visualized by the Twentieth Century Fund only to the extent of rises in user-tax rates, which the program marks up about 15 per cent. The Conference Board points to the increasing need for highways as reflected by a projection of past trends over the period from 1955 to 1965: average miles per vehicle rise by 10 per cent from 9,300 miles, and motor-vehicle registra-tions by a fourth from nearly 65 million.

Expenditures on water transportation are forecast on the assumption that new river-valley agencies will be set up. The switch from radio to electronic patrol of aviation is expected to result in a slight decline in expenditure for aviation patrol. Expenditures for local transit services are expected to rise in view of the problems of urban traffic congestion.

Under agriculture and natural resources, purchases by the Commodity Credit Corporation are estimated at the 1948–51 average. Because of increased farm production, higher expenditures are anticipated for soil and conservation programs, marketing and distribution, extension services, nutritional and other education and research. Federal expenditure on land and water resources is projected to decline on the basis of maturing projects, commitments on power policy, and checks with estimates by the Corps of Army Engineers. A substantial increase over 1950 is pro-jected for atomic energy. On the basis of trends and service requirements the small Federal budgets for forestry, mineral resources, fish and wild-life, and geological surveys are expected to show some increases. State and local expenditures in this area are quite stable, and only a slight increase is projected.

Postal-service expenditures are projected in accordance with the in-crease in mail handled after 1949; other methods were found to be less satisfactory. Federal interest payments are projected principally on the basis of a higher interest-rate charge projected on the assumption that

[28] Hyman Steinberg, "New Highway Program," *Conference Board Business Record,* 13:537–539, 1956.

a larger proportion of the debt will be in the higher-rate, long-term issues.[29] In projecting state and local interest, the rapid growth in debt from 1947 to 1952 is projected, leading to a doubling of interest payments in the decade.

Detailed considerations like those noted on the basis of a functional distribution of expenditures provide a more confident basis for anticipating growth in government expenditures than does the tracing of changing relation to gross national product. That the two methods tend to corroborate each other is reassuring, but the fact remains that projection in the area of government expenditure must be founded on guesses regarding public policy. Appeal cannot be made to factors comparable with productive ability and market demand in the private economy.

The Twentieth Century Fund study distributes the rise in government expenditures from 1913 to 1950 with regard to whether the rise originated from growth in population, higher prices, or larger services. Although this is an imaginative technique, the larger-services category is so predominantly influenced by national-security expenditures that estimates of its future growth are still left principally dependent upon guesses regarding international amity.

NET FOREIGN INVESTMENT

Net foreign investment relates to the increase (or decrease) in our ownership of foreign assets as a result of current transactions. Three major propositions are guiding in making judgments as to secular change: (1) aside from established controls or temporary conditions, a healthy foreign-trade relationship requires balance such that net foreign investment would come to zero; (2) in a world where countries are very unequal in their industrial development, an exception must be made to allow for long-term foreign investment from the industrially developed to the undeveloped countries, which might well last indefinitely; (3) in a world where great inequality of income as well as political instability exists between countries, large foreign aid from the high-income countries may be desirable.

The long-term movement of net foreign investment, thus, cannot be reasonably projected at zero. In any case, interest resides in the major components of net foreign investment rather than in the total as such. These components may be designated as exports, imports, flow of factor

[29] Attention should be called to the fact that the Twentieth Century Fund is projecting gross interest payments before subtraction of interest received, and thus the figure is at a higher level than the net-interest figure used earlier in the section. Also, a higher interest rate was assumed by us, in view of the higher rate prevailing by 1956.

payments, government foreign aid, and private international gifts. Although the growth in each of these factors influences the others, the components are not divisional parts of a whole, as is true of the division of other major expenditures considered in this chapter. In particular, what we have here are not merely different types of expenditure. Exports and imports are contrary flows and, to a lesser degree, factor payments, aid, and private gifts are netted to eliminate flows in our favor.

Imports and factor payments made by us are different forms of foreign purchase, and at least partially offset the requirement put on foreigners to pay for our exports. However, aid and gifts provide similar funds; they must be added to net foreign investment to estimate the export surplus.

Private foreign loans and repayable government foreign loans increase net foreign investment because they increase our claims to foreign assets. Such investment secularly is less dependent upon trade balances than upon our visualization of opportunities for foreign investment. If foreign investment is made, however, funds are provided to buy our product, and our exports are proportionately increased. One way to study the rest-of-the-world influence is to add up investment factors directly. The net result has to be equal to the balance of net current payments, because investment media must be given for any deficit or investment credit obtained for any surplus.

More directly, an alternative analysis can be made of product flows. Of major importance here are exports and imports of merchandise. Our merchandise imports depend upon our requirements for raw materials available principally from abroad or needed to supplement domestic supplies, or they depend upon relative advantages other countries may acquire in supplying us goods, provided we do not raise defensive trade barriers. Our exports depend on the detailed trade development of many foreign countries.

Secondarily, consideration must be given to the cross flows of factor payments, which again depend upon contrasting developments at home and abroad. If added by the methods employed by the Department of Commerce, our gifts and aid are treated the same as imports, and, as noted above, they must be added to net foreign investment to derive an estimate of export surplus. The growth of such unilateral payments is largely dependent upon the degree of unsettlement in the world.

National Planning Association Study.[30] The dynamic factor most influential in the long run is assumed to be private foreign investment. As the most probable secular expectation in 1960, long-term private investment is projected at the 1951 level of $1 billion and government aid at $2 billion; long-term government loans, capital import, and flow of

[30] Colm and Young, *op. cit.,* pp. 130–136.

short-term capital and gold are put at zero. Private gifts are put at a half billion.

Since there is no capital import, the $1 billion of private investment abroad is taken as net foreign investment. Because government aid and private gifts provide payments additional to investments made, the $2.5 billion of aid and gifts must be added to derive an export surplus of $3.5 billion. The net foreign investment is necessarily smaller because aid and gifts provide no claim to foreign assets.

An estimate thought essential for full-employment levels, although considered high, is spelled out somewhat more fully. For 1960, long-term private investment of $3 billion is assumed. The other figures are kept the same as stated above, except that long-term capital import is put at a half billion, on the assumption of an easing of balance-of-payment difficulties which had led to liquidation of many American investments held abroad in the early postwar period. A net foreign investment of $2.5 billion is thus projected. Adding the $2.5 billion of aid and gifts, a total export surplus of $5 billion is implied, including net receipt of investment income.

A figure for net receipts of investment income from abroad is projected at $2 billion in 1960. Direct investment income is principally responsible. The stock of such investment is projected to rise from about $12 billion in 1950 to some $30 billion in 1960, partly through the reinvestment of earnings. At 10 per cent, a return of $3 billion is produced; about a third of this is assumed to be reinvested. Portfolio investments, over which the American investor has no operational control, produce a much lower return; investment return of $0.3 billion is assumed for 1960. Also, a return of $0.2 billion is assumed for investments of the U.S. Government. Projecting our pay of about a half billion on foreign investments in American securities, there is left a net receipt of investment income of $2 billion.[31] If this is subtracted from the $5 billion export surplus, a net export of $3 billion in goods and services is obtained (including merchandise, tourist travel, transportation, and other services).

By the mid-fifties some growth had occurred in our investment abroad and the projected $3 billion in 1960 would represent an extension of the approximate expansion from 1950. Personal gifts had remained approximately stationary. Merchandise exports had risen in proportion to the rise in gross national product.

Twentieth Century Fund Study.[32] The return on direct foreign investment is projected at 12.5 per cent instead of the 10 per cent used in the National Planning Association study because the high rate prevailing

---

[31] This is obtained by adding $2 billion in net receipts of direct investment income, $0.3 billion of portfolio investment income, and $0.2 billion receipt of investment income by the United States government; less $0.5 billion payment of investment income. We have rounded slightly the figures given in the study here summarized.

[32] Dewhurst and Associates, *op. cit.*, pp. 711–717.

in 1950 continued to hold in the mid-fifties. As a result, the yield on foreign investment is expected to outpace the outflow of private investment. The tendency would be to lower or eliminate any net export of goods and services.

Projections of imports are derived from the evidence developed in the President's Materials Policy Commission.[33] Merchandise imports at constant prices are projected to grow 90 per cent as fast as gross national product from 1950 to 1960.[34] Raw materials on the average are expected to rise slightly more rapidly than other imports, but less rapidly than gross national product, ranging from a very rapid rise in petroleum to a decline in tin. Foodstuff imports are expected to rise more slowly because of a relatively slow expansion in coffee and sugar.

On exports, the general principle is held to be that expansion will depend on the supply of dollar funds made available to the non-U.S. world, minus (or plus) the increase (or decrease) in gold and dollar reserves on which the monetary authorities of foreign countries decide. The uncertainties regarding the flow of foreign aid are thought to be so great that only a qualified projection is considered possible.

PERSONAL CONSUMPTION EXPENDITURES

Personal consumption expenditures represent the major proportion of gross national product. In 1955, they amounted to 65 per cent—$254 billion out of $392 billion. They are by far the most stable component of total expenditures. If a secular-growth level is accepted for gross national product, the close relationship of personal consumption expenditures provides a plausible projection.

The relationship is, of course, even better with disposable income, for then comparison is made with the parts of income available for consumer spending. In the pressure of postwar demand, consumer expenditures rose to the level of disposable income in 1947, but this was abnormally high. During the 6 years 1951 to 1956 consumer expenditures never rose above 94 per cent or fell below 92 per cent of disposable income, averaging slightly more than 93 per cent. Stability of this type, aside from unusual conditions or extreme business-cycle movements, is to be expected.

It has not been demonstrated, however, that 93 per cent represents the long-run relationship. It is true that the 94 to 96 percentage holding from 1948 to 1950 was influenced by a high level of deferred demand.[35]

---

[33] *Resources for Freedom*, 5 vols., 1952.

[34] Not allowing for any differences in the rise in prices of imports compared to the rise in prices of gross national product, imports grew faster than gross national product from 1950 to 1955.

[35] Careful note should be made of the fact that the particular definition of consumer expenditures and disposable income made by the Department of Commerce are here employed. See further Chap. 2.

But the six years 1951 to 1956 constitute a short period for establishing a long-run relationship, and no equally valid period is available since 1929. Figures before 1929 are less reliable.

Total consumption expenditures show greater stability than separate types of expenditure. The consumer is limited by the total amount he has to spend; although consumption is expansible for a time in individual cases, disposable income is controlling in the long run. Furthermore, over a long period of time, consumers in the aggregate can be expected to follow a traditional pattern of spending some large proportion of their total disposable income. Less aggregatively, shifts may well develop from one type of expenditure to another.

Projections of consumption expenditures have been made recently by the Twentieth Century Fund and by *Fortune*.[36] In both of these cases the projection is at a level higher than 93 per cent of disposable income: for 1960, 94.5 per cent was projected by the Twentieth Century Fund and 95.6 per cent by *Fortune*. The reasons for assuming so high a percentage are not clearly stated in either study, but the relatively high consumer expenditures in the early postwar period may have been given major weight. In both studies, total expenditures are broken down to show the various types of goods and services which would be purchased, a subject to which we shall turn in the following chapter.

AGGREGATING EXPENDITURE DIVISIONS

Aggregating the expenditure projections developed in this chapter to obtain a total gross national product is an important exercise because it provides a check of the projection made in Chapter 2 and because it forces us to face the relations between expenditure divisions. We can summarize the 1960 gross-national-product percentage distribution developed above approximately as follows (in some cases the percentages are inferred from the income relations assumed):

	Per cent
Personal consumption expenditure	62.0
Residential housing	4.0
Other private construction and durable equipment	11.0
Inventory investment and net foreign investment	1.0
Government expenditure *	22.5
Total	100.5

* The percentage projection for government expenditures indicated earlier in the chapter is 28.2, but 5.7 per cent is government transfer and interest payments, which are not final product, and therefore must be eliminated in aggregating for gross national product.

[36] Dewhurst and Associates, *op. cit.*, pp. 123–470, 1003–1004; Gilbert Burck and Sanford S. Parker, "What a Country!" *Fortune*, October, 1956, pp. 127 ff.

The total can of course be no more than 100 per cent. The least satisfactory technique is that developed for projecting government expenditures. Furthermore, a slight weight might be given to the growing demand for tax relief and for curtailment of government expenditures. Therefore, we have marked the government-expenditure percentage for 1960 down to 22.

On that basis, the 1960 trend projections can be compared with the actual figures in 1955 as follows (billions of dollars in 1955 prices):

Expenditure divisions	1955	1960
Personal consumption expenditure.................	255	280
Residential housing.............................	17	19 *
Other private construction and durable equipment...	39	49
Inventory investment...........................	4	3
Net foreign investment.........................	0	3
Government expenditure for goods and services......	77	97 †
Total..	392	451

* This is taken to represent approximately 1.2 million housing starts, somewhat more elaborate houses, plus allowance for additions and alterations, plus an increase in summer homes and vacation cottages not effectively counted in starts.

† On a basis comparable to Table 4–1, where transfer payments and gross interest payments are included, the projected government expenditures would be $124 billion, with $19 billion representing transfer payments and $8 billion gross government interest.

In this distribution there is a decline from 65 to 63 per cent for personal consumption expenditure along with a percentage rise for construction and equipment and for government. With such high expenditures in the latter categories, the relative importance of consumption expenditures will have to shrink. The income implications of such an economy in 1960 are presented in the following appendix. It will be noted that the figures for personal consumption expenditure projected for 1960 come to 93 per cent of disposable income, a percentage found to be plausible in the earlier analysis in this chapter.

APPENDIX FOR CHAPTER 4

The integrated projection for 1960 presented in the above section assumes the following income relations:

Divisions of income and expenditure	1960 (billions of dollars in 1955 prices)	1960 percentage of next preceding aggregate	1955 percentage of next preceding aggregate *
Gross national product.................	451		
Capital-consumption allowance..........	38	8.4	8.0
Net national product....................	413	91.6	92.0
Subsidies minus current surpluses.........			
Indirect business taxes.................	40	9.7	9.0
Business transfer payments.............	2	0.5	0.4
Statistical discrepancy.................	...	....	0.5
National income........................	371	89.8	90.1
Undistributed corporate profits..........	13	3.5	3.1
Corporate profits tax...................	24	6.5	6.6
Social insurance.......................	18	4.9	3.4
Subtotal............................	55	14.8	13.1 †
Net interest paid by the government......	6	1.6	1.6
Government transfer payments..........	19	5.1	5.0
Business transfer payments.............	2	0.5	0.4
Subtotal............................	27	7.3	7.0
Personal income........................	343	92.5	94.4
Personal taxes: Federal.................	37	10.8	10.2
Personal taxes: state and local..........	5	1.5	1.4
Disposable income......................	301	87.8	88.4
Personal saving........................	21	7.0	6.1
Consumption expenditure.................	280	93.0	93.9

* The 1955 figures are derived from *Survey of Current Business*, July, 1956.

† There was a negative inventory valuation adjustment of 0.5 per cent of national income in 1955. Net, therefore, this figure should be 12.6 per cent.

The implied relation between gross saving and gross investment in 1960 is as follows (in billions of dollars at 1955 prices):

Gross domestic investment.............	71
Net foreign investment................	3
Total..............................	74
Personal saving.......................	21
Undistributed corporate profits.........	13
Capital-consumption allowances........	38
Government surplus...................	2
Total..............................	74

The way the figures are set up a government surplus of $2 billion is assumed. The following 1960 projections are in billions of dollars at 1955 prices:

Personal taxes.................................	42
Corporate profits taxes........................	24
Indirect business taxes........................	40
Contributions for social insurance..............	18
Total...................................	124
Government purchases of goods and services.....	97
Government transfer payments.................	19
Net interest payments paid by the government...	6
Subsidies minus current surpluses..............	
Total...................................	122
Government surplus........................	2

CHAPTER 5

Forecasting Growth in Particular Industries

In forecasting the growth of individual industries we face the methodological question of whether each individual industry should be considered separately or whether all industries should be considered in relation to each other. The fact is that the most important determinant of growth in most individual industries is the growth of total industry. Furthermore, the use of total industry as a determinant is a short cut which conceals significant interrelations between various industries. The gross effect of other industries is no doubt reflected in total industry, but the movement of total industry is only more or less correlated with the various influences bearing on the particular industry in which we may be interested. The difficulty is partially avoided by picking an appropriate industry aggregate for comparison or, when necessary, relating the particular industry to several different industry aggregates. Even so, it is clear that the use of relations to many individual industries might be revealing. Some blunting surely occurs when chief reliance is placed on the movement of a few aggregates.

Since various industries are more or less dependent upon one another, greater confidence can be placed in the projection of growth developed for any one industry if its relation to the growth of others is understood. Unfortunately, the problem of giving recognition to growth interrelations has not as yet been solved satisfactorily. Input-output tables have often been suggested for the purpose. In such a table the rows show industry outputs flowing to the various other industries appearing in the boxheads of the columns; the columns show industry purchases distributed among the other industries appearing in the stubs. The same list of industries appears in the boxheads and stubs. From such a table one can deduce conclusions regarding distribution of the output of any industry flowing to other industries. Also, one can deduce conclusions regarding the distribution of purchases from other industries that each industry must make in order to achieve a given total product.

94

The columns of the input-output table, for instance, can be converted to percentages showing the distribution of purchases an industry has to make from other industries. These percentages are called "flow coefficients." Table 5–1 is an illustration. For the industry at the top it gives the proportion of dollar output purchased by industries shown in stubs at the left.

The input-output table does not forecast total industry, but distributes total-industry expenditure, as shown in projections of such measures as gross national product, among the various industries represented in the table. Flow coefficients are employed for this purpose. Use of constant flow coefficients assumes that the proportional distribution of expenditures for each industry's product will not change. The difficulty is that competition changes the relative distribution of an industry's sales. Relative price advantages arise, shifting sales from one industry to another. Similarly, the quality of products in one industry may improve relatively more than in others and may draw increased sales with or without price changes. Some industries may do a superior job in adapting their product to particular needs, with a similar effect. It will scarcely do in forecasting the growth of individual industries to ignore such influential forces. Constant flow coefficients do ignore such forces.

Shifts in the flow coefficients may be assumed in order to make secular forecasts. The difficulty is that the projection of flow coefficients may be just as involved or even more involved than separate projection of secular changes in industry outputs. Certainly all, or nearly all, of the forces given consideration in the industry forecasts would have to be considered in forecasting flow coefficients. The job of predicting changes in flow coefficients may well be worthwhile but the enormousness of the task must be recognized.

Possibly a better procedure, at least at the present stage of our knowledge, would be to make separate output forecasts for each industry and develop from them implied flow coefficients. Such a procedure should highlight any improbable changes in flow coefficients implied by the interrelated forecasts. Stated in another way, any improbable interindustry relations implied would be brought to light and could then be employed to revise the industry forecasts. No such elaborate integrated set of forecasts is available.[1] The best we can do in this chapter is to

[1] If it were, it might be effectively employed to compute a weighted measure of productivity change which could be used to revise the over-all productivity assumed in the forecast of gross national product, which again could be distributed in the input-output table, thus leading to circular successive approximations. The closest approach to a detailed, integrated set of forecasts is found in J. Frederic Dewhurst and Associates, *America's Needs and Resources: A New Survey* (New York: The Twentieth Century Fund, Inc., 1955), but these are not complete enough, and there are no developed flow coefficients with which a comparison can be made.

TABLE 5–1 INTERINDUSTRY TRANSACTIONS, 1947 (Direct purchases per dollar of output)

INDUSTRY PURCHASING

INDUSTRY PRODUCING

Columns (purchasing industries):
1 AGRICULTURE & FISHERIES
2 FOOD & KINDRED PRODUCTS
3 TOBACCO MANUFACTURES
4 TEXTILE MILL PRODUCTS
5 APPAREL
6 LUMBER & WOOD PRODUCTS
7 FURNITURE & FIXTURES
8 PAPER & ALLIED PRODUCTS
9 PRINTING & PUBLISHING
10 CHEMICALS
11 PRODUCTS OF PETROLEUM & COAL
12 RUBBER PRODUCTS
13 LEATHER & LEATHER PRODUCTS
14 STONE, CLAY & GLASS PRODUCTS
15 IRON & STEEL
16 NONFERROUS METALS
17 PLUMBING & HEATING SUPPLIES
18 FABRICATED STRUCTURAL METAL PRODUCTS
19 OTHER FABRICATED METAL PRODUCTS
20 AGRIC'L, MINING & CONST. MACHINERY
21 METALWORKING MACHINERY
22 OTHER MACHINERY (except electric)

Producing \ Purchasing	1	2	3	4	5	6	7	8	9	10	11	12	13	14	15	16	17	18	19	20	21	22
1 AGRICULTURE & FISHERIES	.260935	.404140	.294104	.213932	.001496	—	—	—	—	.032107	—	.001198	.087035	—	—	—	.012851	.000046	—	.001717	—	.000010
2 FOOD & KINDRED PRODUCTS	.057168	.131870	.005524	.006206	.000057	.005478	—	.000663	.003804	.003864	—	.049224	—	—	—	.000408	—	—	—	—	—	.001728
3 TOBACCO MANUFACTURES	—	—	.310990	—	—	—	—	—	—	—	—	—	.000021	—	—	.000252	.000044	—	—	—	—	.000162
4 TEXTILE MILL PRODUCTS	.001543	.000046	—	.134117	.295538	—	.003439	.099330	.005513	.003899	.000965	.000118	.157283	—	—	.006774	—	—	—	—	—	.006476
5 APPAREL	.001667	.005478	—	—	.149402	—	.001738	.002556	—	.002129	—	—	.000392	—	—	.000641	—	.000071	—	.000086	.000039	.000506
6 LUMBER & WOOD PRODUCTS	.003568	.002174	.006188	.000177	.000689	.182243	.133882	.034158	.000094	.003232	.003232	.034477	.003558	.002205	.002536	.004551	.002180	.003772				
7 FURNITURE & FIXTURES	—	.001052	.001295	—	—	.001295	—	.002433	.000725		.000043		—	—	—	—	.000112	—	—	—	—	.000506
8 PAPER & ALLIED PRODUCTS	.000038	.012165	.008046	.008046	.008046	.012549	.000902	.000758	.009253	.332409	.168256	.023798	.005805	.007041	.014306	.037024	.000038	.000006	.000469	.002194	.001225	.003772
9 PRINTING & PUBLISHING	—	—	.000247	.000247	.000247	—	—	—	—	.000132	.119509	.000132	—	—	—	.000239	—	—	.000678	—	.000558	.000500
10 CHEMICALS	.019942	.038979	.000052	.063102	.010810	.004359	.021779	.023454	.015073	.190897	.000458	.005073	.214162	.033459	.014306	.023855	.013528	.004555	.012260	.007595	.013568	.005993
11 PRODUCTS OF PETROLEUM & COAL	.002984	.001557	.000087	.003102	.000371	.012315	.000347	.008069	.000480	.000102	.274762	.353491	.000442	.000536	.015323	.001286	.000021	.006871	.004090	.000856	.002557	.002715
12 RUBBER PRODUCTS	—	.000238	—	—	.000406	.001449	.000175	.000148	.000620	.000043	.014385	.013323	.000749	.000003	.007861	.007781	.007095	.001473	.002298			.005994
13 LEATHER & LEATHER PRODUCTS	.001555	—	.000177	.004003	.004003	.000661	.002354	.003541	—	.274762	—	—	.002467	—	.000098	.001015	.005624	.000637				
14 STONE, CLAY & GLASS PRODUCTS	.000046	.000076	.000027	.000027	.000027	.002398	.001642	.000642	—	.000036	.002467	.004822	.001400	.088765	.014600	.005260	.004966	.000021	.005721	.005500		
15 IRON & STEEL	—	—	—	—	—	—	.000071	—	—	.003386	.004479	.004822	.000239	.004787	.322796	.005336	.236712	.213267	.161568	.078202	.090225	
16 NONFERROUS METALS	—	—	—	—	—	—	—	.036136	.002149	.013614	.000051	.000031	.000122	.028646	.026282	.413611	.053370	.027247	.042245	.007335	.012442	.035547
17 PLUMBING & HEATING SUPPLIES	—	—	—	—	—	—	—	—	—	—	—	—	—	.000122	—	—	.001216	—	.001132	.001174	.003371	
18 FABRICATED STRUCTURAL METAL PRODUCTS	—	—	—	—	—	—	—	—	.000722	.002231	—	—	—	—	.000562	—	—	.017674	.022322	.002831	.000142	.006528
19 OTHER FABRICATED METAL PRODUCTS	.002003	.014592	.000041	.005584	.000480	.005884	.045717	.002231	.009333	.005668	.004089	.004311	.000990	.000909	.041433	.038996	.033105	.028352	.036275	.031639	.006818	.006528
20 AGRIC'L, MINING & CONST. MACHINERY	.001414	—	—	—	—	.001218	—	—	.009191	—	—	.004311	—	.001245	.000632	.001245	.009997	—	.034863	.01916	.036275	.009332
21 METALWORKING MACHINERY	—	—	—	—	—	—	—	—	—	.000114	—	—	—	.000617	.000981	—	—	.008123	.004039	.031080	.031080	.008697
22 OTHER MACHINERY (except electric)	.000352	.003655	.001602	.002325	.003703	.003655	—	.001727	.005496	.000114	.000394	—	—	.000436	.002146	.000597	.000597	.063161	.018488	.006381	.093214	.054843

SOURCE: W. Duane Evans and Marvin Hoffenberg, *The Interindustry Study for 1947* (Washington: U.S. Department of Labor, 1951). Shown in the table are only 22 of the 45 industries classified. The other 23 industries appear both in the stubs as producing and in the boxheads as purchasing, as do the 22 industries shown.

show some illustrative forecasts for a limited number of individual industries.

The projections shown in the various individual-industry forecasts illustrated below are not always entirely consistent one with another. The reason is partly that there is a variation of a few years in the time at which the forecasts were made and partly that there is a lack of maturity in this kind of work. For our purposes the methods employed are most important, and their development will lead to added consistency. The difference in methods between industries is, at least to some extent, explained by the diversity of the problem.

PURPOSE OF INDUSTRY FORECASTS

A major reason for industry forecasts is to estimate the increase or decrease in need for plant and equipment. Indicated growth shows the proportional increase required, allowance being made for geographical redistribution, as noted below. Some understanding of expansion requirements makes for better management. Temporarily favorable markets can be used to advantage if long-term capital needs are fairly well in mind. Also, a rounded program of expansion is easier to develop. The risk of disproportions in specialized facilities can be reduced. With the needs kept in better perspective, the program can be continuously evolved and revised with less chance of dangerous oversights.

In some cases, notably in the steel industry, company managements state that the major purpose of long-term forecasting is to plan for raw-material needs. The steel companies, for instance, have found it necessary to go into South America to develop sufficient supplies of iron ore, and many years are required. Illustrations of the surprising conclusions to be derived from conservative forecasts of future raw-material needs came from the report of the President's Materials Policy Commission.[2] Given proper notice we can hope to develop new resources or fashion substitutes for raw materials whose supplies might otherwise become deficient.

It must not be thought, however, that the growth of individual industries can be estimated with finality. Even if the needs are estimated quite accurately, new industries may arise which better satisfy them. Of course, a satisfactory forecast of needs is helpful in understanding what can be accomplished in making adaptations which will meet the competition of new products. In fact, this may be considered an additional reason for developing industry forecasts.

Demand for plant and equipment obviously depends on the life of

[2] Frequently called the Paley Report. See *Resources for Freedom,* 1952, especially vols. II and III.

capital as well as on future capacity requirements. The rate of depreciation does not provide a faithful picture of needs for replacement, because obsolescence may shorten the period of usefulness. With rapid technological change, such as that now widely occurring, shorter life may be anticipated for a great deal of equipment. Even the rate of depreciation is not fully known, for, with the constantly changing character of capital, past history provides only limited evidence on the life of new units.

Geographical distribution, as well as the needed level of capacity, influences an effective building program, for in many instances, product cannot be economically shipped more than a limited distance. In such instances, capacity may become excessive in one area and deficient in another. The problems of regional forecasting are not unique, though great detail is involved, and they can be treated only cursorily in this book.

For any given company, an industry forecast is useful only after some estimate of the company's share is developed. It is not difficult to list the broad forces which determine a company's share, but estimating the future position of the particular company may be a challenging problem. Some of the broad forces are efficiency and integration of the company's plant and equipment, its geographical location, the effectiveness of its marketing organization, its alertness to increasing efficiency, skill in handling employee relationships, and adaptation to shifting product demands. This problem is discussed more fully in Chapters 10 and 11.

DIFFERENCE BETWEEN GROWTH FORECASTING AND SHORT-TERM INDUSTRY FORECASTING

In Chapter 9 we consider industry forecasting into the near-future months. The purposes and methods differ fundamentally from those involved in growth forecasting. The short-term forecast provides little leverage for decisions regarding investment in plant and equipment; rather, it is useful in supporting decisions on inventory accumulation, operating rates, sales activity, and the handling of cash accounts.

The growth forecast relates to the relatively stable advance which will occur, on the average, over a period of years. The short-term forecast relates to actual levels, which are much more variable. Although the facts taken into consideration are quite similar for many industries, the analysis is different. The growth forecast deals with fundamental tendencies, whereas the short-term forecast faces temporary distortions. In the following pages we inquire into the basic forces on which advance depends in each individual industry. These basic forces may not be of primary importance in the procedures for short-term forecasting outlined in Chapter 9.

THE STEEL INDUSTRY

The growth of the steel industry is dependent upon the growth of almost the entire economy, for steel is essential to nearly all types of activity in the economy. This fact has led to the assumption that growth

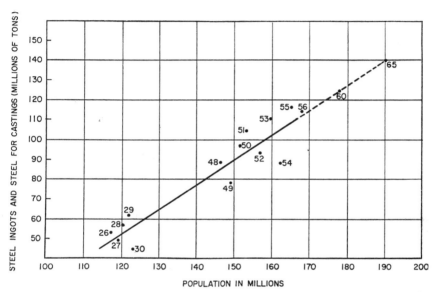

CHART 5–1. Relation of Steel-ingot Production to Population Growth. Years 1931–47 are omitted as being essentially unrepresentative of growth. The equation of the regression line is $Y_c = -98.3 + 1.258\,X$, where Y_c stands for steel ingots and steel for castings in millions of tons and X stands for United States population in millions. The correlation should be considered as illustrative only and not, in itself, an adequate basis for forecasting.

in steel production is dependent upon growth of the population or upon growth of industrial production. The correlation with population for selected years is shown in Chart 5–1.[3] Approximately the same result

[3] The years 1931–47 are omitted in computing the relationship because they fail to represent the growth conditions projected into the future. The regression line is $Y_c = -98.3 + 1.258\,X$. Y_c stands for estimated steel ingots and steel for castings in millions of tons, and X stands for United States population in millions. The population projections are Census A and B assumptions for 1960 and 1965—177.8 million and 190.3 million. See *Current Population Reports*, ser. P-25, no. 123 (Washington: U.S. Bureau of the Census, Oct. 20, 1955).

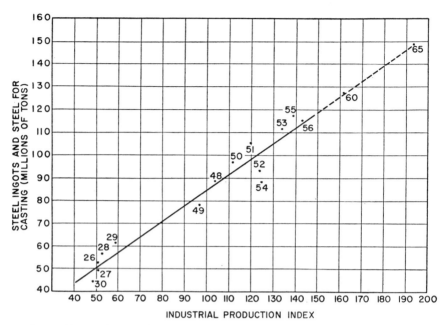

CHART 5–2. Relation of Steel-ingot Production to Industrial Production. Years 1931–47 are omitted as being essentially unrepresentative of growth. The equation is $Y_c = 16.6 + 0.681\ X$, where Y_c stands for projected millions of tons of steel ingots and steel for castings and X stands for the Federal Reserve industrial production index, stated in percentage of 1947–49. The correlation should be considered as illustrative only and not, in itself, an adequate basis for forecasting.

is obtained if steel production is reduced to pounds per person and a secular-trend line is fitted to the same years.[4]

The result is also similar if correlation is with industrial production as shown in Chart 5–2.[5] The projected industrial production index employed

[4] The equation is $Y_c = 1087.1 + 15.906\ X$. Y_c stands for estimated pounds of steel ingots and steel for castings per person, and the trend origin is the year 1941. Data for the years 1931 to 1947 were not used in the fitting. The projection for 1960 is 1,389 pounds and for 1965 1,469 pounds. These projections must be multiplied by population to obtain the steel-production projection.

[5] The equation is $Y_c = 16.6 + .681\ X$. Y_c stands for estimated millions of tons of steel ingots and steel for castings, and X stands for the industrial production index, stated in percentage of 1947–49. Data for the years 1931 to 1947 were not used in the fitting.

This method may be contrasted with one advocated by Boschan, proposing that productive capacity as well as industrial production be considered an independent variable. The method is not illustrated here because of the uncertainties regarding measurement and projection of industrial capacity at the present time. See Paul Boschan, "Productive Capacity, Industrial Production, and Steel Requirements," in *Long-range Economic Projection,* vol. XVI in Conference on Research in Income and Wealth, *Studies in Income and Wealth* (Princeton, N.J.: Princeton University Press, 1954), pp. 233–272.

in this relationship was obtained by correlation with gross national product, as shown on Chart 2–3. Steel production is closely dependent upon industrial production, and for that reason the correlation shown in Chart 5–2 might be thought superior. However, commensurate industrial-production levels are implicit in Chart 5–1, for increasing population levels are partly responsible for advances in industrial production.

A major difficulty in using so aggregate a relationship as population or industrial production is that much more steel is used in some types of activity, like construction, than in other types, like services, and shifts in the product mix of total activity may well occur. For those reasons, more dependable results can be expected by relating steel production to expected growth of different types of product. Each type of product considered is thought of as an outlet for steel, and therefore this method represents a projection by outlet industries. The use of steel per unit of product in each of the outlets is essential for getting an estimate. Table 5–2 is an oversimplified illustration of the industry-outlet method. Much more detail is essential to provide an effective breakdown representing significant differences in relative steel use, but the table illustrates the method more simply than a more complicated and more useful breakdown could. The figures as shown were taken from the American Iron and Steel Institute's market classification of shipments of steel products for 1955.[6] The 1955 figures in the table are those actually reported; and the secular-trend levels for automobiles, railroads, agriculture, and consumer durables in 1960 do not assume that the 1955 secular trends were at actual levels.

The four projections are compared in Table 5–3. The different production comparison in 1955 for each method is due to the fact that except for the outlets method, trend or regression estimates, as indicated by the method, are shown, not the actual level of steel production. However, except for the outlets method, the comparison between 1955 and 1960 and 1965 is a faithful representation. In the outlets method, automobiles, for instance, are obviously above trend levels in 1955, while the 1960 figure is an estimate of trend. The relatively low increase of the outlets

---

[6] *Annual Statistical Report* (New York: American Iron and Steel Institute, 1956). The following market classifications, because they have no obvious industry implication or because of the small amounts involved, were allocated to gross national product: converting and processing; forgings; bolts, nuts, rivets, and screws; warehouses and distributors; shipbuilding and marine equipment; aircraft; oil- and gas-well drilling; mining, quarrying, and lumbering; other domestic and commercial equipment; containers; ordinance and other military; exports; and shipments of nonreporting companies. If the example were offered for direct application rather than for illustrative purposes only, many of these market classifications would be classified according to industry by a technique of distributing the shipments. Cross-classifications by type of product in the American Iron and Steel Institute's data help make this possible.

TABLE 5–2

OUTLET DISTRIBUTION OF STEEL SHIPMENTS FOR 1955

(Units stated in footnotes)

Industry	1955 steel shipments *	1955 product †	Ratio ‡	1960 product †	Projected steel shipments, 1960 *
Gross national product §..	38.29	390.9	0.098	450.5	44.15
Construction............	13.66	43.0	0.318	50.0	15.89
Automobiles............	18.72	7.9	2.364	7.5	17.73
Railroads..............	3.52	7.1	0.494	7.1	3.52
Agriculture............	1.34	16.0	0.084	19.5	1.63
Producer equipment.....	6.99	23.7	0.295	29.0	8.55
Consumer durables......	2.20	36.7	0.062	36.0	2.22
Total...............	84.72	...	...	...	93.69

* Steel shipments are in millions of tons.

† Gross national product, construction, producer equipment, and consumer durables are stated in billions of dollars of final product; automobile product is in millions of automobiles produced; railroad and agricultural products are in billions of dollars of national income because artificial assumptions would be necessary to allocate final product of these industries. Note that the product columns are in noncomparable units and must not be added.

‡ The ratio column expresses the 1955 relationship between shipments and product. On the assumption that this relationship will remain the same in 1960, the final column of the table is obtained by multiplying the 1960 product column by the ratio column.

§ For the classifications allocated to gross national product see footnote 6.

SOURCE: *1955 Annual Statistical Report* (New York: American Iron and Steel Institute, 1956).

method is accounted for by that weakness, as the method is used in Table 5–2.

The last three methods summarized in Table 5–3 *may* point to an unrealistically rapid expansion, partly because the slope developed depends upon a comparison of the use of steel during the most recent decade with use in the late twenties. (The years 1926 to 1930 and 1948 to 1956 are employed in making the computations.) Although the late twenties represent a very prosperous period, they do not involve the making up of deferred demand for durable goods to the degree occurring in recent years. The slope may be wrong even if we assume that the proportionately high level of durable-goods production will continue; what the slope implies is that future increases in the relative position

TABLE 5–3

CONTRASTING PROJECTIONS OF STEEL PRODUCTION
(Steel production in millions of tons)

Method *	1955 steel production	1960 steel production	Per cent increase	1965 steel production	Per cent increase
Outlets..............	117.0	129.4	10.6		
Trend, pounds per person...............	108.4	123.5	13.9	139.8	29.0
Correlation with population.............	110.0	125.3	13.9	141.0	28.2
Correlation with industrial production.....	111.2	127.1	14.3	147.7	32.8

* Methods employed are described in the text. 1955 steel production represents the figure on the trend or regression line for all except the outlets method. For that reason, the outlets method is essentially noncomparable with the other three. Therefore, it is not projected to 1965. The production figures shown for the outlets method and for the pounds-per-person trend involve the use of additional data. For the outlets method the steel-shipments figures have been blown up to the ingot-output level (the difference in level is due to shrinkage in rolling operations). The trend in pounds-per-person requires a projection of population figures to derive the steel-production figures shown in the table (Census Bureau projections were used for the purpose; see footnote 3).

of steel will represent a continuation of the *increase* from the twenties to the present.

Secondly, consideration has not been given to the relative position of steel in relation to other raw materials. Steel has maintained its preeminent position in the past thirty years by effective development of steel alloys, which tailored the steel product more closely to actual needs. Developments in aluminum and in chemical plastics have been remarkable in recent years, and it would be foolhardy to assume, without examination, that competitive materials will fail to make any significant inroads into the steel market. Furthermore, in tailoring the steel product to needs, technological changes have developed a saving of weight for the same uses, for instance, in the building of bridges.

On the other hand, consideration should be given to the possibility that changes in the product mix may tend to increase both the use of steel and the use of competitive materials. With rapidly rising standards of living, demand may shift to more durable products, requiring a large volume of basic materials and involving greater use of tin cans and possibly other consumer conveniences. It is true that services tend to grow rapidly with higher living standards, but this might not prevent disproportionate growth in material-consuming uses; steel consumed in the performance of services is becoming relatively greater, as indicated by the equipment now used in a dentist's or doctor's office.

The growth of the steel industry measured by trends over other long periods is substantially similar to that shown since the late twenties, and this fact may well add to our faith in that trend. The further the data are pushed back, however, the greater the danger of making a spurious comparison. The earlier estimates of gross national product and of industrial production are less firmly founded on widely developed factual information; the growth of the steel industry is less effectively represented by steel-ingot production.[7]

Satisfactory answers to the questions raised in the above paragraphs have not been provided by any available study of the growth of the steel industry. To some extent they are imponderables, or at least relatively impossible to quantify. Hence, forecasts are made by methods like those summarized in Table 5–3. If the forces broadly indicated above will be offsetting, a satisfactory answer may be provided.

The growth shown by the last three methods compared in Table 5–3 is about 14 per cent from 1955 to 1960, only slightly less than our estimate of 15.2 per cent for gross national product, indicated in Table 3–5. Analyses prepared by the United States Steel Corporation's commercial research department show nearly the same result: that the over-all economy is growing at the rate of approximately 3 per cent per year and that steel demand is growing at a rate only very slightly, if at all, less than this.

At the 1957 annual meeting of the United States Steel Corporation, the chairman of the board of directors, Roger M. Blough, stated that "steel demand in 1975 is likely to exceed 150 million ingot tons on what we call a normal level." In supporting his forecast, he stated that the upward trend in per-capita demand for steel will continue. He cited the substantial increase expected in number of families and disposable income. Calling attention to outstanding progress in making new alloys, he reported: "Right now, our scientists are working toward many types of steel with such distinctive qualities as to merit being called entirely new metals."

AUTOMOBILES

Factors responsible for the growth of the automobile industry contrast with those responsible for the growth of steel. Steel is a fabricated-

---

[7] The major reason is that the replacement of iron by steel products was occurring to an increasing extent as we move further back in time. See the author's "How Can the Growth of the Steel Industry Be Measured," *Iron Age*, vol. 137, Mar. 19, 1936.

material ingredient required, in one way or another, for nearly all economic activity. This is the fundamental reason for believing that growth of steel is dependent upon growth of total industry. Automobiles, representing a final product, relate to a specific use, although that use has widely diverging applications.

To a minor extent automobiles are employed as business equipment, but if we exclude trucks and other motor vehicles especially adapted for business use, as we do here, demand is principally for consumer use. As in the case of almost all final products, demand is most conveniently divided into new and replacement components, but also, like applications to other final products, these divisions are somewhat fuzzy.

New-owner demand is most clearly dependent upon new family formation and rise in disposable income. In earlier stages of growth, when the automobile was less fully integrated into American life, the most important factors of growth were related to a rapid increase in the proportion of families owning automobiles (dependent upon the relative desire to own automobiles rather than other products and services). Acceptability of the product and adaptation of the automobile into the pattern of life were at first more important than rises in disposable income. Some minor increase in relative family ownership is still occurring, but that is now largely dependent upon rising disposable income. In only a few geographical regions, principally in the South, does there remain a sizable potential of new-family demand.

Replacement demand is dependent upon the number of automobiles in use and, in the long run, on the average life of the automobile. Over a shorter period the age of automobiles in use at any given time is important, but, as explained in Chapter 9, this produces variation rather than growth. The life of an automobile is a function of mechanical perfection, obsolescence, and disposable income. The relative importance of these factors is difficult to determine at any given time, and changes with conditions. Replacement does not bear a one-to-one relationship with scrappage. On an individual basis, some scrapped cars are never replaced, because of the old age, incapacity, or death of the owner; or because the owner moves to an urban location where an automobile provides little economic advantage or because other economic circumstances become unfavorable. Due to a highly developed secondhand-car market, ownership and scrappage are indistinctly related in any case. For a majority of car owners, disposal does not mean scrappage but resale. Perhaps dealers are more likely to scrap old cars in their possession than are individual owners, so a high rate of turnover of old cars may lead to increased scrappage. Replacement comes to be defined only as the number of new-car sales required to maintain the number of automobiles in use. Any increase in automobile ownership is credited to new-owner demand.

Fortune published in the fall of 1956 the most imaginative study of the growth of the automobile industry which has been made available to the public.[8] In 1956, replacement sales represented about 60 per cent of a 6-million-car market; in 1961 they are expected to represent a somewhat larger percentage of a 7.5-million-car market, as shown in Chart 5–3. Replacements are projected on the assumption that the scrappage rate of total automobiles in use will remain the same as in the mid-

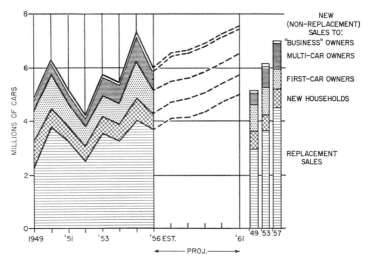

CHART 5–3. New-car Unit Sales, Classified by Type. The classification and forecast are as made by *Fortune*. SOURCE: The chart is reproduced, with permission, from Gilbert Burck and Sanford S. Parker, "The Biggest Car Market Yet," *Fortune*, November, 1956. The chart was copyrighted in 1956 by Time Inc.

fifties.[9] Since the average age of automobiles in use has been declining and is now slightly low, the implicit assumption is that the average life of automobiles will decline. This assumption may not be unreasonable in view of accelerated model changes with rapidly rising disposable income; the rate of obsolescence may be stepped up. The number of automobiles in use, the other factor responsible for replacement, is added to by the extent of new-owner demand.

As shown in Chart 5–3, new-owner consumer demand is the sum of new-household owners, first-car owners among existing households, and added sales because of multi-car ownership. In 1955 slightly less than 3 million cars were bought by these groups, and slightly more than 3 million are projected for 1961. Somewhat less than a third of new-owner

[8] Gilbert Burck and Sanford S. Parker, "The Biggest Car Market Yet," *Fortune*, November, 1956, pp. 109 ff.

[9] See analysis at the end of this section.

sales is represented by new households. The assumption is that new households will buy cars in the same proportion as the car ownership of present households, which appears to be borne out by past experience. A larger proportion, but still slightly less than a third of the total new-owner sales, is expected to come from first-time buyers. At the present time only about 20 per cent of all households do not own cars.[10] Many of the non-car households are concentrated in large urban centers where the economic advantage of car ownership is questionable. Largely because of the rapid rise in disposable income in previously low-income regions, especially in the South, the number of non-car households is projected to drop to 13 per cent in 1961. If this happens, the first-car owner demand will continue at about the 1956 level.

Multi-car-ownership demand is expected to take over a third of the new-car-ownership demand, as shown on Chart 5–3. Multi-car ownership has been expanding rapidly in the recent past. In 1949 it represented only about 2 per cent of the households, rose to 5 per cent in 1953 and to about 10 per cent in 1956. The rise has been especially rapid in high-income groups. The rate of rise seems to have been slowing down. The increase in multi-car ownership may have been partially dependent upon low prices for secondhand cars, but these prices are not expected to continue to show large relative declines. On the other hand, the proportions of youngsters reaching the age of sixteen, the number of families with more than one wage earner, and the number of families moving into the suburbs are increasing; all of these factors are strong incentives to buy a second or third car. On a qualitative evaluation, the percentage of households with multi-car ownership is projected to 18 in 1961. This leads to the large new-car demand by multi-car buyers shown on the chart.[11]

New-passenger-car demand for business and government use is projected at 100,000 cars in 1961, as shown on the chart. This is a very rough figure because there is no good information on segregated business demand. Business replacement demand is well over a half million,[12] and is included in the replacement sales noted on the chart.

Two critical factors implicit in the *Fortune* forecast are the rapid economic development in low-income regions of the country and scrappage rates. On the first point, there is great need to develop information on

---

[10] This is a far more effective figure than the number of cars per household, because of multi-car ownership. At the present time there are more than 90 cars per 100 households.

[11] As stated in the *Fortune* article, "all in all, therefore, multiple-car ownership in the next five years can be expected to rise a little faster than it did in 1953–56, and creates demand for an average of 900,000 cars a year." Burck and Parker, *op. cit.*, p. 276.

[12] Actually, the general practice is for business cars to be retired early and to find their way into the consumer secondhand market.

the percentage of households owning cars in different regions of the country and to relate this information to expansion of disposable income in these regions. Presumably, such analysis is most important in the South. No good information is at hand, but if the percentage of Southern households owning cars is as low as suspected and if it is associated with rapid rises in disposable income, the expected rise in the national percentage may be plausible. On the other hand, even slight increases in the percentage owning cars in the populous regions would be important, so that a need for regional studies throughout the country is indicated.

As noted above, a rise in scrappage rates at the present time would imply some decline in the average life of automobiles. Prewar cars have declined to relatively minor proportions; about three-quarters of the automobiles in use have been made in the last seven years. Continued scrappage at current rates, about 4 million cars per year out of approximately 50 million cars in use, will quickly exhaust the prewar cars available for scrappage and take sizable bites out of the postwar product.

As always, there are contradictory factors in the automobile-mortality experience. Some *decline* will tend to occur because of the extension of multi-car ownership; the second car frequently does not need to be as mechanically perfect as the first. It is possible that new small cars may come to take an important place as second cars, in which case multi-car ownership may not extend the life of used cars as much as sometimes expected. Acceleration of model changes may step up obsolescence and *reduce* car life.

To produce a reliable analysis, scrappage rates must be studied in relation to cars in each age group rather than to the total. R. L. Polk and Company makes an analysis of this kind each year.[13]

Possibly, more fundamental information on the probable expenditure for automobiles may be obtained from a study of income-demand functions, which provide clues to the proportion of income, particularly proportion of increased income, which will be spent for automobiles.[14] The

[13] It is published in *Automobile Facts and Figures,* an annual publication produced by the Automobile Manufacturers Association, Detroit 2. See the analysis of these rates by George P. Hitchings of the Ford Motor Company, in Herbert V. Prochnow (ed.), *Determining the Business Outlook* (New York: Harper & Brothers, 1954), pp. 254 ff.

The relationship between the demand for cars and stock of cars and useful life is carefully developed by Hans Brems in "Long-run Automobile Demand," *Journal of Marketing* 20:379–384, 1956.

[14] The most exhaustive work of this kind to date has been undertaken by the Wharton School Study of Consumer Expenditures. See Irving B. Kravis, "Expenditure-Income Relationships for Consumers Durable Goods and Problems in Their Derivation," *Proceedings of the Business and Economic Statistics Section,* American Statistical Association, Washington, 1956, pp. 106–121. See further analysis from the point of view of short-term forecasts in Chap. 9.

work on income-demand functions is new and has not been tested effectively. Furthermore, the postwar data may be unrepresentative since deferred demand has been of major importance. Consumer expenditures for automobiles and parts have held at about 45 per cent of total consumer durables in most of the postwar period, compared to around 30 per cent in prewar years.

ELECTRIC UTILITIES

The growth of electric power has been spectacular. Projections frequently have been on a comprehensive secular-trend line—a rule of

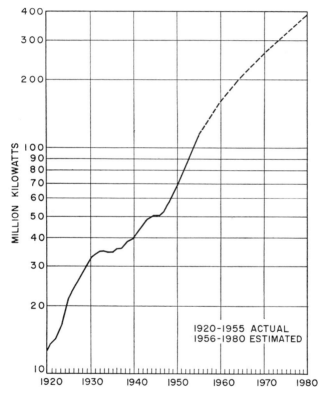

CHART 5–4. Installed Generating Capacity of Electric Utility Systems in the United States. SOURCE: *Estimated Future Power Requirements of the United States, by Regions, 1955–1980* (Washington: Federal Power Commission, December, 1956).

doubling every ten years has often been cited. Actually, the geometric rate of growth has not been so consistent as the statement implies. Growth in the earlier part of the century was greater than it is now. Chart 5–4, picturing installed generating capacity, reflects shifting growth since 1920. However, there has been an approximate doubling in the past ten years, and Table 5–4 below shows a projected increase of more than 80 per cent from 1955 to 1965.

The growth forecast presented here is that of the Federal Power Commission, which has at its disposal the work of regional offices as well as studies of all of the major companies in the country. Conferences are held between the Washington office and key personnel in the regional offices. Many power-market surveys have been made, and these provide useful background on both data and methods of procedure.[15]

The most useful breakdowns to employ in forecasting the power market are (1) residential, commercial, and industrial, and (2) regional. The major controlling factors are developed for each breakdown, and projections are made on a judgment basis.

Residential sales have grown more rapidly than commercial and industrial, and continuation of their relatively rapid growth is projected into the future. Nonfarm residential sales are projected to rise from 19.6 per cent of total utility sales in 1955 to 23.8 per cent in 1980. The most important influence visualized is the use of home appliances. Twenty separate appliances are studied, and forecasts are made of the development of market saturation. The most important appliances from the point of view of energy consumption are found to be electric water heaters, air coolers, ranges, refrigerators, television sets, deep freezers, and clothes dryers. Electric heating and lighting are projected to account for nearly a third of total consumption in 1980, as compared with more than a third in 1955, with twice as much going for electric heating as for lighting. By 1980, 14 per cent of homes are expected to have electric heat, of either the resistance or the heat-pump type. The percentage will be kept down because of the relatively high cost of electric heat. Lighting and cooking are expected to become more efficient, and this will retard the growth of their use of electric power. A generous allowance is made for increased electric consumption arising from new developments, analogous to market changes in the past.

Electric energy used on farms is expected to grow less rapidly than the total because the number of farms is projected to decline slightly. The potential use of electricity on farms is considered to be very great, greater even than in nonfarm homes, but saturation is not visualized by 1980. Although the sales to farmers are projected to double, they would account for only 3 per cent of total sales in 1980 as against 5 per cent now.

Commercial customers are expected to grow in number from 6 mil-

---

[15] The forecast and major factors involved are presented in *Estimated Future Power Requirements of the United States, by Regions, 1955–1980* (Washington: Federal Power Commission, December, 1956).

lion in 1955 to 9.5 million in 1980. Although the use per customer is expected to be more than doubled, the percentage of total sales is projected at approximately the same level as in 1955—nearly 15 per cent. The analysis has been made in terms of the record of commercial-energy sales, by revenue and number of customers, for each utility system. It is recognized that because of the complex variety of commercial customers, this method does not deal very effectively with major controlling factors.

Electric-utility sales to industrial customers have accounted for approximately half of total sales for a long time. In 1955 they accounted for 48.2 per cent, and it is anticipated that they will account for 44.4 per cent in 1980. In addition to utility sales, industrial companies, especially in primary metals, chemicals, and pulp paper, generate electricity in their own plants. This came to nearly a third of the amount purchased in 1955, but the proportion generated by the companies has been declining.

The largest industrial customers are the primary-metals industries, especially aluminum-processing plants. Other major users are chemical, paper and pulp, and atomic-energy industries. Of considerable importance is the consumption by small industrial establishments. Trends are developed for all of these major uses, and they are added to project total industrial consumption.

Separate breakdowns of energy consumption are made for each of eight major regions. These are helpful in projecting the customer breakdowns noted above. It is found, for instance, that the Northeast, which has the greatest industrial concentration, has one of the lowest per-capita rates of consumption in the country. The location of industrial plants has been an important factor in determining the growth of energy sales in many parts of the country. Rapid development of electric energy has occurred in the Southeast, but since no further expansion of nuclear loads in that area is now contemplated, slower growth is expected in the future. In the Pacific Southwest, electric-energy consumption has been increasing at about the same rate as in the nation as a whole, in spite of the fact that population gains have far outstripped those in other parts of the country. Nevertheless, because of the industrial expansion under way in that area, a greater rate of growth in electric-energy consumption is forecast for that region than for any other. Forecasts by regional breakdowns make it possible to relate the analysis more closely to specific industrial and other developments.

The electric-utility industry is primarily interested in the generating capacity required for electric-energy sales. The industry must plan programs of plant expansion on the basis of growth in energy sales. Actually, not only the total level of sales is important, but also the peak

TABLE 5–4

FORECASTS OF ELECTRIC ENERGY AND PEAK-LOAD REQUIREMENTS
(Energy in billions of kwhr; peak loads in millions of kw)

Year	Energy sales	Peak loads	Quinquennial percentage increases	
			Energy sales	Peak loads
1955	533.5	102.7		
1960	779.9	143.9	46.1	40.1
1965	1006.3	185.9	29.0	29.1
1970	1253.2	231.2	24.5	24.4
1975	1523.5	280.8	21.6	21.5
1980	1821.3	335.3	19.5	19.4

SOURCE: *Estimated Future Power Requirements of the United States, by regions, 1955–1980* (Washington: Federal Power Commission, December, 1956), p. 14. The peak-load figures were obtained by summing the highest of the 12 monthly peaks in each of the eight major regions; the sum of the noncoincidental utility-system peaks during the peak month represented were taken in each case. Nonutility industrial generation is not included; it represented 82 billion kilowatt-hours in 1955.

These forecasts are quite conservative in comparison with those made by the *Electrical World;* see Ary Mossiman and Arthur J. Stegeman, "7th Annual Electrical Industry Forecast: Steady Growth," vol. 146, Sept. 17, 1956. The differences are especially proncunced after 1960; the contrasting quinquennial percentage increases projected are:

Year	*Electrical World*	Federal Power Commission
1960	48.4	46.1
1965	44.3	29.0
1970	44.3	24.5

The *Electrical World* visualizes substantially greater increases from 1955 to 1970 for residential and commercial sales than the Federal Power Commission does for 1955 to 1980; only in industrial sales are the two projections about the same. The differences presumably are explained by contrasting visualizations of the growth of the total economy, but the Federal Power Commission does not publish its gross-national-product forecast. The *Electrical World* projection for gross national product represents a 40 per cent increase from 1955 to 1965, compared to our projection of nearly 37 per cent shown in Table 3–5.

amount required at any given time. Peak loads are estimated by regions and totaled to find the requirement for the country as a whole. As shown in Table 5–4, it turns out that the growth in peak requirements parallels energy sales for the country as a whole; peak loads are projected to increase 226 per cent from 1955 to 1980, compared to a 229 per cent increase in energy sales. A safety factor of 15 per cent is added to determine the required level of installed energy. The forecasts are pictured in Chart 5–4.

PETROLEUM

We present here a forecast made by the staff of the Chase Manhattan Bank.[16] Past forecasts have frequently underestimated petroleum demand, as depicted in Chart 5–5.

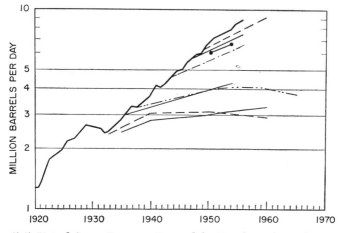

CHART 5–5. United States Domestic Demand for Petroleum (Actual versus Earlier Forecasts). The heavy line indicates actual demand and the lighter lines earlier forecasts from the dates indicated. SOURCE: Taken from Kenneth E. Hill, Harold D. Hammar, and John G. Winger, *Future Growth of the World Petroleum Industry* (New York: The Chase Manhattan Bank, 1957), with permission.

A first step in the forecast is the projection of total energy requirements. This is based on expected over-all growth in the economy and changing efficiency in the use of energy. Although energy consumption has grown at 3.3 per cent per year in the postwar period, the basic growth has been obscured by the conversion of railroads to diesel locomotives, which was virtually completed by the mid-fifties. If railroad consumption is excluded from the total, the postwar growth for re-

[16] *Future Growth of the World Petroleum Industry* (New York: Chase Manhattan Bank, 1957). The staff has had long experience in following petroleum markets.

maining uses is 4.3 per cent per year. The growth from 1956 to 1966 for total consumption, on the expectation that no growth in efficiency similar to the dieselization of the railroad will occur, is projected at 3.8 per cent per year.

The growth of total energy resources—natural gas, coal, and water power—is thought to be more readily projected than petroleum. The utilization of the other energy resources is not as broad as petroleum because of greater difficulty in transporting and because a narrower range of products is available. With the potentialities available in petroleum, possible uses can be visualized only with considerable difficulty. The growth visualized in other sources of energy, total energy, and the residual (petroleum) is as follows:

Energy resources	Quadrillion Btu consumed					
	1956		1961		1966	
Total energy............	42.1		51.0		61.3	
Other resources..........	23.7		27.5		31.2	
Natural gas...........		9.9		13.1		15.6
Coal.................		12.0		12.6		13.8
Water power..........		1.8		1.8		1.8
Residual (petroleum).....	18.4		23.5		30.1	

Next, the similarities in origin and markets made it seem desirable to project oil and natural gas together. The projected growth is shown in the accompanying chart. Since 1920 the growth has averaged 6 or 7 per cent per year. To a large extent this growth has represented the displacement of coal, but that cannot be carried much further. A continuation of the past rate of growth in the next ten years would virtually eliminate coal uses. The projection shown on Chart 5–6 is at 4.9 per cent per year.

The plausibility of the 30.1 quadrillion Btu shown above is checked by various methods, and the conclusions derived from a study of end uses are spelled out to some extent. The past trend in the use of motor fuel is expected to continue. The competition from natural gas as a domestic fuel is expected to diminish because it is less versatile and because its markets are thought to be largely developed. This may offset in the growth of petroleum the slackened possibility of conversion from solid fuels. A growing proportion of the total market will be taken by the "minor products"—jet fuels, asphalt, liquefied petroleum, and others. New technology is almost certain to open additional markets as it has in the past, but these are not readily spelled out. All in all, the 30.1 quadrillion Btu forecast for 1966 appears to be within the range of plausibility. A growth of over 5 per cent per year is represented, which contrasts with an annual average growth of 6 per cent per year since World War II and for the full period since World War I.

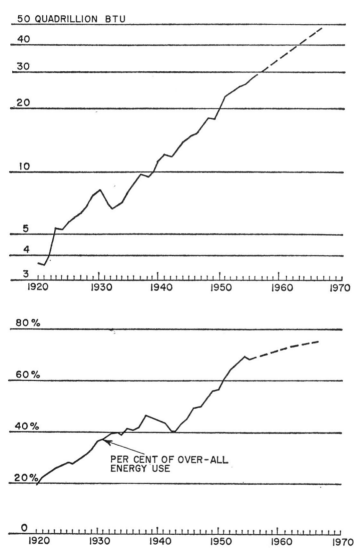

CHART 5–6. Combined Demand for Liquid Petroleum and Natural Gas in the United States. SOURCE: Taken from Kenneth E. Hill, Harold D. Hammar, and John G. Winger, *Future Growth of the World Petroleum Industry* (New York: The Chase Manhattan Bank, 1957), with permission.

It was found useful to forecast the growth in demand in the "free" foreign world. Less satisfactory data are available for that purpose, and we are confronted with the sum of heterogeneous markets. Because there is little access to natural gas and because expansibility in the use of solid fuels is more limited than in the United States, the growth of petroleum uses in free foreign areas has grown more rapidly than in the United States; it has averaged 7.5 per cent per year since 1920. Industrial uses have been almost entirely responsible for past growth, but consumer use is likely to shift slowly to the American pattern if the standard of living rises as it is expected to do. An annual rate of growth of 7.7 per cent is projected from 1956 to 1966. At that rate, alongside the rate of 5 per cent in the United States, the total consumption in the free foreign world would approximately reach ours for the first time in the mid-sixties.

A study of United States reserves, the annual discovery rate, the dwindling rate of added supply per exploratory well, per drilled well, and per foot of hole drilled, the increasing average depth and number of wells drilled, and the increasing number of dry holes—all lead to the conclusion that imports of only 10 per cent, as in the past, would be insufficient to satisfy demand by 1966. But the output in free foreign countries has grown more rapidly than in the United States, and it can be expected to grow rapidly enough to satisfy the total of their own demand and the required increasing proportion of our demand by 1966.

GAS UTILITIES

A long-range forecast of the gas industry's customers, sales, and revenues is made by the American Gas Association.[17] Number of customers and consumption per person are projected separately. For increases in residential customers, a correlation is developed between new housing starts and added customers. The forecast of new customers is thus derived from a forecast of new housing starts. The rate of increase in residential customers is applied to develop the increase in commercial customers, the two classes of service having grown at relatively similar rates in the past. Increase in industrial customers is projected from a trend of past growth.

A separate trend is developed to project the proportion of residential customers using gas for heating. The saturation method is employed; i.e., the trend of past proportions is expected to level off as the proportion becomes larger. Obviously, only a certain proportion of the total houses will be heated by gas, and in effect such a proportion is taken as an upper limit.

---

[17] The material in this section was furnished in a personal communication from Mr. Daniel Parson, Director, Bureau of Statistics, American Gas Association.

The gas consumption per customer is forecast from past trends. Separate trends of consumption per customer in the postwar period are fitted for residential heating customers, residential nonheating customers, commercial customers, and industrial customers. The sales forecast in millions of therms for 1960 and 1965 is as follows:

Gas sales	1955	1960	1965
Total sales............	66,915	92,750	117,050
Residential............	22,387	33,390	43,490
Commercial............	6,029	8,350	10,550
Industrial and other....	38,499	51,010	63,010

Sales to residential customers are projected at a more rapid rate than other classes of service. It is anticipated that the number of residential heating customers will nearly double from 1955 to 1965.

The methods employed do not reflect to any substantial extent the possible use of new types of gas appliances, such as gas air conditioners. The adoption of new appliances is considered too difficult to pinpoint, and the gas consumption involved is considered indeterminate. Nevertheless, the indicated expansion is greater than for natural gas only as projected in the preceding section.[18] The American Gas Association does not expect residential gas heating to level off as rapidly as does the Chase Manhattan Bank.

The American Gas Association's forecast is higher than that indicated by a survey conducted among individual gas-utility companies. In the past these companies have consistently underestimated growth requirements as more remote future years were brought into consideration. The precise reason for such conservatism is not entirely clear, but ap-

---

[18] The forecasts are not precisely comparable, since the forecast made by the Chase Manhattan Bank noted in the above section applies to natural gas only and runs from 1956 to 1966. However, natural-gas consumption will probably grow faster than the total, and the American Gas Association's forecast for 1965, considering all classes of service, is nearly 60 per cent above the 1956 level; the Chase Manhattan Bank's for the full ten-year period to 1966 represents an increase of about 58 per cent. As another comparison, the text table above indicates a growth of 75 per cent in the American Gas Association's computation from 1955 to 1965. The Chase Manhattan Bank argument, as presented in Lyon F. Terry and John G. Winger, *Future Growth of the Natural Gas Industry* (New York: Chase Manhattan Bank, 1957), is as follows: "The spectacular growth rate of natural gas in the postwar period was due in an important degree to the displacement of coal. In urban areas gas also competed successfully with oil for new markets. But the cream has now been skimmed off. The number of potential conversions to gas from coal has been sharply reduced. Most of the urban markets have been penetrated and oil will be able to compete more effectively in the rapidly growing suburban areas."

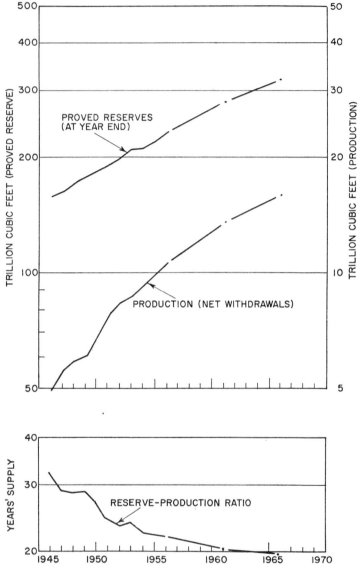

CHART 5–7. Natural Gas Production and Reserves in the United States. SOURCE:
Taken from Lyon F. Terry and John G. Winger, *Future Growth of the Natural Gas
Industry* (New York: The Chase Manhattan Bank, 1957), with permission.

parently it is common to most surveys of growth projections for any considerable period into the future.[19]

To maintain the growth rates anticipated, substantial additions to reserves will be necessary. Presumably this will not curtail the rate of growth in production, however, for discovery during the past decade has been consistently near 2 cubic feet for every cubic foot produced. Nevertheless, the reserve-production ratio has been declining as shown in Chart 5–7.

BITUMINOUS COAL

Long-term coal demand has been forecast by studies of the amounts which would be taken in various major applications—a kind of industry-outlet study.[20] The forecast shows a 61.4 per cent rise in domestic demand for bituminous coal from 1950 to 1975, less than the growth ordinarily visualized for gross national product for that period but a reversal from the past horizontal movement. Bituminous-coal production was no higher in the early fifties than in 1929, although gross national product was nearly 80 per cent greater in 1950 than in 1929. Inroads on the coal market were made by oil and gas, but by the early fifties some shift back to coal was already occurring in some markets. As shown in Table 5–5, a large part of the increase in coal consumption expected between 1950 and 1975 is by coke ovens and electric utilities. Consumption in these classifications rose substantially from 1925 to 1950, although at a slightly lower rate than that projected from 1950 to 1975.

To develop the industry-outlet analysis, we may follow the consumer classification shown in Table 5–5. The more than 50 per cent rise of consumption in coke ovens is built up from forecasts of (1) pig-iron production, (2) foundry uses, (3) unspecified industrial uses, (4) gas making, and (5) household fuel. Growth in pig-iron production is projected at 54 per cent, in iron castings at 62 per cent, and in gross national product at 100 per cent. These percentages are applied to the first three consumption categories to forecast coal consumption. Coal consumed in gas making is forecast to remain constant; It is expected to decline as a household fuel at the same rate as combined residential and commercial consumption decline (65 per cent, as shown in Table 5–5). For consumption in steel and rolling mills the forecast of increased steel making is used (62 per cent). Diesel oil is expected to make further inroads into the railroads' consumption of coal. The increase in use of coal in cement making is expected to rise with cement

[19] The American Gas Association has found a consistent pattern of underestimation in anticipated construction expenditures shown in the survey of utility companies.
[20] *The Outlook for Key Commodities,* vol. II in *Resources for Freedom,* p. 130, and *The Outlook for Energy Resources,* vol. III in *Resources for Freedom,* pp. 24–30.

TABLE 5–5

CONSUMPTION OF BITUMINOUS COAL BY CLASS OF CONSUMER

(In millions of tons)

Consumer class	1925	1950	1975
Coke ovens................	75	103	157
Steel and rolling mills.......	n.a.*	8	13
Railroads..................	137	61	15
Residential and commercial..	n.a.*	87	30
Cement mills..............	n.a.*	8	20
Electric utilities............	36	88	300
General industrial uses......	n.a.*	98	196
Total..................	506	453	731

* Estimate not available.

SOURCE: President's Materials Policy Commission, *Resources for Freedom,* vols. II and III, Washington, June, 1952.

demand (150 per cent). Electrical generating capacity is expected to rise by 300 per cent, but because of increased efficiency of coal utilization, consumption of coal by electric utilities is expected to rise only 240 per cent. General industrial uses are expected to rise at the same rate as the projected increase in gross national product.

Since the percentages stated were developed in 1952, they may now be somewhat out of date. Nevertheless, the study provides a convincing demonstration of probable rise in coal demand, contrasting with the earlier horizontal or falling market for coal in all uses combined.

WATER

The Department of Commerce has estimated that nonirrigation water use will approximately double between 1955 and 1975 and that less than 7 per cent of the increase will come from ground sources.[21] As shown in Table 5–6, four categories of nonirrigation use are studied separately.

The domestic category represents individual water-supply systems for farm, rural, and suburban-fringe homes. The population served is estimated to increase about 8 per cent from 1955 to 1975, and the per-capita consumption to increase by a third.

[21] *Water Use in the United States, 1900–1975,* Business Service Bulletin 136, Water and Sewerage Industries and Utilities Division, Business and Defense Services Administration, U.S. Department of Commerce, January, 1956.

TABLE 5–6

NONIRRIGATION WATER USE IN THE UNITED STATES
(Daily average use in billions of gallons)

Year	Self-supplied use			Public water supplies	Total	Quinquennial percentage increases
	Domestic	Industrial and miscellaneous	Steam electric power			
1900	2.00	10.00	5.00	3.00	20.00	
1950	4.60	46.00	38.40	14.10	103.10	
1955	5.40	60.00	59.80	17.00	142.20	37.9
1960	6.00	71.90	77.60	22.00	177.50	24.8
1965	6.50	87.70	92.20	25.00	211.40	19.1
1970	6.90	103.00	107.80	27.80	245.50	16.1
1975	7.20	115.40	131.00	29.80	283.40	15.4

SOURCE: *Water Use in the United States, 1900–1975,* Bulletin BSB-136, Water and Sewerage Industries and Utilities Division, Business and Defense Services Administration, U.S. Department of Commerce, January, 1956. The actual level of current estimates is considered subject to revision.

Industrial and miscellaneous use of water has doubled since 1940 because of increased water required for new products and for air conditioning. These trends are expected to continue.

Water use for steam electric power has almost tripled since 1940, and it is expected to more than double from 1955 to 1975. This is predicted on a slightly more conservative growth in electric-energy sales than is shown in Table 5–4; these sales are assumed to increase about 170 per cent instead of 185 per cent. About 85 per cent of the electric-power production is assumed to be steam or atomic generated.

The three-fourths increase in public water supplies from 1955 to 1975 is partially accounted for by an increase of nearly 35 per cent in the population served. Domestic, commercial, and industrial uses are lumped together.

Irrigation now takes nearly 85 per cent as much as the other four uses combined, but it is expected to grow more slowly and to take only 60 per cent as much by 1975. The recent rate of increase in irrigation use has been lower than the rate of increase in the industrial and electric-power self-supplied use. Irrigated acres rose from 7.7 million in 1900 to 29.5 million in 1955, and are expected to rise to 37.4 million by 1975.

It is stated that the projections were obtained by "correlation with

basic assumptions developed from experience of the past twenty years."
Population is assumed to increase slightly more than 25 per cent and
industrial production to rise 50 per cent from 1955 to 1975. These assumptions are rather conservative by comparison with those now usu-

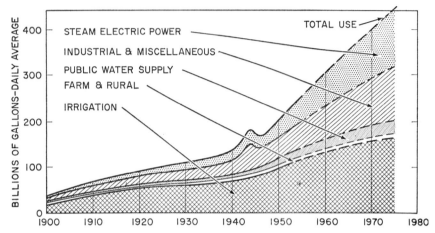

CHART 5–8. Total Water Use in the United States. *Water Use in the United States,
1900–1975,* Business Service Bulletin 136, Water and Sewerage Industries and Utilities
Division, Business and Defense Services Administration, U.S. Department of Commerce, January, 1956.

TABLE 5–7

IRRIGATION USE OF WATER IN THE UNITED STATES

(Daily average use in billions of gallons)

Year	Water use	Quinquennial percentage increases
1900	20.19	
1950	100.00	
1955	119.84	19.8
1960	134.95	12.6
1965	148.07	9.7
1970	159.01	7.4
1975	169.68	6.7

SOURCE: *Water Use in the United States, 1900–1975,* Bulletin BSB-136, Water and
Sewerage Industries and Utilities Division, Business and Defense Services Administration, U.S. Department of Commerce, January, 1956.

ally made. Even so, the water projections are remarkably large and for the first time provide a national background on the growth of water uses, essential for a profitable study of supplies. The forecasts are pictured in Chart 5–8.

FARM PRODUCTS

Growth in the demand for farm products depends primarily on population growth, rise in disposable income, and a redistribution which is occurring in the demand for different foods. Besides domestic food consumption, there is a relatively small demand for domestic nonfood use, especially important in the case of some products.

We summarize here a study made in the Department of Agriculture.[22] Population is projected to grow 30 to 35 per cent and per-capita disposable income nearly 60 per cent from 1953 to 1975. Assuming past income elasticities to hold, per-capita food consumption is projected for various products. Care must be taken to segregate the effect of outlays for marketing and processing, because the rise in per-capita farm production with a rise in income is relatively much less than the rise in outlays for marketing and processing.

Little increase is indicated for the volume of food taken per person with a rise in income, but shifts are indicated to higher-unit-cost foods —increases are notably concentrated in livestock and citrus fruits. These shifts are indicated by the differences in per-capita income elasticity for various products. An increase of about 10 per cent in total per-capita consumption is indicated from 1953 to 1975, giving effect to relatively large increases in high unit-cost foods. A rise of about 45 per cent in domestic food consumption is expected, giving consideration to a projected population increase of 30 to 35 per cent. Chart 5–9 (page 124) shows the wide differences in anticipated growth in per-capita consumption of various products.

Nonfood domestic consumption of farm products accounts for 12 to 14 per cent of farm production, concentrated in such commodities as cotton, wool, tobacco, some oils, and grains. The nonfood use of these products as a whole is projected to increase only slightly less than domestic food consumption, between 40 and 45 per cent. Several factors will prevent rapid increases in consumption. Synthetic fibers compete with cotton and wool, and synthetic detergents compete with farm-produced fats and oils; per-capita consumption of tobacco has trended upward, but publicity on possible adverse effects of smoking cannot be

[22] Rex F. Daly, "The Long-run Demand for Farm Products," *Agricultural Economics Research,* July, 1956.

ignored. There may be a wide potential for the use of farm products as industrial raw materials, but past growth provides no clear indication.

Agricultural exports account for less than a tenth of total farm output, but are concentrated in wheat, corn, cotton, fats and oils, and tobacco. Each type of product must be analyzed in terms of particular conditions, but growth of world population and living standards, to-

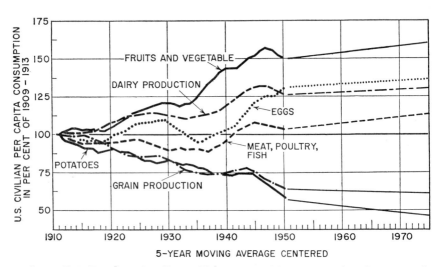

CHART 5–9. Trends in Our Eating Habits, 1911–75. SOURCE: Taken from *Agricultural Programs of the United States, Current and Prospective: A Report to the Food and Agriculture Organization of the United Nations* (Washington: U.S. Department of Agriculture, November, 1952).

gether with differential rates of growth in different parts of the world, are taken into consideration in all cases. The net result of a detailed examination is that exports of farm products will rise little. A much greater rise is to be expected in imports of complementary farm products such as rubber and coffee, about in line with the domestic increase in consumption of domestically produced farm products.[23]

Required increases in output will be less than the projected rises in demand because of the stock buildup which has been occurring. Total cropland is expected to increase little, but substantial increases are usually projected for crop production per acre and livestock production

[23] Daly is careful to speak of projections rather than forecasts, because his extrapolations are the expectations to be derived from the particular assumptions made. However, that is all a proper forecast can be. Fairly faced, the only argument which could arise from calling the projections forecasts would refer to whether the most appropriate assumptions were made.

per breeding unit. These are in line with recent history and give effect to the improved practices being adopted.[24]

TELEPHONES

The forecast of telephone growth is made separately in each operating company of the American Telephone and Telegraph Company. As an illustration, we shall describe briefly the work in central Pennsylvania.[25] The basic forecast needed is the number of "main stations"—the number of households equipped with one or more telephones. Residential demand for telephones is forecast by projecting the trend of main-station telephones per hundred households. This projection is made separately for each telephone-exchange area.[26] The trend is modified qualitatively by judgment regarding the economic potentiality of each exchange area. Saturation is assumed at 96 to 98 per cent, although at lower levels for some exchanges. Each forecast is for a fifteen- to twenty-year period. Revisions are made when short-term appraisals show the trend to be in error or when building additions are required in any particular exchange area.

Projections of the growth of main-station telephones in the total of central Pennsylvania are employed as a control—the independent exchange-area forecasts are summed and checked with the total for the district. Economic aggregates, such as gross national product, are employed as explanatory variables in projecting main-station telephones in the total district, but not in a precise quantitative way.

Forecasts are also developed for telephone lines and extensions. The number of lines required is increased with a movement toward one-party phones. The growth of lines and extension phones is thought to depend partly on sales effort, contrasting with the dependence of main-station telephones on basic economic factors.

Forecasts of different lengths are required for different types of expenditure. For buildings it is thought that 10- to 15-year forecasts are needed; for cable installations, 5- to 8-year; for equipment, 1- to 3-year; for labor-force requirements, 1- to 2-year; and for number of telephones,

[24] See *Agricultural Programs of the United States: Current and Prospective* (Washington: U.S. Department of Agriculture, November, 1952); Glen T. Barton and Robert O. Rogers, *Farm Output, Past Changes and Projected Needs,* Agricultural Information Bulletin 162, August, 1956.

[25] The information described in this section was provided by Mr. Howard C. Towle, Jr., General Commercial Engineer, Bell Telephone Company, Pennsylvania.

[26] Difficulties are involved in developing the population and household figures because apportionment is frequently involved for parts of counties. Primary dependence is placed on the intercensal counts of the Pennsylvania State Department of Education.

only 1-year forecasts. In each case separate forecasts are used for each individual telephone-exchange area.

FURNITURE

Demand for furniture is closely related to disposable income and to new housing. Income elasticity is relatively high because the durability of furniture readily makes possible the delaying or speeding up of expenditures. Also, for the vast majority of the population, felt need for more or better-quality furniture is virtually unlimited. There is a strong tendency to install new furniture in new houses.

In a study made by the Department of Commerce, furniture expenditures in constant dollars were found to be closely correlated with constant-dollar disposable income per household, constant-dollar new private residential construction per household, and the ratio of furniture prices to the average prices of all consumer goods and services.[27]

Using the Census Bureau's estimate of an increase in number of households from about 48 million in 1955 to about 52 million in 1960, our estimate of 11 per cent increase in disposable income, and our estimate of approximately the same new housing construction,[28] and assuming no change in relative furniture prices, we can estimate the secular level of furniture expenditures in 1960. We shall not try to defend the price assumption, but there is no clear basis for projecting secular changes in furniture prices, and it is not clear that ordinarily any important secular change would occur. Applying the assumptions noted to the Department of Commerce equation, we obtain an estimated increase of less than 5 per cent in furniture expenditure from 1955 to 1960. Furniture expenditure in 1955 is estimated at $3.7 billion. An estimate of over $3.8 billion is developed for 1960.

The method used implicitly assumes that furniture demand was at secular-trend levels in 1955. It may have been somewhat high because of the large volume of housing construction in that year, but, as noted in Chapter 4, the trend level of housing expenditures will surely be as high in the early sixties as the actual level in 1955.

---

[27] The equation is $Y_c = 0.0002X_1{}^{1.469} \times X_2{}^{0.137} \times X_3{}^{-0.948}$. Y_c is estimated expenditure for furniture in 1939 dollars per household; X_1 is disposable personal income in 1939 dollars per household; X_2 is the value of new private residential construction in 1939 dollars per household; and X_3 is the ratio of furniture prices to prices of all consumer goods and services. The fitted period from which the constants were derived was 1923, 1925, 1927, 1929–41, and 1948–51. See *Markets after the Defense Expansion* (Washington: U.S. Department of Commerce, 1952), pp. 56–57, 90, and Walter Jacobs and Clement Winston, "The Postwar Furniture Market and the Factors Determining Demand," *Survey of Current Business*, May, 1950. The equation quoted is the one reported in *Markets after the Defense Expansion*.

[28] The estimates of disposable income and housing construction are at secular-trend levels. See Chap. 4.

Furniture expenditures calculated from the equation tend to follow actual year-to-year movements part of the time. Substitution of secular values for the independent variables may give estimates of the approximate level of growth in furniture expenditures even better than do actual yearly levels if the explanatory variables have been correctly forecast.

PETROCHEMICALS

The use of natural gas and petroleum to make chemicals is relatively so small in the petroleum industry that it will play only a minor part in the growth of gas and petroleum. Growth in this application, however, has been extremely rapid. A long-range survey was made by the Standard Oil Development Company for the President's Materials Policy Commission.[29] The various petrochemicals are used for a wide range of products, and if output is not limited by available capacity, a pattern of end-use requirements may be established so that demand can be traced back to chemical production.

The major end uses are synthetic fibers and rubbers, plastics and plasticizers, and nitrogen products. The detailed procedures employed in forecasting the end products are not explained, but a consensus of industry was obtained on the outlook for synthetic fibers and plastics. The largest volume is accounted for by plastics and nitrogen products and rapid growth is projected for these products. The use of plastics is expected to increase more than threefold in the ten years from 1955 to 1965 and nitrogen products to nearly double. The wide consumer use of plastics in various applications and the use of nitrogen in the fertilizer industry are well known. Forecasting such uses is very difficult and is frequently done on a short-trend projection. This trend may be modified by knowledge of cost-price advantages and an understanding of quality and adaptation to uses superior to competitive products.

Even if known products are perfectly forecast, total petrochemical requirements will remain indefinite until new undetermined end-product demands are estimated. The best method is to project the trend of past miscellaneous uses, modified by technical information on new product developments.

The conversion of end-use demand to chemical requirements would be a mechanical problem if particular uses could be traced to a single chemical, but generally this is not possible. Furthermore, some of the chemicals are raw materials used to produce others. Technical questions are involved and they lie outside our main purpose. It is easily seen, however, that estimating the growth of any particular raw material may become quite involved.

[29] *Resources for Freedom,* vol. IV, pp. 205–212.

The growth visualized for some of the petrochemicals is almost astronomical. For instance, ethylene and acetylene for use in synthetic fibers (the two are largely alternative raw materials for such use) are projected to grow more than fifty-five fold from 1950 to 1975 by the President's Materials Policy Commission.[30]

MAN-MADE FIBERS

Part of the rapid growth of petrochemicals is accounted for by the increased use of synthetic textile fibers. It will be seen on Chart 5–10 that the growth of rayon twenty years earlier was of the same order of magnitude as that of synthetic fibers at the present time.

Chart 5–10, prepared by Arthur D. Little, Inc., presents a forecast of textile fibers broken down into major types.[31] The basic assumption is that per-capita consumption will remain constant,[32] so that total consumption of textile fibers is expected to grow proportionately with population. It will be seen that man-made fibers are expected to grow at the expense of wool and cotton. Growth is forecast on the basis of past trends, chemical properties which partially determine demand (in consumer markets, for instance, wear, washability, and appearance), and likely competitive price relationships.

These factors are traced to major uses in industrial, household, and apparel markets. In the industrial market a major new use is cigarette filters. The other major uses are related to the automobile. Nylon is replacing rayon in the tire-cord market. A shift to vinyl-coated fabrics is anticipated for car interiors because they are more easily installed and cleaned. A decline in seat-cover fabrics is expected because of their increased durability. In the household market, a notable shift has been from wool to viscose rayon because of price advantage.

WOOD

In 1954 the Weyerhaeuser Timber Company published a study of growth in the use of wood, as reported by the Stanford Research Institute.[33] The whole range of the demand for wood is traced to explanatory variables. For construction, demand is traced to growth in population and gross national product. Within construction, increase in

---

[30] *Resources for Freedom,* vol. IV, p. 200.

[31] The material presented in this section was furnished by Arthur D. Little, Inc., Cambridge 42, Mass., from current unpublished studies and earlier published studies, notably *The Technology behind Investment,* 1952.

[32] A slow increase in per-capita consumption occurred in the past. The precise reasons for expecting no increase in the near-future years are not stated.

[33] Stanford Research Institute, *America's Demand for Wood, 1929–1975* (Tacoma, Wash.: Weyerhaeuser Timber Company, 1954).

school buildings is traced to a large increase in school-age population; residential housing demand is traced to new housing starts, but a substantial decrease in lumber used per unit is noted. The growth in shipping

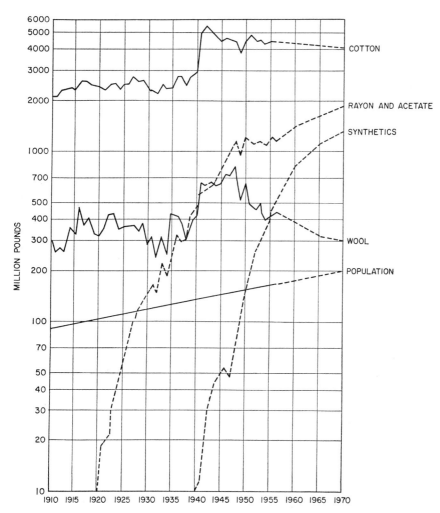

CHART 5–10. United States Consumption of Textile Fibers, 1910 to 1970. SOURCE: Taken, with permission, from chart furnished by Arthur D. Little, Inc., based on data in U.S. Department of Agriculture Statistical Bulletin 89 and *Textile Organon*.

materials is projected at the rate of increase in the Industrial Production Index, but competing materials are expected to make substantial inroads on the lumber market so that the use of wood will increase less.

In manufacturing, demand is traced principally to furniture and fixtures, railroad freight cars, and motor vehicles. Personal disposable income is used as the explanatory variable for furniture and fixtures. Use in making railroad freight cars is projected by estimating total stock of cars, distributed by type, and taking into consideration expected average age in each type. Trucks, trailers, and busses are expected to increase in relation to changes in population and disposable income.

The demand for pulp and pulpwood is traced to paper and paperboard. The demand for paper is traced to population, disposable income, and secular trend. Paperboard demand is separately traced to the same factors, resulting in a projection which checks with the sum of estimates for various uses, including shipping containers and building board.

The demand for fuelwood is expected to decline drastically, especially for home heating, because the relative disadvantages of heating with wood become important with rising living standards. Miscellaneous uses, including wood used in the production of chemicals, are broadly estimated to absorb a constant amount of wood representing between 2 and 3 per cent of total wood consumption.

Wood demand is converted to log and bolt requirements by multiplying domestic production, commensurate with total demand, by converting factors and subtracting (1) imports of logs and bolts and (2) utilization of mill residuals. Estimates of scalable sizes are made by subtracting those below minimum scaling standards which are expected to be used. These projections are worked out separately for various major uses.

For all uses, as shown by log and bolt requirements, wood demand is expected to increase very slowly, reaching only slightly more than 1 per cent above the early fifties by 1965. Total lumber requirements on a finished basis are projected to increase very little more by 1965 but to increase 10 per cent by 1975. A major factor responsible for the slow increase, in addition to the competitive inroads of other materials, is technical improvements which reduce the wood needed. It may be noted also that the Stanford Research Institute in this study is projecting explanatory variables at a slightly slower rate than shown in more recent revisions.[34]

Lumber prices are projected to increase more than the prices of competing materials because of the reduced supply of readily accessible timber and higher transportation cost. The lumber supply in the East is expected to come largely from the West until about 1975. Logging costs will be higher because of the shift to remoter areas with rugged terrain. Manufacturing costs will be higher with declining size of logs,

---

[34] Gross national product, for instance, is projected to grow at slightly less than 50 per cent from 1950 to 1965 in *America's Demand for Wood, 1929–1975,* 1954, but it is projected at about 65 per cent in Bonnar Brown and M. Janet Hansen, *Production Trends in the United States through 1975* (Menlo Park, Calif.: Stanford Research Institute, 1957).

increasing labor costs in the South, and increased dependence on high-cost small mills in scattered locations.

OTHER INDUSTRIES

The industry forecasts presented above may be considered illustrative. They cover critical areas and represent some of the best work done to date. In most cases more mechanical detail would be required in order to follow precise procedures, but adaptations are still being made on details employed, and the broad methods are certain to be of major importance for some time to come.

Most of these studies properly refer to "particular" industries only in relation to the broader categories of the preceding chapter. Problems of forecasting at a still more detailed level, actually more directly applicable to problems faced by the majority of businessmen, are covered in Chapters 10 and 11 on the sales forecast.

For our purposes, it is not essential to add further to the illustrations given. It may be helpful, however, to state the summary methods employed in other cases, especially when the problem is to make a broad range of industry forecasts.

The Twentieth Century Fund study employs many growth projections.[35] A few illustrations of consumer demand may be given. In almost all industries, disposable income is assigned critical importance. For furniture, number of households is also emphasized. House furnishings are thought to be trending to a shorter life and to relatively lower original cost. More rapid replacement is implied. Mechanical appliances are also expected to be replaced more rapidly with stepped-up obsolescence. Total transportation expenditures in constant dollars are visualized to increase only slightly more rapidly from 1950 to 1960 than the growth in population, largely because the expenditures for private transportation (automobiles and maintenance) were considered relatively high in 1950. On the basis of past trends airline traffic is expected to grow rapidly and to surpass intercity railway traffic by 1960. Overseas travel is expected to double from 1950 to 1960 because of larger disposable income and improved travel services, especially airline.

The Twentieth Century Fund's forecasts of the growth of expenditures for private productive facilities are related in most cases to growth in gross national product. Where this method is not considered satisfactory, major reliance is placed on the past percentage of total capital expenditures accounted for by expenditures for private productive facilities in the particular industry.

[35] Dewhurst and Associates, *op. cit.*

In the *Fortune* studies,[36] new demand is forecast for productive facilities in each separate industry by estimating the capacity requirements for the projected levels of gross national product. Replacement requirements of each industry are estimated from survival tables, indicating the part of the total stock of productive facilities expected to survive each year. Special conditions are also considered in each industry. In the metal-manufacturing industries, for instance, additions to capital stock were so rapid in the mid-fifties that no increase in new capital demand is expected to 1959. Although some industry executives expect the growth of oil consumption to slow down from 6 to 4 per cent per year, the growth of plant and equipment expenditures is predicted to rise as rapidly as in the past, because of rising exploration and drilling costs, particularly for offshore operations.

[36] Gilbert Burck and Sanford S. Parker, "Another Big Decade for Capital Goods," *Fortune,* December, 1956, and earlier articles, September to December, 1954.

CHAPTER 6

Indicators of Business Conditions

We now turn our attention to short-term forecasting. For this purpose current measurements are of crucial importance. Changes which occur are dependent upon what is currently happening rather than upon any fundamental relationships, so that the relevance of historical trends is much less than in growth forecasting. In fact, the assumptions made in short-term forecasting must relate to current unbalance, rather than balance, which exists between variables and to the forces which perpetuate unbalance for a limited time. This is closely related to the way businessmen visualize requirements in the near future. Analysis in terms of requirements implies the use of current indicators and necessitates an interpretation of what they mean.

Output or expenditure is basic in seeing what is happening. We have already noted measurements of gross national product and industrial production in Chapter 2. Gross national product is the sum of final expenditures made in the economy, and thus is in terms of current dollar values. It reveals the areas supporting or curtailing total expenditure. On the other hand, it provides a framework for tracing any expected change in total expenditure to specific areas. Since gross national product is expressed in current prices, the changes traced represent the combined influence of quantity and price. Initially this is an advantage, for price and quantity work together in effecting the changes which occur. In analyzing the unbalance which is developing, it is important to segregate these influences once the total effect has been traced. The segregation leads into an analysis of price changes.

The Federal Reserve Index of Industrial Production is measured in quantitative terms, for it aggregates individual series which are representative of quantitative movements. Its coverage is restricted to manufacturing and mining. Activity in these areas represents only about a third of the total product covered in gross national product. Most of the sensitive types of activity are included, however, so that the Index is of substantial importance in watching current changes.

Movements in the gross-national-product measure are greatly influenced by activity which changes sluggishly, so that the influence of sensitive indicators tends to be swamped in that measure. By use of weight factors, changes in the separate series combined in the Industrial Production Index can be related to changes in the total index, but less effectively than in gross national product. The difficulties are that the weight factors in the Industrial Production Index do not express the relative final-expenditure influence of the components, and the effect of price changes on expenditures is ignored.

Another measure reflecting expenditures is the monthly dollar amount of manufacturing and trade sales as reported by the Department of Commerce.[1] This measure covers a wide range of commodities and thus is helpful in summarizing the broad changes which are occurring. The fact that it omits services is to some extent helpful, for services tend to move sluggishly and, if added in, would tend to smooth out the changes which are occurring elsewhere. Manufacturing and trade sales are, nevertheless, less useful in showing current changes in final output or expenditure than gross national product, for the series cover many sales made between businesses (in contrast with final sales), and changes are significantly dependent upon inventory accumulation or runoff at critical times. The sales series is most usefully studied in relation to the movement of orders and inventories, as noted below.

Many other series have varying utility in measuring output and expenditure. There are relatively comprehensive measures of input, such as electric-power production, and of spending, such as bank debits. There are various published indexes of business activity which purport to reflect current economic changes. These and other measures have limited importance in measuring product and expenditure. While anyone fully conversant with forecasting problems should understand such measures, their consideration lies outside the major objectives of this book.[2]

CHANGE IN PRICES

With regard to the total economy, there are four measures of price change which may be singled out for particular consideration. They are the Bureau of Labor Statistics' Indexes of Wholesale Commodity Prices,

---

[1] Currently published in the *Survey of Current Business* and in the *Industry Survey*. See the first reference in the first part of the appendix to this chapter.

[2] A description will be found in the author's *Business Cycles and Forecasting*, 4th ed. (Homewood, Ill.: Richard D. Irwin, Inc., 1953), pp. 357 ff.

of Spot Market Prices, and of Consumers' Prices; and the Department of Commerce's Implicit Price Deflator for gross national product. These indexes reflect change in, and not level of, prices. The level of prices is shown only by unit prices of individual commodities. Price indices fictionally take some base period as 100 and show average prices at other times in proportion to the base price. Price indices thus show whether prices are high or low only in relation to prices at some other particular time. In showing change in prices they do provide material information for forecasting short-period changes.

The Wholesale Price Index is reported on a monthly basis as the weighted average of about 2,000 items and on a weekly basis as the weighted average of about 200 items. It represents the average change of prices in primary markets, generally the price in large lots at the first important commercial transaction for each commodity. The Index is a reasonably faithful measure of the change in average prices in primary markets and thus reflects the strength or weakness in basic demand. It is possible, however, that at critical times actual prices paid may be influenced by unquoted, possibly informal, discounts and premiums or extras which cannot well be represented. Furthermore, the timing relation between the Index and prices actually paid on current shipments may shift slightly from time to time; if orders have been made substantially in advance at one time, past price quotations may apply, and at another time short ordering may lead to a close approximation of current quotations to current shipments. A shrewd qualitative allowance for these factors will make the Index even more relevant to current conditions. The Index shows separately the major industry groups, each of which is further subdivided.[3]

The Daily Spot Market Price Index is an unweighted average of the relative prices of 22 commodities. The commodities included are in markets showing frequent price changes, traded on open markets, and generally important in world trade. They quickly reflect shifts in market conditions; the Wholesale Price Index is heavily influenced by administered prices and thus may be tardy in reflecting competitive conditions. On the other hand, the Spot Market Price Index is so narrowly based on a limited group of commodities that it might be overinfluenced by changes in particular markets.[4]

The Consumer Price Index represents the effect of price changes in the living costs of city wage-earner and clerical-worker families. A sample

---

[3] For a description of the Wholesale Price Index, see *Monthly Labor Review*, February, 1952.

[4] See *Monthly Labor Review*, September, 1952. There are several similar indexes available from private sources. See A. H. Cole, *Measures of Business Change* (Homewood, Ill.: Richard D. Irwin, Inc., 1952), pp. 119 ff. These measures are often called sensitive price indexes.

of 46 cities is employed in computing the Index. It represents price changes in a fixed "market basket" of goods and services. The prices cover a rather broad range of purchased products—apparel, food, housing, medical care, personal care, reading and recreation, transportation, and others. Subindices are reported for each of these groups. About three hundred items are regularly priced to obtain the weighted over-all Index. If a change occurs in market sources at critical times, e.g., a shift to purchasing from discount houses, the Index may not fully reflect it. Also, markdowns and special deals may not always be fully reflected. The Index is not devised to represent the prices paid by all consumers, although it is generally employed for that purpose; no other available measure is as effective in any case. Not the least important value of the Consumer Price Index in forecasting is the way it highlights the differential movement of prices paid for various consumer products. For instance, the relatively steady rise in prices paid for most services since the war is explicitly shown.[5]

The Department of Commerce's Implicit Price Deflators for gross national product, personal consumption expenditures, and other component expenditures are important because they provide the most suitable means of taking price changes into account in dealing with expenditure aggregates.[6] The implicit price deflator for gross national product provides the best available measure of the change in average prices for final expenditure of all sorts. From the point of view of forecasting, the fact that the Implicit Price Deflators are computed only on an annual basis is a disadvantage in obtaining short-term perspective. Qualitative judgments made currently in the *Survey of Current Business* may represent as useful an indicator of current prices in the shorter period as can now be obtained, considering the limited basis for computing short-period measures. Furthermore, the Deflators are published in the first quarter of the following year, when the expenditures for the final quarter of the preceding year first become available.

THE INDUSTRY SURVEY

The "industry survey," conducted by the Department of Commerce, obtains monthly figures on sales and inventories in manufacturing and

[5] For a description of the Consumer Price Index, see *Monthly Labor Review,* February, 1953, and Bureau of Labor Statistics Bulletins 1140 and 1165.

[6] These price indices are called "implicit" because of the way they are developed. Segmental price indices are obtained, and the expenditure series affected by them are deflated; the deflated expenditure series thus obtained are added to find the total level of deflated expenditure. This total is then divided into the current-dollar aggregate-expenditure series to obtain the price index. The implicit price indices are published in the February and July issues of the *Survey of Current Business.*

trade, and in some cases on new and unfilled orders.[7] The relation between sales and inventories is important information in forecasting because of the part inventories play in most business-cycle movements. If inventories are low relative to sales and the prospects for expansion are good, an important factor reinforcing the expansion is indicated. If inventories are high relative to sales and activity is leveling off, a possible culminating influence may be emerging in the inventory situation. The breakdown provided for sales and inventory figures is helpful in spotting the greatest discrepancies in the inventory-sales relationship and in showing how universally the discrepancy indicated by total figures may be spread.

For manufacturing, inventories are classified within durable and non-durable divisions according to stages of fabrication—purchased material, goods-in-process, and finished goods. This is very helpful, for it aids in judging the extent to which inventory change has been desired or undesired. For instance, if sales are increasing very slowly or beginning to decline, increase in finished-goods inventories should be examined as a possible indication of undesired inventory increases. The logic is that production scheduling may at first tend to ignore slight and irregular falling off in sales and thereby push up inventories. Rising inventory of purchased material under similar circumstances might imply desired increases in inventories, since variation in scheduling will not so greatly affect purchased material; checking for the supply of purchased material and its price movements would be indicated. Note should be taken of the fact that the stage-of-fabrication classification used is in accordance with the way the classification would be made in each business, even though what may be finished goods for one manufacturer may be purchased material for another. This is advantageous for our purposes, for we are interested in the combined outlook of the individual companies, not in the total movement of inventory of any particular type of product as such.

For some of the major divisions of manufacturing, especially the durable-goods industries, a useful distinction between sales and orders is found. In manufacturing, sales mean billings or shipments. Orders mean the placing of new business, usually without regard to when the orders will be delivered.[8] New orders move with greater irregularity than sales, but do tend to lead sales. More important than checking for leads at turning points is the indication given by the extent to which new orders are running ahead of or falling behind sales. This shows whether new

[7] Published in a release entitled "The Industry Survey" and in the *Survey of Current Business.*

[8] Besides durable-goods industries, the distinction is made for textile, leather, paper, and printing and publishing industries.

business is outstripping or falling behind activity. Series on unfilled orders show this fact by the direction of movement. Unfilled-orders series must be employed with care, however, for they are affected by the combined influences of change in sales activity and change in new orders, which sometimes move in opposite directions. Furthermore, unfilled-orders series may be affected by order cancellations and other manipulations.[9]

RETAIL TRADE

The personal-consumption-expenditure component of gross national product is comprehensive and is the best representation of final purchases made by consumers, but some other retail-trade measures are also useful in short-term forecasting. The chief value of the alternate measures is that they can be obtained monthly and fairly promptly and may be compared to inventory-stock levels; their chief disadvantages are that they may include intermediate sales, are of uncertain comprehensiveness, and are not broken down into as useful subdivisions as the personal-consumption-expenditure series.

The retail-sales component of the industry survey is derived from the monthly movement of a sample of large independent retailers and chain stores. It is thus a relatively comprehensive measure. It is broken down by major type of durable and nondurable goods stores, and by major type of store. Comparable inventory holdings are shown.

Department-store sales have been collected by the Federal Reserve since 1919. The series is widely used, partly because of its long availability and partly because comparable movement in the Federal Reserve districts provides a consistent regional comparison for sales and inventories. For a sample covering about half of total department stores, outstanding orders, receipts, and new orders are reported; data are available only back to 1948, and the order relations indicated are still considered experimental. Figures are also reported comparing sales on charge and installment accounts to cash sales.

EMPLOYMENT AND EARNINGS

At the end of Chapter 2 we described briefly the Census figures on labor force, employment, and unemployment. These figures are available monthly and are useful in short-term forecasting. Also important is the essentially noncomparable, nonagricultural employment reported by the

[9] As the industry survey is now computed, new orders equal change in unfilled orders plus monthly sales. In some other series the unfilled orders are not set in close arithmetical adjustment with new orders.

Bureau of Labor Statistics, derived from reports from business establishments rather than from direct household interviews.[10] Although less comprehensive, these figures are useful because of the detailed industry breakdowns available and because somewhat comparable weekly and hourly earnings and weekly hours are available. Estimates of employment are published for more than 140 manufacturing and mining industries as well as for the 48 states.[11]

MONEY SUPPLY AND CREDIT

The best single measure of money supply is the series reported by the Federal Reserve, which covers currency outside banks and adjusted time and demand deposits, sometimes called privately held money supply. The adjustment of time deposits involves subtraction of interbank and United States government deposits and addition of the total of postal savings. The adjustment of demand deposits involves subtraction of interbank and United States government deposits and cash items in process of collection (known as "float"). The *use* of money throws more light on evolving economic change than total money supply does, and progress is being made in measuring money flows, although standard measures have not been developed. Some approach is shown by the series on bank debits, representing the private check payments made.

The banks are creators of credit. The total loans and investments of commercial banks constitute the best aggregate to represent their total credit influence. More important in developing the current picture are the movements of various types of loans. A classification of commercial and industrial loans of Federal Reserve member banks by major industry is helpful in getting some idea of direction of flow. The Federal Reserve report on outstanding consumer credit, classified by installment and other, is indicative of the consumers' current debt position and the broad types of purchase responsible. Particularly helpful are the amounts shown for automobile and other consumer-goods paper. The evolving influences arising from credit extension are better portrayed by the series now available for the same industry breakdown on credit extensions, repayment, and changes in outstanding credit.

The Federal Reserve issues a quarterly report on mortgage debt

[10] The principal differences result from the following: (1) the BLS figures do not include domestic-service workers, the self-employed, and unpaid family workers; (2) they may include some workers under fourteen years of age and may count more than once workers who hold more than one job or who change jobs in the reported week; and (3) they exclude employed workers temporarily away from work but receiving no pay in the surveyed week.

[11] These figures are currently reported in *Employment and Earnings,* monthly report of the Bureau of Labor Statistics.

outstanding. Classification shows separately one- to four-family houses, multi-family and commercial properties, and farm mortgages. The series on one- to four-family houses makes apparent the rapid rise which has been occurring in home mortgages. It would be more helpful if extensions and repayments could be shown separately, but as long as rapid rises occur, the general influence is apparent.

Commitments to purchase mortgages present an interesting type of data from the forecasting point of view. Data of this sort have not been made available publicly, but the Life Insurance Association of America now collects a series which is disseminated to a limited group.[12] The series is somewhat experimental, but presumably an early point in investment planning is represented.

OTHER MEASURES

The list of available barometric measures is long and detailed, and it would overburden this book to aim at any degree of comprehensiveness. The development of an approach to a wider understanding is outlined in the Appendix at the end of the chapter. No simple classification will indicate the potentialities because the type of data depends not only on the nature of the economic system but more importantly upon the various facets of data which have been developed, many of them quite accidentally. A few broad generalizations may be helpful to the person unacquainted with the area. Major value figures, like gross national product and its breakdown, are needed. Indexes of physical quantity, like the Index of Industrial Production and its breakdown, are similarly desirable. Price indices relate the two above types and independently tell something about demand. Money and credit data give some idea of the influence added to the economic round of events by monetary flows. Inventory accumulation and sales at successive stages of distribution show the flow of goods through the system. The relation of employment to production is basic in our present methods of studying economic change. Measurement of these processes has been outlined above. Although the exact information is partly the result of accidental developments, the broad fundamental needs are represented. Further detail which is available provides information on foreign trade, agricultural conditions, changes in business population, advertising, life insurance, security markets, the labor market, transportation, and many individual industries.

In the rest of this chapter we look at the problem of economic measurements from the point of view of the way data are organized for forecasting rather than in terms of the economic relations between the series. This involves the extent of lead in timing, relations shown in "diffusion indices," surveys or indicators of expenditure plans, and surveys of general-business expectations.

LEAD, LAG, AND CONCURRENCE IN TIMING

The hunt for timing leads in economic series has been largely a delusion. No series lead with complete consistency. Some show a short average lead but often actually lag. A few show a long lead, but with so great a variation that they are of little aid in locating turning points. Furthermore, the actual dating of turning points, upon which the determination of leads depends, is to a considerable degree accidental. An erratic factor, such as weather or labor disturbance, may create a temporary interruption or speedup and shift the actual occurrence of peaks or troughs by several months, when the movement of the series is substantially horizontal. The use of timing, long considered to be the ultimate objective in forecasting, is of value principally as a supplementation of other methods.

Nevertheless, there are series which historically have shown a significant tendency to lead and for which a lead is logically to be expected.[13] We may single out business births, business deaths, common-stock prices, new orders, length of the workweek, and sensitive price indices. Business births should lead because they represent expansionary business anticipations; when anticipations fade late in a period of prosperity, business births can be expected to decline, and when anticipations show some improvement late in a contraction, business births should begin to rise. Similarly, business deaths represent market conditions which lead businessmen to make contractionary decisions. Business births are best represented by the Department of Commerce series on New Businesses. Business deaths are best represented by the Department of Commerce series on Discontinued Business and the Dun and Bradstreet series on Industrial and Commercial Failures.

Representing major equities, common-stock prices are sensitive to business anticipations, and therefore should lead business activity. A

---

[13] The lead, lag, and coincident series described here have been statistically developed by the National Bureau of Economic Research. See Geoffrey H. Moore, *Statistical Indicators of Cyclical Revivals and Recessions,* Occasional Paper 31, 1950, and W. C. Mitchell, *What Happens during Business Cycles,* 1951. A more detailed analysis of the timing of the series described is given in *An Appraisal of Data and Research on Businessmen's Expectations about Outlook and Operating Variables* (Washington: Board of Governors of the Federal Reserve System, September, 1955), pp. 119–149.

common-stock price index represents the aggregation of detailed antici-pations of many separate individuals on future prospects.

The rate of ordering can be expected to rise and fall with business anticipations; since new-orders data principally represent durable goods, an additional reason for leading is the prompt movement of durable-goods activity. Construction contracts awarded, a special type of new order, tends to lead for similar reasons.

The length of the workweek is probably the most reliable lead series available. This is because businessmen make interim adjustments to de-mand by raising or reducing the hours of work. The effect of change in demand is thus usually first seen in a shift in the length of the work-week. The workweek may decline temporarily, however, even when the expansionary phase is continuing.

Spot price indices, such as provided in the Daily Spot Market Price Index, tend to lead because they quickly reflect shifts in demand. Many other series which show some tendency to lead might be considered.[14] The series briefly noted above are those for which the best statistical evidence is available or for which the best case can be made.

Recognition of important concomitant and lagging series is probably as important in forecasting as recognition of lead series. Statistical evi-dence indicates that employment, unemployment, corporate profits, bank debits outside New York, freight carloadings, nonfood wholesale prices, and industrial production are timed with total business activity. Simi-larly, personal income, retail sales, installment credit, bank rates on busi-ness loans, and manufacturing inventories tend to lag after the turns in activity. Probably partly through wishful thinking, the high or rising level of these series is often employed to justify expectations of con-tinuing expansion when a prosperity phase is ending. Particularly, refer-ence is frequently made to the high level of personal income, retail sales, employment, and corporate profits at such a time. On the other hand, the continued low levels of these series is often cited as evidence of con-tinued contraction as a business upturn is approached.

DIFFUSION INDICES

Although few particular series show highly useful leads, a large number of series lead at any given turning point. Evidence which can be obtained from many series is probably far more important than that shown by a few series which can be singled out because of consistency of lead. Evidence of this kind can be obtained by a method known as "diffusion indices." The term relates to the indication given of the spreading of influences throughout the economy. The measure can be

[14] Other measures are described in the Federal Reserve study noted in footnote 13.

obtained historically by developing the percentage of series which is expanding. Theoretically, for instance, we can expect that the percentage of companies showing rising profits will decline well before a business-cycle downturn and rise well before a business-cycle upturn, although the statistical evidence is somewhat sketchy.[15] The reasons ordinarily accepted for the ending of a phase of expansion are closely related to

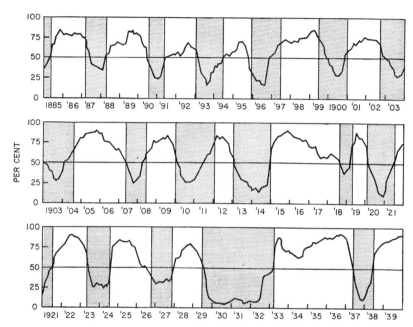

CHART 6–1. Diffusion Index. (Per Cent of a Large Number of Series Which Is Expanding.) Only series which conform well with business-cycle movements are included; they number over 300 from 1920 to 1940. Shaded areas represent contractions. SOURCE: Reproduced with permission from A. F. Burns, *New Facts on Business Cycles* (New York: National Bureau of Economic Research, Inc., 1950), p. 12.

increasing difficulties many companies experience in making profits. Similarly, the reasons for the ending of a phase of contraction are related to increasing profit possibilities.

The most convincing evidence on diffusion indices is an index of the percentage of a large number of available series which is expanding at any given time, as shown in Chart 6–1. It will be noted that there is a strong tendency for business-cycle turning points to occur when approximately 50 per cent of the series is expanding. No one would expect all series to turn at once; at any turning point, some lead and some

[15] See Thor Hultgren, *Cyclical Diversities in the Fortunes of Industrial Corporations,* Occasional Paper 32 (New York: National Bureau of Economic Research, 1950).

lag. That about half should be still rising when over-all downturns occur and half rising when over-all upturns are finally achieved is reasonable. If such 50-per-cent points are typical, a considerable lead is shown
by diffusion indices. Historical evidence strongly indicates that this is
so.

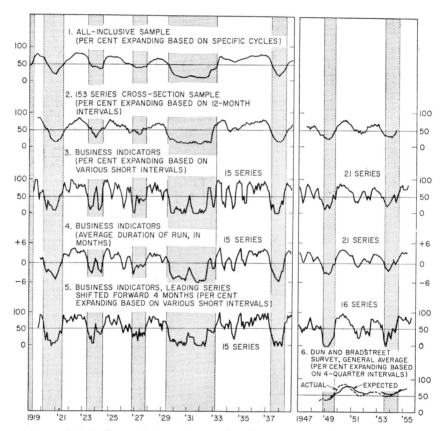

CHART 6–2. Diffusion Indices Compared with a Duration-of-Run Index. Shaded
areas represent contractions of general-business cycles; unshaded areas, expansions.
SOURCE: Taken, with permission, from Geoffrey H. Moore, "Diffusion Indexes: A Comment," *American Statistician*, October, 1955.

Some adaptation is necessary to make use of diffusion indices currently. Prospectively, we do not know whether the peak or trough has
yet been achieved in any particular series, and therefore we do not know
whether or not the series is in an expanding phase. A reasonable substitute for the per cent of series expanding has proved to be statistically
reliable: "Average duration of run," as indicated by the number of un-
interrupted months a series rises or falls. A rise is a plus and a fall

is a minus; the maximum figure to be added for any single series is taken as 6, in order to avoid overweighting stable series. Continued rises are representative of expansions, and continued falls are representative of contractions. Duration-of-run indices are now reported by several publications to provide a current indication of diffusion.[16] Chart 6–2 shows a duration-of-run index compared with various diffusion indices.

WRIGHT'S STATISTICAL-INDICATOR METHOD

An alternative procedure for making use of any leads which may appear has been developed by C. Ashley Wright.[17] The idea is that if a reasonable number of series that conform well with business-cycle movements are timed about any particular turning point, a distribution pattern which is quite similar to that for any other turning point will be obtained. Nothing is implied about the timing of any particular series. At any particular turning point, some series will lead and some will lag. Wright does not presume to know what the shape of the distribution pattern is, but has found satisfactory results by employing the normal frequency distribution.

Forty closely conforming and sensitive series were picked and turning points were determined currently by a method described below. At an extreme point on the distribution, one of the series will make an early turn, and as the months go by, more turns will occur. A relatively few early turns will describe the "tail" of the distribution of turning points. The center of the distribution will locate the business-cycle turn. Having given the tail described by the early turns, the full distribution curve can be projected by statistical methods. The date of the center of the distribution will thus have been estimated, and that date is taken as the forecast of the turning point. As more and more turns occur, the entire distribution curve can be forecast more accurately, so that increasing confidence can be placed in the forecast. As noted above, the normal frequency curve is employed to project the distribution.

Turning points are determined currently in each of the individual series by fitting a trend to recent data and measuring the deviation of

---

[16] Representative cases are *The Value Line Investment Survey*, 5 East 44th Street, New York 17; *The Conference Board Bulletin,* published monthly by the National Industrial Conference Board, 460 Park Avenue, New York 22; *Statistical Indicator Reports,* published by Statistical Indicator Associates, Great Barrington, Mass. It is now thought that equally satisfactory results may be obtained by applying smoothing moving averages to each component series to determine whether it is rising or falling. Both methods increase reliability at the expense of delay in registering indications.

[17] C. Ashley Wright, "Business Cycle Research and Business Policy," in *Conference on Business Cycles* (New York: National Bureau of Economic Research, Inc., 1951), pp. 339–374.

the current point in the series from the trend line. When the current point moves two standard deviations away from the measured trend, a turning point is considered to have occurred in that series. There is no information available on the effectiveness of this rule in practice. The method has been employed less widely than the diffusion index, and there is little empirical data available on its performance, but it has performed best with sharp peaks or troughs.

SURVEYS OF EXPENDITURE PLANS

The two most important areas covered by surveys of expenditure plans are represented by the Survey of Plant and Equipment, jointly made by the Office of Business Economics of the Department of Commerce and the Securities and Exchange Commission, and the Federal Reserve Survey of Consumer Finances, conducted by the Survey Research Center of the University of Michigan. The Survey of Plant and Equipment Anticipations provides both annual and quarterly expenditure anticipations. The annual-expenditure anticipations have been remarkably close to actual. The quarterly anticipations have not been so close, especially the first anticipations reported near turning points, but nevertheless they have been good. The survey has been approximately comparable since 1948 to that presently reported. The relative stability of the period may partly account for the good record.[18]

The McGraw-Hill Department of Economics conducts a similar survey, except that information is obtained principally from large companies and the survey refers only to annual periods.[19] A preliminary checkup is obtained by telegraphic reports in the fall, and this is followed by a survey made during March and April with the cooperation of correspondents of *Business Week*, the staffs of other McGraw-Hill magazines, and the American Gas Association. As in the OBE-SEC Survey, information is obtained on planned sales to compare with the anticipated capital expenditures; also, the companies are asked to state the per cent of capacity, on their own definition, at which they are operating as well as the per cent at which they prefer to operate. These percentages are useful in indicating capital demand in relation to capital supply. If, for instance, the preferred rate of operation is substantially

---

[18] For further study of this Survey see Irwin Friend and Jean Bronfenbrenner, "Plant and Equipment Programs and Their Realization," in *Short-term Economic Forecasting*, vol. XVII in *Studies in Income and Wealth* (Princeton, N.J.: Princeton University Press, 1955); Vito Natrella, "Forecasting Plant and Equipment Expenditures from Businessmen's Expectations," *Proceedings of the Business and Economic Section, American Statistical Association*, 1956; Murray F. Foss and Vito Natrella, "Ten Years' Experience with Business Investment Anticipations," *Survey of Current Business*, January, 1957.

[19] Published in *Business Week* and also in special releases.

higher than the actual rate, a considerable part of capital demand may have to depend on modernization plans. There may be some industries in which the preferred rate is below the actual rate, however, as was true in early 1957.

Other types of surveys which obtain complementary information on capital-expansion plans are now becoming available. The Securities and Exchange Commission issues a release early in the year showing the anticipated financing plans of manufacturing and public-utility companies for the year in progress. These industries, of course, may indicate greater or less reliance on the securities market, and hence the survey might properly show a different movement from anticipated expenditure plans.

The National Industrial Conference Board started an experimental quarterly Survey of Capital Appropriations in 1956.[20] It is too early to evaluate the survey, but it may prove to be very useful in providing early information on a change in capital plans. As reported in 1956 and 1957, the backlog of capital appropriations was large, even though a slackening was occurring in newly approved appropriations.

In connection with both the joint survey by the Office of Business Economics and the Securities and Exchange Commission and the Mc-Graw-Hill survey, sales expectations of manufacturers are obtained. These have been consistent in movement with the expenditure anticipations. It will be interesting to see if sales anticipations inverse to the direction of movement of expenditure anticipations develop at any time.

The Federal Reserve Survey of Consumer Finances is founded on a relatively small sample of "spending units," related individuals living together who pool their incomes. Questions are asked on money income, past change in income, expected change in income, liquid-asset holdings, evaluation of own financial situation, expected general-business conditions, plans to purchase automobiles, houses, home improvements, furniture, and appliances. This survey is still experimental, and it is difficult to say how far into the future consumers make plans to purchase. The information developed is generally considered useful, however, in forecasting consumer expenditures, especially to the extent that such expenditures depend on factors other than change in disposable income.

In both the capital and the consumer surveys, the reports provide indications regarding psychological attitudes. This is very important in forecasting and would justify use of the surveys even if the anticipations were usually quite different from the actual outturn. Single fig-

---

[20] The results of the survey are issued quarterly in the *Conference Board Business Record*. A useful analysis has been made in an unpublished paper by Morris Cohen of the National Industrial Conference Board, "The National Industrial Conference Board Survey of Capital Appropriations," scheduled for publication in a forthcoming volume of the National Bureau of Economic Research *Studies in Income and Wealth*.

ures do not give us the full meaning of the attitudes revealed by the surveys, for there tends to be a wide dispersion of decision makers about the average anticipation. In fact, one of the most striking things about these surveys—both capital and consumer—is that only a small per cent of the respondents expect changes close to the average. Furthermore, the anticipated expenditures of individual respondents tend to be quite different from the expenditures which are actually made. For instance, in reviewing the 1955 survey made by the Office of Business Economics and the Securities and Exchange Commission, it was found that in a manufacturing sample a fourth invested more than twice as much as anticipated, a sixth invested between 40 and 100 per cent more, and nearly a tenth invested less than 40 per cent as much. With so great a variation among individual respondents, it is a striking fact that the average anticipation comes close to the outturn.

SALES ANTICIPATIONS

In addition to the sales anticipations of manufacturers, surveyed in connection with expected capital expenditures, several other investigations are made. We may consider here the *Fortune* and Dun and Bradstreet surveys. *Fortune* surveys retail trade, farmers, homebuilding, business inventories, and capital-goods sales.[21] Except for inventory, the *Fortune* surveys refer principally to sales anticipations. The retailers' anticipations are expected to throw light on consumers' expenditures; the anticipations of companies selling to farmers are expected to show farm expenditures, especially nonconsumer; contractors' anticipations are expected to indicate the trend of homebuilding; and capital-goods producers are looked upon to point the movement of expenditures for capital goods. The results have been encouraging. The inventory survey is obtained directly from individual firms and is useful in highlighting anticipated inventory changes.

The Dun and Bradstreet surveys cover the anticipations of a large group of businessmen on sales, inventories, employees, prices, and, in the case of some manufacturers, new orders. The average results obtained by surveying the anticipations of these businessmen provide rather unsatisfactory forecasts. It has been found, however, that a diffusion index turns the survey figures into more reliable indicators. For instance, the excess of the percentage of concerns expecting an increase in sales [22] over the percentage of concerns expecting a decrease has faith-

---

[21] See *An Appraisal of Data and Research on Businessmen's Expectations about Outlook and Operating Variables*, pp. 75–96.

[22] The increases and decreases are stated in relation to the corresponding period the year before; in order to avoid reflecting seasonal changes, the respondents are asked to make their own forecasts in that way.

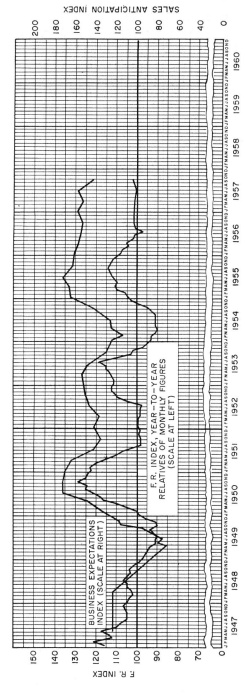

CHART 6–3. Index of Sales Anticipations as Shown by Dun and Bradstreet Survey and Index of Industrial Production. The index of sales anticipations is developed by taking the excess of the percentage of concerns expecting an increase in sales relative to the previous year over the percentage of concerns expecting a decrease plus 100. Measured in this way, those businessmen who say they expect no change are ignored, and this group frequently is relatively large. The Federal Reserve Index of Industrial Production is cast in the form of year-to-year relatives for comparison. The Sales Anticipations Index was developed by Ralph J. Watkins, Director of Economic Studies, Brookings Institution.

149

fully led the Industrial Production Index (see Chart 6–3). The cumulative shift in anticipations is thus represented; it is interesting that it tends to provide a reliable indicator although the average anticipation does not.[23] An increasing number of firms foresee the change in direction of sales as the turning point in total activity is approached, even though the total dollar amount anticipated has been a poor indicator.

GENERAL-BUSINESS EXPECTATIONS

In comparison with expenditure plans or individual anticipations, general-business expectations are usually much vaguer and may be developed more casually. It would seem that very often expectations regarding changes in the total economy are obtained from general reading or chance conversation. Probably this is the best method of attaining an intelligent appraisal if one is not fortunate enough to have an effective economic-analysis department at one's disposal. For purposes of forecasting, however, hope is often held out that the business situation may be forecast by surveys of general-business expectations because the interviewers are closely acquainted with the sales prospects of many companies. It would appear that, for this reason, the monthly business survey of the National Association of Purchasing Agents is helpful in developing general-business forecasts.[24]

Many surveys ask for general-business expectations as well as expenditure expectations or sales anticipations. This is true, for instance, of the *Fortune* "mood" surveys, which refer to general expectations. The question in the Federal Reserve Survey of Consumer Finances relating to expected general-business conditions provides similar information from typical consumers. Although we may not usually obtain a great deal of leverage on the forecast of general-business activity from such surveys, they do throw light on psychological expectations. Probably they will continue to be more useful in this respect than in any other.

APPENDIX FOR CHAPTER 6: SOURCES OF DATA

1. *Sourcebooks Describing Series*

Business Statistics, 1957 Biennial Edition: A Supplement to the Survey of Current Business (Washington: Office of Business Economics, U.S. Department of Commerce, 1957).

    Detailed notes in the back of the book give quite satisfactory descriptions of the many series carried in the *Survey of Current Business*.

[23] See pp. 25–54 of the reference in footnote 21.
[24] See pp. 54–66 of the reference in footnote 21. A sample of purchasing agents who jointly represent most branches of industry are canvassed. See also discussion of the price forecasting of the Association in Chap. 9 below.

Cole, Arthur H.: *Measures of Business Change* (Homewood, Ill.: Richard D. Irwin, Inc., 1952).

This book gives brief descriptions of 449 series representing the volume of business, commodity prices, construction costs, employment, finance, and regional measures.

Selected Economic Indicators (New York: Federal Reserve Bank of New York, December, 1954).

Lists and describes some key indicators.

Snyder, Richard M.: *Measuring Business Changes: A Handbook of Significant Business Indicators* (New York: John Wiley & Sons, Inc., 1955).

Provides helpful descriptions of widely used barometers.

Statistical Services of the United States Government (Washington: Office of Statistical Standards, Bureau of the Budget, 1952).

Describes principal types of economic and social statistics; explains co-ordination and general areas of responsibility.

Techniques of Preparing Major BLS Statistical Series, U.S. Department of Labor Bulletin 1168, 1954.

Provides careful descriptions of consumers' price index, work-stoppage statistics, national housing volume, labor turnover, wholesale price index, wage and hour series, industrial employment, earnings of workers, new construction, industrial injuries, and occupational wages.

2. Publications Covering the Most Generally Useful Data

The Economic Almanac, prepared by the National Industrial Conference Board (New York: Thomas Y. Crowell Co.).

Annual publication with relatively comprehensive coverage of economic data.

Economic Indicators, prepared by the Council of Economic Advisers (Washington: Government Printing Office).

A monthly publication of charts and tables of critically important series. A historical supplement published in 1957 provided a useful description of the series.

Economic Report of the President (Washington: Government Printing Office).

Annual publication with an up-to-date statistical appendix containing limited but very frequently needed statistical data.

Federal Reserve Bulletin (Washington: Board of Governors of the Federal Reserve System).

A monthly publication which covers financial data relative to the banks in the United States, international data on banks and gold, interest rates, savings institutions, Federal finance, business finance, consumer credit, mortgage debt, indices of business activity—basic publication of the industrial production index and department-store statistics.

Federal Reserve Charts on Bank Credit, Money Rates and Business (Washington: Board of Governors of the Federal Reserve System).

A relatively comprehensive monthly chart book with an annual historical supplement.

Monthly Labor Review (Washington: U.S. Department of Labor).

A monthly publication showing a major part of the data developed by the Department of Labor, including various phases of labor data, prices, and housing.

Statistical Abstract of the United States (Washington: Government Printing Office).

Annual publication providing the most comprehensive coverage on an annual basis, but not particularly pointed at forecasting problems.

Survey of Current Business (Washington: Office of Business Economics, U.S. Department of Commerce).

This is a monthly publication, accompanied by a weekly supplement containing the most current figures and occasional supplementary volumes on *National Income, Personal Income by States, Business Statistics,* and other topics. The coverage of monthly and quarterly data is superior to that of any other single publication for forecasting purposes. Omissions are principally matters of detail which are covered more fully in specialized sources. Few data which are available only on an annual basis are reported.

3. *Sources of Data on a Select List of Subjects*

AGRICULTURE

Principal data are published by the U.S. Department of Agriculture. Out of a wide range of reports, we may note *The Farm Income Situation* (monthly), *Agricultural Outlook Charts* (annual), *Agricultural Statistics* (annual).

AUTOMOBILES

Weekly assemblies by make are reported by R. L. Polk; ordinarily published in summary form in the leading newspapers. *Automobile Age* carries a price average for secondhand cars from prices recorded in car auction markets. The annuals, *Automobile Facts and Figures* and *Motor Truck Facts,* published by the Automobile Manufacturers Association, contain much useful information.

CAPITAL SPENDING

Plant and equipment expenditures are developed in a survey made jointly by the Office of Business Economics and the Securities and Exchange Commission, published in the *Survey of Current Business.* See also the discussion earlier in this chapter of the survey made by the McGraw-Hill Department of Economics. The Machinery and Allied Products Institute reports intermittently a series on new plant and equipment outlays, published in the Institute's *Capital Goods Review.*

The most comprehensive measure is the construction and equipment component of gross national product. Coverage varies between the series. On construction, the Bureau of Labor Statistics reports residential building permits and starts. The F. W. Dodge Corporation reports contract awards; summary information is carried in the *Survey of Current Business* and the *Federal Reserve Bulletin.* Data on construction expenditures are developed by the government and reported in the *Construction Review,* a monthly publication available from the Government Printing Office; this publication also carries allied information on construction, such as costs, material production, and contract employment. Data on inventories are covered below.

CONSUMER CREDIT

The chief data on consumer credit are reported in the *Federal Reserve Bulletin,* including a series on installment credit extended and repaid by type of credit. A six-volume study on consumer credit was made by the Board of Governors of the Federal Reserve System in 1957 and is available to the public. It is entitled *Consumer Installment Credit* and can be ordered from the Government Printing Office.

CONSUMER AND RETAIL PRICES

The Consumer Price Index is available in all major sources. Further details are published in a monthly release of the Bureau of Labor Statistics, *Consumer Price Index*. The *Survey of Current Business* carries a Retail Price Index developed by the Department of Commerce.

CORPORATE PROFITS

Several sources should be used to trace the movement of corporate profits. As a division of national income, corporate-profit estimates most closely approximate the true level, but these figures *currently* are not satisfactory as to level, for temporary methods of extrapolation must be employed by the Department of Commerce in making the estimates. The Bureau of Internal Revenue figures, on which they are based, become available three or four years late. The Federal Reserve reports on a sample of manufacturing and electric-power companies and on virtually complete coverage of railroads and telephones, showing quarterly profit figures (published in the *Federal Reserve Bulletin*). The Federal Trade Commission and the Securities and Exchange Commission estimate total profits of all manufacturing corporations quarterly from a large sample (published in the *Survey of Current Business*). The National City Bank shows the change in profits for a total of more than 3,000 corporations and for many industrial groups for the previous year in the April issue of the *National City Bank Letter*. Each quarter it shows the combined result for about four hundred corporations. The various series noted, except those of the Department of Commerce, accept the profits reported by the companies themselves in estimating the profit component of national income. Conceptual adjustments are made to conform with national-income concepts in the Department of Commerce estimates.[25]

DIVIDENDS

Like corporate profits, dividends as a component of national income most closely approximate the true level, but such figures are available only very tardily. The surveys of the Federal Reserve and of the Federal Trade and Securities Commissions, noted above, likewise report on dividends. Dividend series are additionally reported by Moody's and by Standard and Poor's Corporation (currently published in the *Survey of Current Business*).

GOVERNMENT FINANCE

The most comprehensive measures are annual data appearing in detailed Tables 8 and 9 in *National Income*, published by the Department of Commerce as a supplement to *Survey of Current Business*. For the Federal government only, the *Daily Treasury Statement* and the monthly *Treasury Bulletin* present official data on financial operations; similarly, *Budgetary Re-*

---

[25] See Table 38 of *National Income*, published by the Department of Commerce, for a reconciliation of national income and Internal Revenue estimates of corporate profits. This indicates the principal differences between the national-income component and original profit reports.

ceipts and Expenditures and *Cash Receipts from and Payments to the Public* provide official data on receipts and expenditures and cash flows.

INTEREST RATES, BOND AND STOCK YIELDS

Short-term interest rates as reported by various agencies are published currently in the *Survey of Current Business* and the *Federal Reserve Bulletin*. There is a considerable range of variation between rates on various types of loans, covering bank rates on business loans, various open-market rates, Reserve bank discount rates, and rates on government securities. Bond yields by quality ratings and also by industrial classification are reported by Moody's and by Standard and Poor's Corporation; bond yields representative of issues of large cities are reported by *The Bond Buyer* (the major aggregates, but not all of the detail of these series, are published in the *Survey of Current Business*). The *Federal Reserve Bulletin* reports on yields on U.S. Government bonds and Moody's series on state and local government bonds by quality ratings. The *Survey of Current Business* reports on Moody's dividend yields on common stocks and Standard and Poor's Corporation dividend yields on preferred stocks. The *Federal Reserve Bulletin* reports an earnings–common-stock-price ratio.

INVENTORIES

Inventory investment is represented by change in inventory stocks, preferably after inventory valuation adjustment (to avoid incorporating inflationary factors which may be involved in the price of the inventory stock). The only available series of this type is the inventory-investment component of gross national product. The early figures are not very reliable, being subject to substantial revision as time goes on. The most comprehensive data on inventory stocks are developed in the Industry Survey made by the Department of Commerce (reported in the *Survey of Current Business*). Department-store stocks are reported in the *Federal Reserve Bulletin*. Inventory stocks are available on many individual products; many of the most important series are currently published in the *Survey of Current Business*, notably on copper, lead, zinc, coal, fuel oil, gasoline, rubber, rubber tires, glass containers, cotton, rayon, and other products.

NATIONAL INCOME AND PRODUCT, INCLUDING GROSS NATIONAL PRODUCT, NET NATIONAL PRODUCT, NATIONAL INCOME, PERSONAL INCOME, DISPOSABLE INCOME, AND PERSONAL CONSUMPTION EXPENDITURE

These measures are computed by the Office of Business Economics of the Department of Commerce. Quarterly figures are reported in the *Survey of Current Business* nearly two months late. However, the Council of Economic Advisers recently has released early estimates to the newspapers only about three weeks late. The measures, together with breakdowns and supporting tables, are shown since 1929 in the Department of Commerce's supplement *National Income*. The figures are brought up to date each year in the July issue of the *Survey of Current Business*. The supplement *Personal Income by States* is published occasionally, and the figures are brought up to date each year in the August issue of the *Survey of Current Business*. Although other work has been done on national income and product measurements, no other series are published currently. The National Bureau of Economic Research was a pioneer in this field and has published several fundamental studies on the subject.

NEW ORDERS

The most important data on new orders are those for durable-product manufacturers and some nondurable-product manufacturers reported in the Industry Survey by the Department of Commerce and published in the *Survey of Current Business*. Some individual series showing a historical tendency to lead can be singled out: southern pine lumber, oak flooring, steel forgings, and machine tools (these are reported in the *Survey of Current Business*, but they are not subdivisions in the Industry Survey). Other new-order series are of value; reports are made by various trade associations. The series on new orders reported for department stores in the *Federal Reserve Bulletin* is interesting in tracing commitments back from the retailer, but its anticipatory value has not been demonstrated.

PHYSICAL PRODUCTION

The most important series on physical production is the Federal Reserve's Index of Industrial Production. The Federal Reserve also reports on an index of the output of consumer durable goods, subdivided into autos, furniture and floor coverings, appliances and heaters, radio and television sets, and other items (published in the *Federal Reserve Bulletin* and *Survey of Current Business*). The Department of Agriculture develops an index of the physical volume of farm marketings, subdivided into crops and livestock and products (published in the *Survey of Current Business*). There are a great many monthly series showing the volume of production of individual products (most of the important ones are published in the *Survey of Current Business*). Major weekly production series are bituminous coal mined, cars and trucks assembled, electric power distributed, freight car loadings, paperboard production, and steel production. These are reported in leading newspapers.

POPULATION AND LABOR FORCE

Population projections developed by the Bureau of the Census are presented in the *Economic Almanac*, based on information supplied in *Current Population Reports;* a recent population projection is in ser. P-25, no. 123, dated October 20, 1955. Similarly, the Census Bureau makes available projections for households and the labor force (see current *Economic Almanac*). Recent projections are in *Current Population Reports:* for households and families, ser. P-20, no. 69, August 31, 1956; for the labor force, ser. P-50, no. 69, October, 1956.

SALES

The most important series are those representing manufacturing, wholesale trade, and retail trade in the Industry Survey of the Department of Commerce. Also noteworthy is the series on corporate sales in detailed Table 29 in *National Income*. The report in the *Federal Reserve Bulletin* on sales in divisional manufacturing groups is useful. Other sales series, such as for capital goods, are covered elsewhere in this outline. A great many series representing sales of individual products are reported, part of which are published in the *Survey of Current Business*.

SAVINGS, PERSONAL

There are two major sources of personal-savings data. The Department of Commerce reports a total quarterly figure, obtained by subtracting personal consumption expenditures from disposable income. The Securities and Exchange Commission reports quarterly personal savings as the amount of change in various asset items. The first is published in the *Survey of Current Business* and the second in the Securities and Exchange Commission's *Statistical Bulletin*. A reconciliation of the two sets of figures is given in Table 38 in *National Income*.

SPOT PRICES

The most important spot price series is the Bureau of Labor Statistics' Daily Index of Spot Market Prices. Somewhat similar indexes are the *Journal of Commerce's* Daily Price Index of Sensitive Commodities and Dun and Bradstreet's Daily Wholesale Price Index of Basic Commodities. Also, Dow Jones and Company compiles a Commodity-Futures Index and a comparable Daily Spot Commodity Price Index. All of these are published in leading newspapers.

STOCK MARKET PRICES

The Dow Jones stock price averages are the outstanding measures of the stock market because of their wide use among persons interested. Many other equally effective measurements of the market are available, but they are generally less useful, for the information ordinarily desired is less what actually happened than what is thought to have happened by those financially interested. Nearly all stock price indices are reported daily in leading newspapers. From the point of view of prompt measurement of actual changes taking place in the market, the new Standard and Poor's Corporation hourly index computed by rapid electronic equipment and weighted scientifically is superior.

WHOLESALE COMMODITY PRICES

The outstanding measure is the Bureau of Labor Statistics Wholesale Price Index, together with its breakdown to represent various parts of the economy (reported in all of the standard compilations, including the *Survey of Current Business*). Several other indexes are reported. Depending on the degree of weighting placed on various parts of the economy, these indexes show different relative movements, usually greater than those depicted by the Bureau of Labor Statistics Index. A great deal of detail on individual prices can be obtained in various releases issued by the Bureau of Labor Statistics. An especially useful reference on the price of raw, unfabricated materials is the *Commodity Yearbook* of the Commodity Research Bureau.

CHAPTER 7

Short-term Forecasting of Aggregate Industry

Compared with long-term forecasting, the near future might seem quite simple to anticipate because of the factor of inertia, but actually it is very difficult to tie the near future to any simple formula. Long-term forecasts are aimed so far into the future that many changes cannot be perceived. On the other hand, we have shown in earlier chapters that the secular-trend level of the future is obviously dependent on forces which are reduceable to mechanical form. Short-term changes are not so reduceable because possible changes must be traced to too many sources and on rather complicated patterns.

PROCEDURES EMPLOYED BY EARLIER GENERATIONS

Favorable-Unfavorable Factors. The earliest method employed to make short-term forecasts involves setting favorable factors in the outlook against unfavorable ones. Such a procedure necessarily is highly subjective, and when it is used in a naïve way it must be considered quite unreliable. No technique is available for quantifying the factors. Let us assume that we have increasing employment as a favorable factor and the leveling off of profits as an unfavorable one. It is impossible to say that the sum of these two factors add prospectively either to an expansionary or to a contractionary result.

Nevertheless, when carefully employed, the method provides an indispensable integrating procedure even today. If the factors are sharply related to the business outlook, and listing according to any criteria other than outlook is avoided, the method can bring attention to critical factors otherwise ignored. This represents a desirable step at a preliminary stage in forecasting.

At a somewhat later stage in the forecasting process, a determination of turning points—shifts in general direction of movement—may be made by judging a list of evidential factors quite akin to an enumeration of factors dealing with the outlook. For the purpose of judging turning points, however, more specialized outlook evidence is required. If effectively employed, the list will include the conclusions derived from as many other methods of forecasting as are applicable. The technique is illustrated below in forecasting the 1957 recession.

The Single Leading Index. The dream of a single measure which will show the movement of total business activity before it occurs has played an important part in the history of forecasting. Much effort was exerted to this end in the twenties, but we have little that is constructive to show for it. Slowly and reluctantly, forecasters came to recognize the dream as an unattainable goal because of the diversity of the factors which make up aggregate business activity and because of the irregularity and uncertainty of leads in the best leading series.[1]

The Harvard Index Chart. Although there were many isolated attempts to develop a forecasting index which would lead the movement of business activity because of the logical forces represented in it, illustrated by the Smith index described in footnote 1, the general tendency was to put faith in empirical leads. The acme of the period was reached by Warren M. Persons in the Harvard Index Chart.[2] Persons studied empirically the timing of all available economic series and grouped them according to their timing patterns. He finally chose three timing groups and picked the most consistent series to represent each. The result was the prewar Harvard Index Chart, shown in Chart 7–1. The leading series are represented by the *A* curve, the coincident series by the *B* curve, and the lagging series by the *C* curve. A close study of this chart will convince the reader that the timing difference between these curves is remarkable; the *A* curve always leads, and the *C* curve always lags at the cyclical peaks and troughs over this long period of thirty-nine years.

[1] A most striking and now nearly forgotten leading index was developed by B. B. Smith in 1930. It was not founded simply on empirical relations, as many of these indices are, but the leading factors were set down by Smith on the basis of what appeared logically to be responsible factors. His forecasting index was a weighted combination of (1) the deviations of short-term interest rates from bond yields, (2) variation of monetary gold plus Federal Reserve bank holdings of United States securities about a trend line, (3) measurement of the rapidity of rise or fall in the security markets, and (4) the twelve-month trailing total of new corporate and municipal long-term bond flotations in the United States, excluding those of investment trusts, shown in percentage deviations from their trend. See B. B. Smith, "A Forecasting Index for Business," *Journal of the American Statistical Association* 26:115–127, 1931. Like most of the logically developed forecasting indices originating in this period, the responsible factors were assumed to be monetary. Partly because of the depression and partly because of shifting institutions, the monetary factors later appeared to lose much of their logical influence.

[2] See early issues of the *Review of Economic Statistics* and a pamphlet by the Harvard Committee entitled *The Harvard Index of General Business Conditions: Its Interpretation* (Cambridge, Mass.: Harvard University Press, 1923).

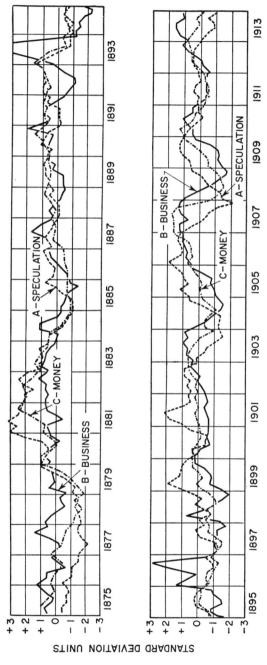

CHART 7-1. The Prewar Harvard Index Chart. Adjusted indices of (A) average stock prices and New York bank clearings, (B) wholesale commodity prices and outside bank clearings, and (C) rates on 60–90-day commercial paper: bimonthly, 1875–1902. Adjusted indexes of (A) speculation, (B) business, and (C) money: bimonthly, 1903–1913. SOURCE: Reproduced, with permission, from J. L. Snider, *Business Statistics*, 2d ed. (New York: McGraw-Hill Book Co., Inc., 1932).

Actually, the Harvard Index Chart might have been developed logically instead of empirically. It will be noted that the *A* curve represents stock prices, the *B* curve commodity prices, and the *C* curve interest rates; logical arguments regarding these timing differences are presented elsewhere.[3] Substantially this same chart was employed by the Brookmire Economic Service as early as 1911, and it is likely that the Service was guided principally by the logic of the timing differences in developing the chart.

Unfortunately, the Harvard Index Chart never performed very satisfactorily, once it was put into use in the early twenties. The 1920 downturn was forecast perfectly, but thereafter the timing was never quite right, and usually very wrong. Publication was discontinued in 1941, and the method has fallen into disuse. The Harvard Committee attributed failure in the twenties to Federal Reserve control and stockmarket speculation. For instance, stock prices failed to decline in the 1927 recession. The control of rediscount rates to stabilize business was thought to have influenced the timing. Large gold imports exerted an abnormal influence on the short-term money market.

Conditions in the thirties were also unfavorable for the operation of the Harvard Index Chart. No substantial demand existed for short-term money, and monetary policy was frequently used to keep interest rates low. Stock prices both at the downturn in May, 1937, and at the upturn in June, 1938, led business turns by only two months. The forties were dominated by war controls and inflationary conditions thereafter. The major decline in stock prices in 1946, unrelated to any business contraction, is explicable if we recognize that the danger of commodity-price inflation greatly decreased in that year.

The performance of stock prices and interest rates has been better in the 1948–50 and 1953–55 experiences. Stock prices peaked in May or June of 1948, whereas the business peak was not reached until October, and short-term interest rates did not decline until mid-1949. Compared with the business trough at October, 1949, stock prices began rising in the preceding June, and short-term interest rates did not begin to rise until mid-1950. Compared with the business peak at July, 1953, stock prices began declining in the preceding March, and short-term interest rates began declining at the downturn in July. Compared with the business upturn in August, 1954, stock prices began rising in September, 1953, and short-term interest rates did not begin to rise until January, 1955.

Thus, it will be seen that the leads and lags specified by the Harvard Index Chart actually were reasonably well borne out at recent business-cycle turning points. The forecasting significance is doubtful, however.

[3] See especially Chap. 6 and the section below on leading series.

It is difficult to disentangle the cyclical turning points from intermediate movements in the stock market until the perspective provided by later changes is available, so that slight leverage actually was provided by the stock-market leads. The movements of the money market reflect national policy more than they do competitive market conditions, at least in so far as the turning points are concerned, and therefore their aid in establishing the turns is easily exaggerated. Recent experience is, however, consistent with the belief that stock prices tend to lead and interest rates to lag.

LEADING SERIES

Faith in the indications of leading series has not disappeared. Continued work at the National Bureau of Economic Research is the most important along this line.[4] Under Moore's direction, considerable care has been given to evaluating the business-cycle conformity [5] and timing of about 800 monthly and quarterly series. These series are classified into 24 major groups,[6] and in each group the proportion of accepted series and the characteristic timing of accepted series is shown. A major criterion employed in fixing attention on a limited number of 225 of the total series, accepted according to the criteria of conformity and timing, is the extent to which the series belong to a group with relatively consistent timing. An effort is made to choose series which represent the consistently performing groups, whether or not a long impressive record is available for the particular series.[7]

The 21 series chosen from the total group to represent leading, coincident and lagging processes in the economy is shown in Chart 7-2.

[4] See Geoffrey H. Moore, *Statistical Indicators of Cyclical Revivals and Recessions,* Occasional Paper 31 (New York: National Bureau of Economic Research, Inc., 1950). This represents a continuation of an earlier study, W. C. Mitchall and A. F. Burns, *Statistical Indicators of Cyclical Revivals,* Bulletin 69 (New York: National Bureau of Economic Research, Inc., 1938).

[5] By conformity is meant how closely and consistently series have moved with the general-business cycle. See Moore, *ibid.,* pp. 23 ff.

[6] Retail sales, wholesale sales, imports, exports, new orders, construction contracts and permits, inventories, production, transportation and communication, employment, average hours per week, earnings per employee, payrolls and other income payments, prices of commodities, banking and money, interest rates and bond yields, stock-exchange transactions, stock prices, corporate security issues, business profits, business failures, bank clearings and debits, business-activity indexes, and unclassified. *Ibid.,* pp. 34–35.

[7] In the leading series, new incorporations from the unclassified group and the Bureau of Labor Statistics' Index of Wholesale Prices of 28 Basic Commodities (chosen because the Index bears a similarity to Bradstreet's Index, which has an extraordinary cyclical record) are added because of the performance of the particular series rather than because of their group behavior. In like manner, manufacturers' total inventories and consumer installment-debt series are added to the lagging series.

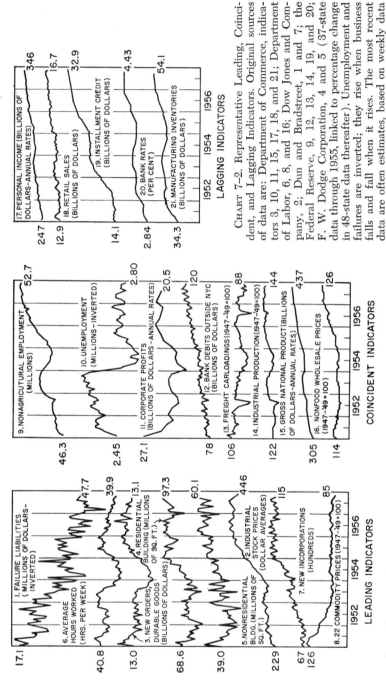

CHART 7–2. Representative Leading, Coincident, and Lagging Indicators. Original sources of data are: Department of Commerce, indicators 3, 10, 11, 15, 17, 18, and 21; Department of Labor, 6, 8, and 16; Dow Jones and Company, 2; Dun and Bradstreet, 1 and 7; the Federal Reserve, 9, 12, 13, 14, 19, and 20; F. W. Dodge Corporation, 4 and 5 (37-state data through 1955, linked to percentage change in 48-state data thereafter). Unemployment and failures are inverted; they rise when business falls and fall when it rises. The most recent data are often estimates, based on weekly data (2, 8, and 16) and bank rates. Indicators 1, 4, 5, 6, 7, 10, 12, and 19 are adjusted. Only indicators 8, 13, 14, and 16 are indices. Indicators 6, 9, and 16 are on an arithmetic scale because monthly percentage changes are too small to be seen on a ratio scale. All others are on a ratio scale; thus, equal vertical distances measured in the same direction anywhere on the charts represent equal percentage changes. SOURCE: Chart furnished by Statistical Indicators Associates, Great Barrington. Reproduced, with permission, from the weekly report regularly sent to subscribers.

and news releases by original sources. All series are seasonally adjusted except the price series

Although a new technique has been employed to combine the showing in each of these timing groups, as described in the following section, the National Bureau of Economic Research has avoided the use of orthodox index-number methods for this purpose. With a limited number of series, there is much to be said for looking at each individually rather than in combined indices, for in this way idiosyncratic movements of individual series can be readily discounted. Although adding to the difficulties of interpretation, this method of presentation perhaps should be rated as an advantage over the Harvard Index Chart; otherwise, the basic technique bears a close resemblance to the Chart. The National Bureau timing classification is, of course, a distinct improvement, because it has produced series which relate more closely to currently existing timing differences and which rest to a minimum extent on pecuniary processes more descriptive of earlier institutions.

Further, it can be shown that Moore's leading group of indicators all reflect, among other forces, action taken because of expectations regarding the near-future business picture.[8] Business failures represent closings because of unsatisfactory anticipations; common-stock prices, action founded on anticipated profits; new orders, action to provide protection in future markets; similarly for building contracts; average hours per week, action in adjusting to quick changes in demand; new incorporations, anticipations of expansionary conditions; and basic-commodity prices, highly competitive market action reflective of future requirements.

Notwithstanding these facts, the limitations inherent in any classifications of timing differences are so great that rather unsatisfactory forecasting aid is provided. Moore found that the behavior of the total series tested was somewhat less satisfactory from 1919 to 1938 than earlier. The erratic fluctuation of economic series is well known, and its existence means, as a practical fact, that the spotting of turning points in leading series is dependable only after a lapse of time.

In sophisticated use of timing differences for forecasting, seldom is sole reliance placed on leading series. With substantially the same logic as formerly employed by the Harvard Committee in explaining the use of the Harvard Index Chart, comparison of the timing of leading, coincident, and lagging series is recommended. For instance, a downturn in leading series while coincident and lagging series are still rising signals a downturn in total activity. If, after a few months, the leading series continue to decline, the coincident series also begin to decline, and the lagging series still rise, the downturn is confirmed. Use of combined

[8] See the report of the Federal Reserve Committee on General-Business Expectations, *An Appraisal of Data and Research on Businessmen's Expectations about Outlook and Operating Variables* (Washington: Board of Governors of the Federal Reserve System, September, 1955), pp. 119–149.

timing relationships does make it possible to avoid the confusion of erratic movements to a slight extent. The erratic movements still confuse the picture, however. For instance, although substantial consistency in timing movements of the 21 series is shown by the record at the 1953 downturn, the National Bureau was able to do little better by use of the method than to recognize the turn when it occurred. As noted elsewhere, such a performance is actually of some significance, and should not be underrated.

THE DIFFUSION INDEX

The diffusion index offers considerable promise in forecasting turning points.[9] In all of the applications made of this index, the lead ahead of total business activity is substantial and reasonably consistent, as illustrated by Chart 6–1. The performance is a reasonable expectation if various unit activities (which in combination total to significant aggregates) end their rise, as expansion proceeds, in a fashion indicative of a spreading effect, and if they end their decline in like manner in contraction. The implication is that an origination and spreading of cyclical movements within diverse activities, somewhat independent of the movement of the aggregate, is represented. The statistical record itself certainly has been most important in supporting a conviction that this type of index is valid. We must remember, however, that, almost without exception, earlier experience has shown that convictions about the validity of timing relationships, though they be similarly supported, have proved to be unwarranted. Therefore, it is important to ask if there are any logical reasons for believing that the diffusion index will fare better.

The logical case to be made for the diffusion index turns on the fact that the test performance of earlier indices apparently was dependent upon institutional relationships whose influence declined substantially in the operating period to which it was applied. Notably, monetary factors played a major part in the Harvard Index Chart, but institutional changes in our monetary system and new circumstances, as outlined above, were responsible for unsatisfactory performance in the operating period. Rather similar conclusions can be drawn regarding other forecasting indices for which high hopes have been held.

Institutional shifts are unlikely to influence markedly the performance of the diffusion index. To make a case for such shifts, it would have to be established that the independence of movement of individual units is becoming substantially less in relation to the aggregate. Under unusual

---

[9] For detailed description of the method and some of the applications made, see the preceding chapter. Briefly, what is shown is the percentage of a group which is rising.

circumstances, it might seem that a case could be made. Overriding influences may develop from rapid shifts in particular expenditures. For instance, the rapid rise in defense expenditures after the beginning of the Korean engagement produced a very marked effect on the economy. Chart 6–2 shows that diffusion indices generally tended to provide a false indication in 1950, although, if the influence of the Korean engagement is discounted, later indications of the 1953 downturn are furnished. Under the extreme conditions of a major war, the diffusion index could not be expected to have much value, but this is merely a clear case of the dependence under war conditions of all expenditures on government decree.

Possibly, the indications of the diffusion index could be improved by assigning weights to the various unit factors. As the index is now constructed, unit divisions vary in importance and each unit is counted the same as any other. Practically nothing has been done in experimenting with weighting the diffusion index, and it is unprofitable to speculate on the improvement such weighting might provide. It should be noted, however, that the total from which the unit parts are drawn is obviously a weighted aggregate of the unit factors of which the total is composed, and in all cases the total fails to show the lead developed by the diffusion index. In fact, the total establishes the turn with which comparison is made.

As in all series employed to show early leads, problems arise in distinguishing irregularity of movement from cyclical turns. A series may decline in a particular month, but this may be only an irregular fluctuation, with offsetting rises occurring in the following months. As past history, of course, it is possible to look back and see that the cyclical turn is dated in each component series at a particular point in time, but no such leverage is available in currently facing the future. In 1950, Moore proposed the "duration of run" as an approximate method of establishing cyclical turns in unit series. For each component series the number of months of rise was called a run, and the runs in all of the unit series were added together to get the index, with the limitation that six was set as the maximum allowable figure to be added in for any unit series.[10] Such a measure is illustrated in Chart 6–2. The duration-of-run measure represents merely a smoothing average. Recently, a short-period moving average, the standard technique for averaging out irregularities, has frequently been used in its stead. In this application it is necessary to use the moving average of each series in computing the diffusion index.

The current practice is to lay most emphasis on a diffusion index developed from a group of leading series. To the extent that the leading

[10] Moore, *op. cit.*, pp. 78–91.

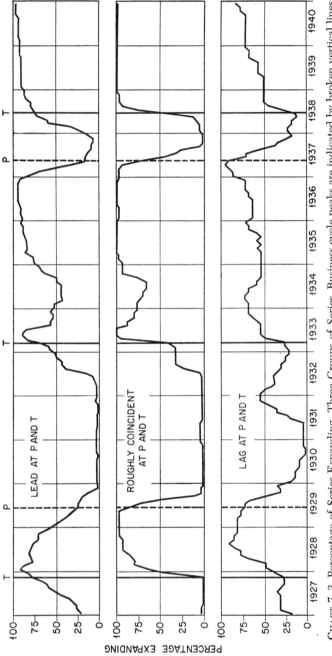

CHART 7–3. Percentage of Series Expanding, Three Groups of Series. Business cycle peaks are indicated by broken vertical lines; troughs by solid vertical lines. SOURCE: Taken with permission from G. H. Moore, *Statistical Indicators of Cyclical Revivals and Recessions*, Occasional Paper 31 (New York: National Bureau of Economic Research, Inc., 1950).

166

series actually do show a significant lead, one would expect this to be an advantage, and the record bears out this expectation, as shown by Chart 7–3. The record does not indicate, however, that the lead is substantial, and because of what we know regarding the irregularity of leads, even in the most reliable leading series, the advantage of using only leading series in the diffusion index may be questioned. A considerable number of series which show no consistent lead do show leads at various turning points. Advantage can be taken of such leads in a diffusion index if it is not limited to leading series. Furthermore, many more series are available when this limitation is avoided, and a broader index is likely to provide a smoother picture. If attention must be concentrated on only a few series, the use of leading series does appear to be advantageous.

THE IMPORTANCE OF STRAIGHT THINKING ON METHODOLOGY

Before passing on to a discussion of several other methods of forecasting, it is well to consider the broad principles of evaluation. The need for appraising the effectiveness of past forecasts is often noted, and we summarize available information on this subject in Chapter 13. For various reasons, appraisals of past forecasts will not provide us with all of the information necessary in choosing forecasting methods to employ.

Actual forecasts represent conclusions drawn from a variety of methods, and generally there is a shifting in the various methods employed as time passes. In appraising actual forecasts, therefore, it is nearly impossible to develop ratings by methods. Instead, ratings are usually assigned to the individuals or organizations which make the forecasts. Though it is possible to develop a hypothetical rating by checking the indications of any particular method against the record of what actually happened, the resulting evaluation cannot substitute effectively for an evaluation of what would have happened if the method had been actually employed in forecasting. The reasons are that actual forecasts may be to some extent self-defeating and that what one would actually have done surely is not precisely equal to the showing obtained from mechanical results. Generally, the methods outlined above have shown an excellent performance in long test periods but frequently have been ineffective when put into operation.

The method of appraising, in and of itself, as developed in Chapter 13, introduces distortion. Considerable judgment is required in deciding precisely what various forecasts actually intended, and equally plausible rating scales will result in some differences in appraisals.

For considerable periods, bias in forecasts may be of such a nature that forecasts are substantially closer to what actually happens than unbiased forecasts. Any method with a built-in optimistic bias would have achieved good results in the decade following World War II, just as a pessimistic bias would have been an advantage in the decade following 1929.

If we cannot place implicit faith in the mechanical testing of forecasts, emphasis must be placed upon their rational foundation. It certainly is unnecessary to belabor the proposition that forecasts based on causal relations will work better in the long run than those which are not. Causal relations involved in business-cycle changes are not always clearly discernable, however, and therefore, as a practical policy, dependence on them must always be somewhat tentative in nature. The underlying assumptions made by forecasts, whether they be implicit or explicit, should be those which best fit causal relations. But disagreement can readily arise as to which underlying assumptions meet this criterion. Rationalizations may be readily available, but they are not always convincing.

In view of these facts, about all that we can do is to question continually the rational foundations of the methods of forecasting being pursued. In spite of the fact that empirical relations holding in the past are not, in and of themselves, a good basis for forecasting, they do provide many of the most plausible methods when they are checked against causal relations and found not to be unreasonable. Needless to say, a major burden is placed on the forecaster by the constant need for reappraising the causal significance of empirical data.

BUSINESS EXPECTATIONS

Surveys of business anticipations provide made-to-order information for critical sectors of the economy. Initial estimates of plant and equipment expenditures are universally obtained from survey data. Wide attention is given to the possibility of developing an extensive range of other anticipatory data—inventory investment, homebuilding, farm expenditures, retail sales, wholesale sales, new orders, employment, and prices—to provide similar estimates; in none of these cases can present surveys be accepted as a satisfactory initial estimate in developing the general-business forecast. They are principally helpful as contrasting information.

Direct surveys of general-business expectations have frequently been emphasized. Seldom have they been found reliable, and most such surveys have been discontinued. A difficulty is that most respondents may rely on common published sources, so that little or no independent information may be obtained. The survey of the National Association of

Purchasing Agents may be something of an exception in this respect, for considerable attention has been given to specific company prospects by each respondent. The survey thus reflects various points of view colored by the prospects of the industries represented. The independent information obtained should be useful when employed as a contrasting estimate of the general-business outlook.

The greatest value in all surveys, including those of plant and equipment expenditures, derives from the fact that they provide good estimates of psychological attitudes. What businessmen are thinking should be set in a framework of forces responsible for the decisions they make. This use of survey information to describe current plans surely must ultimately prove more valuable than the use of analytical forecasts as a starting point. One difficulty at this stage of development is that we know too little about the probable effect of various types of expectations on business decisions. If reliable expectations can be developed for several contrasting processes, likely decisions may be simply deduced. If, for instance, level or declining sales, price weakness, and rising finished-goods inventories were anticipated, it would be clear that businessmen generally would make contractionary decisions. At the present time the surveys do not point to clear enough conclusions at an early stage to make possible many important generalizations of this sort. Efforts to watch for such information will be rewarded, especially if the quality of the survey information continues to improve.

A major reason for the forecasting effectiveness of plant and equipment surveys is that advanced programming is required for such expenditures. This is particularly true of large companies and of large programs. That it is not uniformly true is indicated by the fact that actual outlays of individual firms tend to deviate substantially from reported anticipations, especially in manufacturing. Clearly, changes in the general-business outlook may have an important effect on the maturation of plans. Dependence on changes in general-business conditions should not be overlooked.

However, it is only in developments which deviate widely from the expected that major revisions of plans will materially reduce the forecasting effectiveness of anticipatory data. In the relatively mild recessions of recent history, the surveys forecast satisfactorily, as indicated in Chapter 13. Barring a considerable increase in instability, we may expect that pattern to continue. A large part of plant and equipment expenditures manifests greater inertia than the total business outlook.

For the other surveys there is less assurance that firm plans are made far enough in advance to provide useful forecasts. It is true that all of the other anticipatory series do tend to point in the right direction and frequently indicate turning points, as shown in Chapters 6 and 13. Unfortunately, the leads are relatively slight and the actual amount of movement is poorly judged.

Improvement of surveys is to be expected, but confidence is lacking that early plans are made or that they are reasonably stable when made. Advanced planning is clearly required in house construction, but the indications are that the plans are subject to rapid revision. Increasing attention is given to planning inventories, but it remains probable that even a moderate change in business prospects will lead to unplanned inventory changes. The businessman ordinarily has no control over sales and only limited control over prices, so that his plans in these areas depend on implicit or explicit general-business forecasts. Nevertheless, if the total business picture is reasonably stable, contrast of anticipations with independently developed forecasts should prove useful. Providing knowledge of the plans themselves and the relations between them is the most promising role of surveys, as noted above.

CONSUMER ANTICIPATIONS

The principal information on consumer anticipations is provided by the Survey Research Center of the University of Michigan, for use by the Board of Governors of the Federal Reserve System, as outlined in the preceding chapter. The surveys show changes in consumer finances and expected purchases of housing and consumer durables. Information available in March on consumer plans to purchase houses has shown a tendency to indicate the direction of movement of the housing market as compared to the preceding year. The consumer survey makes available useful checking information, especially if it is coordinated with the financial condition of consumers and with their broad expectations.

The consumer cannot be expected to make an effective forecast of his disposable income, but he may be expected to tell us something about how he will spend in relation to a given level of disposable income. Such information is invaluable, for general analysis of data has been only moderately successful in projecting consumers' durable expenditures. Doubt exists regarding the stability and significant lead time of consumer plans to buy durable goods, but it is very possible that consumers do have in mind, in a vague way, whether they will buy on credit or spend accumulated liquid funds, whether they will be greatly influenced by speculative gains or losses or by expected changes in income, and whether they will purchase differently with price changes or purchase less because they feel their stock of durables is adequate. Such influences make the consumer vary his purchases in relation to the level of disposable income. The surveys provide some effective information regarding such influences, especially in the case of automobiles. Perhaps more attention to some of these influences, especially the consumer's attitudes regarding his stock of durables, is needed in the Federal Reserve survey.

The forecasting value of the Federal Reserve survey is largely lost because it is not available before March of the year forecast. By that time the year's developments have thrown much light on consumer expenditures. For most forecasting needs, information on consumer outlook is desirable before the year begins or at least very early in the year.

ANALYSIS OF THE MARKET SITUATION

To a considerable degree, a direct analysis of market data can be said to be an alternative to using sales-anticipations data in forecasting. The businessman's chief tool in anticipating his future sales is his analysis of the market picture. In this work he has substantial advantages; he can take specific detailed factors directly into account, and he avoids the blunting effect which develops when this method is used for broader groups, with many movements averaged out.

The most essential information in making an aggregative analysis of the market situation relates to prices, inventories, sales, and new and unfilled orders. Some approach to disaggregation can be made by studying relations between these factors by groups, but far less successfully than is possible in dealing with an individual-company unit. The aggregation of anticipations is a correct procedure; what we are looking for in aggregative forecasting is the net sales-anticipation figure. Nevertheless, the relations between aggregated market factors tends to be blunted in the process. Discordant influences are cancelled out in the over-all data, and it is difficult to trace the influence of specific economic factors.

We cannot afford to neglect aggregative relations in the market situation at the present time because sales-anticipations data are still in an early stage of development. An examination of relations between market factors is required.

Attention has frequently been given to the inventory-sales ratio. Although the most common use has implicitly assumed past averages to represent an approximately adjusted figure, the procedure is poor because required inventories generally do not rise relatively quite as much as sales. A better procedure utilizes a regression-line relationship between inventories and sales.[11] Even here the indications are no more than suggestive. Changes may have occurred in the distribution of sales since the period in which the correlation between inventories and sales

---

[11] See Louis J. Paradiso and Genevieve B. Wimsatt, "Business Inventories—Recent Trends and Position," *Survey of Current Business*, May, 1953, especially charts on p. 13.

was developed, so that the current position with regard to the regression line may be somewhat deceptive. Again, standards of inventory requirements change with the condition of the market. If prices are expected to rise, inventory needs will be looked on as relatively large. Rising sales expectation will also add to desired inventories. It will be seen that an evaluation of the whole market picture is required and that simple mechanical deductions regarding the relation between sales and inventories are of limited importance.

The distribution of inventories into "planned" and "unplanned" can throw a great deal of light on the expected movement of inventories. If the inventory changes occurring are approximately those intended by businessmen and if no abrupt change in the business outlook appears to be in sight, inventories can be expected to move in the near future approximately in line with expected changes in sales (bearing in mind the limitations noted in the preceding paragraph). Although we have never found any way of making a clear distinction between intended and unintended inventory changes, it is often valid to accept a large part of the change in raw-material inventories as intended and a large part of the change in finished-goods inventories as unintended. This is especially true near the turning points. If a contraction is under way, if prices and sales are declining while finished-goods inventories are rising and raw-material inventories are constant or falling, it is usually safe to deduce that inventory increases are unintended. Under these circumstances, businessmen can be expected to reduce finished-goods inventories at the first opportunity. On the other hand, if an expansion is under way, if prices and sales are rising and finished-goods inventories are falling, it is usually safe to deduce that inventory declines are unintended. After sales begin to level off, businessmen can be expected to increase inventories substantially.

The order position is frequently considered a direct indication of the general-business outlook. The correct interpretation to be given to changes in new or unfilled orders depends on accompanying circumstances. The order position in any given industry is dependent upon a long list of mechanical factors, e.g., the delivery period into the future for which orders will be accepted, the existing type of cancellation privileges, and other conditions specified in the order contract, such as the extent of unstated precise specifications as to size, quality, etc. Not only may changes in one or more of these mechanical factors result in abrupt breaks in the new orders received, but some of the factors may produce discontinuity in the backlog of orders. For instance, when, in an expansionary period, order books are opened up for an additional quarter in the steel industry, orders may rise rapidly only to decline until the books are opened for another quarter.

Order data apply principally to durable manufactures, in which the practice of administered prices is strong. In these circumstances, prices tend to change infrequently, and advance notice is often available before price rises are posted. At such times orders may rise rapidly for a brief period only to slacken for a time thereafter, even though no fundamental change has occurred in the market situation in the meantime. In a contractionary market, orders may decline for a time in anticipation of price declines. When the price decline occurs, orders may rise briefly and decline thereafter, even though no fundamental change may have occurred in the market picture.

It has been frequently suggested that the level of inventories should be compared with new orders instead of with sales. These suggestions appear reasonable to the extent that new orders reflect the future market better than sales do. When we consider the limited areas for which new-order data are available and the difficulties involved in interpreting the new-order position, it appears that little is to be gained at the aggregative level by comparing inventories with new orders rather than with sales. Rapid changes in new orders will, however, aid substantially in judging the degree to which inventory changes are to be interpreted as intended. With due allowance for nonmarket influences arising in new-order data, inventory changes which are intended should be positively correlated with changes in new orders.

Jacobs and Wimsatt made a tentative suggestion that new orders lead sales in the ratio of unfilled orders to sales and that sales will rise if unfilled orders have been rising.[12] The first of these rules would mean, for instance, that if unfilled orders are three times the current level of monthly sales, orders may be expected to lead sales by three months. The rules are characteristic of behavior in the postwar period, which admittedly has been an era of high demand, and behavior might be somewhat different under other conditions. Nevertheless the assumption underlying these rules—that order data tend to reflect future demand—is a reasonable one.

Price changes are of major importance in reflecting market conditions. Rising prices are probably the best single indication of high demand, and falling prices of low demand. In the relatively inclusive price indices, however, prices which are administratively set get important weight, and such prices frequently do not move promptly with changes in demand.

The most effective analysis of the market situation appears to be a rather loose one, with major emphasis being placed on interrelations between all of the market factors. Rises in a price index may mean vari-

---

[12] See Walter W. Jacobs and Genevieve B. Wimsatt, "An Approach to Order Analysis," *Survey of Current Business*, December, 1949, pp. 20–22.

ous things, depending upon the movement of the other market factors. If new orders are rising while sales are not, rising prices may well mean no more than that administered prices are catching up with the demand situation. This conclusion would appear still more plausible if inventory changes may be assumed to be about as intended. Many other possible cases could be argued in a somewhat similar way.

It must be remembered that optimism and pessimism tend to be justified by the market itself, and therefore an analysis of the market situation is more convincing if checked against the kind of changes which occur because of advances in investment demand. These are relatively high inventory investment and a starting rate greater than the completion rate in building durable capital. Their utility in forecasting is considered in the following section.

CYCLE HYPOTHESIS

Several methods are directly dependent upon characteristic changes in the business cycle. Timing relationships and the diffusion index are of this type, but they were discussed earlier because they provide a useful contrast with the methods of historical interest which we found helpful in introducing the problem.

Investment plays a major part in the business-cycle movement. Measures of the momentum it produces would be of great significance if they were available. The important characteristic of this momentum is that it adds to demand factors without adding to supply factors in an expansion and adds to supply factors without adding to demand factors in a contraction. The influence is readily illustrated in the case of inventory investment. Any positive inventory investment adds to income available for buying goods but does not add to the goods which may be purchased with that income, since the production involved goes into inventory.

Although inventory investment of any amount produces the momentum effect noted, normal growth of the country requires a minimum increase in inventory stocks, at a percentage rate nearly equal to the growth in gross national product. Any inventory investment in excess of that approximate rate can be thought of as a temporary expansive factor, and any deficiency can be thought of as a temporary depressive factor. Of course, the controlling condition in the business cycle is the *extent of the increase or decrease* in such expansive or depressive factors. The method throws no light on forecasting inventories, and therefore the basic forecast must be developed by other methods. Some perspective is gained by visualizing inventory investment as a momentum factor, but no simple mechanics are readily available for doing it. The method aids in visualizing expected changes in prices and in judging the general degree of instability which may have been reached.

The discrepancy between starting and completion rates in the process of durable-capital formation might, with the proper data, be of even more direct forecasting value because in this case a substantial inertia is necessarily developed. Completion follows starting by an approximately constant construction period, and therefore it is subject to relatively accurate prediction. The momentum which the difference in starting and completion rates engenders, like inventory investment, throws light on expected price changes and on the degree of instability reached, and, since reasonably effective forecasts of the difference in the rates appear plausible, a better understanding could be made available on changes in momentum. Cyclical momentum of the kind indicated may be the most important influence supporting the continuation of a cyclical expansion or contraction.

Much remains to be done in measuring starting and completion rates. Completion rates could be obtained by using length-of-construction periods, now employed to estimate the dollar amount of construction put in place. The dollar amount of all construction initiated could be readily estimated by analyzing such data as contracts awarded and building permits. Reported expenditures on producers' equipment are approximately on a completion-rate basis. No facile scheme is available for developing starting rates for producers' equipment, but the timing difference between starts and completions is short enough to be of minor importance.[13]

There are various types of cyclical analogy which are somewhat helpful in forecasting, although they all provide only crude applications. The average length of the business cycle in the past aids somewhat in gain-

---

[13] Completions, as visualized here, add to potential supply, and starts add to demand. Some intermediate measurements might also throw light on the support that construction work is giving the cyclical movement. For example, the amount of construction work yet to be completed provides an estimate of demand forthcoming from the construction program. This may be a major support in recession even though businessmen may continue the programs only because they are already under way.

The Department of Trade and Commerce in Canada has developed an index of construction work not yet completed, and completions could be estimated by the same general methods. See Dominion Bureau of Statistics, *Appraisal of Construction Prospects. Housing in Canada,* quarterly publication of the government's Central Mortgage and Housing Corporation, contains similar data on housing.

Another indication of cyclical momentum might be developed from data on changes in the expected life of the stock of consumer durables. It might be represented by the average age of various categories of consumer durables. It would give some indication of deferred demand and thus aid in estimating saturation. It would not, by itself, be a sensitive indicator of cyclical change, however, partly because of the possibility of forelog demand and partly because of the importance of new-owner demand.

ing perspective. For instance, if an expansion has been running only a few months, inability to visualize a continuation of current expenditure rates may be heavily discounted. For the last century, expansions have averaged slightly less than thirty months, and only two have run less than a year and a half.[14] Many forecasters were misled in the early months of 1955 because it was difficult to see how expenditures would arise to replace those lost from an anticipated decline of automobile production and housing construction. Although crude, deductions derived from the fact that the expansion had lasted only a few months would have added some perspective. On the other hand, the forecaster should be wary of drawing deductions from the average length of the expansion phase when scare buying is driven to excessively high levels, as occurred in the second half of 1950. This experience did not lead to a prompt downturn because defense production rose with great rapidity.

Contractions have averaged not more than about twenty months, but they have been quite irregular in length. Past averages help little in judging the continuation of a contraction under way unless some clear estimate is available on the severity of the depression. In mild depressions, contractions have been short; in deep depressions, they have been long. These differences account for most of the over-all irregularity in length.[15] In deep depressions, contractions can be expected to last two or three years or even more. In minor recessions, contractions usually last only about eight months to a year.

A simple measurement of rates of change in business indices provides some perspective because the expansion or contraction almost always slows down before a turning point is reached. One of the principal difficulties involved in the use of a rate-of-change measure is the irregularity with which the cyclical movement occurs. A moving average smooths out the irregularity but, at the same time, automatically delays the indication available.

Because the business cycle develops considerable inertia, "naïve" extrapolations lend some slight degree of perspective. In the naïve extrapolation, the following month or quarter may be forecast at the same level as the most recent reported figure or at a level obtained by adding to the most recent figure the amount of change recorded between the two most recent figures. Obviously, this method is of little help in forecasting turning points, but when a turning point is not imminent, it repre-

---

[14] The two are expansions ending in January, 1913, and in January, 1920. Special conditions existed in both; the first is related to the outbreak of World War I, and the second started with an almost imperceptible trough in April, 1919, dated in accordance with the National Bureau of Economic Research reference dates. See Moore, *op. cit.*, p. 6.

[15] See Moore, *loc. cit.;* also E. C. Bratt, *Business Cycles and Forecasting*, 4th ed. (Homewood, Ill.: Richard D. Irwin, Inc., 1953), pp. 272–275.

sents a simple procedure for making an estimate which is usually helpful.

Forecasts are frequently based on an analogy with a past movement which occurred when approximately comparable conditions are thought to have existed. Although this method has produced quite unsatisfactory results in the past, it appears to be unavoidable, at least to some extent. For instance, in an effort to gain perspective after World War II, analogies with the period after World War I were commonly employed. The conclusions so obtained had only limited reliability, but they compare favorably with some analytical forecasts of the postwar period developed during World War II. However, analogies to cyclical movements less dependent upon a particular expenditure influence have given indications so mistaken that one should not be tempted to use them.[16]

NATIONAL INCOME AND EXPENDITURE MODEL

The advantages of the national income and expenditure model have led to its wide application wherever forecasting has been given careful consideration in recent years. It is highly flexible. Changes expected in the aggregate can be checked with specific changes, and specific changes can be translated into income or expenditure effects and summed to develop the aggregate effect. The quantitative effects indicated by any other method can be integrated in the model. For example, anticipation surveys can be introduced as expected expenditures. This is in striking contrast with the use of leading series which merely tend to summarize an aggregative effect and cannot be dissected to determine the specific effects involved. Leading series develop anticipated changes from past patterns. If important structural changes have occurred in the economy, past patterns may not apply well.

The expenditure model performs with maximum effectiveness when no change in direction is occurring. Past rates of change in various types of expenditure, modified by the indications summarized from all bits of evidence, can be projected into the future. As a first step, illustrated by the fourth quarter of 1956 in Table 7–1, the amount of change may be projected. The projection would have been off more than a billion dollars only for consumer durables and inventory investment. In both of these cases it appears that adjustment in the correct direction might have been made. The introduction of new automobile models probably would have led to an upward revision in consumer durables. A decline in in-

---

[16] A striking illustration is the forecast of an upturn of business conditions made by Warren M. Persons in January, 1931, in analogy to the depression of 1884–1885. See Warren M. Persons, *Forecasting Business Cycles* (New York: John Wiley & Sons, Inc., 1931), pp. 14–17.

TABLE 7–1

GROSS NATIONAL PRODUCT MODEL—PROJECTION TO FOURTH QUARTER, 1956
(In rounded billions of dollars at seasonally adjusted annual rates)

Expenditures	2d quarter	3d quarter	3d quarter plus change	4th quarter	Difference
Gross national product........	408	414	420	424	+4
Consumer durables...........	33	33	33	35	+2
Consumer nondurables.......	132	134	136	135	−1
Consumer services...........	98	100	102	101	−1
New construction............	34	34	34	33	−1
Producer durables...........	28	30	32	32	0
Inventory investment........	4	2	0	4	+4
Net foreign investment.......	1	2	3	2	−1
Federal government..........	46	47	48	48	0
State and local government....	33	33	33	34	+1
Total....................	409 *	415 *	421 *	424	

* Error in the total is due to rounding. The figures shown here are those published early in 1957. Later revisions will probably produce changes, minor for the most part. The revisions would illustrate forecasting less well, for the forecaster has to use the figures available at a given time.

ventory investment to zero would scarcely have been accepted unless a recession were expected, for it would definitely have indicated a marked change in sentiment. Broad knowledge of what is happening will ordinarily indicate whether the rise (or fall) is accelerating or slowing down. Thus, adjustment of the projected change will frequently be in the right direction.

At turning points, more attention to factors which might indicate a culmination of the expansion or contraction may be required. This is particularly true when a sharp peak or trough occurs. If the movement rounds off gradually, a study of the recent rate of change in various expenditure groups may help to indicate the turn, because some groups probably will be declining before the turning point in gross national product is reached.

To illustrate the forecast of a trough which is rounding off, we may take the Stein Roe and Farnham forecast published June 28, 1954.[17] The

[17] Distributed privately by Stein Roe and Farnham, Investment Council, 135 South LaSalle Street, Chicago 3, June 28, 1954, under the title "Business Review and Forecast." The forecast for the whole 1953–54 period is analyzed more fully

TABLE 7–2

STEIN ROE AND FARNHAM FORECAST OF FINAL EXPENDITURE,
THIRD QUARTER, 1954

(All figures are given in billions of dollars, seasonally adjusted at annual rates;
the change from the preceding quarter is shown)

Expenditure	1953–54 4th quarter to 1st quarter	1954 1st quarter to 2d quarter		1954 2d quarter to 3d quarter	
		Projected	Actual	Projected	Actual
Gross national product................	−5.7	−0.8	+0.2	+1.0	−0.5
Consumer durables..	−0.9	+0.3	+0.7	−0.5	+0.1
Consumer nondurables..............	−0.1	+0.2	+1.2	+1.0	+1.1
Consumer services...	+0.8	+0.7	+0.7	+0.5	+0.5
Residential construction..............	+0.7	+0.2	+0.5	−0.3	+0.3
Other construction...	+0.5	0.0	+0.5	−0.1	+1.0
Producer durables...	−1.3	−0.8	−0.3	−0.4	−0.6
Inventory investment	−1.8	+0.3	+0.4	+0.8	−1.0
Net foreign investment..............	0.0	0.0	+0.1	+0.5	+0.8
Federal government..	−4.4	−1.6	−3.7	−1.0	−3.4
State and local government.........	+0.8	−0.1	+0.1	+0.5	+0.7

SOURCE: The change from the 4th quarter, 1953, to the 1st quarter, 1954, and the projected changes are taken from "Business Review and Forecast" (Chicago: Stein Roe and Farnham, June 28, 1954). The "actual" figures shown are taken from the earliest available publication after the date shown. As revised for publication in the July, 1956, *Survey of Current Business*, the total change in gross national product from the second to the third quarters of 1954 was +0.9, very close to the projected figure; similarly, inventory investment was −2.9 and Federal government expenditure was −0.5. The "actuals" as shown in the table, however, are the appropriate figures with which to check the forecast.

change projected to the second quarter and from the second to the third quarter is shown in Table 7–2. The forecast was published more than two months before the measurements became available for the second quarter. It will be noted that about as much difficulty was faced in de-

by Kenneth D. Ross, "Business Review and Forecast," in A. G. Abramson and R. H. Mack (eds.), *Business Forecasting in Practice* (New York: John Wiley & Sons, Inc., 1956), pp. 180–223.

veloping the second-quarter figures as in making the forecast for the third quarter. This illustrates the point that current estimates are forecasts of no mean importance.

The projection of a turning point in the third quarter (the upturn is now dated at August, 1954) was not a marked break with the past, since rises were already occurring in all areas except producers' durable equipment and Federal government expenditure. However, the most recent facts actually at hand in June, 1954, were the changes from the fourth quarter of 1953 to the first quarter of 1954, at which time only four components were positive, as shown in the table. There is no mechanical, naïve way to turn the negative changes of the past into the positive changes of the future.

The Stein Roe and Farnham forecast does not begin with a simple table of past changes in final expenditures, but with detailed analysis of changes occurring in a wide range of factors. In the summer of 1954 these included defense spending, labor force and employment, income and profits, output and productivity, prices and the price level, individual savings, residential construction and various other types of capital expenditure, the financial position of business, the inventory-stock position, the foreign-trade position, and others. Specific assumptions were made in all of these areas. For instance, the OBE-SEC Survey of Plant and Equipment Expenditures was used as a partial base in projecting capital expenditures, and the elements of strength in this area, partly the non-statistical, such as geographical redistribution and the development of new products, were cited. The plan to cut defense spending was clearly stated, and a decline in the area of Federal expenditure was a strong assumption. It would appear that the strength of consumer spending for services was recognized in terms of lagging prices, increases in service expenditures, and the inertia of such spending backed by a strong liquid-asset position and relatively well-maintained employment. Many additional detailed assumptions were required to develop the changes shown in Table 7–2.

In the interest of convenience and simplicity we have covered only the forecast of the third quarter of 1954, but actually the Stein Roe and Farnham report included a forecast to mid-1955, clearly indicating that an upturn was anticipated. The increase in gross national product projected to the second quarter of 1955 was $8 billion. Although this fell considerably short of the increase which actually occurred, the projection of an upturn was the critically important indication.

The "actual" changes noted in Table 7–2 are properly taken from current estimates made in 1954. Revisions by 1956 had raised substantially the estimate of Federal government expenditure and lowered the estimate of inventory investment, showing on net an increase in gross national

TABLE 7–3

STEIN ROE AND FARNHAM FORECAST OF INCOME CHANGES,
THIRD QUARTER, 1954

(All figures are given in billions of dollars, seasonally adjusted at annual rates;
the change from the preceding quarter is shown)

Income	1954 1st quarter to 2d quarter	1954 2d quarter to 3d quarter
Wages and salaries.....................	−1.2	+1.2
Dividends............................	0.0	0.0
Interest..............................	+0.1	+0.1
Rental income........................	+0.2	+0.1
Unincorporated enterprise income..........	−0.7	−0.1
Transfer payments and other labor income less employee contributions...........	+0.9	+0.2
Personal income......................	−0.7	+1.5
Minus:		
Government interest....................	+0.1	0.0
Transfer payments.....................	+0.7	+0.2
Plus:		
Corporate profits in excess of dividends.....	−1.0	−1.0
Inventory valuation adjustment...........	0.0	+0.2
Contributions for social insurance..........	−0.2	0.0
National income......................	−2.7	+0.5
Plus:		
Capital consumption allowance...........	+0.3	+0.4
Indirect business taxes..................	−0.4	0.0
Business transfer payments..............	0.0	+0.1
Government enterprise surplus less subsidies.	−0.1	0.0
Statistical discrepancy..................	+2.1	0.0
Gross national product.................	−0.8	+1.0

SOURCE: "Business Review and Forecast" (Chicago: Stein Roe and Farnham, June 28, 1954). Since the 2d-quarter figures could not be reported until several months after the end of the quarter, the 2d-quarter as well as the 3d-quarter figures are projections. Income payments in this table correspond with final-expenditure projections shown in Table 7–2.

product from the second to the third quarter of 1954 almost precisely equal to that projected by Stein Roe and Farnham.[18] It has been necessary to make marked revisions of the estimate of inventory investment at many times in the past, but so large a revision in the estimate of Federal government expenditure is unusual.

An income model is an essential complement of an expenditure model because it shows where the funds come from to make the expenditures. Table 7–3 is a brief summary of the balancing income model employed by Stein Roe and Farnham. It will be seen that the major shift indicated is from declining to rising wage and salary disbursements. Later facts indicate that wages and salaries actually were already increasing slightly in the second quarter.[19]

Forecast of a downturn is illustrated by the author's projection for 1957, made originally in November, 1956, and successively revised to April, 1957. Through all revisions the downturn was set at the third quarter, but the estimated degree of the decline was successively reduced. Initially, gross national product in the fourth quarter of 1957 was estimated at 93.5 per cent of that a year earlier, but the April, 1957, model, shown in Table 7–4, represents a decline to slightly less than 97 per cent.[20] Revision of the forecast was largely founded on the strength shown by anticipatory data taken together with the prompt inventory adjustment indicated in the first quarter. If inventory adjustment were to occur early, while the strength of past momentum, notably in the case of construction projects under way, was maintained, the urgency to cut inventories would be reduced later on. As widely noted at the time, it was possible that forecasting was beginning to pay off.

It is true that anticipatory data may be found most unreliable at turning points. Plans are most likely to be revised when unexpected change in total expenditures is superimposed upon the businessman's market. This is possible even though many businessmen may have seen the contraction coming and were preparing for it by reducing inventories, because the degree of decline may have been poorly forecast and some businessmen will have failed to prepare for it.

[18] The decline in Federal government expenditure was marked down to −0.5 billion from −3.4 billion, and inventory investment was lowered from +1.0 billion to −2.8 billion. *Survey of Current Business,* July, 1956, p. 29.

[19] As reported in the November, 1954, *Survey of Current Business,* this increase was very slight. As later revised and reported in the July, 1956, *Survey of Current Business,* the increase was as great as between the second and third quarters. The first report is the one which should be used to judge the forecast.

[20] The actual change, measured by the preliminary estimate in February, 1958, with allowance for known revision of bench-mark data, was an increase of 1.5 per cent. The estimated decrease from the third to the fourth quarter did not differ materially from the estimate published in February, 1958. The principal error in the forecast was failure to project a rise in prices; as shown in the February, 1958, estimate, prices rose 2 per cent from 1956 to 1957.

TABLE 7–4

1957 EXPENDITURE MODEL

(In billions of dollars)

Quarter and year	(1)*	(2)	(3)	(4)	(5)	(6)	(7)	(8)	(9)	(10)	(11)	(12)
4–6	423.8	34.8	134.7	101.4	14.9	18.0	31.5	4.1	2.4	43.2	5.1	33.7
1–7	427.0	35.5	136.5	103.0	14.2	18.2	32.5	0.0	2.6	44.3	5.2	35.0
2–7	427.0	36.0	138.0	103.0	12.0	18.0	31.0	1.0	2.0	45.0	5.0	36.0
3–7	418.0	35.0	138.0	103.0	10.0	16.0	30.0	−3.0	2.0	46.0	5.0	36.0
4–7	410.0	33.0	136.0	103.0	10.0	15.0	28.0	−5.0	2.0	46.0	5.0	37.0

* The columns refer to the following expenditures:

(1) Gross national product
(2) Consumer expenditures for durable goods
(3) Consumer expenditures for nondurable goods
(4) Consumer expenditures for services
(5) Expenditures for nonfarm residential building
(6) Other construction expenditures

(7) Expenditure for producers' durable equipment
(8) Inventory investment
(9) Net foreign investment
(10) Government security expenditures
(11) Other Federal government expenditures
(12) State and local government expenditures

It is obvious in September, 1957, that gross national product did not level off and decline beginning in the second quarter of 1957. From other evidence, it appears possible, however, that the business-cycle peak did occur not later than mid-1957. If that proves to be the case, the model may have forecast general economic conditions better than it forecast gross national product (principally implying that adequate allowance was not provided for rising prices). The changes projected from the third quarter of 1957 to the fourth quarter should be compared with the changes rather than the levels which actually occurred.

The expenditure model itself does not readily generate a turning point except when the turn is gradual, with many of the major sectors showing a shift in direction in advance of a turn in the total. Somewhat analogous to a list of favorable and unfavorable factors, employed to avoid overlooking any substantial development, a running list of indicators of the direction of movement in total activity may be maintained. Included are forecasting techniques particularly sensitive to changes in direction, analytical conclusions, conclusions derived from a review of forecasts by others, and the showing of leading series. The list employed in the fall and winter of 1956–57 indicating the imminence of a downturn is as follows:

1. It was conceived that if a diffusion index representative of the

profits of a widely distributed group of companies were available, a decline would have been in evidence. The conception was partly supported by known cases of costs pinching on selling prices.

2. The diffusion index of Moore's eight leading indicators had shown a general decline during 1955 and 1956.

3. Durable private investment was leveling out. This was indicated by (a) expenditure surveys, (b) the new survey of capital appropriations, (c) the development of bottlenecks, such as shortages in heavy rolled-steel products, and (d) higher interest rates.

4. The leveling out of durable private investment meant that the completion rate would be catching up with the starting rate, that capacity would be rising more rapidly than expenditures being made for it.

5. There was evidence that the demand for inventories would level off, producing an influence similar to that noted in item 4.

6. A wide group of consumer durables appeared to be approaching a temporary saturation.

7. Rising public-utility rates, the adoption of new taxes in various local communities, and rising prices for various services appeared to be pinching the available funds for other personal spending.

8. The average weekly hours per worker in the total of manufacturing industries, a most reliable leading series, began to decline in the fall of 1956.

9. A check of various currently reported forecasts led the author to believe that those persons forecasting a contraction were appealing to more appropriate arguments than those forecasting a continued rise or a level movement.

The contrary evidence related generally to more basic influences, in contrast with the culminating nature of the above factors. This evidence tended to indicate that a contraction would be mild rather than that no contraction would occur:

1. Government expenditures were rising and could be expected to offset partially declines in private expenditure.

2. Technological improvement was substantial, and large research expenditures could be expected to sustain it.

3. Optimism, except for the short run, was universal.

4. A rapid rate of population growth was continuing and would make widespread needs for expansion obvious.

5. The time was fast approaching when the generation beginning with the fillip in birth rates immediately after the war would be reaching maturity, creating a major increase in demand.

6. Prices and wage rates would be well maintained or even increased, and for various reasons demand would not be greatly curtailed.

A rather rigid forecast of this type may be compared with one stated in more flexible terms. It must be granted, in any case, that the above statements do not permit simple quantification. The Union Service Corporation's forecast, under the direction of Joseph B. Hubbard, may be employed as an excellent example of a flexibly stated forecast.[21] In "The Business Situation," the report issued April 4, 1957, the following statements are made in substance: activity lies at exceptionally high levels, and there is over-all statistical stability; weak spots have been developing, with some layoffs reported in a substantial number of production lines; the money market has eased slightly; sensitive prices are down, and the advance in general wholesale prices has been checked; little positive indication has appeared, and high levels might continue for a considerable period, but it is more necessary now than for a number of years to appraise weaknesses evident in the economy. Hubbard states that he attaches "much importance . . . to changing valuations appearing in commodity prices, stock prices, bond yields, and money rates and the connections between them." [22] This is an informal appeal to market prices as indicative of strength of demand, to stock prices as indicative of the profit picture, and to stock prices, bond yields, and money rates as indicative of financing operations. Hubbard thus carries forward in detailed analysis the major relation incorporated in the Harvard Index Chart. He states that the "basis for anticipating a downturn lies in reaching a business position that displays maturity: activity high judged by the past, gains slowing down, business earnings under pressure, unbalanced production or demand, and firm conditions in money." [23] This position is substantially similar to that taken by the author in the forecast summarized above, although the procedure is fundamentally different.

The many details faced in projecting income and expenditure models cannot be described here. We must give our attention to major procedures. The first step involves obtaining, from whatever source, the best available estimate of expected income and expenditure streams for use in the models.

The anticipation surveys should be given substantial weight in choosing figures for expected plant and equipment outlays, although care must be taken to adjust for biases shown by similar figures in the past. Furthermore, when a turning point is imminent some examination should be made of the firmness of current programs and of the availability of funds; a changed outlook may result in increased vulnerability. Also, attention should be given to the influence of new companies, which are especially important in the investment market because usually they must

[21] A description of the forecast made for the 1948 downturn and the 1949 upturn will be found in Hubbard's chapter in Abramson and Mack (eds.), *Business Forecasting in Practice: Principles and Cases*, pp. 78–116.

[22] *Ibid.*, p. 97.

[23] *Ibid.*, p. 107.

rely entirely on new capacity. At the end of an expansion, fewer new companies will be depressive, and this influence would not be counted in the surveys.

Inventories reflect the movement of sales which occurred a few months earlier, except at turning points. At most times the method for obtaining the most reliable initial information on inventory investment is therefore developed from sales and anticipated-sales figures. Some comparison should be made with inventory-anticipations data.[24]

Near and at turning points, lagging relationships of inventories to sales tend to break down because inventory levels depart from intended levels. Under these circumstances, the best initial estimate of inventory investment must be derived from some crude approximation of the extent to which inventories are expected to depart from intended levels. Such an approximation can be best derived from projections of departures shown by current measures. Purchased-material inventories follow closely with intended levels, because, in most cases, these are subject to quick correction by instructions given to suppliers.[25] Finished-goods inventories tend to depart from intended levels. For instance, when purchased-material inventories are declining in contraction and finished-goods inventories are rising, it is usually clear that the rise is unintended. The extent of unintended inventory accumulation or reduction can be roughly estimated from the difference in movement of finished-goods and purchased-material inventories.

The projection of inventory investment into the future from a time when unintended investment is substantial requires first an estimate of the time it will take to bring the inventory movement under control. Such judgments depend on various factors. The extent to which the movement of finished-goods inventories may be leveling off will provide an important clue. The analysis in this case is best conducted in some detail, for related movements in the commodity areas most affected will provide insight into the progress of adjustment. Also, the extent to which the total economy is leveling off is important information. Unintended investment is easier to avoid when the rate of expenditure change is moderate.

When it becomes clear that unintended investment is about at an end, the extent of reaction in inventory investment must be estimated. This will depend partly on the degree to which unintended investment has occurred. A clue is provided by the movement which has been experienced in the ratio of finished-goods inventories to sales; an attempt to restore this ratio to the point reached before unintended investment began may often be postulated. Of course, allowance must be made for expected

---

[24] *Fortune* now conducts the most important survey of inventory anticipations. The Department of Commerce is instituting a trial survey in 1958.

[25] Exceptions, of course, occur where the period of delivery is a long one.

changes in sales. Putting all of these factors together requires considerable judgment, and the process cannot be readily formalized.

Net foreign-investment estimates for the model should be obtained by making separate projections of imports, exports, and foreign aid, using the equation:

$$\text{Net foreign investment} = \text{exports} - \text{imports} - \text{foreign aid}$$

Foreign aid can be estimated only by making judgments regarding expenditures for aid programs under consideration or already appropriated. The amount of such expenditures is most closely related to the momentum of programs under way if appropriations are available or sure to become available. If judgments must be formulated regarding appropriations to be made, reliance should be placed principally on the urgency or changing urgency which foreign situations are thought to involve.

Exports may be projected from recent levels, with allowance being made for any expected changes in foreign aid and in business activity in foreign countries. Imports are best understood in terms of major types of imported commodities. Raw materials are especially important, and the demand for them tends to rise more rapidly than increases occur in gross national product. In a recession, care must be taken to make allowance for expected changes in inventory investment, since quick changes in our imports relate principally to adjustments we make in inventory stocks of such goods. Such inventory reduction relates not only to raw materials but to an important extent to major imports of processed goods. The runoff of inventories of British textiles in the 1949 recession is a case in point. Because of the tendency to cut inventories of imported goods, imports may decline sharply, and a rise in net foreign investment may result.

Government expenditures can be crudely projected from present levels by extending the recent trend of movement, if allowance is made for any changes indicated by government budgets. The interpretation of government-budget figures requires some care, however, for at times expenditures are underbudgeted with the intention of asking for deficiency appropriations; also, the budget frequently does not give a clear indication of probable public-works programs. This may be due to delayed legislation or to failure to draw careful budgets for such items. The best indication of these practices is the relation of public-works budgets to actual expenditures which were made in the recent past. It is essential to consider separately (1) Federal security expenditures, (2) Federal expenditures other than for security, and (3) state and local expenditures,[26] for the influences involved in these three cases differ substantially.

[26] An experiment is now under way on surveying state and local public-works expenditures which may prove to have importance in forecasting. See "Survey of

Personal-consumption expenditures are best estimated last because they are most closely dependent upon the level of aggregate activity. For this purpose, a procedure sometimes followed involves multiplying the total of predicted nonconsumption expenditures by some figure, say 2.5,[27] to estimate gross national product; personal-consumption expenditures are then derived as the difference between gross national product and nonconsumption expenditures. Before such a figure is entered into the projected model, it should be checked against various other estimating procedures which assume less rigidly that consumption expenditures are completely dependent upon the level of total expenditures. In the light of some detailed knowledge of the movement occurring in the demand for various products and services, near-future levels of detailed items may be projected. For instance, it was clear as the 1953–54 recession got under way that no decline would occur in the total dollar expenditures for consumer services because of the support resulting from rising rents.[28] Anticipatory data derived from surveys are helpful in estimating automobile demand and, to a lesser extent, other durable goods. A further check should be obtained by taking the projected figure on disposable income and applying to it a trend derived from the recent movement in the ratio of consumer expenditures to disposable income. Judgment will be required in resolving any disparities which develop from these various projections.

The largest part of personal income is closely dependent upon the level of total expenditures and cannot be estimated without relation to it. Wage and salary payments, representing about 70 per cent of personal income, are determined by the level of total final expenditure. They may be initially estimated by a regression relationship to gross national product; some judgment is needed in evaluating how reasonable such a projection is in the light of other known facts. Consideration should be given to movements occurring in wage rates and employment, and to whether the estimate derived from the preliminary projection of gross national product is reasonable in the light of these facts.

Dividends, personal interest income, and rental income of persons can all be estimated with reference to recent trends. In projecting dividends, attention should be paid to the movement of corporate profits and to

Construction Plans of State and Local Governments," U.S. Department of Commerce, Bureau of the Census, released Apr. 4, 1955. A new survey is to be made in 1957.

[27] See, for instance, Nathan M. Koffsky, "Economic Forecasting Methods as Used by the U.S. Department of Agriculture," *Midwest Conference on Forecasting Techniques Applied to Business Problems* (Chicago: Monarch Printing and Publishing Corp., 1954). The 2.5 ratio represents the average experience 1929–41 and 1947–51. The fact that consumption expenditures lag means that the figure varies. It tends to be greater than 2.5 in contractions.

[28] See, for instance, E. C. Bratt, "Consumer Expenditures on Nondurables and Services in 1954," *Journal of Business*, 27:77–86, 1954.

business investment. A rise in the former and a fall in the latter will lead to a rise in dividends. Personal interest income changes very slowly and recent rates of change can often be effectively projected into the future. Similarly, rental income of persons is a continuation of the recent movement, but consideration must be given to the influence of changes in rent-control laws. When such laws are first eliminated, rental income increases rapidly, but it levels off as prices come to be adjusted to market relationships.

The proprietorship income of business proprietors is sensitive to the movement of business activity, but that of professional proprietors is not affected for a period of a few months into the future. Unfortunately, separate estimates are not currently available for these two types of proprietorship income. We can do little better than estimate their changes as a regression relationship to gross national product.

Proprietorship income of farmers is separately available; the most important determinant in this case is the prices received by farmers. These prices are related to the volume of farm marketings, disposable income, and agricultural exports.[29] The volume of farm marketings is obtained principally from actual and forecast crop and livestock output, as shown in Department of Agriculture estimates. The nonseasonal variation in agricultural exports can be taken to follow total exports over short periods. Since changes in farm costs can usually be ignored over short periods, proprietorship income of farmers may move in conformity with the product of farm prices and farm marketings.

The principal variation in transfer payments is related to unemployment. The coefficient required to multiply by changes in unemployment in order to derive changes in transfer payments is subject to successive adjustments as allocations for direct relief and unemployment benefits change. Crude approximations should be made from recent history, making allowance for slight changes which may occur in maximum periods for which unemployment benefits are payable.[30]

The forecast of individual industries is considered in more detail in Chapter 9. With a different perspective, the purpose there is to look at each individual industry forecast as an end in itself rather than as a step toward obtaining a forecast of total industry. For the total-industry forecast, the purpose is frequently best achieved by making use of divisional forecasts developed by those who specialize in studying the outlook of

[29] Koffsky estimates farm prices to move 1.66 per cent, 1.24 per cent, and 0.14 per cent for a 1 per cent change, respectively, in each of these factors. *Op. cit.*, pp. 65–66.

[30] Considerable work has been done on developing more precise methods. See, for instance, David W. Lusher, "The Stabilizing Effectiveness of Budget Flexibility," in Universities-National Bureau Committee for Economic Research, *Policies to Combat Depression* (New York: National Bureau of Economic Research, Inc., 1956), pp. 77 ff.

each division. However, such forecasts are not uniformly available for the range of needs covered above, and since the assumptions made in individual-industry forecasting often are not stated, it is best to judge such figures, when obtainable, against at least a minimum independent analysis. The summary statements on the projection of each major division are made with that view in mind in the above paragraphs.

Once divisional estimates have been entered in projected models of income and expenditure, interrelations between them must be studied with care. This study is best conducted by a highly flexible, if rather elementary, type of analysis. The input-output procedure achieves the same purpose by an elaborate and orderly process, but it is not adaptable to short-term forecasting at the present time because current estimates are not available to fill in the cells of the input-output table and because considerable "slack" is possible in the interrelations over a short period of time, owing to irregularity in the flow of inventories. The less elaborate, elementary procedure involves simply going through the projected models and checking the plausibility of the relations implied. This is frequently referred to as a "recycling" procedure, for it may require making a series of successive adjustments. Checked against a plausible pattern, one figure or several may appear too high or too low in relation to one or more of the other figures. Changes are then made in order to bring the figures into better alignment with the pattern applied. The process may be repeated by centering attention on other patterns of relationship.

In the early stages of the development of model building, it was assumed that relatively rigid patterns should evolve. For instance, the relation between consumer expenditures and disposable income was thought to be effectively described by a formula, and if the projected figures did not fit into the implied relation, adjustments were made. It is now widely recognized, much more realistically, that considerable variation about such average relationships occurs over a short period of time. The essential objective is to avoid assuming an unwarranted combined situation. Many illustrations could be given. For instance, an increase in government security expenditures, which implies substantial inventory accumulation by manufacturers who are beginning the kind of production called for, may be written into the model. On investigation, it may be discovered that there is no reason to believe that other types of inventory stocks are likely to decline, although, let us assume, the initial projected model showed zero inventory investment. If, now, some inventory investment is to occur, expansion will attain greater momentum, and slightly greater rises may appear likely in certain other expenditures, for instance, in consumer durable-goods expenditures. The need for recycling to develop empirically justified relationships of this sort becomes clearer as the model is set up in greater detail. In the input-output tables, for instance, a material industry must be high enough to provide the amount which will be used in the industries appearing in the various columns. Given changes in certain types of expenditures will imply consonant changes in other types.

Recycling of the projected model should also be employed to incorporate other types of information. Some study should be made of the control measures the government is likely to employ, and deductions should be developed as to the influence such measures are likely to have on income and expenditure, if any. If the controls represent increases in government expenditures or decreases in taxes, their net influence should already appear under government expenditures and disposable income, but the potential influence may wisely be checked through to assure attention to the coordinated information.

If the control measure is monetary or of a similar type, its influence on expenditure or income is much less obvious, and a separate analysis is highly desirable to make sure that its influence is not ignored in the forecast. Although attention to control measures may thus be assured, the conclusions reached are not likely to be too satisfactory. In relation to monetary measures whose purpose is to limit credit expansion, the problem is to estimate the extent to which credit expansion will be curtailed. If consumer credit or credit for purchase of inventories actually is to be curtailed, an estimate of the influence would provide a basis for revising the consumer-expenditure and inventory-investment figures in the projected model.

The results obtained by all other methods of forecasting can be compared with the projected model; any indicated revisions can be made in the expenditure or income figures, and the model may be recycled to develop consistent relations. By checking through a list of favorable and unfavorable factors, attention may be directed to probable changes in certain incomes or expenditures which had not previously come to the forecaster's attention.

If leading series and diffusion indices indicate that a turning point is likely to occur in the near future, the various income and expenditure divisions should be carefully checked for the plausibility of changes in direction of movement.

Conclusions derived from an analysis of the market situation should throw light on the probable movement of various types of inventory investment. Consideration of the discrepancy between starting and completion rates in the process of durable-capital formation, together with the rate of inventory accumulation, throws light on the momentum of the expansion or contraction under way and provides a rational basis for projecting the inflationary effect induced by investment expenditures.

Unfortunately, current measurements of inventory investment and of the discrepancy between starting and completion rates are unsatisfactory.

Comparison with the average duration of past expansions and contractions will lend some reassurance if projections do not assume durations longer or shorter than the average; if they do, comparison will focus attention on the need to explain the unusual factors present. The results of any other analogies to average or specific past cyclical changes can be checked against the projected model, and judgments may be made as to the desirability of revisions in the light of indicated differences.

The expenditure model is a particularly appropriate device for recording data on anticipations and planned expenditures. The alternative to data on anticipations is analytically derived data. The latter may be more carefully developed from past patterns of behavior, but the patterns of short-term behavior are at best poorly understood. In the realistic forecasting process much insight may be developed by direct use of anticipations and plans if these actually provide important guides to action. It may be granted that the anticipations and plans of decision makers usually do not derive from the most carefully developed analysis of patterns of behavior, but this fact may sometimes actually increase their importance. To the extent that an influence independent of past patterns is brought to bear on the activities of the near future, its incorporation in the forecasting procedure is of primary importance.

The most desirable procedure, therefore, would be to employ figures indicated by anticipations and expenditure plans in the initial projected-expenditure model and, perhaps to a lesser extent, even in the income model. Included in the summary recommendations made on the development of the projected-expenditure model earlier in this section was the incorporation of data on anticipations and expenditure plans, along with the use of analytical conclusions. Such a procedure is quite different from putting only data on anticipations and expenditure plans in the initial model. The implied set of models cannot be effectively developed at the present time; for some of the expenditure divisions there is little information which truly represents anticipations, most strikingly in the case of net foreign investment.

If an initial expenditure model based on anticipation and expenditure-plan data were available, a second step in its use would involve recycling the model to develop figures which represent expenditures the analyst may rationally expect to be achieved. This step would be necessary not only because of the inadequacy of the data on anticipations and planned expenditures employed but, just as significantly, in recognition of the fact that all the plans will not materialize. Plans fail to materialize because of the force of the conditions which develop. Change of plans will shift income and expenditure streams. If we can become analytically astute enough to discover what income and expenditure changes will be forced upon the plans which are being evolved at the time the forecasts are being made, the recycling of the expenditure model representing anticipations and expenditure plans will typify the realistic process of evolving decisions and their fulfillment or nonfulfillment occurring in the economy.

The author believes that the above paragraphs demonstrate that the expenditure-and-income-model method of forecasting can satisfactorily incorporate the conclusions developed from all other useful procedures. This inference may make it easier to understand the growing use of such models as the central procedure in forecasting.

We have not given significant attention to alternative models—notably, models based on input-output tables and the Federal Reserve Index of Industrial Production—because they have obvious weaknesses which are thought to make them inferior to the expenditure-income model. The input-output tables must depend on data representative of conditions several years past, and they face the particular difficulty that technical coefficients relating sales to other industries do not satisfactorily incorporate the effect of inventory flow. The Industrial Production Index incorporates only a small part of the total economy and suffers from duplications which result from representing successive stages of production without regard for the development of net aggregate relationships.

Brief note should be taken of structural expenditure models founded more carefully on econometric equational relationships, such as the model developed in the Michigan Research Seminar.[31] The Michigan model, first of all, attempts to make a clear distinction between dependent and independent variables. The dependent variables are those the model is designed to forecast; the independent variables are predetermined or historically developed from other information. The most important dependent variable is gross national product; the predetermined variables are illustrated by last year's profits, actual levels of capital stock and liquid assets, and last year's consumption expenditures; historically independent variables may be represented by forecasts of government expenditures. In the Michigan model, 25 equations are employed to develop forecasts of the dependent variables. Compensatory modifications and approximate adjustments of the coefficients in the equations are made to take advantage of new information. Elaborate recomputations are required when the basic data are revised. For instance, in 1955 the equations had not yet been adjusted to take into account the changes made by the Department of Commerce on income

---

[31] See Daniel B. Suits and Arthur S. Goldberger, "A Statistical Model for 1955," *Michigan Business Review*, 7:25–28, 1955.

and product data in the 1954 revision. In view of these difficulties, question may be raised as to whether the more empirically founded approximation procedures outlined above will not, at least for the time being, give better results. Furthermore, the equations upon which the econometric method relies describe principally a type of equilibrium relationship. As has been repeatedly emphasized, short-term changes do not tend to represent equilibrium relations.

SEASONAL FORECASTING

The above discussion refers to the forecasting of any aggregate short-term change not due to expected seasonal shifts. In general, a change greater or smaller than the typical seasonal change, whether "irregular" or closely related to the business cycle, is readily brought into consideration by these methods. It should be carefully noted that actual seasonal changes which are greater or smaller than the amount indicated by seasonal indices are included in the short-term changes considered above. The seasonal index measures the only kind of seasonal movement which can be forecast by appeal to past seasonal patterns.

Since the typical seasonal change is measured by a seasonal index, its forecast is dependent upon the extent to which future seasonal movements can be expected to duplicate those experienced in the past. Except for periods of urgent demand, recent measures of typical seasonal variation will provide very satisfactory indications of the normal seasonal variation to be expected in various industries in the near future. Should demand become highly urgent, as in an emergency call on all resources during an all-out war, any seasonal variation dependent upon demand rather than supply conditions may largely disappear. Typical seasonal movements of the future will differ little from those of the recent past unless abrupt shifts occur in seasonal conditions. Such shifts could occur with the introduction of a seasonal stabilization program. This is a rare occurrence. Changing the date of new models in the automobile industry in 1935 is perhaps the best illustration.

It might appear that the problems involved in forecasting the component part of aggregate-industry changes represented by typical seasonal movement are relatively simple. Such a conclusion is not wholly warranted, however, for seasonal movements are characteristic movements of individual industries, and their effect in total industry is merely the aggregate effect of separate, independent seasonal variations. Seasonal variation in total manufacturing, for instance, is the combined effect of seasonal movements in many separate companies in various industries. In each of the industries it is easy to see why the seasonal movement occurs. On the other hand, the business-cycle movement in each industry must be explained by reference to the influence of aggregate activity.

The normal seasonal movement in aggregate activity will change from year to year, even if it remains unchanged in each component industry, because of fluctuations in the "product mix," i.e., in the relative importance of various individual industries from one year to another. If, for example, major industries experiencing autumn seasonal peaks lose

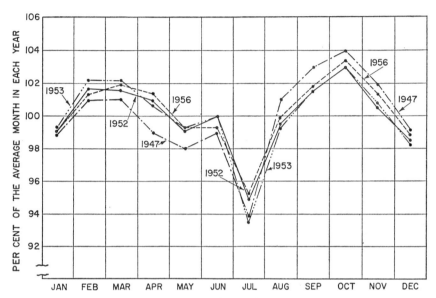

CHART 7–4. Implied Seasonal Indices of Manufacturing Production, Several Years (Federal Reserve Unadjusted Index of Manufacturing Production divided by Adjusted Index). See statement in footnote 32 for indication that these measures understate the differences between years.

relative to other industries, the total may show a lowered seasonal bulge in the latter part of the year. Therefore, to forecast seasonal changes in aggregate industry, it is necessary to anticipate shifts in industry distribution rather than simply to employ a fixed, weighted combination of seasonal indices within industry. So far, little constructive work has become available along the line of anticipating the influence of industry shifts on seasonal variation in industry aggregates.

Chart 7–4 shows some of the changes occurring from year to year in the typical seasonal movement in total manufacturing.[32] The seasonal

[32] The implied seasonal indices shown are somewhat inferior to those developed before the 1953 revision because the procedures for making seasonal adjustments were changed to facilitate a more flexible review program. As stated in "Revised Federal Reserve Monthly Index of Industrial Production," *Federal Reserve Bulletin,* December, 1953: "In the old index all individual monthly series were separately

movements differ in the years shown, especially in periods of recession and prosperity, largely because of the varying relative importance of industries with unlike seasonal patterns. Actually, such changes are not fully reflected in Chart 7–4, as explained in footnote 32. Since the Federal Reserve makes available seasonal indices for some manufacturing industries, how changes result from shifts in industry distribution can be illustrated. In the case of seasonals in the aggregate of all industry, changes cannot be fully explained because current seasonal indices are not available for all industries which experience seasonal variation.

It is not too difficult to explain that the type of seasonal variation which can be forecast in individual industries is that which recurs year after year. Such a seasonal movement is generally expected by those who are concerned with the industry, and plans are made accordingly. Since this type of seasonal may be reflected in a kind of average of past movements, it may be measured by the seasonal index. Individuals in specific industries readily understand extreme seasonal movements, which actually are seasonal changes greater or smaller than those typically occurring in the past. In a specific industry no one would expect to be able to forecast extreme seasonal movements of this sort. In aggregate industry, the distinction becomes less clear because typical seasonal movements are readily explained only at the specific-industry level. Hence it is not surprising that confusion frequently arises in interpreting seasonal changes in aggregate industry.

A case in point is presented by the difficulties which were faced in interpreting seasonal changes in unemployment in the summer of 1954. For instance, seasonal unemployment typically increases from May to June, largely because all of the students leaving schools of various types are not promptly placed. In June, 1954, practically no increase in unemployment occurred. Because of the difficulty of disentangling the various facets of seasonal changes, the Census Bureau did not report a seasonally adjusted unemployment figure, but instead merely stated in its release that practically no increase occurred in unemployment, contrary to the

---

adjusted for seasonal variation and were combined to obtain the adjusted subtotals and totals, including those for major groups. In the new index seasonal adjustments are determined directly for each of the 26 major group indexes, and the adjusted indexes for the major divisions and the total are obtained by aggregating the adjusted group indexes. . . . Selected individual series are also being seasonally adjusted for other purposes. These adjusted series for individual products and industries will not be used currently in obtaining the adjusted group indexes or larger aggregates."

The implied indices shown in Chart 7–4 are obtained by dividing the unadjusted data by the adjusted data in each year for the total-manufacturing figures. It will be seen that the methods employed involve a certain amount of smoothing out of the seasonal variation of particular industries since the group indices are averaged. Also, some individual seasonal movements are not averaged in by the process, as indicated by the last two sentences of the quotation.

usual seasonal pattern. In the Congressional hearings before the Subcommittee on Economic Statistics in the summer of 1954, it was found impossible to provide a clear-cut interpretation of the seasonal movement in unemployment which had just occurred.[33]

[33] *Hearings before the Subcommittee on Economic Statistics of the Joint Committee on the Economic Report,* 83d Cong., 2d Sess., July 12 and 13, 1954, pp. 203–204, 319–323.

CHAPTER 8

The Commodity Price Forecast

Prices play a key role in business thinking about the future, for they are indicative of shifting demand. Rising prices are a simple, direct reflection of demand expansion and falling prices of demand contraction. Not only is this a plausible conclusion regarding the behavior of the market under conditions of shifting demand, but it is usually borne out by experience. Furthermore, rising prices lead to a temporary bulge in sales because buyers try to make purchases before higher prices come into effect, and falling prices induce buyers to wait for lower prices. Thus there is enough of a "feedback" effect for a change in price partially to justify itself. Such a situation, however, reflects only the striking, clearly understood price changes.

Buying, or waiting to buy, in anticipation of price changes implies inventory speculation, and businessmen generally state that they do not engage in it. They do make exceptions, though, when price changes are striking and clear, justifying their actions in terms of the shifts occurring in demand or the need for special measures to protect their supply positions. This kind of adaptive behavior adds to the difficulties of price forecasting, but does not reduce interest in it.

Price movements influence shifts in inventory investment and at the same time are influenced by these shifts. A price forecast is of major assistance in forecasting inventory investment.[1] When inventory investment shrinks rapidly in contraction, prices are vulnerable, for a critical margin of demand has been eliminated.

It is well known that all types of investment demand are subject to rapid change. Any such change produces a disproportionate shift in expenditure. If inventory investment advances rapidly, as it often does, demand is accelerated, especially for certain key products, including

[1] Inventory-stock figures are available more promptly than inventory-investment figures, and because of inventory valuation adjustment, the change in dollar stocks of inventories requires price adjustment in estimating inventory investment. See discussion of inventory valuation adjustment in Chap. 2.

many raw materials. The prices of the particular products advance because supply cannot be expanded with sufficient rapidity, and the price increase spreads to demand-related products. Similarly, plant and equipment investment frequently undergoes rapid expansion, with a pinch arising in major raw materials, forcing price rises which spread to other parts of the economy. Investment shrinks during contraction even more rapidly than it rises in business expansion, producing the opposite result.

Of major importance, no doubt, is the shifting relation between starting and completion of durable investment. As starts slow down or decrease, the income-producing effect is blunted, and with a rise in completed installations, the increase in capacity is accelerated. Both slowing down of starts and increased capacity weaken prices. The opposite effect occurs, of course, when starts rise rapidly before a substantial amount of capacity is being completed.

Price changes are generated to some extent by all expenditures if a wide fluctuation occurs. This is partly reflected by the fact that some of the decline in expenditures in a major contraction is accounted for by price changes. Areas of price weakness depend on demand conditions in different parts of the economy at a particular time. In 1949 the inventories of nondurable consumer goods appeared excessive, and prices paid for such goods generally declined, although the total physical amount purchased for consumption actually increased for the year as a whole. A similar situation appeared for consumer durables in 1954, although the general average price of consumer nondurables did not decline in 1954. The prices of consumer services have not declined in any of the recessions since the early thirties, and the lagging inflationary rise occurring in these prices in 1949 and 1954 tended to support the total dollar volume of expenditures.

Short-term conditions are best represented by total expenditure, reflecting both quantity and price. If rising prices lead to increased expenditure in a given area and if there are no counterbalancing decreases in expenditures in other areas at the same time, the price increase has reduced the contraction.

Major price declines are largely indicative of reduced investment. A contraction with prompt and substantial price declines may reflect a readier market adjustment than one exhibiting little price decline.

Industry-administered prices principally rule in consumer markets, and they may reflect demand conditions very tardily if no important shift occurs in inventory demand. Much of the vagueness in price forecasting arises from the fact that changes in industry-administered prices are not closely timed with the forces responsible for changes in demand. Price changes are most basically explained by demand conditions. The actual change in prices may be delayed in many administered-price areas, but when the analysis of demand conditions is fully developed, it will indicate the future changes to be expected, even though the timing may not always be clear.

It will be seen that there are many reasons why short-period price forecasts are of critical importance in judging the outlook. Unfortunately, methods of short-term price forecasting are but little developed. In view of their importance, however, we review possible procedures in the present chapter.

THE SEGREGATION OF PRICE AND QUANTITY MOVEMENTS

Prices and quantity sold are intimately related in the marketing process. In the case of many products, what is directly observable is neither the change in price nor the change in quantity sold, but the change in total value paid. Partly, this is due to changes which occur in quality, so that unadjusted prices and quantities become somewhat noncomparable from one time to another. But it is also due to the fact that the market is more concerned with total values than with prices and quantities. Thus, in Chapter 7 we have dealt with a value, rather than a quantity, forecast. Starting with a value forecast, one may attempt rough judgments as to what part of the change in value will be due to price. For this purpose it is essential to consider separately different phases of the business cycle.

Case I—Increase in Demand Early in the Expansion Phase. Prices frequently register substantial increases in this period. When that happens, it is related to factors which may be picked from the following list: a considerable price decline in the relatively recent past; a critical shift in the inventory position; increase in non-inventory demand; and expectation of further increases in demand. A relatively common occurrence at this juncture is a critical shift in the inventory situation, producing an increase in inventory demand. The extent of price increases resulting will depend on the degree to which prices were beat down late in the preceding recession. If prices were cut to out-of-pocket costs, any increase in requirements will lead to an advance in prices. If prices declined only slightly, little if any advance is to be expected with a slight increase in inventory demand. Any increase which may occur in non-inventory demand—for instance, because of a rapid increase in public spending—is an accentuating factor. Any expectation of further increases in demand is to be similarly considered. Generalizations regarding these influences must, it is true, be very qualitative, but the general magnitude of price increase can be partly judged by analogy to what happened in similar cases in the past.

Case II—Peak Prosperity. It is sometimes argued that weakening of demand is a precursor of recession. If so, it would be reasonable to expect, as many persons have concluded deductively, that price declines precede declines in quantity. Past records, however, do not substantiate that conclusion. Examination of the following conditions will lead to a firmer conclusion: current attitudes regarding inventory levels; rate at which investment facilities are being completed; conditions in major consumer durable-goods markets; changes occurring in credit conditions; condition of unused resources; and the development of critical levels.

If current beliefs are that inventory stocks are inadequate, inventory demand may not decline. The attitude is more important than the actual rate of inventory accumulation, because shortages of goods may prevent buying at the desired rate, and the level of pressing unfilled orders may keep up the price. If, on the other hand, there is a wide belief that inventory stocks are adequate, inventory demand will dry up and be a price depressant.

If capital facilities are being completed at an ever increasing rate, increased capacity will be a price depressant, especially if slackening payments for capital formation are acting as a brake on purchasing power at the same time. The contrasting situation, smaller increases in the rate of completion of capital goods and rising payments for capital formation, occurs early in prosperity, as in the latter half of 1955 and the first half of 1956.

Inquiry should be made into the market for consumer durable goods as well as that for capital goods, because the development of saturation there is also important. The significance of shift in market conditions for capital goods turns on the fact that demand experiences violent fluctuations, and the same is true of consumer durable goods. The direct price influence of consumer durable goods, however, is less. Their prices are largely administered, and fall promptly only through the avenue of the price of secondhand goods. Tailing off of demand for consumer durable goods is certainly a price depressant, although the price of most types will not decline promptly without pressure to deplete inventories.

Shifting credit conditions are indicative of the vulnerability of prosperity. Businessmen are not primarily motivated by the cost of borrowing, but in vulnerable markets, substantial increases in interest rates are a retarding factor. The unfavorable effect of a rise in interest rates on commodity prices depends on the extent to which the rise increases costs already advancing in the face of unfavorable markets. Rising interest rates are more likely to add to unfavorable conditions than to initiate them.

Continuation of prosperity depends principally on expectation of expanding business conditions. Business expansion, however, will be disappointing if the cost of added resources is abnormally high and market demand shows little resilience. The best resources are usually first brought into use, and the small proportion of unused resources in prosperity tends to be inferior; costs are abnormally high in developing them. As long as market prices are rising, the increased cost may be readily absorbed. But as soon as market demand begins to falter, the increased cost of inferior resources may appear intolerable and may discourage adding to activity at points in the economy where some increase in demand is still apparent.

The reaching of so-called critical levels refers to reaching a point at which additional resources are both limited and markedly inferior. The critical level literally means the limit of available supply, but seldom, if ever, is it impossible to expand supply by a minor amount if increased costs are not prohibitive. It is, of course, true that what is sometimes involved is an expensive increase in the output of a plant already operating above optimum capacity. The increased cost may make the added output impractical. Failure to add to output will limit expenditures. If expenditures do not increase, prices will be weakened.

Other types of critical levels are related to costs out of line with market prices. Interest rates and related monetary factors are cases in point, but the critical level cannot be set at any particular point, for the limiting condition is relative to other factors. If stock prices remain high because of conviction regarding the growth potential, in spite of higher interest rates, the essential funds for capital expansion may be obtained in the equity market. Limitation may arise not because the individual businessman thinks higher interest rates add unduly to cost but because the financial community fears this is true and refuses to ration him credit.

All of these factors will, of course, reflect on quantity output as well as on price. The price effect will be most pronounced in the more competitive markets. If inventory levels come to be considered excessive, highly competitive prices will fall promptly. The addition to capacity principally affects the bargaining position. Clues to saturation in consumer markets usually are developed from price weakness, such as the showing indicated by prices of secondhand cars in auction markets (reflected in the *Automobile Age* price index).

Credit weakness is quickly reflected in the commodity prices that bidders are willing to offer. The primary effect of limited resources is to increase certain prices, but for industry generally the increased price of resources leads to increased costs and may effectively provide a test of the strength of the market for goods made of the resource materials.

Case III—Early Contraction. The degree of price decline in early contraction is related to prevailing attitudes regarding inventory levels, the rate at which investment facilities are being completed, the rapidity of decline in demand, the degree of competition in saturated markets, the monetary policy pursued, and the expectation of government price-support programs.

A very powerful depressive factor in early contraction is the urge to reduce inventories. Declines in physical output will be drastic, and price declines will accompany them if inventories are considered excessive. In the inventory runoff at the end of 1937, the industrial production index declined approximately 25 per cent between September and December while the wholesale price index declined nearly 7 per cent. In the runoff of textile inventories in 1948–49, the production index for textile-mill products dropped approximately 30 per cent from October, 1948, to July, 1949, while the wholesale price index for textile products declined approximately 7 per cent.

When a large volume of capital facilities remain to be completed, output declines slowly, and prices may decline nearly as much. Between the peak in 1929 and mid-1930, the index of industrial production declined less than 20 per cent while the wholesale price index declined considerably more than 10 per cent. With the institutional changes which have occurred, doubt may be raised as to whether prices would fall as freely now as they did in 1930, but substantial declines in durable investment will induce price declines, probably to a greater extent than induced by declines in inventory investment.

Declines in demand may be initiated in other areas. Most important are consumer durable goods. If no urge exists to reduce inventory, substantial price declines are not likely to occur promptly because prices are administered in these areas. However, inventory curtailment usually accompanies any substantial reduction in demand.

If the markets which become saturated are competitive, price declines are certain to occur. Rapid shifts are occurring in the development of consumer durable goods, and the field tends to be increasingly competitive, with many companies keeping the market in a state of flux. Such has not always been the case. Mechanical refrigerators, for instance, were priced for a narrow market in the late twenties, and prices did not quickly react to the slide in business conditions. The modern tendency to employ "dynamic pricing"—setting prices in line with the visualized potential market rather than principally in relation to past costs—makes holding the line on prices of consumer durables more difficult.

The price effect of decreased demand in consumer nondurable-goods markets is even more dependent on efforts to reduce inventory than the price effect of decreased demand in durable-goods markets. Of course, prices may react quickly in competitive markets when an important change in supply occurs if demand is inelastic, as in the case of farm products. But the price is reacting to supply rather than demand and reflecting an increase in inventories.

The monetary policy pursued by the monetary authorities in early contraction will have an influence on the price decline, at least in a negative way. If credit restrictions are not promptly relaxed, an approach to the old type of monetary crisis could appear. With money in short supply, prices would be beat down. There is little likelihood that this will happen. The monetary authorities may, however, hold rigidly to credit restriction until contraction becomes obvious as prices continue to go down. Any great easing of credit by the authorities at that point is unlikely to keep prices up, for easier credit would not immediately counter the market-demand influences.

Supply-induced price declines are likely to be countered to a substantial extent by government price-support programs. These not only cover agricultural areas, but may influence other raw materials through stockpiling programs. Similarly, any demand factors which threaten to induce major declines in raw-material prices may be countered by government programs. The forecaster will find it necessary to anticipate what the government is likely to do.

Case IV—Later Contraction. Prices are likely to level off in late contraction, but not to rise immediately even when an upturn occurs in physical output. For instance, the wholesale price index continued to decline until February, 1950, even though the business-cycle upturn occurred in the preceding autumn. In the 1953–54 recession, the wholesale price index continued to decline slightly until the end of 1954 even though the upturn in activity occurred at mid-year. On the average, resources are relatively ample near the business-cycle trough, and market demand is usually insufficient to raise the price level. It should be noted, however, that early price increases occur in markets where drastic price cuts and substantial inventory depletion have been experienced.

In any particular recession, leverage can be gained by giving specific consideration to the following factors: the character of the inventory situation; construction work remaining to be completed; the extent of the output decline; the credit situation; and expected support programs. Unless the contraction has been spotty, no great amount of unplanned inventory increase is likely to remain. Since unplanned inventory increases largely arise in finished goods, an indication of their continuance can be obtained by examining change in the ratio of finished-goods inventories to raw-material inventories. If finished-goods inventories are not increasing and raw-material inventories are, it is probable that the latter are being increased intentionally and that the former are under control.

How much construction work remains to be completed depends on the length of the business contraction and the completion time required for the projects which are under way. As long as the construction projects still under way are such as would not have been started under the prevailing economic conditions, construction is providing more support to physical output than to prices. The work involved necessarily calls for output, but provides little support in the price market because the work would not have developed if decisions had been comparable to current ones.

If the decline in output has been great, there will be a poor competitive position for supplies put on the market, and prices will show considerable weakness even though no further decline in output is indicated. The financial authorities are likely to have developed ample credit, and interest rates will have become relatively low. These influences will not raise prices or directly raise the level of physical activity, but they will make funds easier to obtain for those firms which visualize profitable opportunities for expansion. Under the kind of conditions now existing, the presence or absence of currently operating government price supports will be a major influence on the price level.

In all of these cases the extent to which physical activity rises or falls depends on the condition of business inventories, the condition of consumer inventories, the mood of consumers, the durable-investment situation, the expenditure generated by government programs, and the expenditure generated by foreign demand. The quickest and most violent force affecting physical output is business inventories. The most important questions relate to the amount of planned inventory accumulation, the extent to which planned inventory accumulation is achieved, and the extent to which unplanned inventory accumulation occurs. Inventory demand represents an adjustment to the past changes which have occurred in demand, so that the effect of inventory action is to accentuate any increase or decrease in physical output which arises from final sales. When sales exceed anticipated levels, so that planned inventory increases fail to be achieved, the stimulating influence of inventories becomes even more expansionary in the following period. Unless a considerable supply of unused resources is available, the influence of trying to catch up with unachieved inventory expansion will reflect more on prices than on quantity of output.

When inventories rise more than desired because current sales fail to extend the rate of increase of the recent past, a desire to shrink inventories is carried over to the next following period. Physical production falls rapidly, but considering the desire to reduce inventory stock at successive stages in distribution, inventory may continue to be higher than desired, especially at early production stages such as in manufacturing. Rapid and uninhibited cuts in production schedules follow. Rather violent price cuts might be expected, but experience indicates that declines in the rate of production far exceed those in prices.

Relatively low consumer stocks in association with high disposable income, as occurred with the large deferred demand at the end of the war, drive up physical production to about the limits of available resources and increase very substantially the prices actually paid by the consumer. The market price registered in the price indices may understate the actual price increase because of the subtle effect of trade-in values and shifts in discounts or premiums charged in comparison to list prices. Relatively high consumer stocks, even with high disposable income, have the opposite effect. The price influence may be difficult to determine.

Confidence of consumers that now is a good time to buy and that adequate individual buying power will be available in the future, possibly even in the face of temporary shrinkage in employment, may increase the proportion of disposable income spent in contractions. This will limit somewhat the shrinkage of dollar purchases by the consumer. It would appear that the retailer is induced to cut prices to maintain sales in these circumstances, and the shrinkage in physical quantities sold may be limited. The prices consumers paid declined from 1948 to 1949, for instance, while the physical volume of goods bought actually increased. Expansionary attitudes of consumers at peak prosperity, with very limited unused resources, are likely to result chiefly in rising prices. Very pessimistic attitudes on the part of consumers in a deep depression may lead to some shrinkage in spending relative to disposable income and may lead to drastic price cuts.

Change in durable investment does not usually produce sharp and violent reversals, unlike change in inventory investment, but it is most important in extended periods of prosperity or depression. The pressure on dwindling unused resources becomes intense if investment continues to expand in a lengthy period of generally prosperous conditions. Prices will rise at least as much as physical production. If decision makers desire a substantial cutback from high levels of durable investment in recession, long-drawn-out construction periods will temporarily support physical production above levels which are then desired, and prices will be cut substantially.

Considerable increases in government expenditures, such as occur with the onset of war or fear of war, will advance prices substantially if prosperous levels are current, barring the institution of very rigid controls. If increased government expenditure starts with depressed business levels, price increases may be kept quite restricted until the time comes to reduce government expenditures and eliminate emergency controls.

At that time, deferred demand and large increases in the money supply may lead to rapid price rises.

Foreign demand is not relatively great enough to be an important price factor, but it often has been important in advancing the physical output of certain kinds of products. Machinery is an illustration in our recent history. In earlier times, when agricultural products bulked relatively larger and we depended on an export market, shifts in foreign demand brought important price changes because agricultural supply could not be voluntarily changed significantly in the short period.

AGGREGATIVE ANALYSIS OF DEMAND AND SUPPLY FACTORS

Change in price is a result of shift in demand for, and supply of, money. The demand for money is best examined in relation to expenditures and the supply of product. The supply of money is an elusive magnitude, for it depends largely on Federal Reserve actions. Furthermore, an increase or decrease in the velocity of circulation can stretch or shrink the influence of a given volume of money.

The total money funds required are largely dependent on the volume of expenditures. The critical elements are business inventories, durable investment, and major consumer durables, for funds have to be obtained to finance a large proportion of these purchases. Contrastingly, most consumer nondurable and service purchases are made directly out of income payments received. These require no lesser money funds per dollar of expenditure, but the money funds arise from money payments made automatically in the economic process. Investment funds have to be bid for, and their availability depends on the discretion of those who made savings or of the banking authorities in extending credit. The distinction relates to the supply of money, rather than to the supply of goods.

As long as expenditures are substantially below the capacity of the economic system to produce goods, little or no average price rise will occur. With a redundancy in the supply of goods at least potentially available, the competitive process provides little inducement to mark up prices. Nearly always, a few types of goods will be in short supply temporarily, but their effect is swamped by the excess supply of most goods. There is no satisfactory measure of total capacity to supply goods.[2] The best indicator is relative unemployment. When unemploy-

---

[2] Repeated efforts have been made to develop measures of capacity. The most noteworthy at the present time is reported by the McGraw-Hill Department of Economics. The manufacturing companies interviewed are asked to state, using whatever definition is most convenient, the per cent of capacity operation and the rate of operation preferred. If the preferred rate is substantially higher than the actual,

ment has been about 10 per cent or more of the labor force historically, prices have tended to fall and when less than about 5 per cent, have tended to rise. The labor resource is the most critical one.

If the monetary authorities are moderately successful in making needed money funds available, critical points in the neighborhood of 10 and 5 per cent unemployment may be expected. The exact monetary policy pursued will fix more precisely the level at which deflationary and inflationary conditions arise. With very easy money, rising prices will develop at relatively high unemployment, and with a tight money policy, prices may not rise until unemployment is somewhat less than 5 per cent. The monetary policy may of course exert a greater influence on quantity of output than on prices, in which case prices are influenced only indirectly. In most cases, in fact, monetary policy is likely to exert the major direct effect on quantity when it is effective. If ineffective, an increased supply of money is merely spent more slowly. The effect on prices develops secondarily when important changes occur in the per cent of capacity used. Of course, there may be exceptions, as when prices are widely expected to rise or fall substantially.

Monetary control involves manipulation of the interest rate as well as of the supply of money, but the relation to interest rate is usually less useful in price forecasting than the relation to money supply. The pinch produced by mild advances in the rediscount rate is likely to be influential only after considerable delay.

Interest rates lagged after a turn in commodity prices before the institution of the Federal Reserve System. The lag now is less apparent, but concomitant interest-rate changes are unlikely to result from Federal Reserve action.

Although we may question the forecasting effectiveness of more precise statements of relations between supply and demand at the present time, two of the most promising statements may be noted, partly because we can hope to develop more trustworthy formulas. Charles F. Roos suggests as a first approximation:

$$\text{Price} = (\text{new orders})^a \times (\text{money gradient})^b \times (\text{inventories})^c \times \text{constant}$$

The exponents a, b, and c are measures of elasticity—a of the demand for goods, b of the demand for money, and c of inventory supply. The "money gradient" is defined as the rate of change of bank deposits measured by taking the ratio of demand deposits this month to a weighted average of demand deposits for the past twelve months. Roos looks on

---

a soft price situation is to be inferred. If actual rates are nearly equal to or greater than preferred rates, a hard price situation is indicated. The effectiveness of the system remains to be tested. The extent to which the capacity measures employed are comparable, one with another, is unknown.

the money gradient as a measure of the expansive or contractive forces originating in the banking system.[3] The money gradient alone has some forecasting value. Roos holds that its turns lead those in production and prices by six months to a year.

Major difficulties faced in using Roos's price-forecasting formula may be summarized. New-orders data are available for only a small part of the total economy, notably for the manufacturing of durable goods. (Production or shipments can of course be used as a substitute in other areas.) Changes in the value level of inventories may be largely due to price, and prompt segregation of the price effect is possible only on a very crude basis. The assumption of constant elasticities, as indicated by fixed values for *a, b,* and *c* in the formula, is probably unwarranted.

Roos notes that "the ratio of inventories of raw materials to production of finished goods, or months' supply as it is often called, has long been used by purchasing agents as a guide to the future of raw material prices." He holds that "even better results are obtained by using the ratio of inventories of raw materials to new orders for finished goods." [4] This is a crude kind of supply-demand relationship. If raw-material inventories should change rapidly without a change in demand, a price reaction usually would occur. As an exception we may note the possibility that raw-material inventories may be purposively run down rapidly with a low level demand, under the assumption that additional raw-material supplies are readily available. The supply-demand ratio suggested probably would not be helpful when unanticipated changes are occurring in demand or supply because of waiting by buyers or sellers. Price forecasting should give due regard to unique supply and demand factors, but need for supply-demand ratios has not been clearly established.

By using yearly statistical data from 1921 to 1949 (with the war years 1942–46 eliminated), Lynip has developed the following equation:[5]

Wholesale prices = 0.215 industrial production index, 1926 base + 3,470 reciprocal of steel capacity in millions of tons + 10,500 reciprocal of labor force in millions + 1.26 price of gold in dollars per troy ounce + .331 public debt in billions of dollars + .452 private debt in billions of dollars − 298.

The logic of the equation is readily explained. Increased production is positively correlated with price because higher levels indicate an increased

---

[3] Charles F. Roos, "Survey of Economic Forecasting Techniques," *Econometrica,* 23:363–395, 1955.

[4] *Ibid.,* p. 379.

[5] B. F. Lynip, Jr., *Factors Affecting the Wholesale Price Level* (San Francisco: California and Hawaiian Sugar Refining Corporation, Ltd., 1950). In making use of current data, a conversion must be made for the price and production indices, since the coefficient for the wholesale price index is expressed on the old 1926 base and the coefficient for the industrial production index on the old 1935–39 base.

pressure on the supply of resources. Steel capacity and labor force are inversely correlated because a rise in capacity would tend to reduce prices. There is at least a theoretical positive correlation between commodity prices and the price of gold because we have a modified gold standard. Historically, prices have been positively correlated with the amount of outstanding debt, since an increase in debt increases the volume of money.

The most important influential forces are represented in Lynip's equation. Change in expenditures or buying pressure is represented by the industrial production index. Available supply or capacity to provide product is represented by steel capacity and size of the labor force. The effect of increased money supply is represented by change in debt. It is not surprising therefore that the yearly movements of prices since 1921 have usually been fairly closely matched by computations based on the equation.[6] Exceptions can be at least partially explained by the particular conditions existing in some of the years. The computed equation indicates a price rise of slightly more than 4 per cent between 1955 and 1956, compared with a rise of slightly more than 3 per cent in the wholesale price index.[7]

Lynip's equation may be of some aid in forecasting prices, but important limitations must be recognized. The key independent variables are industrial production and debt levels. These must be forecast to make use of the index in forecasting prices. The mechanics of the index indicate that the rise or fall in prices will be commensurate with the rise or fall in industrial production (if we make the logical assumption that private-debt levels will move with industrial production). A mechanical estimate of change in prices is facilitated by Lynip's equation, but frequently particular conditions may make questionable the assumed rigid relationships to the levels of industrial production and debt. Use of the equation may give some "feel" of the expected change in prices, but particular conditions, developed from examinations similar to those suggested earlier in the chapter, may provide a better indication. Since Lynip's equation was fitted on a yearly basis, the coefficients may not provide the best weights to use in developing a quarterly or half-yearly forecast.

The long-term price forecast, considered in Chapter 3, assumes a con-

[6] *Ibid.*, p. 13. A chart shows the comparison for the test period.
[7] Because of revisions, the levels of most of the series included in the equation now differ from those published at the time Lynip made the computations. For instance, public debt is now reported at $239.4 billion in 1950 as compared with the estimated $215 billion used by Lynip. The changed levels reduce the appropriateness of the coefficients in the equation, but should make no material difference in indicating the percentage change from one year to the next.

tinuation of the average change in the conditions of supply and demand since the 1880s. Under these circumstances it was unnecessary to examine the relative influence of high- and low-demand conditions in as much detail as is necessary in the present chapter. Adapting the analysis presented here, the forecast in Chapter 3 could be reformulated with different assumptions. If low-capacity use were anticipated in the future, perhaps a declining trend instead of a rising one should be expected to represent the secular price movement.

PROJECTION OF RATE OF CHANGE SHOWN IN THE RECENT PAST

An inescapable method in price forecasting is the projection of changes occurring in the recent past. Roughly similar price conditions tend to continue for a limited time. The inertia seldom exhibits a constant rate of change, but it is frequently represented by a slight tapering off or speeding up of the rise or fall which is under way. The movement must be followed in several time periods in order to develop an approximation of the pattern of deceleration or acceleration. Because of the similarity between price and quantity movements, it is wise to contrast the movement of prices with the rate of change in gross national product and major expenditure divisions.

The projection of rates of change can be more usefully employed in connection with an index than with individual prices. In the general average, offsetting rises and falls cancel, and any general momentum prevalent in the economy makes for more stable movements. It is very useful, however, to study divisional indices and find where the price strength or weakness centers. Nearly 60 group indices are available as divisions of the wholesale price index. Their movement throws a good deal of light on the stability of the rate of change in the over-all index. Obvious illustrations are: (a) most of the group indices may be experiencing rate-of-change movements quite similar to the over-all index, and exceptions may appear to be due principally to temporary factors; or (b) most of the group indices may be moving differently from the over-all index, and a few group indices, apparently in response to transient factors, may be largely responsible for the movement of the over-all index. A continuing study of the changes in the group indices often reveals a diffusion of strength or weakness spreading throughout the economy and may represent the most important use of rate-of-change studies.

A mechanical use of rate-of-change projection is not advisable. It would provide a fair forecast most of the time, but is likely to fail at the turning points or when important autonomous forces are arising. Better results are obtained if attention is given to the reasons for expecting similar or different price movements in the future. This amounts merely to an integration of rate-of-change analysis with other forecasting procedures. Rate-of-change analysis does add to our understanding. Of no mean importance is the fact that it forces us to explain why we may be willing to project a movement unlike the recent trend.

PRICES IN RELATION TO THE GENERAL MARKET SITUATION

In markets where price reflects market forces with fair promptness, the relation of price to market factors provides the most important basis for a forecast. Individual prices are more effectively analyzed in this way than are indices, for the canceling effect of different price movements in an index blurs the reflection of specific market forces. The relation to sales and various types of inventory is frequently very revealing. It is important to develop a clue to whether inventory investment is planned. Different bits of information available in different industries throw light on this question. Frequently, the movements of raw-material and finished-goods inventories are indicative. Raw-material inventories in many industries move about as planned. It is probable that persons connected with a specific industry can judge pretty well whether that is true in a given case. Finished-goods inventories often move in accommodation to production scheduling and to the maintenance of relatively steady employment. Inventories of finished goods may, therefore, rise embarrassingly when sales turn out to be fewer than implicitly expected. Such a situation tends to make prices decline, but other factors, such as nearly full-capacity operation or rising wage rates may be counteracting. On the other hand, if the level of sales is higher than implicitly expected, inventories may fall below the levels considered most desirable, and prices tend to rise.

The ratio of finished-goods inventory to raw-material inventory tends to move rather steadily (except for year-end values) when finished goods are not being piled up or depleted unduly. Thus, a rise in the ratio is indicative of falling prices and a fall indicative of rising prices.[8] In the first case, the indication is most useful when sales are declining and substantial unused capacity exists; in the second case, it is most useful when the opposite conditions exist. For building materials, the extent to which buildings are being completed in order to avoid the loss involved in closing down building operations should be construed as adding to undesired inventory accumulation. When the ratio of finished-goods inven-

---

[8] To avoid the inverse regression, the ratio is sometimes expressed as raw-material inventory to finished-goods inventory.

tory to raw-material inventory is steady, other methods of forecasting, such as demand and supply analyses and rate-of-change projections, are likely to give good results. Indicative changes in the inventory ratio occur at critical times, when a price forecast is most needed.

A high level of unfilled orders indicates strength and a low level indicates weakness, but the level may not be too helpful in indicating the immediate movement. Many businessmen place major reliance on unfilled orders in forecasting volume. Because of this fact, unfilled orders clearly give an indication of the extent to which businessmen are likely to believe that the market will stand an increase in prices or that the market is likely to dictate reduced prices before long. Unfilled-orders data are available only for limited sectors of industry, notably in industries manufacturing durable goods. In many of these cases, inventory data are relatively poor, and unfilled-orders data are a useful supplement. This is especially helpful if prices are industry-administered, as in the case of steel, for administered prices are unlikely to move promptly in response to market factors in any case.

There are many specific factors available in individual industries. The relative use of available capacity is usually known in the industry, at least in a vague way. As noted earlier, there is no generally successful summarization of capacity use for total industry. Special demand factors, such as government stockpiling, are of major importance.

Recently, use of productivity measures has come into vogue. Short-term changes in productivity are very difficult to predict, especially on an individual-industry basis. Rising productivity increases available supply and may reduce costs, so that reliable estimates would throw light on price changes. Owing to erratic movement on an individual-industry basis and inadequacy of measurement, the method cannot be recommended at the present time. For total industry, short-term changes in productivity are so dependent upon shifting product mix that attempts to anticipate productivity changes do not help a great deal in price forecasting.

USE OF DIRECT COSTS IN FORECASTING
ADMINISTERED PRICES

Administered prices react to the demand and supply pressures of the market, but slowly or through subterfuges, so that the timing of price changes is not well reflected. In a case like steel, prices are not marked up as much or as fast as the demand would warrant in periods of high demand, so that the companies resort to a certain amount of rationing. The quoted price is not the whole story, however. There are published extras, and sometimes other payments of one kind or another are involved. Quoted prices fall only after a considerable period of hesitation in a weak market, but again customer charges may actually decline faster than price quotations through reduction or elimination of extras and other types of payment. The automobile is an even more difficult case. Price augmentation or reduction comes largely through the avenue of trade-in prices, and it is fair to say that few buyers realize what they actually pay for a new car.

The forecast of quoted administered prices therefore involves two major difficulties. The price itself is more or less fictitious, in that it does not entirely reflect the actual charges. Even if a satisfactory system of forecasting quoted prices were developed, it would fail to reflect the information frequently desired—actual unit charges. A forecast of what market conditions indicate the price should be is unsatisfactory, for if weakness or strength is transient enough, declines or rises in charges paid actually may never correspond with market requirements, for conditions may change in time to make adjustment unnecessary.

No effort will be made here to outline a system of forecasting actual charges. The forecast of quoted prices must for the present rest largely on the movement of direct costs, principally wage-rate changes and advance notices of price changes. Quoted price changes are closely related to changes in wage costs when a strong market prevails. Any substantial increase in wage rates is almost certain to be reflected in quoted prices under these conditions. The exact timing of the price change is arbitrary and may be approximated by taking the average lag in the industry in the past. The lag may be modified in a given case if intimate knowledge is available on how urgent price changes are felt to be in the industry. Frequently, notice of an expected price *advance* is given and may be substituted for information on the lag after wage-rate changes which occurred in the past.

In weak markets, forecasts of price declines are even more difficult. Charges additional to the quoted price may be eliminated rather promptly, but quoted prices are usually cut back reluctantly and belatedly. About the only guide is how long a time after past declines in activity the price line was held. This method is not too satisfactory at the present time because periods of price decline have been short and rare in recent history. The ability to resist cuts in the price structure may well have changed with time. Before cuts are made in the quoted price structure, chances are that various forms of discounts and other types of reduction in charges will be instituted. Once a cut has been established in quoted prices, the probabilities are that further declines will occur. One of the major reasons for reluctance to cut prices is that customers are likely to wait for further cuts.

NATIONAL ASSOCIATION OF PURCHASING AGENTS' PRICE FORECASTS

We turn now to a brief summary of some current price-forecasting work. Apparently, the National Association of Purchasing Agents is reasonably successful in anticipating the price outlook. Committees have been set up to follow the markets in various industry groups, notably fuel oil, coal, steel, nonferrous metals, lumber, textiles, and paper. Current reports on these markets are published in the Association's *Bulletin.* In analyzing the outlook in each market, price trends, stocks, production, and other pertinent conditions relative to the particular market are reviewed, and conclusions are reached on the price outlook. Analysis of the "general market situation" and administered-price forecasting, the methods analyzed in the two preceding sections, can be illustrated by material in these reports.

One device developed in the reports on the steel market is the "steel products barometer." This shows the market availability of various steel products at warehouses and at the mill. For most of the markets, a breakdown is shown by important regions, and this often reflects some important differences in market conditions in different parts of the country.

It may well be that the survey of anticipations conducted by the NAPA survey committee is most important in the area of commodity-price forecasts. An important piece of information developed in the survey is how many days ahead buying commitments are made. A shortening of the time presumably represents a weakening of market conditions. Heinz Luedicke has suggested that the work of the survey committee would be more valuable if a summary were made of the differences between the percentages of those surveyed reporting expected declines and the percentages reporting expected rises. He worked out such a summary for several of the reported series. The promptness of the movement of the NAPA survey of prices on that basis in 1953 indicated an early understanding of the price weakness accompanying the recession.[9]

HANEY'S PRICE INDICATORS

In current reports Lewis H. Haney uses two barometers which merit special attention. A supply-demand ratio is obtained by classifying im-

[9] See *An Appraisal of Data and Research on Businessmen's Expectations about Outlook and Operating Variables* (Washington: Board of Governors of the Federal Reserve System, September, 1955), pp. 54–66. In addition to price anticipations, the NAPA survey asks questions about new orders, production, employment, and inventories. All of the summaries are essentially on a qualitative basis. About two hundred hand-picked respondents are included, but the nonresponse rate is sub-

portant series as demand or supply indicators. For instance, production and employment series are generally taken to represent supply, and payrolls, orders, and sales are taken to represent demand. The ratio is interpreted principally in relation to a base line at which demand and supply are supposed to be in equilibrium. Excess supply leads to a high ratio and indicates vulnerability. A rise in the ratio from a low point is interpreted as the working off of excess supply.

Another ratio Haney uses is called "P/V," the price index over the physical-production index. A rise indicates price strength and a fall indicates price weakness, but Haney holds that only the "general direction" counts for this ratio. No effective evaluation of these ratios is available.[10]

McGILL COMMODITY SERVICE

The McGill Commodity Service [11] may be taken as a representative service reporting on price trends. It covers all types of commodities, whereas some commodity services cover only particular areas. Each month a general summary report details the major recognized influences in different important sectors of the economy, and conclusions are drawn regarding expected price changes.

Various commodity services frequently foster studies on the forecasting of individual commodities. An illustration is the article by T. A. Hieronymus on "Forecasting Soybean Prices," published in the 1956 *Commodity Yearbook*.[12]

DEPARTMENT OF AGRICULTURE ANALYSIS
OF AGRICULTURAL PRICES

The Department of Agriculture develops forecasts of the price of individual farm commodities and of general, average farm prices. The forecasts for individual commodities are under the direction of "commodity men" who specialize in various fields of agricultural activity. The whole range of factors thought to be responsible for agricultural prices is taken into consideration by each specialist, although a few specific factors are usually considered critical. For instance, the government loan program is most important in wheat and cotton prices; the

---

stantial. The chairman of the survey committee exercises considerable freedom in interjecting his own evaluations in the prepared summaries.

[10] Haney's barometers are currently reported in the *Bulletin of the National Association of Purchasing Agents*. A good statement of his methods is contained in the Oct. 10, 1956, issue (vol. 27, no. 36).

[11] McGill Commodity Service, Inc., Auburndale, Mass.

[12] New York: Commodity Research Bureau, 1956.

movement of disposable income is looked to for critical guidance on meat prices. Levels of production and inventory, shifts in consumption patterns, and special factors which may arise are taken into consideration in each case. Mechanical models are used to a greater or lesser degree in making these forecasts, but only broad conclusions are reached, and the forecast is usually stated in qualitative terms.

To forecast average farm prices, a gross-national-product model is developed to obtain a forecast of disposable income. This is done because consumer demand, based on income flow, is considered to be a most important determinant of farm prices in general. Also, forecasts are made of exports of farm commodities and the expected level of agricultural production. After these forecasts are made for the following year, a model is developed which sets farm prices equal to a function of disposable income, exports of farm products, and level of agricultural production. The precise figures obtained from the model are considered to be somewhat misleading, and the published forecast is stated in qualitative terms or in a broad quantitative range. The general levels expected for disposable income, exports, and production are stated with the forecast. The formula used is not ordinarily given, however, so that if the reader wishes to make different assumptions about the determining variables, he cannot follow the Department's procedure in a precise way.[13]

[13] The forecasts of both individual-commodity prices and the average price of farm products are presented in *The Demand and Price Situation,* a monthly periodical issued by the Agricultural Marketing Service of the U.S. Department of Agriculture. The individual-commodity forecasts are presented monthly and the forecast for the general average is presented near the end of the year for the following year. See also the section on farm products in Chap. 9.

CHAPTER 9

Short-term Forecasting
of Individual Industries

The growth relationships between industries, discussed in Chapter 5, do
not necessarily hold in the short run. Because future demand is not
entirely clear and because of temporary fluctuations of total demand in
the economy, activity in an individual industry may deviate from its
growth level at a particular time. Production is speeded up or slowed
down to accommodate inventory requirements and shifting consumption
patterns.

It is true, as explained in Chapter 7, that the activity of particular
industries is closely related to that of aggregate industry even in the short
run. This relation, however, differs between industries. Some, like the
steel industry, for instance, may rise and fall much more than others with
the rise and fall of aggregate activity, even though the growth of the
industries may not differ substantially. Furthermore, the reactions of
particular industries to fluctuations in the total market differ somewhat
from one time to another. One may conclude from these facts that the
potential of the input-output table in short-run forecasting is quite
limited. The essential nature of the input-output table involves inter-
relationships between industries. The temporary relationships between
industries in the short run are too fluid for the input-output table to be
of value in forecasting.[1]

As explained in Chapter 7, short-term movements are reactions to
temporary situations and are not to be explained by fundamental forces.
Nevertheless, many of the controlling factors are frequently the same.
Their influence may be somewhat more variable, and it may be related
to temporary adjustments rather than to basic requirements. As in
growth forecasting, leverage is gained by relating to aggregates such
as gross national product or disposable income. In fact, as we saw in

[1] This contrasts with a much more favorable potentiality in long-term forecasting.
See discussion in the early part of Chap. 5.

Chapter 7, the relationship is sometimes traced the other way around: the movement of total industry is traced to the movements of many particular industries. There is nothing the matter with such circular procedures if they are recognized as a form of "cycling," tracing relationships from the whole to the parts and from the parts to the whole. This is a useful method of uncovering interrelated effects moving through the economy.

In this chapter we carry the analysis from total industry to particular industries. Our attention is centered on the forecasting of a few industries. It is believed that in this way we can make the most progress toward clarifying the problem involved: the short-term forecasting of individual industries.

STEEL INDUSTRY

Short-term forecasts of the steel industry are often obtained by projecting activity in steel-consuming industries. The major consuming industries usually covered are passenger cars, appliances, furniture, and metal cans, largely in the consumer market; and private construction, government construction, oil and gas drilling, machinery, transportation equipment, agricultural equipment, ordinance, shipbuilding, and aircraft, principally in the capital-goods market. Additionally, consideration must be given to inventory investment and net exports; they may either add to steel demand or add to its supply.

The analysis would become unduly involved if we should become concerned with the forecasting of each consuming industry at this point. Such forecasting is basically the same, whether undertaken as a step in the steel forecast or for other purposes.

"Use" factors are applied to measures of activity in the consuming industries in order to convert them into an estimate of amount of steel consumed.[2] Use factors may be developed for consuming-industry outputs or for expenditure divisions of gross national product. Although available use factors are of uncertain accuracy, the process of making continuing forecasts makes it possible to increase their consistency. Differences in activity implied may be resolved by contrasting and reexamining expenditure relationships in the consuming industries and major gross-national-product divisions. When discrepancies are located within limited expenditure groups, accountable differences may become apparent; if not, hunting for new evidence is essential.

Direct forecasting of steel-consuming industries is most important

[2] The best current information on the amount of steel taken by various levels of activity in different industries is developed from the American Iron and Steel Institute's survey of shipments of steel products by market classifications, published yearly in the *Annual Report of the American Iron and Steel Institute.*

in annual forecasts made for the following year. Concentrated work on such a forecast usually begins in July or August, is subjected to successive revisions, and is made available by the end of October. Obviously, the annual forecast must be further revised in the following months as new evidence becomes available. By the end of the first quarter its importance has faded, and principal attention is given to shorter current forecasts for the remainder of the year. A more elaborate scheme is to make current annual forecasts beginning with each quarter in the year. Because much of the necessary information for forecasting consuming industries is available only on an annual basis, difficulties are multiplied when other than calendar years are forecast.[3]

Forecasts for periods of less than a year are critically related to the movement of steel inventories. Inventory flows are far more volatile than takings by consuming industries and account for a large part of the accelerated variation which occurs in steel production schedules.[4] Furthermore, inventories reflect rather quickly the demand situation in consuming industries. Inventories accumulate principally at the plants of consuming industries and at the warehouses of jobbers. Their level is readily varied. Actual consumption may poorly reflect the market demand for steel near turning points because of the buildup or runoff of inventories.

No measurements are available on steel inventories, so that a first step is the development of a measurement. Major reliance must be placed on estimates of steel consumption. Such estimates have to be obtained by the application of use factors to measures of activity in the consuming industries. The level of steel consumption so indicated is contrasted with reported levels of steel production; the difference is taken to represent change in inventories.

Inventory forecasts may be developed by contrasting three types of information: (1) qualitative evaluation of the current mood found among executives in consuming industries and among warehousemen; (2) estimates of activity to be expected in the various consuming industries;

[3] Unfortunately, no recent forecast employing steel-use factors has been made available to the public. The procedure involved can be simply followed. Some rough indication of use factors can be developed by classifying American Iron and Steel Institute figures on shipments of steel products by market classifications according to consuming industries (the appropriate classification will not be obvious in all cases and, in some, crude assumptions have to be made), and dividing the resulting shipments figures into the product figures for the consuming industries. Projections of the products of the consuming industries can be divided by the use factors to obtain forecasts of steel requirements. Work of this kind improves with experience.

[4] For instance, W. W. Sebald, President of Armco Steel Company, estimated that perhaps a third of the decline in steel production from 1953 to 1954 was accounted for by a runoff of inventories in 1954. Production of steel ingots was 112 million in 1953 and 88 million in 1954. Sebald's estimate of steel consumption in 1954 was 96 million. See "Outlook for Steel," *Blast Furnaces and Steel Plants*, 43:232, 1955.

and (3) forecasts of change in gross national product. The mood of buyers can be judged from reports of personnel having direct contacts and from reports of such organizations as the National Association of Purchasing Agents. The other estimates come from economic-analysis work. The reports on mood and the estimates of activity in consuming industries must be judged against the current situation. The outlook visualized is often closely related to current inventory change. The essential problem is to decide whether or not the current trend in inventory flows will continue. The forecast of gross national product should be set against the past indications of correlated movements in steel production. The expectation has to be modified by the particular distribution of demand by steel consumers at the time.

Considerable emphasis is frequently placed on the order-book position in forecasting the steel industry. The level of unfilled orders does provide a crude indication of the extent to which buyers are willing to anticipate future needs. The extent of shrinkage in the steel industry when a recession occurs may be partially indicated by the level of unfilled orders.

Unfilled orders do not forecast well the timing of turning points in the business cycle. It is true that a downturn in general business activity is usually preceded by a downturn in unfilled orders, but there is little to indicate that this movement differs from the frequent sagging periods in unfilled orders during the expansion phase of the business cycle. Unfilled orders may not rise prior to a business-cycle upturn. Advance ordering is usually unnecessary at the upturn because mills will have plenty of capacity to fill new orders.

Unfilled orders have helped, however, in providing leads with regard to the relative strength in different parts of the steel market. A relatively high level of unfilled orders for one kind of product usually indicates that this part of the market will be relatively well sustained.

When no major change of direction occurs in aggregate activity, the movement of steel activity may be fairly well indicated by unfilled orders. Rising unfilled orders usually precede a speeding up of sales, and a leveling or slight sagging in unfilled orders may lead to slight irregularity in sales.

AUTOMOBILES

Short-term forecasts of automobiles are made for the following year and for a few months in advance, once the new-model season gets well under way.[5] Following-year forecasts are made in the preceding fall and successively revised until about the end of May.

---

[5] For instance, these two types are clearly distinguished by George P. Hitchings, of the Ford Motor Company; see his "Forecasting in the Automobile Industry,"

In the yearly forecast, consideration must be given to a wide range of facts. Repeated efforts have been made to develop an equational relationship showing automobile sales as a mechanical function of determining factors. The most famous and most successful of these equational relationships was published in 1939.[6] Its functional determinants are supernumerary income, the reciprocal of an index of automobile prices, number of cars in use relative to "maximum car ownership," [7] and "replacement pressure." [8] The equation forecast automobile sales reasonably well until World War II brought an interruption in car production. Poor postwar results have been obtained because of the large deferred demand and possibly other factors. Apparently the quantitative coefficients used in the equation have not been revised in the light of more recent data.

In practical work, mechanical equations are little used because of the difficulty of forecasting the determining variables and because the rigidly stated relationships do not usually describe well the most appropriate assumptions. However, the quantitative evidence on the relationships made available by thorough studies increases confidence in using the relationships in a more qualitative way.

A first step in the yearly forecast is to estimate new-owner and replacement demand. The new-owner market discussed in connection with the growth forecast in Chapter 5 includes sales to new households, advance in ownership among existing households, and multi-ownership sales. Starting with secular-growth figures, adjustments depend principally on expected disposable income. Similarly, replacement demand must be estimated from automobile survival tables, and allowances must be made for any expected change in disposable income deviating from secular growth.

The extent to which consumer credit is being used is important in that expected acceleration in installment sales leads to a higher forecast

---

Midwest Conference on Forecasting Techniques Applied to Business Problems, sponsored by the Chicago Chapter of the American Statistical Association and the Chicago Association of Commerce and Industry (Chicago 5: Monarch Printing and Publishing Corporation, 1954).

[6] C. F. Roos and Victor von Szeliski, "Factors Governing Change in Domestic Automobile Demand," in *The Dynamics of Automobile Demand* (New York: General Motors Corporation, 1939). Possibly, demand functions developed in the University of Pennsylvania study may come to be used in somewhat the same way. See Irving B. Kravis, "Expenditure-Income Relationships for Consumer Durable Goods and Problems of Their Derivation," *Proceedings of the Business and Economic Statistics Section, American Statistical Association,* 1956.

[7] Maximum car ownership is a function of real supernumerary income, number of families, and durability of cars.

[8] A function of disposable income, index of automobile prices, and theoretical scrappage rate, developed from survival and scrappage curves.

than independently indicated by rising disposable income. Ordinarily, changes in disposable income and installment sales are positively correlated, and the combined effect will indicate a large part of the wide nonsecular movement which occurs in automobile sales. Installment sales are forecast principally on the basis of the recent trend; a flattening out tends to be continued, etc. If installment sales and disposable income are not expected to experience comparable movements, sales are projected to change less than they ordinarily do.

An important indicator of new-car demand is the ratio of used-car prices to new-car prices. The major part of new-car demand originates in the used-car market—most first-car buyers buy a used car. When used-car prices are low, new buyers are more readily obtained. Also, lower used-car prices advance the scrappage rate because scrap prices may not drop proportionately. Relatively low used-car prices may slacken the purchase of new cars by the high-income groups, but this influence often is largely offset by rising disposable income.

The expected public acceptance of new models is often given weight independent of changes in disposable income. For instance, sales were expected to rise substantially with drastic changes in new models in 1957. Although the total rise in sales was somewhat disappointing, the shifting proportion of sales among companies was partially related to model changes. In the short run, model changes may be of limited importance in changing the total level of automobile sales. In the longer run, however, rapid model changes probably will shorten the life of cars; a decline in used-car prices will step up the scrappage rate.

The market for automobiles is not independent of the markets for other consumer goods, especially other durable goods. Some indication of the relative saturation of other durables is needed, recognizing that saturation in this respect is not a simple mechanical concept. Not only relative use of different products, but attractiveness, price, and importance in living standards, must be considered. The problem is rather vague, and it is usually most effectively indicated by relative trends in the demand for various consumer products. If demand for other types of durable goods is leveling off, for instance, automobiles may have a better chance to capture an increased share of the market. Other possible competitive relationships should not be ignored. As an illustration we may note the possible adverse effect of lagging rises in the price of consumer services in a contraction when the condition of automobile stocks is quite satisfactory.

Any change in established dealer margins will have an important effect on car sales for the following year. Widened margins make it possible for dealers to sell new cars more readily by giving more favorable trade-in allowances, or to sell used cars more readily by reducing the prices below trade-in levels. Reduced margins impede the dealer in making sales.

Naming these factors, as we have done, does not produce a forecast. At the present time, however, the weighing of them requires judgment based on experience. Even with long and effective experience, the yearly forecast may be wide of the mark, as shown by the revisions Harlow Curtice, President of General Motors, found necessary in the spring of 1956 and of 1957.[9] In making these forecasts, it is probable that all of the influences noted above were given consideration. It is also probable, with more experience, that errors will be reduced to a narrower range.

The annual forecast must be distributed seasonally for the forecast year. Recently, this has been a most difficult task. Because of deferred demand, little seasonal variation was experienced in the industry in the postwar years before 1956. The extent to which the prewar seasonal patterns are now being reestablished is difficult to say, for several years' data are required to establish a seasonal pattern.

Chief interest lies in the yearly forecast until about the end of February, at which time currently expected sales for the next few months come to be of central importance. The seasonal movement could loom large in the monthly forecast. In the early part of the postwar period, monthly movement depended principally on the availability of materials. Now estimates must be made of the rate at which consumers wish to buy. An important clue is dealers' stocks of cars, for current information on automobile activity relates to production and not to consumer sales. If dealers' stocks are building up, the production rate is above the buying rate. Under certain conditions, a buildup of stocks is intentional; for instance, after new models come out dealers need stocks, and their needs may be accentuated by the expectation of a surge in spring buying. Aside from the seasonal problem, the change in dealers' stocks in relation to the rate of production offers the best clue to the movement of consumer sales.

The level of spring sales (factory production with a correction for estimated change in dealer inventories) in relation to the experience in recent years offers an effective method of estimating the total sales of the year's models. Also helpful in forecasting the current monthly movement of consumer sales of new cars are used-car prices and installment buying. Declining used-car prices temporarily tend to discourage new-

[9] In May of both years the forecast was cut back to 5.8 million from an early forecast of 6.5 million. *Commercial and Financial Chronicle,* May 17, 1956; *New York Times,* May 25, 1957. Both of the May forecasts turned out to be approximately correct.

car sales, other factors being equal.[10] The forecast of used-car prices depends principally on the estimated level of used-car stocks and the potential new buyers.

Local influences are important, and, as often suggested, a dealer survey should provide useful current information. Dealers may have a good understanding of new-household formation, prospects for selling cars to existing households, and prospects for selling added cars to households already having one or more in use. Without an organized survey, some guessing is necessary to estimate the level of used-car stocks and the current potential for new-owner sales.[11] Current newspaper reports are often helpful. Obviously, used-car prices will go down as automobile stocks rise and new-owner potential fades, and vice versa.

Note should be taken of the question on intention to buy a new or used automobile in the Federal Reserve Survey of Consumer Finances. The Survey has usually pointed in the correct direction from one year to the next. But the forecast is not available until March, at which time interest in the year's forecast is fast being replaced by interest in the outlook for the coming months. If the year's forecast is to be of much value, it should be available no later than the first of the year. In view of valid questions regarding the length of buying plans made by consumers, successive quarterly surveys of buying intentions during the following quarter might be of more help.

DWELLING-UNIT CONSTRUCTION

House-building activity is projected in terms of demand, supply, and cost factors. The most important demand factors are family formation, population migration, and disposable income. Family formation, by type, is estimated annually by the Bureau of the Census, but the figures are based on samples and apparently incorporate a sizable response bias.[12] Mechanical use of changes in yearly figures is therefore of little help. Some aid is given by interpreting changes in light of the Census Bureau's

[10] The effect of used-car prices is somewhat complicated. As noted above, low used-car prices encourage *new buyers* and tend to increase the scrappage rate, which, taken together, will increase the year's sales if disposable income is rising rapidly. A rapid rise in disposable income may encourage the buying of new cars in spite of low turn-in allowances. During months in which used-car prices are falling, some slackening will tend to occur in new-car sales because the disadvantage of trading for a new car increases.

[11] The potential for new-owner sales is the principal measurement sought. Even if a dealer survey did not prove satisfactory for that purpose, it should aid in highlighting new-buyer demand for used cars.

[12] See *Current Population Reports*, ser. P-20, no. 76, July 5, 1957. Growth projections are given in ser. P-20, no. 69, August 31, 1956.

long-term projections of households and families, but here again mechanical procedures give limited aid; wide differences in the increase to 1960 are indicated by the different projections.[13] By using projections making the same assumptions at different times, however, the likely general movement is represented. At the present time, for instance, a slow increase appears to be indicated in the major family groups. Such an increase may reasonably be postulated, with allowance for a minor variation in "doubling" or "undoubling" which might be created by shifts in general economic conditions. (More individuals double up with others in the same household with the onset of unemployment.) Changes in the minor family types are particularly sensitive to shifts in general economic conditions, and therefore projections are closely related to those shifts.[14]

Population migration is best indicated by the Census measurement of the rate of migration to different counties in the United States. Recent reports indicate that migration is continuing at a high postwar rate,[15] but the most recent report available at any given time is from one to two years late. However, general information should be fairly reliable in indicating any marked change occurring in migration, and therefore some reliance may be placed on a projection of past changes.

Disposable income is relatively unimportant as a determinant of the number of housing starts. Under certain supply conditions, such as a disproportionately large number of small houses when the family size is increasing, it may become more important. With rapid increases in disposable income, larger houses may be built even though some of the smaller houses become vacant in the process. In any case, disposable income is an important determinant of the price level of houses built.

The most useful indicators of supply are the vacancy rate, the ratio of the size of the civilian population twenty-one years of age and over to the number of dwelling units, and the distribution of housing supply. The vacancy rate as reported quarterly by the Census, has shown some irregular increase since 1950, but has not reached an abnormally high level. A secular decline is occurring in the average number of persons per household because of an increase in the number of non-husband-

[13] *Ibid.* The indicated increase in husband-wife families from March, 1957, to July, 1960, range from about 0.4 million to about 1.2 million. The difficulty is that comparison is made between actual and different growth projections; therefore any difference in level of growth projections gets counted as a difference in the indicated increase.

[14] The major family types are called "primary families" and are divided into husband-wife, other-male-head, and female-head types. The minor family types are called "primary individuals" and are divided into male and female types. The sensitivity of minor family types probably is declining at present because of aging of the population and because of widening and increased level of old-age pensions.

[15] See *Current Population Reports*, ser. P-20, no. 73, March 12, 1957.

wife households.[16] The ratio of the civilian population twenty-one years of age and over to the number of dwelling units declined from 2.2 in 1950 to about 2.1 in 1957. This is about in line with secular expectations and does not indicate any significant shift in the supply situation.

Postwar housing has been concentrated in houses with few rooms, about in line with earlier demand. But primary families have been increasing in size, and some inadequacy of supply is indicated under high-income conditions. The geographical distribution of vacancies is reported by the Census.[17] Reported vacancies are relatively high in areas which are growing most rapidly, and have been so continuously since 1950. This appears to be indicative of requirements under conditions of rapid expansion, rather than evidence of oversupply.

Major cost factors are the installed price of a house, total interest charges, and financing costs; unfortunately, no good measurements are available on any of these factors. Rapid changes in financing costs would be important, but changes probably tend to occur slowly. Should rapid changes occur, striking cases no doubt would come to the attention of the forecaster. Customer loans may give some indication of changing interest rates. Available cost indices, such as reported by E. H. Boeckh and Associates, are satisfactory when productivity in building houses remains stable, for such indices represent changes in material and labor costs reasonably well.

Changes in FHA interest rates, down payments required, and length of mortgage permissable are readily available and often are critically important in decisions to buy. Required down payments were reduced slightly in mid-1957 and apparently added to activity. With quiescent demand, however, the influence was limited. For short-period forecasting, changes in the down payment required and the monthly payments provide a succinct picture of the major cost influences impinging upon the buyer.

Housing contractors probably plan their building activity well in advance. The Bureau of Labor Statistics conducted a survey of residential builders in 1951 with promising results. *Fortune* has conducted an annual survey of home builders' plans since May, 1951. Answers have been obtained on a questionnaire from builders in 35 cities, covering at least three builders engaged at each of the following levels of activity in each city: less than 10 homes; 10 to 100; and more than 100. The cities are widely distributed and encompass diverse economic condi-

[16] See further discussion of this in Chap. 4.

[17] U.S. Bureau of the Census, "Housing and Construction Reports: Housing Vacancies," ser. H-111, no. 9, October, 1957, indicates a vacancy rate in the West of 7.5, down from a year earlier but higher than the rate of approximately 5 for the country as a whole.

tions. Although the surveys have overestimated housing starts every year since they began, the margin was narrow in 1951, 1952, and 1954. In 1953 and 1955 the actual number was missed by 9 per cent and in 1956 by 13 per cent. In spite of the probability that plans are laid for future building, there is evidence in these figures that builders have been swayed by their recent levels of activity, especially in 1956.

In addition to new house building, "fix-up," covering additions, alterations, and maintenance of homes, represents residential activity of wide interest. No good data are available. Until we know more about the field, little can be done except to assume that the movement of fix-up expenditures will be commensurate with that of disposable income.

ELECTRIC UTILITIES

Frequently, in the past, electric-power production has been forecast yearly and monthly on the projection of a secular trend. In the industrial division, which represents about 55 per cent of total sales, this method is particularly unreliable. Reports made each month to the Federal Power Commission from about 98 per cent of the industry give estimates of anticipated loads. In the expansionary period from January, 1955, to September, 1956, these forecasts had to be raised every month.[18]

There is an increasing tendency in the industry to forecast on the basis of explanatory variables. This is indicated, for instance, by the *Electrical World* forecast for 1957, which posited an increase in total sales of 8 per cent compared with 10 per cent for 1956 because some slowing down was expected in explanatory variables.[19]

The method used by the Cleveland Electric Illuminating Company will be briefly summarized to illustrate procedures now being developed. The residential sales forecast is made on the basis of the estimated increase in customers and average consumption per customer. To estimate added customers, the past trend of the ratio of new customers to housing starts is projected; a forecast is made of housing starts and multiplied by the projected ratio. The number of new customers is derived from added homes, and added homes are shown by housing starts. A projection of the trend of kilowatt-hours per customer is modified by estimates of expected appliance sales and other factors which appear pertinent at the time. The residential sales forecast is the product of projected total customers and average consumption per customer.

    [18] *Estimated Future Power Requirements of the United States by Regions: 1955–1980* (Washington: Federal Power Commission, December, 1956), p. 3.
    [19] Ary Mossiman and Arthur J. Stegeman, "7th Annual Electrical Industry Forecast: Steady Growth," *Electrical World,* vol. 146, Sept. 17, 1956.

Other sales are divided into the following classes: other commercial; large industrial and commercial customers, exclusive of specific groups; specific groups; and other classes. General commercial sales are forecast by computing trends in the number of customers and the average use per customer; and then multiplying the use per customer by total number of customers.

The sales to large commercial and industrial customers, exclusive of some specific cases noted below, were found to be closely correlated

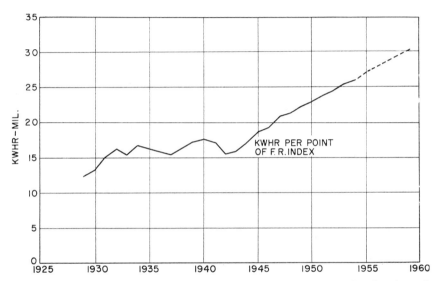

CHART 9–1. Movement of Kilowatt-hour Sales to Large Commercial and Industrial Customers per Point in Index of Industrial Production (illustrating work of the Cleveland Electric Illuminating Company). SOURCE: Reproduced with permission of the Cleveland Electric Illuminating Company.

with the Federal Reserve's industrial production index. The trend of kilowatt-hour consumption for these customers per point of the Federal Reserve's index has been found to be stable and arithmetically linear since the beginning of the war. This is shown in Chart 9–1. The trend is projected and multiplied by the company's forecast of the Federal Reserve's industrial production index to develop the sales forecast.

The specific cases excluded from the forecast of the large customers noted above are electrochemical plants and some others. These customers are very large consumers, and their loads are likely to fluctuate widely. Forecasts of sales are made after analysis of special factors, obtained partly from the market research department of the company.

The other classes represent relatively small consumption from such outlets as street lighting, railways, sales to public authorities, etc. Their consumption of electricity tends to be quite stable. Any contemplated increases, like additional schools or rapid-transit facilities, are uncovered by the market research department. The past stable trend is modified to take account of such changes.

Two methods are employed to forecast peak loads. Separate formulas are applied to residential and rural, small light and power, large light and power, and other classes. These formulas utilize the Federal Reserve Index of Industrial Production, the length of the work week, and average use. For the residential, rural, and small light and power customers, experience indicates that the principal determinant of change in the load factor is increasing use per customer.

For large light and power customers, the conditions in December and the pressures for second- and third-shift operation determine peaks. The December peak is estimated by forecasting how high the December industrial production index will be in relation to the yearly average, and by projecting the secular trend of the quotient of two ratios: the ratio of December kilowatt-hours to December industrial production index divided by the ratio of annual kilowatt-hours to annual industrial production index. Arithmetically, this quotient multiplied by December industrial production over annual industrial production equals December kilowatt-hours over annual kilowatt-hours.

Second- and third-shift pressures are found to correlate positively with the length of the workweek in manufacturing. Peak loads are forecast for most of the other classes of electrical consumers by relating to average use per customer, although special factors are required for railroads and street and traffic lighting.

The second method of forecasting peak loads is to survey all customers who use 500 kilowatts or more. The historical relationship between the sum of the peaks of these customers and the total for all company sales is developed. The trend of the historical relationship is projected and divided by projected sales (obtained by the methods outlined above). The resulting figure is used to check the sum of the forecasts for each type of service.[20]

FARM PRODUCTS

The Department of Agriculture forecasts are standard, and the description presented here will be based entirely on them.[21] The two most

[20] Memoranda were furnished by the Cleveland Electric Illuminating Company to guide the author in making these statements.

[21] See especially James P. Cavin, "Forecasting the Demand for Agricultural Products," *Agricultural Economics Research*, July, 1952; Nathan M. Koffsky, "Economic Forecasting Methods as Used by the United States Department of Agriculture," in *Forecasting Techniques Applied to Business Problems*, sponsored by the Chicago

critical forecasts are cash receipts from farm marketing and the average prices received by farmers. The principal determining variables are conceived to be disposable income and the exports of farm products. Mechanical correlation with more independent variables is not considered very profitable. Generally only approximate ranges or qualitative statements are used in the published forecasts. Koffsky holds that "if there is an art in forecasting, it is the art of disregarding a statistical relationship when circumstances warrant it." [22]

The cash receipts from farm marketings of all commodities except cotton, wheat, and tobacco are found to be principally dependent upon disposable income, although when a minor weight is given to exports, the relationship is slightly improved. For cotton, wheat, and tobacco, exports are much more important and are assigned greater weight as explanatory variables, although disposable income is also given substantial weight. Forecasts of disposable income are derived from aggregative forecasts of the economy starting with gross national product.

The procedure in forecasting exports of farm products has varied somewhat since the war, depending on what currently appeared to be the most indicative factors. As late as 1952, the total amount of foreign aid to be used in financing agricultural exports, plus indications given by the programming agencies about the distribution of aid among principal agricultural products, provided the major basis for the forecast. By 1954, the most important determining variables were conceived to be the level of gold and dollar holdings by foreign takers, farm-product supplies abroad in both importing and exporting countries, bilateral trade arrangements in force, and price competition from other exporting countries. The change in procedure grew out of improvement in the food situation abroad.

Disposable income and exports of farm products are also used to forecast the average prices received by farmers. Actually, most of year-to-year changes in cash receipts from farm marketings are due to prices, for the physical volume of total farm marketings changes little within most years. Changes in demand can have little effect on production within the yearly production cycle. The first approximation of prices received by farmers is developed from a logarithmic relationship to disposable income, value of agricultural exports, and the volume of farm

---

Chapter of the American Statistical Association and the Chicago Association of Commerce and Industry (Chicago 5: Monarch Printing and Publishing Corporation, 1954); *The Agricultural Estimating and Reporting Services of the United States Department of Agriculture,* Miscellaneous Publication 703, 1949; Karl H. Fox, *The Analysis of Demand for Farm Products,* Technical Bulletin 1081, 1953.

[22] Koffsky, *ibid.* He points out, however, that experiments are being made with sets of equations, and that these may come to supersede the single-equation approach with the development of better data and a better understanding of interrelations.

marketings. Prices are expected on the average to change 12 per cent with a 10 per cent change in disposable income and 1.5 per cent with a 10 per cent change in agricultural exports; an inverse change of 17 per cent is expected with a 10 per cent change in physical volume of agricultural marketings.

The final estimates of cash receipts from farm marketings and average prices received by farmers depend upon checks against price and income forecasts by commodity specialists for each individual commodity. The necessary adjustments to the over-all forecasts are usually few since a consistent set of over-all assumptions is made by the commodity specialists.

Detailed commodity projections can be illustrated by forecasts for meat animals. Forecasts of meat production for each quarter in the succeeding year are made on the basis of the size of pig crops, hog-breeding intentions (see discussion below), hog slaughter, and the number of cattle and sheep on feed, moving into feed lots, and going to slaughter. Demand is conceived to have little effect on production within the year. Domestic consumption takes about 95 per cent of the production and therefore depends principally on the production forecast.

The price to be received on domestic consumption is obtained by relating to disposable income. A "price-structure approach," starting with the retail price of meat and ending with the price received by farmers, has been reasonably successful. In 1950, for instance, expected pork production indicated a consumption of 75 pounds per person. The proportion of disposable income spent on pork had held at about 2.3 per cent in 1935–39 and in 1949 and therefore was projected to 1950; a forecast of $28 per person was obtained. Relating to the forecast of 75 pounds per person, a retail price of 40.5 cents per pound was derived (making allowance for a lower price on lard). A study of costs and margins indicates that about 40 per cent goes for marketing charges, leaving about 60 per cent of the retail price of 40.5 cents as the price at the farm.

Crop-production forecasts were made as early as 1912. Until recently, they have been based on correlating reports from voluntary crop reporters with outturn in the past. A probability sampling method is now being developed to obtain these forecasts.

The Department of Agriculture pioneered in "intention" reports, i.e., reports on production plans. Intentions to breed sows have been reported since 1922 and intentions to plant principal crops since 1924. Promulgation of intention reports together with price forecasts may produce some change in farmers' plans, and thus the forecasts may partially defeat themselves. Apparently, however, the influence of intention reports on the intentions themselves has been relatively minor.

Forecasts are made in 18 areas: (1) farm income; (2) farm cost; (3) national food; (4) marketing and transportation; (5) farm real estate; (6) agricultural finance; (7) wheat; (8) feed; (9) cotton; (10) wool; (11) tobacco; (12) sugar; (13) fats and oils; (14) fruits; (15) vegetables; (16) dairy; (17) livestock and meat; and (18) poultry and eggs. The forecasts are made principally for extension experts, who pass the information along to farmers.

PETROLEUM INDUSTRY

Petroleum Week and *Petroleum Processing* conducted a survey of leading oil economists which showed an anticipated increase in demand of 4.6 per cent in 1957.[23] Separate projections were obtained for each major petroleum product, and substantial variation in expansion was indicated, with petrochemicals and jet fuels projected to increase more than three times as fast as gasoline. Petrochemicals had increased about 20 per cent in 1955 but only 10 per cent in 1956; they were expected to increase 14 per cent in 1957 with expanded demand for plastics and synthetic rubber. Distillate fuel oil was expected to show the major increase in volume of product. The increase in demand for distillate fuel oil relative to gasoline in recent years has led to growing inventories of gasoline because a proportionate adjustment in yields has not been made at the refineries. Because of the accumulated gasoline stocks, the projection of new supply needs was substantially less than the projection of demand.

The increased demand visualized for 1957 was about an eighth less than for 1956. By May, unusually large exports had changed the picture somewhat,[24] with stocks of gasoline worked down to more desirable levels. Domestic demand was rising in the first half of the year, about as predicted, and a new survey conducted in May, 1957, showed practically unchanged anticipations for the year, allowance being made for the unusually large export demand in the first half.[25]

---

[23] H. A. Yocum, "The Petroleum Industry," in *The Pulsebeat of Industry: 1957 Business Forecast* (New York: McGraw-Hill Publishing Company, Inc., 1957).

[24] The 4.6 per cent rise in demand had assumed "normal" export volume, with no allowance for the disruption of supply in the Middle East. The forecast ignored special factors in foreign demand and avoided anticipating them.

[25] The May, 1957, statement was for a demand increase of 5.7 per cent for 1957, but the large increase in export demand in the first half accounts for the excess over 4.6 per cent. "Paired" economists' predictions varied from a rise of 3 per cent to a rise of 6.8 per cent from the second half of 1956 to the second half of 1957. The individual economists' predictions were considered confidential. In May, 1957, the survey was obtained from 16 economists chosen geographically and also divided between major and "middle-sized" integrated companies. This kind of sampling may develop a forecast which tends to approximate the average forecast made in the industry, but does not necessarily represent the more promising forecasts. No infor-

TEXTILE INDUSTRY

By their own admission, most of the major textile companies "fly by the seats of their pants," i.e., take action on the basis of market developments. The short-term movements in textiles are closely related to a usual two-year cycle and to the business cycle.[26] As to the former, it is said that "for a great many years, the industry has followed a more or less rhythmic (a) expansion of unfilled orders accompanied by a contraction of inventories and rising price, followed by (b) contraction of unfilled orders, increasing inventories and falling price." [27] By watching interrelated changes in the market situation along this pattern, prediction is frequently made of the two-year cycle movement. Specific conditions, however, may make the outlook differ from the two-year-cycle blueprint. On a chronological basis and in relation to evolving market changes, at the beginning of 1956 the two-year-cycle low was to be expected at mid-year. However, it was generally agreed that, barring a change in the general-business picture, any decline experienced at mid-year would be slight and short-lived because of the closeness with which buying was approaching mill capacities in almost all lines. Forward buying early in the year on the basis of anticipated price increases was visualized as producing some slackening at mid-year. The actual outturn well bore out these predictions.

Predictions have not always been so successful, especially at business-cycle downturns. Notable cases are the rapid, unanticipated inventory contractions in 1937 and 1949. Since the textile industry is often extremely sensitive to short-term changes in the business cycle, a consistent application of the industry's relation to over-all conditions might prove particularly valuable in making short-term analyses.

OTHER INDUSTRIES

Each industry presents a unique problem and cannot be satisfactorily forecast without familiarity with the particular conditions existing in it as well as an understanding of forecasting methodology. In practice, forecasts are frequently made at the company level without the benefit of over-all analysis, so that heavy reliance may be placed on the particular market conditions without adequately testing the validity of over-all relationships. On the more theoretical level of analysis, quick

mation on methods employed in forecasting is obtained in the survey. These statements are drawn from personal correspondence with the editors of *Petroleum Week* and from *Petroleum Week*, vol. 4, May 24, 1957, pp. 9–11.

[26] Sources of the observations offered here are conferences with economists in the industry and the annual forecast articles in *Textile World* during the last ten years.

[27] "Commitments go well into 1956." *Textile World*, February, 1956.

applications of over-all relations are frequently made without a thorough understanding of the particular conditions existing in the industry.

The major methods employed are: correlation, often partially qualitative, with an over-all aggregate such as disposable income; analysis of the market situation; projection of recent trends; a study of the prospects in sales-outlet industries; and projection of recent technical advantages or disadvantages apparent in recent sales trends. Several of these procedures are usually employed in combination, as is clear from the cases briefly detailed above.

Attention may be called to techniques employed in some other industries. In the case of railroads, the problem is principally the outlook for total activity, because shipment and travel are directly related to it. Increasing competition from other transportation systems is also important. Bituminous-coal production was expected to increase in 1957 in line with recent trends (which reverses the general tendency prior to 1954), largely because of the advances in use in major consuming industries, notably electric utilities. The metal working industries were expected to show rising sales in 1957 along with a projected rise in gross national product, because of large new orders for machinery, indications shown by plant and equipment surveys, the passing of a low point in farm machinery and tractor sales, and satisfactory conditions in other outlets.[28]

Electronics were expected to experience sales increases in 1957 approximately similar to the 5 per cent increase in 1956 because of a large backlog of orders and because of the sales stimulation due to new applications such as the use of transistors in radio receiving sets.[29] The dollar volume of sales of electrical goods by wholesalers was predicted to rise 7 per cent in 1957, in accordance with the annual survey of anticipations of electrical-goods wholesalers conducted by *Electrical Wholesaling.*[30] Although petrochemical sales rose only about 10 per cent in 1956, about half as much as in 1955, a somewhat greater increase was expected in 1957 because of new uses becoming apparent in plastics, especially in polyethylene, used in squeeze bottles, and the growing new applications for synthetic rubbers.[31]

Reassurance regarding food manufacturing was given in 1957 by the fact that dollar sales in grocery stores had risen as fast in the postwar period as disposable income. This was due partly to the fact that with

[28] Burnham Finney, "The Metalworking Industries," in *The Pulsebeat of Industry,* 1957, pp. 63–65.

[29] W. W. MacDonald and Vin Zeluff, "Electronics," in *The Pulsebeat of Industry,* 1957, pp. 45–47.

[30] George Ganzemuller, "Distribution of Electrical Products," in *The Pulsebeat of Industry,* 1957, pp. 30–31.

[31] William F. Bland, "Petroleum Processing," in *The Pulsebeat of Industry,* 1957, pp. 69–71.

the increasing commercial employment of housewives and changes in living habits, a trend toward the use of processed and conveniently packaged goods was growing rapidly. A Nielson study showed that 40 packaged commodities experienced a 33 per cent increase in sales in 4 years, contrasted with a 10 per cent gain for other items in the same group. Continuing increases in prepackaging were evident, including a rapid shift to frozen, prepackaged red meats. The use of new flexible packaging materials such as "Mylar" and "Saran" was inducing a spread of the movement. Modernization of equipment used by food processors was keeping prices down, so that the consumer was not paying higher prices for equal convenience and quality. A minimum gain of 5 per cent in food sales was therefore forecast for 1957.[32]

[32] Frank K. Lawler, "Food Manufacturing Moving Fast," in *The Pulsebeat of Industry*, 1957, pp. 48–50.

CHAPTER 10

The Sales Forecast: Methods and Uses

A forecast which throws no light on sales prospects is of limited value to an individual company. In the business world, therefore, most forecasting work points to the sales forecast. The sales forecast builds to a greater or lesser degree on other types of forecasting detailed in this book. By centering attention on the sales forecast, we may put the relation between it and other forecasting in perspective and avoid attributing values to other forecasting which are properly attributed to sales forecasting.

Sales forecasting relates to the prospects for the individual company. Industry, or "market," forecasting is identical only in the unusual case of one-company industries, or when one company completely dominates the industry. As we shall see, the industry forecast is often of major importance in developing the sales forecast, but there are many exceptions, including the cases in which no industry forecast or even industry data are available. Sometimes the sales of an individual company cover diverse industries, as industries are commonly classified, and it may be hopeless to trace sales to industry classifications in these cases.

THE SALES FORECAST AND THE BUDGET

The sales forecast came of age with cost accounting. As Compton says, "with the introduction of standard costs, in one sense, accountants became forecasters. That is, we no longer said an article *had* cost so much. Instead, accountants began to say this article *will* cost so much, and it was here that budgetary control began." [1]

On the other hand the budget has been employed to establish sales control: "each salesman is assigned a certain sales quota. The total of

[1] J. P. Compton, "How an Index Helps Make Accurate Sales Forecasts—The Heart of the Budget," *Journal of Accountancy*, 92:473–474, October, 1951.

all salesmen's quotas is equal to the sales budget."[2] The sales quota could not be set effectively for the purpose of a sales budget without a peek into the future, and sales forecasting came to be recognized as essential for this purpose.[3]

In line with the functions which the yearly budget came to serve, notably the development of sales targets and financial planning, the practice of making yearly forecasts has spread widely since the war. Furthermore, the yearly forecast, put in perspective by the monthly or quarterly forecast, has been found helpful in scheduling production and controlling inventory. The uses of sales forecasts are discussed more fully at the end of the chapter.

SALES FORECAST AND MARKET ANALYSIS

Sales forecasts are sometimes confused with a static market analysis. The two might be about the same for long-term forecasting, but a static analysis of the past market does not provide a good short-term sales forecast. A static market analysis is likely to relate to past conditions rather than to prospective sales. The purposes differ. Sales forecasts project the effect of economic conditions, whereas market analysis emphasizes the size of the total market rather than its near-term change.[4]

MAJOR SOURCES OF THE SALES FORECAST AND ADMINISTRATIVE PROCEDURE

The information for a sales forecast is derived from salesmen in the field and from analysis at the central office. Although information is usually obtained from both sources, there is often a tendency to emphasize one source or the other. Unfortunately we do not know at the present time, as noted below, which is the more reliable source for many industries. The fact that a given company organizes its sales forecasting in a certain way may indicate no more than that the original administrative procedure is being followed. Possibly, the form of organization of the company may make a continuation of this administrative procedure desirable, whether or not it produces the most re-

[2] Walter Rautenstrauch and Raymond Villers, *Budgetary Control* (New York: Funk & Wagnalls Company, 1950), p. 179.

[3] J. Brooks Heckert, *Business Budgeting and Control* (New York: The Ronald Press Company, 1946), pp. 81 ff.

[4] It may sometimes be true that the standard type of market analysis is called sales forecasting. See description of a market survey preliminary to forecasting in *Forecasting in Industry,* Studies in Business Policy, no. 77 (New York: National Industrial Conference Board, Inc., 1956), pp. 41–45.

liable forecasts.[5] If the procedure is somewhat flexible, experiments in shifting emphasis on the source of information may be found desirable. Care is required in judging such experiments, however, for performance during an expanding period may give little indication of how much reliability the forecast will have at the downturn. The more sensitive method is more likely to spot the downturn, but it is also more likely to yield a false indication if the expansion weakens only temporarily.

FORECASTING WITH INFORMATION DERIVED FROM THE SALES FORCE

Forecasting sales with information derived from salesmen in the field is often called a "sales-force-composite method." This is a grassroots approach in that it represents a compilation of anticipated sales by those men who are in closest contact with the market. It is thus a kind of anticipation survey. The chief difficulty, however, is that what is represented probably varies from salesman to salesman—what he thinks the customers' anticipations are, what he thinks he can sell perhaps with added effort, or in some cases the salesman's own analysis of the market situation. The meaning of the compiled information may therefore be vague.

The vagueness of the collected information accounts for the weaknesses usually cited. Aside from the problems of adding subsidiary responsibilities to the duties of the sales force and the efforts and difficulties of integrating the information received by the company executives, the following disadvantages are recognized:

1. Salesmen are poor estimators, being either too optimistic or too pessimistic.

2. If estimates are used as a basis for setting quotas, salesmen are inclined to understate the demand in order to make the goal easier to achieve.

3. Salesmen are often unaware of broad economic patterns which are shaping future sales and are thus incapable of forecasting trends for extended periods.[6]

The advantages often cited, on the other hand, include: the comprehensiveness of information received from all sales fronts; the specialized knowledge possessed by salesmen; the possibility of breaking the

---

[5] The possible reasons are various. For instance, because of their responsibility to provide effective operation, the management may wish to give sales and plant officials a hand in the forecast in any case.

[6] Slightly adapted from *Forecasting in Industry*, Studies in Business Policy, no. 77, p. 6.

forecast down by product and territory since it was built up from that level of detail; and the fact that the forecast responsibility is coordinate with the sales responsibility. From the point of view of accuracy of the forecast, the collection of specific knowledge of customer demands for the entire market offers intriguing possibilities. It is hard to evaluate, however, because of the probable vagueness of meaning of salesmen's forecasts.

To overcome the disadvantages of the sales-force-composite method, several companies, for instance, International Harvester, Cherry-Burrell, and A. O. Smith,[7] have adopted an "area sales manager composite." The area sales managers may be in a better position to make forecasts of their areas than the salesmen themselves, especially if they maintain frequent contacts with the salesmen. The sales manager is likely to have a better understanding of competitors' activities and of general economic conditions in the area; he knows more about the plans of the management, an essential ingredient in a sales forecast.

An even more promising adaptation of the sales-force-composite method may be to eliminate entirely the fiction that forecasts are being made in the field, and to emphasize that salesmen are playing a crucial part in providing for the forecast the information available to them. One method of gathering information from the sales force is described by Crawford as follows: [8]

Early in the forecast preparation period, the forecaster notifies each salesman of the estimates desired from him. Instructions are given regarding the period to be forecast, the products to be included, the extent to which he should draw on the opinions of customers, and the time and manner of collecting the forecasts. Soon thereafter, the salesman goes over each account with his sales manager and gives consideration to any expected changes in his selling effectiveness. The estimates that result are forwarded to the forecaster for consolidation.

A salesman must be prepared to make forecasts. He may be provided with past sales figures, with special charts, and with statistical analyses of past sales variations. In many cases, however, he is not fitted either temperamentally or by training to analyze this material.

It is possible that a carefully drawn up survey could elicit desirable information without asking either the salesmen or the area sales manager for a forecast. What the sales force knows relates to the plans of customers, local conditions, and shifting sales effectiveness. Relatively simple questionnaires might readily elicit the information. Compilation in making the forecast at the central office would then be more reward-

[7] C. M. Crawford, *Sales Forecasting: Methods of Selected Firms* (Urbana, Ill.: University of Illinois Press, 1955), p. 41.
[8] *Ibid.*, p. 24.

ing because the meaning of the information would be clearer. The field information could more readily be coordinated with other forecast information developed at the central office; actually, few cases remain where sole reliance is placed on forecasts by salesmen. The salesmen could still be made to feel that they play a vital part in the forecasting process, that they are contributing the information they have at hand to the company's efforts to formulate future plans. It might be highly useful to find out from salesmen what they feel their unique understanding to be, and in so far as possible, integrate these reactions into the formulated questionnaire. Being relieved of a forecasting responsibility for which they may be poorly fitted might raise the morale of the salesmen rather than lower it.

CENTRAL OFFICE PROCEDURES IN ORGANIZING SALES FORECASTING

All sales forecasts which are used by management are coordinated in one way or another in the central office. Forecasts originating in sales offices usually pass through the hands of the sales forecaster, when there is such an officer, but in any case go to the sales manager for revisions and adjustment and in most cases are submitted for final revision to a forecasting committee composed of top executives. Somewhere in the process, the product managers are likely to review and criticize the forecasts. This procedure is typical at the present time even if other information is employed in forecasting.

A method called "jury of executive opinion," more common in the past than now, begins and ends with the "forecasting committee," whatever that group may be called in the particular company. The top executives sit down and decide what is probably going to happen. Decisions may be made by the group, or coordinated and revised by the chief officer of the committee, who may be the president of the company. Personal opinions necessarily play a large part if no source material feeds into the committee.

Even if the forecasting work actually starts with the committee, it is unlikely to end there unless an over-all company sales forecast is all that is required. The translation of the over-all forecast into product, area, financial, and other detailed estimates is likely to be delegated to assistants. Suffice it to say that at the present time it would be difficult to find many sizable companies which depend entirely on the jury-of-executive-opinion method. Forecasting work has expanded to such an extent that most companies which can afford it have some specialized personnel.

If the source material used in forecasting does not come entirely from sales offices, forecasting will originate to a greater or less extent in specialized forecasting offices. In large companies at the present time there is a tendency to have specialists making sales forecasts placed in the product divisions or in connection with these divisions. The economist's office in such cases is usually called on to supply forecasts of general economic variables, and these forecasts may be used as explanatory in making the sales forecast. The economist's office also supplies other general economic information.

The process of making the sales forecast in a company has progressed on many fronts. At one time forecasts were the sole responsibility of a forecaster who was expected recurrently to come forth with forecasts for the guidance of responsible officials in the company to the extent that the officials might decide to use the forecast. A more recent tendency is to make forecasting the responsibility of a forecasting committee composed of responsible company officials. The forecasting and planning functions thus become coordinate. The job of the forecaster becomes one of providing first approximations. He may be asked to defend these approximations, but he may be overruled. The management decides on what the forecasting guide shall be. Operations are planned in accordance with that guide. The forecasts are appraised by the forecasting committee not in terms of their accuracy, for which the forecaster is responsible, but in terms of feasibility. In this way sales forecasts become an integral part of the company's planning procedures. Crawford found that many large companies were still separating planning and forecasting in 1954 by bottling forecasting up with a forecasting specialist, although an increasing number of companies were coordinating forecasting and planning.[9]

In the following sections we discuss the most common methods employed. In actual practice, several methods are usually used in combination. The difference in application of methods is outlined below in the section on sales forecasting methods used.

USE OF INDUSTRY FORECASTS

If a comparable forecast for a particular industry is available and considered reliable, it may often be very helpful in making a sales forecast. One procedure is to project the ratio of company sales to the industry output. If the ratio has remained constant in the past, the ratio projection is merely a horizontal line; company sales are forecast as the past percentage of industry output. On the other hand, the company sales may have fluctuated more or less widely than industry output; if a rise or fall is projected in industry output, company sales will be

[9] *Ibid.*, pp. 38–39.

projected to rise or fall at a somewhat higher rate in these cases. The company may be found to have been slowly gaining or losing in relation to the growth of the industry. Growth may need to be taken into consideration, although possibly the influence will be so minor over a short period that it can be ignored.

The industry-percentage technique is attractively simple, although seldom, if ever, is it followed implicitly in practice. Company sales correlated perfectly with industry output would indeed be unusual. Even if the past relationship were found perfect, the company should be on the alert for changing relationships. If there has been a close relationship in the past, any likely deviation may be readily apparent upon careful examination. It is more probable that many exceptions have occurred, and if the relationship is to be emphasized in future forecasting, all of these exceptions should be convincingly explained. If such explanations cannot be made, the relationship can scarcely be considered of first importance in future forecasting.

Interest in industry forecasts is indicated by current surveys made by the National Electrical Manufacturers Association. Some companies are asked to estimate future sales, and the figures obtained are added to develop an industry forecast. Other companies are asked to report their own forecasts of total industry, and these are averaged to show the general expectation in the industry.

The majority of companies do not have sales which are directly comparable with those of any one industry. Breaking the company sales down into subtotals comparable with known industry groupings then becomes an essential first step. Instead of one industry comparison, several are necessary.

The distribution of the company's sales according to industry totals may be possible for only a part of the total. In such a case the other parts are not related to any industry aggregates. In some of the more specialized companies none of the company sales can be profitably compared with industry totals. And there are cases in which no industry figures are collected, although the company sales relative to industry totals may be comparable with those of other companies. Industry comparisons have limited value in some cases.

END-USE ANALYSIS

End uses vary greatly in different industries. In companies in basic industries, end uses ordinarily apply to important industries which consume the company's product in further fabrication. In industries making consumer products, end uses are a part of consumption expenditures, with the possible exception of some inventory accumulation.

The tracing of end uses may thus be quite comparable to industry comparisons, although in this case the comparison is not with the industry of which the company is a part but with industries to which it sells. If a consumer-goods industry is involved, the problem is comparable, although the tracing is to sales of consumer goods.

Probably a more dependable and convincing relationship can be developed if sales are traced to customers by given industries or consumer-expenditure groups. The sales to specific customers on which the company depends, placed in their industry relationship, makes it possible for the company to figure on its share of the markets. If a reasonably good forecast can be developed for its markets, a highly dependable sales forecast may result.

In this connection it is very important to know the current purchases of ultimate buyers. The Market Research Corporation of America is one service, among others, which offers to develop information of this kind. The ultimate-buyer information is obtained from a consumer panel, in which a sample of consumers maintain weekly records of their purchases.[10]

There are of course difficulties. If the customer relationship is not stable, little can be gained. If new customers are constantly an important and variable factor in sales, the historical relationship may be of little value. The method, however, has proved its worth in many cases. A notable case is the sale of new products to a single outlet. Such a method was used earlier for nylon and "Dacron," but when their uses multiplied, the outlet analysis became too complicated.

Even if customer relationships cannot be effectively traced, the end-use analysis may be more useful than industry-percentage analysis. The sales of a company depend on the outlook for its outlets. If the relationships are entirely commensurate, the industry sales also depend on the same outlets, but even in such a perfect case the relationship is being traced, more indirectly, to the industry rather than to the market.

ANALYSIS OF THE MARKET SITUATION

Studying the relationship of sales to orders, prices, and inventories is probably a more common tool in sales forecasting than now stated in the published summaries. Considerable reliance, apparently, is placed on these relationships by company managements in their directional influence on the work of their forecasting specialists, especially when sig-

---

[10] Other services are the A. C. Neilsen Company, which estimates bimonthly consumer purchase of grocery and drug products by studying the sales and inventories of a sample of retail stores, and Audits and Surveys, which estimates consumer purchases of consumer hard goods by a similar method. See *Business Week*, June 18, 1955, pp. 132–135.

nificant changes are occurring in market factors. Managements are impressed by changed levels shown by order books, shifts in net prices received, and changes in inventories held. The contention that these changes reflect past market conditions is generally correct, but there is an irresistible tendency to project them into the future. The projections are usually made on the basis of astute reflections on the supply and demand changes indicated. Since business executives are not in the habit of publicizing reasoning of this type, it is not readily possible to summarize the methods employed.

On the more analytical level, comparisons are made with the market situation in related industries. That these methods are widely employed is indicated by use of the market situation in forecasting individual industries, summarized in the preceding chapter. Major reliance in making individual-industry forecasts is placed on the work of the principal companies in the industries represented; the market situation is important in both industry and company forecasts.

At critical times, however, the method has sometimes led to serious error because of the deceptive movement of inventories. A manufacturer, looking at his own sales and his own inventories, may fail to recognize an inverse movement of inventories at later stages of distribution when it occurs. Part of his sales may be flowing into inventory at late stages of expansion. Analytical forecasters are more likely to catch changes of this kind than top management. As forecasting work develops, disproportionate inventory changes may come to be better understood.

SERIAL CORRELATION

A good deal of rationalization about future sales is derived from a trend projection of past sales. Crawford recommends a wider understanding of more formalized serial correlation, although it is not widely employed.[11] Several methods are possible; Crawford illustrates a quarterly sales forecast based on projection of the change in quarterly sales a year ago.[12] Such a model is called "naïve" because it is founded on simple mechanical assumptions. Specially tailored (often in a qualitative way) projections of past sales trends which take into consideration known factors in the market situation will probably perform better. But the assumptions made are more complicated and unlikely to be stated clearly. The advantage of the naïve model is that the assumptions may be made clear, stated precisely, and illustrated in a mechanical model.

---

[11] Crawford, *op cit.*, pp. 41–44.
[12] Projection of changes occurring a year ago are employed to avoid the complications of seasonal change which would be involved in projecting the most recently available quarterly change.

The comparison of results shown by the mechanical model with the forecasts actually used by the company may be very revealing. If the performance of the more complicated procedures is not superior to that of the mechanical model, an explanation is in order.

SPECIAL SURVEYS

This method bears close relations to the analysis of customer-classified end uses as well as to the sales-force-composite method. It differs from the latter in that inquiries generally originate in the central office rather than in the field, but if the modifications suggested above were made in the sales-force-composite methods, they would essentially become surveys made from the central office. Pertinent sales information would then be obtained from the sales offices. Special surveys differ from customer-classified end-use analysis in that the opinions of buyers or of persons close to them are sought, rather than following a procedure of analytical judgment in the central office.

Actually, special surveys to develop buying intentions are seldom employed except to analyze markets for very new products. The method is very expensive, and in developed markets the same type of information is obtainable from the sales force. Also, doubt is frequently expressed about whether buyers have planned their future purchases and know what they are going to buy.

In the case of new products the method is not infrequently employed by advertising agencies. Before continuing a large advertising expenditure to publicize a new product, tests may be made to develop facts on market reaction. These can be obtained only through a survey. Most frequently, a sample of potential consumers is interviewed, although in some cases reliance is placed on wholesalers and retailers because of their close contact with consumers.[13]

Other than for new products, surveys of the market for given products are usually conducted by trade associations, publishing companies, or the government. In this way the high cost of a survey can be spread

[13] Controlled experiments are sometimes used in the survey to predict market reaction to new products or to a shift in pricing policy for old products. The selling to be tested is tried out in a sample of sales outlets. The variable studied is not introduced in a paired "control" sample drawn to be otherwise as similar as possible. See William Applebaum and Richard F. Spears, "Controlled Experimentation in Marketing Research," *Journal of Marketing*, 14:505–517, 1950.

Bahm, of the General Electric Company, describes a system developed for the silicon products department to show market reaction, placing main reliance on salesmen's call reports and planning guides for all large, or potentially large, customers. See John F. Bahm, Jr., "Sales Forecasting for New Products," in *Sales Forecasting: Uses, Techniques, and Trends* (New York: American Management Association, Inc., 1956), pp. 75–80.

over many firms. Group surveys are usually one-shot affairs and are useful in sales forecasting only as bench marks.[14]

CYCLE AND SEASONAL ANALYSIS

Seasonal forecasting plays a major role in a great deal of sophisticated sales forecasting. In the petroleum industry, for instance, the sales forecast for heating oil depends largely on the weather influence on home heating. The forecast must be qualified by the statement that normal weather variations are assumed. Actually, the seasonal changes in weather vary substantially from the average, or normal, pattern, and this variation accounts for a large part of the discrepancy between the forecast and the outturn.

Frequently, seasonal changes must be anticipated even though the historical pattern is unsatisfactory for measuring the typical or normal seasonal. Such is the case in the automobile industry at the present time. Forecasters may find it necessary to employ rough temporary expedients to guess at the seasonal movement.

The seasonal problem is often sidestepped in less sophisticated analysis by putting the measurement in terms of changes from the similar month or quarter a year ago, as indicated in the mechanical illustration used in the above section on serial correlation. Although the confusion between seasonal and other short-period changes may thus be partially avoided, the seasonal changes are ignored rather than forecast. These methods are truly useful only if the explicit forecast of seasonal movement in sales is relatively unimportant.

The use of cycles in sales forecasting is largely limited to industries in which a special cycle is of major importance. The two-year textile cycle is a good illustration. Few seasoned forecasters in the textile industry would entirely ignore that cycle, but they are unlikely to make a mechanical projection from it. In the best practice the cycle aids in generalizing on the culmination of forces in the market situation over a period of a year or two, but special factors existing in marketing relations at the given time must also be taken into consideration.

In Chapter 7 we found that only limited use is made of the cycle hypothesis in forecasting changes in aggregate industry. Forecasting the total economy on the basis of the business-cycle or any mechanical-cycle pattern is seldom employed in sales forecasting today. The use of the actual influences responsible for short-term changes is more rewarding.

---

[14] For further study of the utility of special surveys in sales forecasting, see Robert Ferber, "Sales Forecasting by Sample Surveys," *Journal of Marketing*, July, 1955. Also, useful illustrations of surveys applied to new products will be found in Frank D. Newbury, *Business Forecasting* (New York: McGraw-Hill Book Company, Inc., 1952), pp. 249–259.

If the forecaster is inclined to be more mechanical, he has a range of more favorable choices than mechanical-cycle forecasting. He may project the trend which has been occurring in sales, or he may forecast on the basis of correlation with controlling variables, discussed in the following section.

CORRELATION WITH CONTROLLING VARIABLES

After World War II there was a widespread awakening to the fact that the sales of many companies were positively correlated with aggregates representing total industry. Particularly notable was the discovery by many companies that sales moved with gross national product, and time charts plotting gross national product on one vertical scale with the company's sales on the other became common. The scale for the company's sales was adjusted to bring the movement of the two series approximately together along about the same vertical levels; if the company's sales were about one ten-thousandth of gross national product, the scale differences would be adjusted accordingly. Usually, little direct logic could be established for the movement of the company's sales with gross national product. Rather, appeal had to be made to a proposition, long well known among economic analysts, that almost universally variation in individual activities is related to total economic activity. Any mechanical relationship would appear highly unlikely, however.

More promising is tracing the company's sales to some over-all economic variable to which they are logically related; for instance, company sales and F. W. Dodge Corporation contracts awarded are related by the American Radiator and Standard Sanitary Corporation.[15] The contracts series is found to lead the sales series by four months, although moving averages are first applied to both series to smooth out irregularities. The movement of sales-contracts ratios are studied over time; applied to contracts awarded in different sales districts of the company, the movement of the ratios gives some indication of the shifting proportion of the market being taken.

The contracts-awarded figures, however, are not considered to represent the only controlling variable. It is found, for instance, that construction prices show a more pronounced reaction to demand changes than do the company's prices on plumbing equipment, so that not only may the ratio from undeflated figures be distorted in periods of rapid price change, but over-all construction prices may have a greater influence on the demand for plumbing equipment than do the plumbing-equipment prices themselves. It may be desirable to put the series on a constant-dollar basis at times of rapid price change and also to arrive at a qualitative judgment regarding the influence of price change on demand. A

---

[15] See *Forecasting in Industry*, Studies in Business Policy, no. 77, pp. 26–28.

careful contrast with the shifting market situation is made at the sales-district level at all times.

In the automobile companies, great reliance is placed on disposable income as an explanatory variable. As noted in the preceding chapter in connection with the Ford Motor Company's methods of forecasting, many other explanatory variables are employed, including installment credit extended, used car prices, the demand for other durable goods, and dealer margins. Also, other more qualitative factors are taken into consideration, for instance, the influence of model changes.

In the most carefully organized forecasting work of companies which can afford a rounded program, much attention is given to the development of explanatory variables. Certainly, a better understanding of a company's future sales is obtained if the major factors responsible for changes can be developed. It is possible, of course, that no better forecast is available generally for the explanatory variable than directly for the sales themselves. If this is true, mechanical relationships are of little value for the sales forecast most of the time, but cases are likely to arise in which expected changes can be projected for the particular explanatory variable. In these cases, understanding the relationship to the explanatory variable will pay off.

The use of mechanical correlation is not ruled out in companies which build a careful forecasting program. The mechanical relationships, however, are usually used as a guide. The actual forecasting work generally proceeds on a less mechanical basis. With knowledge of the mechanical relationships indicated and understanding of many qualitative factors which should be taken into consideration, the forecast is made on a judgment basis. There may be companies in which econometric methods produce more effective results, and, in any case, the promise of these methods is likely to improve. They are considered more fully in the following section.

USE OF DEMAND FUNCTIONS

Mechanical correlation is not limited to one explanatory variable but can proceed with a multiple set of variables. In theory, the problem of forecasting sales is often considered to be ideally solved by an equation which relates company sales to a multiple set of variables which explain demand for the company's products. Such an equational relationship is properly called a "demand function." Obviously this procedure might be too complicated if the range of products is wide, in which case several demand functions might be needed.

For various reasons the use of demand functions has not usually been successful in forecasting company sales. An effort to develop functions would be worthwhile in many cases, however, if the time and effort could be spared for the work. A frontal attack on the listing and measurement of forces responsible for demand may put the problem in proper focus. If perchance an effective relationship should be developed, the conclusion need not be drawn that the resulting equation would be directly employed in effective forecasting. Clear thinking on what the explanatory variables are might be helpful, with provision of quantitative weights which show the relative importance of each explanatory variable. Furthermore, much may be learned if the best demand function which can be established performs poorly; its failure may lead to a search for the reasons why a logical formalized explanation of demand will not explain changes in demand in the short run.

Although useful, the development of a list of demand factors is far from easy. No criterion is available for making a conclusive decision about what the controlling variables are. Statistical correlation is not decisive evidence, for correlation does not demonstrate cause and effect. Theory must be looked to, but demand theory is incomplete. Furthermore, many known causal factors, such as the mood of buyers, cannot be effectively quantified.

The demand function requires data for a test period, and available data seldom are wholly satisfactory. In some cases what, in theory, appears to be a demand factor may not be representable with statistical data, and less satisfactory substitute data must be accepted as the explanatory variable. Even the company sales are seldom homogeneous and available for a long enough period to be satisfactory in computing the needed relationships.

Forecasts may not be feasible for the accepted causal factors, even if measurable. The use of a demand function to forecast assumes that forecasts can be obtained for the explanatory variables. Furthermore, it is to be expected that several explanatory variables must be used, and statistical correlation becomes less satisfactory as the number of variables is expanded.

Most important of all, even if the demand relations shown in the demand function are highly satisfactory on the average, they are unlikely to describe satisfactorily any particular short-term period. Rising prices, for instance, are negatively correlated with demand, but they may actually add to sales in the short run because still higher prices are anticipated, and thus the price rise may cause a rush to buy. Inducement to accumulate or deplete inventories is complicated and has never been effectively incorporated in a demand function applicable to behavior over a few months; average inventory accumulation over a longer period is much less difficult to describe. Deferred demand is frequently an important demand factor, but it has not been satisfactorily incorporated in a demand function. Buying surges are socially induced frequently, and the associated phenomena are not readily quantified for incorporation in a demand function.

A demand function for a complete industry is simpler than for a company. The industry relations are between total supply and total demand, but for an individual company its proportion of the total market is also a factor. Competitive strategy and the relative advantages of different companies introduce questions which cannot be easily answered by a demand function.

FILTER AND SKEPTIC'S TECHNIQUES

As a means of obtaining a record of sales forecasts made by informal appraisals, checking them against "naïve" mechanical models, and clarifying the potentialities of additional analyses, James H. Lorie has suggested what he calls filter and skeptic techniques.[16] As the mechanical model for the filter technique, Lorie suggests the mechanics outlined in the above section on serial correlation—next month's sales will differ from last month's by the percentage shown in corresponding months last year. An artificial historical forecast can be generated for comparison with the forecast actually made. By comparing both forecasts with the actual sales record, performance can be judged. Try to explain the reasons for great discrepancy of any of the forecasts, Lorie's outline of the technique continues; the reasons developed should lead to new explanatory variables. Incorporate the most promising of the indicated explanatory variables in a new model, making allowance, by a technique such as simple historical averages of past discrepancies, for new qualitative variables deemed important. Repeat the same steps by generating the new model, developing an artificial historical forecast, etc. By this scheme, less effective procedures may be filtered out and new, more promising ones adopted.

The skeptic's technique involves checking sales forecasts actually made against simple trend projections of past sales. Establish a "probability band" of two standard deviations on each side of the projected trend line, Lorie proposes. Check the forecasts made to see if they fall within this probability band. If they fail to do so, ask for reconsid-

[16] James H. Lorie, "Two Important Problems in Sales Forecasting," *Journal of Business*, vol. 30, July, 1957. In relation to the skeptic's technique, see further F. B. Newman, "Better Production Planning from Controlled Sales Forecasts," *Factory Management and Maintenance*, June, 1952, pp. 108–109; also, a description of the use of this method at the Dodge Manufacturing Company in Mishawaka, Indiana, in *Sales Forecasting: Uses, Techniques, and Trends*, pp. 128–130.

eration of the forecasts, and if the forecast still is not within the probability band, elicit reasons for breaking with the historical pattern. These techniques will not work in all cases, but they illustrate the possibility of using simple, mechanical, and economical checks to stimulate improved forecasting.

SALES-FORECASTING METHODS USED

In the spring of 1956 a survey of methods and data utilized in sales forecasting was conducted by the American Management Association among nearly three hundred businessmen attending a conference on sales forecasting in Chicago. More than 70 per cent of the group use past sales trend of the firm, sales department estimates, judgment and hunch, and general economic indicators. Only slightly less use economic data on their own industry and salesmen's field reports. Approximately half use new-product plans, competitors' activities, production capacity, market surveys, and promotion plans. It will be seen that each firm uses a wide assortment of data.[17] More than 80 per cent of the companies conduct a formal sales-forecasting program in which data from internal and external sources are evaluated and combined into a definite forecast presented to top management. The percentage varies from more than 90 for companies grossing $50 million annually to 65 for those grossing less than $10 million.

Nearly all of the companies represented in the survey prepare annual forecasts and 60 per cent prepare forecasts either quarterly or monthly, with a large proportion favoring the former. Sixty per cent of the companies, principally large in size, make long-range, i.e., longer than annual, forecasts. Forty per cent forecast at all time ranges: for a shorter period than annual, annually, and for the long range. About 15 per cent of the companies use high-speed electronic computers in processing data for sales forecasting, and others are preparing to do so. Two-thirds of

[17] *Sales Forecasting: Uses, Techniques, and Trends,* pp. 141 ff. The information used is classified by nine industry groups. Some differences appear between groups, but in general the groups are in accordance with expectation. For instance, relatively more producers of consumer nondurables than producers of consumer durables use general economic indicators. In each industry division, except for producers of consumer nondurables, services, and trade, about the same proportion use salesmen's field reports as use general economic indicators. (In the three excepted divisions, the proportion using field reports is smaller.) The differences in proportions are small enough in most comparisons so that a shift of one or two replies would eliminate the indicated significance. The precise meaning of the different types of information used is not entirely clear; the survey shows that the importance assigned to various types of information is not reflected accurately in data on the types used. Some of the companies place little emphasis on some of the methods they employ. The size of the companies represented is well above average. Almost all of the companies participating are in manufacturing.

the companies are planning some changes in their forecasting program, notably use of more data, better techniques, changes in the organizational status, and adding a forecast at an additional time range.

A furniture company provides an interesting case of a forecast said to be developed from all important available sources.[18] A field forecast is based on estimates made by each dealer and salesman; a product forecast is made by each product sales manager; and a total sales forecast is prepared by the market analyst. The field forecast depends on the "feel" of the market. The product managers' forecast depends on judgment founded on order trends, maturing research developments, competitive products, and management policy. The market analyst gives appropriate consideration to external variables. After discussion with the central office personnel involved in each of these forecasts, the general sales manager determines the sales forecast, which is approved or altered by a top-management forecasting committee. Although seldom spelled out so precisely, the use of information from similarly extensive sources may be fairly common.

A less common situation is one in which the company sales are almost wholly dependent on external influences. This may be illustrated by the work of Swift and Company, a meat packer.[19] No annual sales forecast is made because volume of production and selling prices are largely outside the control of the company management. Forecasts are made of livestock price and supply, which are of critical importance in the company's operations.

There are many companies in which sales forecasts depend principally on forecasts of general-business conditions. The Jewel Tea Company relies principally on per-capita disposable income as an explanatory variable.[20] In the Westinghouse Electric Corporation, all company forecasts are based on estimates of general-business conditions.[21] R. H. Macy and Company relies principally on factors in the general-business outlook.[22] The Eastman Kodak Company places important reliance on sales of the company's products expressed as a per cent of disposable income. A large oil company estimates the company's share of demand in the industry after forecasts are made largely by relating to specific economic aggregates, such as number of motor cars in use, average mileage, and nonhighway demand for petroleum products.[23]

---

[18] Described in *Forecasting in Industry*, pp. 39–40.

[19] *Business Forecasting: A Survey of Business Practices and Methods* (New York: Controllership Foundation, Inc., 1950), pp. 43–45.

[20] A. G. Abramson and R. H. Mack, *Business Forecasting in Practice: Principles and Cases* (New York: John Wiley & Sons, Inc., 1956), pp. 174–178.

[21] *Forecasting in Industry*, pp. 37–39.

[22] *Business Forecasting: A Survey of Business Practices and Methods*, pp. 46–47.

[23] *Forecasting in Industry*, pp. 36–37.

RELATION BETWEEN SALES AND AGGREGATE
INDUSTRY FORECASTING

Sales of most individual companies are closely, but not wholly, dependent upon the movement of total economic activity. No doubt, until recently, assumptions were too glibly made that sales forecasts could be mechanically derived from total-industry forecasts.[24] Roos put the emphasis on general-business conditions in its extreme form in 1948: "In fact, it may be argued that successful management is the result of ability to diagnose external trends quickly and to devise adequate counteracting or reinforcing policies."[25] Successful sales forecasters emphasize the importance of general-business forecasting. For instance, Hoadley, of Armstrong Cork Company, states, "Since the company sales forecast must take full cognizance of 'outside' factors, it is important to begin by directing attention to *general business prospects*. Chart historical relations between company sales and key measures of national or regional business activity."[26]

However, depending on the situation in which the individual company is placed, sales forecasting need not necessarily start with general-business forecasting. In most cases a check against the general-business prospect is needed somewhere along the line, but there are cases for which even that may be unimportant, as noted below. Whether it is appropriate to start with a general-business forecast depends on the importance of general economic aggregates as explanatory variables and on the business policy of the particular company. If business policy emphasizes starting with forecasts developed in the sales offices, material revisions must be considered likely at the central office in case major economic aggregates are explanatory variables.

For some companies the influence of general economic conditions is minor. It is possible, although unusual, that a company's sales may depend almost entirely upon the company's changing competitive position and scarcely at all on prospects in its industry. Some industries, like many services, are insensitive to minor over-all business changes. New and rapidly growing industries may not decline with a business reces-

---

[24] Crawford emphasizes that medium-sized and smaller companies particularly rely on the statements of experts for general-business forecasts and concentrate their own work on sales forecasts. See C. M. Crawford, *op. cit.*, pp. 36–38. T. G. MacGowan, of Firestone Tire and Rubber Company, has expressed the opinion that even an untrained person in a small company could develop a satisfactory general-business forecast. See his "Forecasting Sales," *Harvard Business Review*, vol. 27, November, 1949.

[25] C. F. Roos, *Charting the Course of Your Business: Measuring the Effects of External Influences* (New York: Funk & Wagnalls Company, 1948), p. 7.

[26] Walter E. Hoadley, "Developing and Utilizing the Sales Forecast," *Management Review*, vol. 40, December, 1951, pp. 755–756.

sion, although a slackening of growth is probable; however, the growth may also slacken as much at other times because of market changes within the industry itself.

In any case, the particular conditions in a company usually play some part in explaining its outlook unless the position is like that of Swift and Company, noted above, with sales and prices, over a short period almost wholly dependent on the flow of livestock to market. The company may have broken into a new and expanding market, may have added a new large contract, may be in a particularly desirable inventory position, may have a particularly favorable product capacity in light of current demand, or, of course, the opposite conditions may prevail. As a minimum, the specific conditions of the company should be taken into careful consideration.

LONG-RANGE SALES FORECASTS

Although emphasis has been placed on short-range forecasts in the past, rapid capital expansion in recent years has led to the wide initiation of long-term forecasting work. In a survey conducted by the National Industrial Conference Board in 1956, nearly 150 of almost 200 companies responding say they make forecasts for periods longer than a year. About a third of the companies forecast five years ahead and about a tenth as far as ten years. The majority make long-term forecasts on a regular periodic basis and report frequent revisions.[27]

Sales and industry forecasts are similar at the long-period time range (see industry forecasts in Chapter 5), except that estimates are required for market share. An oil company reports that its "long-term [five-year] forecast of sales is a mathematical projection of share-of-the-market modified by executive opinions on matters such as new product development, competitive activity, price trends, and the company's sales policies."[28] The Westinghouse Electric Corporation makes five-year forecasts of about ten over-all economic aggregates, and these are used as explanatory variables for the company's total- and individual-product sales. The Union Carbide and Carbon Corporation, as revised in 1957, states that it uses various aggregate economic data for long-range sales forecasts, including: gross national product and expenditure divisions; population, labor force and manhour productivity; total industrial production, production of basic materials and of major industries consuming plastics; personal income and distribution; and consumer and wholesale prices.

[27] Arthur D. Baker, Jr., and G. Clark Thompson, "Executives Find Long-range Planning Pays Off," *Conference Board Business Record*, 13: 435–443, October, 1956.
[28] *Forecasting in Industry*, pp. 36–37.

The electric utility companies have had long experience in making long-term sales forecasts. The Cleveland Electric Illuminating Company uses the same explanatory variables in making long-term (five-year) forecasts as in making short-term forecasts; this company's short-term forecast was described in Chapter 9. We noted there the methods employed in forecasting each type of service; for instance, added residential customers depend on residential starts, and the average kilowatt-hour consumption per customer is forecast by a trend projection, qualitative allowance being made for anticipated changes in the use of appliances. The relative stability of the consumer market for power lends some justification to the use of the same controlling variables as for long-term forecasts. The long-range forecasts of the Cleveland Electric Illuminating Company are less detailed than the short-term.

At Lockheed, the sales of aircraft and missiles for defense are projected to rise on a fairly stable trend somewhat less than in the rapid expansion from 1949 to 1954, but smoothing out any wide fluctuations such as those which occurred at the end of the war. In visualizing the secular growth both of military and commercial business, emphasis is placed on corporate capabilities and limitations: notably, ability to make further market penetration, financial ability to acquire new research and development facilities, time required to develop and put new models into production, and limited availability to the corporation of certain types of manpower.[29]

Little is known about the methods of forecasting used by the large number of companies which have recently initiated long-term forecasts. Probably many of these forecasts are on a preliminary basis and under frequent readjustment. Some of the comments made by respondents in the National Industrial Conference Board survey tend to confirm that conclusion: 15 executives of smaller companies indicate lack of faith in their long-term forecasting work; many say they use forecasts only as a guide (possibly meaning they do not place much reliance on them); some point to difficulties in the forecasts of departments, which are thought to use them to outbid each other.[30]

USE OF SALES FORECASTS

The major use of long-term forecasts is in planning capital expansion. The large-oil-company forecast, noted above, is said to be used in planning capital expansion, new product developments, long-range exploitation of markets, and long-term fiscal policies.[31] The Cleveland Elec-

[29] *Long-range Planning in an Expanding Economy*, General Management Series, no. 179 (New York: American Management Association, Inc., 1956).

[30] Baker and Thompson, *loc. cit.*

[31] *Forecasting in Industry*, p. 37.

tric Illuminating Company states that its long-term forecasts are made to help in determining (1) the adequacy of the rate schedule, (2) future loads and proper scheduling of construction to insure sufficient capacity to meet loads required, and (3) the timing, method, and amount of new financing. An executive of an aircraft company states, "We rely on our long-range planning in the short-run situation to analyze and determine the desirability of proposed projects. We rely on long-range planning to promote and guide sales and development of engineering programs as the one formal means we have of tying in the efforts of the company to grow and improve its operations." [32] The controller of a textile company reports that prior to the introduction of long-range planning, there was lack of coordination, inadequate provision for financing, continual disruption of organizational structure, and nothing to force the elimination of marginal operations.[33] Other executives suggest that long-range plans help avoid hasty decisions and provide a way of keeping abreast of competitors in a rapidly growing economy. Some companies suggest that long-range forecasting helps in planning for personnel needs as well as for capital and financial needs. Executives in the steel industry emphasize long-range forecasting in planning material requirements. Some companies find long-term forecasting useful in indicating the size and direction of research and development programs. Long-range forecasting aids in establishing standard costs because these depend on the selection of a normal production level for the distribution of fixed costs.

At the opening of this chapter we emphasized the use of short-term sales forecasts in budget making. The sales budget, however, is not an end in itself. Budget making has often been looked on as a process of coordination only, with proportionate distribution of expenditures considered satisfactory. Budgets which assume an incorrect sales level will require revision, and proportionate revision usually is not satisfactory. With rising sales, some expenditures should increase relatively more than others. The proportionate budget set at past sales levels fails to keep a satisfactory control on expenditures.

Perhaps the most important use of short-term sales forecasting is in scheduling production. With knowledge of future sales, schedules can be set to provide for smooth operations. Unwanted inventories can be at least partially avoided, and, as long as materials and labor time are readily available, inventories can be kept up to satisfactory levels if sales should rise. Cash funds will not be tied up in unwanted inventory expansion or temporarily built up to high levels by embarrassing inventory runoff. Work periods for employees can be established well in advance. Of course, sales forecasts will not help in these respects if completely invalid.

[32] Baker and Thompson, *loc. cit.*
[33] *Ibid.*

The Otis Elevator Company has for many years used sales forecasts to control inventories. The high inventories necessary in relation to sales in this business stimulated the company to develop its plan. Estimated inventories of parts are projected in the light of sales forecasts. Inventory standards are established item by item, but an important point is to recognize maximums and minimums as well as normal levels and ordering points. There are likely to be wide and unpredictable variations in sales from week to week, and inventories have to absorb the shocks. The establishment of maximum and minimum points allows for temporary variations, and the longer-term sales forecast acts as a guide and makes it possible to avoid disastrously high or low inventory levels. In the case of final products, production rates are established by projecting expected backlogs. Starting with actual backlogs, the projected sales (quarterly for a year in advance) establish the movement to be expected for the backlog of unfilled orders. The production schedule is set to move commensurately with the expected level of unfilled orders.[34]

The use of short-term sales forecasts in production planning is considered to be most important in the automobile industry, where procurement of materials and parts is usually scheduled six months ahead, and car assemblies are scheduled about three months ahead. Revisions are made monthly, based on weekly estimates of consumer buying.

Production planning has been extensively used in many companies to stabilize seasonal production schedules. These are cases in which the typical seasonal movement of sales is quite regular and the product is readily storable. Inventories are made to rise in off-season periods and to fall in peak periods, with production rates holding nearly horizontal. The Eastman Kodak Company has been notably successful in applying this method.[35] Probably there are not many companies which have failed to adopt the method if they can use it successfully. On the other hand, with better sales forecasts, many companies would place greater emphasis on production planning for less regular seasonal and other variations.

The flow of cash funds is closely geared to sales. Most large companies plan cash requirements on the basis of sales forecasts. The larger the sales, the larger the receipt of funds. Substantial economies are possible by avoiding either unduly large or unduly small cash balances.

The planning of employees' work time can save money and improve labor relations. Overtime frequently can be largely avoided by scheduling production well in advance. Calling on employees on short notice to work more or less than planned is likely to cause some friction. If

---

[34] *Forecasting in Industry*, pp. 71–73, especially the chart on p. 73.

[35] See Elmer C. Bratt, *Business Cycles and Forecasting*, 4th ed. (Homewood, Ill.: Richard D. Irwin, Inc., 1953), pp. 29–30.

employees feel that production is well planned, they will have more confidence in the management and in the security of their jobs.

Forecasts make it possible to set more realistic sales quotas. The use of such quotas has generally proved worthwhile, but quotas which are too low provide no incentive, and those which are too high are likely to be discouraging. The sales forecast helps direct sales effort. Forecasts are based both on market potentialities and sales effort, and in some sales territories the forecast may be exceeded because of exceptionally effective selling.

Advertising expenditures are planned on the basis of sales forecasts. From long experience it has been found that the effectiveness of advertising depends on the changes which take place in sales.

Industry-administered prices are most profitably established on the basis of the sales outlook. Knowing the volume of sales to expect, prices can be set "dynamically," in accordance with expected future costs and volume rather than in relation to past costs. Actual sales volume tends to be maximized with the maintenance of a fair profit.[36]

[36] See further uses of the sales forecast reported by participants in the American Management Association's conference on sales forecasting, presented early in the following chapter.

CHAPTER 11

The Sales Forecast: Company Practices

For most companies a sales forecast sets a sales goal in an anticipated market. As stated by B. E. Estes of the United States Steel Corporation: [1]

We should recognize that what we are in the habit of calling a "sales fore-cast" is really a market forecast, plus a sales goal in the expected market, based on carrying out successfully a sales plan for achieving a desirable and feasible degree of penetration into that market.

This chapter is devoted to an analysis of procedures and forms of organization that make effective use of a sales forecast possible, and to a description of forecasting methods employed by twelve companies.

By its very nature, the sales forecast is generally less accurate than an industry forecast. This is true for two reasons. (1) The sales forecast implies an estimate of the industry, product, or other market potential to which the company's sales are related. The company's forecast of sales, representing but a part of the total market potential, is likely to reflect greater variation because it is less subject to the averaging-out stability of a larger total. (2) The sales forecast implies an estimate of the company's market penetration. Even if the company made a perfect estimate of the market potential, the sales forecast would be wrong if the influence of marketing methods and practices were wrongly estimated.

Business managements are careful to ascertain in advance whether there is a reasonable possibility that effective performance can be expected. Perfection is not sought, but the forecast must be accurate enough to make planning in terms of the indicated level worthwhile.[2]

---

[1] B. E. Estes, "What Management Expects of Forecasting," in *Sales Forecasting: Uses, Techniques, and Trends* (New York: American Management Association, Inc., 1956), p. 13.

[2] See C. M. Crawford, *Sales Forecasting: Methods of Selected Firms* (Urbana, Ill.: University of Illinois Press, 1955), pp. 15–16. Crawford points out that the company may find purposeful distortion useful; the most likely forecast figure may be raised to provide a goal or lowered to establish a conservative safety limit.

The rapid increase in the use of explicit sales forecasting indicates that managements increasingly expect sales forecasting to be useful.

Expectation that sales forecasting will be useful involves much more than confidence in its accuracy. It represents acceptance of the validity of some approach to the type of business operation described in this chapter. The effective use of sales forecasting changes standards of operation. Planning in terms of sales forecasts usually leads to the adoption of sales and cash budgets and implies a new set of management controls, as developed below.

WHO PARTICIPATES IN MAKING THE SALES FORECAST

The primary responsibility for the sales forecast most often falls on a marketing executive. In the survey conducted by the American Management Association at its sales-forecasting conference in the spring of 1956, two-thirds of the companies stated that control fell in the marketing department.[3] There is some difficulty here, however, because the titles of executives charged with the forecasting responsibility, as well as the names of departments, may be deceptive. A forecasting executive may have various titles, but if his sole job is forecasting, the difference in title is of little moment. Central responsibility for sales forecasting may be placed in the marketing department, but the rules of line reporting may not be the same as those which apply in other marketing departments. Because of the nature of his function, the forecasting executive may, in some cases, be as answerable to other executives as to the vice-president in charge of sales.

In about half of the companies represented in the American Management Association's survey, the market research department participates in developing the sales forecast.[4] Nearly half of the production departments participate. Other participating departments are: finance, slightly over 40 per cent; product development, slightly over 30 per cent; advertising and promotion, slightly over 25 per cent. A scattering of participation by such departments as engineering, purchasing, economic research, and planning and by individual product managers was also reported. The manufacturers of consumer goods use the advertising and

---

[3] *Sales Forecasting: Uses, Techniques, and Trends,* pp. 145 ff. Ninety-five per cent of the companies covered in the survey were in manufacturing. The distribution on the length of forecasts made and on the relation between forecasting effort and size of company agrees in general with John A. Howard's more representative sample of 30 corporations. A summary of 22 cases will be found in *Company Organization for Economic Forecasting,* Research Report, no. 28 (New York: American Management Association, Inc., 1957). For Howard's sample see "A Note on Corporate Financing Practices," *Journal of Business,* 27:101–105, 1954.

[4] *Sales Forecasting: Uses, Techniques, and Trends,* p. 146.

promotion department relatively more frequently in making the forecast than do other companies.

As shown by the survey, the use of the sales forecast is in no way commensurate with participation in making it. The uses are indicated as follows: [5]

	Per cent of companies
Sales	97
Production planning	89
Budget preparation	86
Earnings forecast	76
Equipment and facilities planning	68
Setting sales quotas	63
Manpower planning	57
Raw materials stockpiling	54
Promotion planning	43
Other	8

For various reasons, there is no assurance that these proportions are representative. They do, however, indicate clearly that use of the forecast is wider than participation in making it.

On the average, the survey shows that three departments participate in making the forecast. In a few companies only one department is involved and in some companies as many as six or seven. Five years ago only half of the companies placed centralized primary responsibility for the forecast on one person or at least on one department; today the percentage is over 80.[6]

SUPPLEMENTARY FORECASTS

To be useful, the sales forecast must be broken down to show what its implications are for various areas. The actual breakdown required varies substantially from one company to another. Most companies making more than one product require separate forecasts by products. If the company has formalized a production plan to foster production scheduling, inventory forecasts are required and perhaps forecasts of new and unfilled orders (depending on the nature of the production plan adopted). The production plan may also call for price forecasts, but these are made independently of the sales forecast. Sometimes the forecast is made on a product-unit basis, and when it is, the importance of the price forecast is reduced in some applications.

Financial forecasting is relatively new, but some companies have found it rewarding, and it seems to be spreading rapidly. Full-blown

[5] *Ibid.,* p. 147.
[6] *Ibid.,* pp. 144 ff.

financial planning requires long-term as well as short-term sales forecasts because plant and equipment expenditures represent a major cash drain. The key figures in financial planning are cash flows, and these depend to an important extent upon the funds required for inventories and the funds derived from sales. A forecast of profits becomes essential. The immaturity of forecasting is indicated by the fact that there are still companies which operate with a dual system: one forecast for sales planning and quota making, and another for financial-control purposes.[7] Presumably, a clash occurs between the methods and outlook of the sales manager and the comptroller. Well-developed production planning involves additional problems, and both the sales and the financial perspective might come to depend on the outlook employed in production scheduling. Production planning may be a catalyst that forces a single sales forecast.

In national companies, forecasts probably will be required for each sales territory. Forecasts may be required for different types of customers. If sales go through more than one channel of distribution, forecasts may be needed for sales in each channel. Other special kinds of forecasts may be required, but we may assume that the kind of detail generally needed has been illustrated. Detail like forecast by sales territory and product is useful to the sales organization. Production and financial planning may involve other details essential for building management perspectives, as developed more fully below.

REFORECASTING REQUIRED

If a forecast is worth making, it is worth keeping up to date. One problem is that the forecaster may come to feel that he has committed himself and that a revision implies he was wrong. He may adopt the rationalization that new information does not change the outlook, even though his forecast might have been different if he were starting from scratch with the new information. Rich, of the United States Steel Corporation, has called such a tendency the "law of the too heavy anchor."[8] To be useful, the forecaster must keep an open mind.

MacGowan, of the Firestone Tire and Rubber Company, holds that a forecast should be reviewed once a month, since forecasting and planning should be a continuous process or nearly so.[9] More and more

[7] *Ibid.*, p. 9. Richard D. Crisp states that at the conference a sharp difference in opinion on whether there should be two forecasts was apparent, as well as a sharp difference in practice.

[8] James L. Rich, "Techniques and Uses of Forecasts of General Business Conditions in U.S. Steel," *Proceedings of the Business and Economic Statistics Section, American Statistical Association*, Washington, 1956.

[9] Thomas G. MacGowan, "When and How Forecasts Should Be Reviewed and Revised," in *Sales Forecasting: Uses, Techniques, and Trends*, pp. 98–108.

companies are coming to forecast twelve months ahead at each quarter and to place less emphasis on the annual forecast for the calendar year. This automatically opens the forecast to revision every quarter.

There may be limits to the desirability of revising forecasts. Slight changes in perspective within a very short period may be more disturbing than helpful. The evidence is, though, that sales forecasters almost universally err in the direction of making too little revision. If the forecast is an important management tool, it is necessary that the best current information be applied at all times. The calendar for revision needs to be worked out within each company in terms of the use made of the forecast and the degree of revision which would indicate a significant shift in perspective.

In reviewing the forecast there is an opportunity to study the factors affecting sales. The strength or weakness of the market for given products may be highlighted by the revisions which have become necessary.

THE ORGANIZATION OF FORECASTING

The location of the forecasting function shown in organization charts is often deceptive, because forecasting is a service required by a number of departments. No single department can have exclusive control over the forecasting process because use of the forecast by other departments will entail some responsibility to them. Nevertheless, the organization chart affects the functioning of the forecasting process, and brief notice should be given to it.

In early developments, forecasting work was almost universally attached to the sales department. A parallel, but much less common, development was the establishment of sales forecasting in accounting or treasury departments. The purposes were different, and sometimes two different forecasts came to be made by the same company. The sales manager might be thinking in terms of a "high-level sales forecast to stimulate salesmen's effort or to justify a higher sales department budget or advertising appropriation." [10] The chief financial officer, on the other hand, is faced with holding down expense budgets and maintaining a safe cash position. As noted elsewhere in this chapter, such differences could not exist with well-coordinated planning.

Adding to the patchwork was the superimposing of an office to report on general economic conditions, manned by professional economists and statisticians. Initially this office was usually attached to a top-policy officer or a financial officer. The pressure for adding the office grew out of experience with general business recessions, particularly 1920–21,

---

[10] Frank D. Newbury, *Business Forecasting: Principles and Practice* (New York: McGraw-Hill Book Company, Inc., 1952), p. 17.

1929–32, and 1937–38. In those businesses where general economic conditions play a major part in the set of controlling variables, the sales forecasts often perform poorly when the movement of the general economy begins to attain some momentum. However, the economist's office usually is advisory, and the full step of integrating it with planning has not been made. In the Controllership Foundation survey, 26 of the 37 corporations interviewed in 1949–50 had business research staffs of professional caliber, but in only five cases did the general-business forecast attain the status of an officially approved corporation forecast.[11] It is much more common for the sales forecast to receive official sanction.

Two major methods for seeking agreement on sales forecasts are utilized. Newbury calls them the low-level and the top-level approaches.[12] The low-level approach involves a committee of knowledgeable staff members who develop and use the forecast. The committee is required to come to a majority agreement, with no record being made of minority opinion. Top management sees only the majority report and, if unimpressed, may decide to develop another forecast by a method similar to the jury of executive opinion described in the preceding chapter. The range of opinions expressed in the working committee is unavailable to top management in reaching its decision.

The top-level approach, on the other hand, places the responsibility for a single sales forecast with top management. All the departments interested in the forecast consult with each other unofficially, and agreement may result. If the departments do not agree, each presents its position to top management.

Crawford notes the tendency to shift from a market-research forecasting division under the sales department to a commercial research department attached at a higher echelon, perhaps to the executive vice-president.[13] This occurs in recognition of the fact that sales forecasting is becoming more closely coordinated with planning, which is a top-management responsibility. Crawford suggests further that, instead of a commercial research department attached to the executive vice-president, what may be required is an operation-planning-and-research department attached to the executive vice-president, with production-planning and sales-planning subdivisions. He found no companies which had actually evolved this form, but he felt it to be a logical outgrowth of the emphasis on implementing forecasts with planning. In many companies interviewed by Crawford, there were objections to the trend of pushing the planning function up to higher management levels, the contention being that planning must be tied closely to daily operations.

[11] *Business Forecasting: A Survey of Business Practices and Methods* (New York: Controllership Foundation, Inc., 1950); Newbury, *ibid.*, pp. 18, 21.

[12] Newbury, *ibid.*, pp. 21–23.

[13] Crawford, *op. cit.*, pp. 55–57.

It is unnecessary to attempt to anticipate the outcome of the organizational shifts now in progress. From our point of view the important fact is that increased emphasis is being placed on use of the sales forecast in coordination and planning. We may, however, quote Dodge, of the Aluminum Company of Canada, on the requirements of organization: [14]

> It seems to me that there are only two alternative methods of organization for forecasting. One is to set up a centralized planning or forecasting department, from which all forecasts originate, for use by all departments. The other is to decentralize the forecasting to each department that requires it. The first choice necessitates the accumulation of experts on the detailed problems of each department in order to interpolate them into the over-all situation. This, obviously, is difficult to achieve, and when achieved leads to considerable duplication of effort. The second choice leads to forecasts that do not "hang together." In my opinion, the best system is a compromise of the two basic alternatives, with the sales forecast serving as the central core and being distributed to other departments for the elaboration and detailed interpretation which those departments can most efficiently provide.

PLANNING, COORDINATION, AND EXECUTION

Realization that sales forecasting is essential to planning and coordination is spreading among companies. Forecasting establishes the basis for budgeting the future on an anticipatory basis, and budgeting is an essential background for planning. To avoid the onus of the term "budget," some companies refer to the budget as a "profit plan." The budget in this connection is used as a yardstick to measure performance; distaste for budgets arises largely because they have been used as a goad to greater efforts.

Curran, of General Foods Corporation, states that "forecasting and budgeting are the basis of 'operation planning,' which in turn is the essential basis of efficient management. Forecasting and budgeting together are like the agenda of a meeting. They outline the desired goals of the business and program the managerial decisions by which the goals shall be achieved." [15]

The interrelations of various aspects of the business are increasingly stressed. As these interrelations are more fully traced, the necessity for interchange of information throughout the company becomes obvious.

---

[14] James D. Dodge, "The Use of Sales Forecasts by Other Departments," in *Sales Forecasting: Uses, Techniques, and Trends*, pp. 81 ff.

[15] N. J. Curran, Jr., "Coordinating Budgets with Forecasting," in *Charting the Company's Future*," Financial Management Series, no. 108 (New York: American Management Association, Inc., 1954).

Although the sales department has frequently felt itself to be independent of the planning of financial operations, Robert R. Zisette, of SKF Industries, emphasizes the dependence: "The sales executive cannot possibly discharge his inventory responsibility unless he has the necessary checking tools, which only the financial department can give him. If costs go up but prices stand still, a comfortable inventory position may soon become a distressing one." [16] The tendency is toward business planning which forces close coordination of various types of forecasting work. If uncoordinated, sales forecasting may apply *separately* one or more of the uses noted at the end of the preceding chapter. If top management finds it desirable to plan on the basis of anticipations indicated by sales forecasts, the coordinated effect may be to add to the importance of the sales forecast. G. A. Mitchell, of the National Biscuit Company, states: [17]

> The preparation of a tentative forecast will not, in itself, guarantee maximum profits. It will, however, provide an orderly process for developing the kind of information that will help management to evaluate the profit potential and establish company goals. Of course, conditions vary from company to company, and any such plan must be adapted to the particular problems of each organization. But as a method of developing company objectives and establishing plans and policies to meet these objectives, this procedure is a management tool that has proven its value.

NEED FOR LONG-TERM FORECASTS IN PLANNING

The more highly coordinated the planning of a company becomes, the more long-term, as well as short-term, forecasts come to lay the foundation for current action. Curran says, "Only when we had settled by means of a long-range forecast where we were going and how we were going to get there could we make more specific profit plans for the immediate future." [18] Roberts, of Bell and Howell Company, states, "Flexibility is a must in a 60-month program. Looking ahead five years from a constantly moving current date makes planning for the immediate 12-month period easier." [19]

In a highly coordinated system, short-term plans merge into long-term

[16] Robert R. Zisette, "What the Finance Executive Can Do for the Sales Department," in *Coordination and Communication Problems of the Financial Executive,* Financial Management Series, no. 109 (New York: American Management Association, Inc., 1954), pp. 11–16.

[17] G. A. Mitchell, "Mapping Realistic Company Goals: A Tested Approach," *Management Review,* October, 1956.

[18] N. J. Curran, Jr., *op. cit.,* p. 42. Curran is describing the profit plan for Instant Maxwell House Coffee.

[19] Charles H. Percy and William E. Roberts, "Planning the Basic Strategy of a Medium-sized Business," in Edward C. Bursk and Dan H. Fenn (eds.), *Planning the Future Strategy of Your Business* (New York: McGraw-Hill Book Company, Inc., 1956), pp. 18–37.

plans. Plant and equipment, materials, personnel, and other basic needs are gauged by the long-term plan. Current production and sales as well as expansion plans are to some extent judged against the longer-term anticipation. It is true that the long-term forecast is not just an extension of the short-term; the long-term forecast gives the average, instead of the actual, situation of the future. However, in forcing the elimination of marginal operations and in developing perspective on expanding operations, long-term planning puts current coordination of production, inventories, expenditures, and cash flows on a more solid foundation. The short-period forecast guides the planning from month to month, and the long-period forecast gives the planning direction. Decisions must be made to take chances in the positive or negative direction. The future general level of sales also helps in establishing sound personnel policy and in the setting up of financial arrangements.

THE SALES BUDGET

The two most vital tools in short-range planning are the sales budget and the cash budget. Profit plans, as noted above, are founded on these budgets. Management control of operations is coming to be established by use of these budgets in an increasing number of companies.

The sales budget is based on the sales forecast. Costs are calculated and prorated by procedures adapted to measure performance, as noted below. The sales forecast is broken down by product lines for each time unit and perhaps by geographical regions. A variation which sometimes occurs is the building up of the over-all sales forecast from product and regional projections, but ordinarily the total sales forecast will be controlling, as indicated in the preceding chapter. An indication of profits is obtained by taking the difference between anticipated sales receipts and costs as established for the sales budget.[20]

The profits picture as developed by the sales budget may differ substantially from that shown by the conventional income account. To begin with, the sales budget deals with anticipated rather than actual results, but that is not the only difference. The cost used with the sales budget are standard costs, predetermined figures, setting a pattern for

---

[20] As a method of simplification, we speak of the sales budget as including both cost and profit estimates, although it is a frequent practice to speak of these as separate budgets. For fuller analysis of the sales budget the following references are suggested: Glenn A. Welsch, *Budgeting: Profit Planning and Control* (Englewood Cliffs, N.J.; Prentice-Hall, Inc., 1957); I. Wayne Keller, *Management Accounting for Profit Control* (New York: McGraw-Hill Book Company, Inc., 1957); L. L. Bethel and others, *Production Control* (New York: McGraw-Hill Book Company, Inc., 1942); W. Rautenstrauch and R. Villers, *Budgetary Control* (New York: Funk & Wagnalls Company, 1950).

performance at production levels appropriate for the control established. Furthermore, a technique called "direct costing," which excludes some or all fixed factory expenses from inventory values, is often employed. The fixed expenses are charged directly against the profit or loss of the period in which they are incurred.[21] The resulting profit estimate is a management tool, and more useful to management than if it were based on more traditional accounting procedures.[22] This fact has been illustrated by G. J. Barry, of Continental Can Company: [23]

> I can recall instances where some plants in our company have had an exceptionally heavy production schedule for a few months because it was necessary to build up inventories in anticipation of a seasonal pack of fruits or vegetables. During such months, the volume of production was many times greater than the sales volume. Prior to our use of the direct costing technique, the element of fixed cost was included in the standard cost which was used as the basis for charging inventory with the cost of production. When the actual monthly production was far in excess of one-twelfth of the annual production, we charged inventory with more fixed cost than was actually incurred and an over-absorption of fixed cost resulted. In short, we were creating a profit by producing for inventory. We even encountered instances where the amount of the monthly profit actually exceeded the amount of the month's sales. Obviously, profits were tied to production volume rather than sales volume. An accounting system that produced a profit in excess of sales volume just didn't make sense to our operating executives, and understandably so. Since changing to direct costing, we no longer have to contend with the under- or over-absorption of overhead and its effects on profits.

Production is budgeted to meet the requirements for estimated sales. Inventory variation accounts for the difference between production and sales. In some cases, inventory of finished product is planned to vary somewhat in order to keep seasonal production on a more even keel than sales. Plans will also depend on the adequacy of inventory levels at the beginning of the period and on the general direction of movement forecast for sales. Production budgets usually start with individual manu-

---

[21] See I. Wayne Keller, *ibid.*, pp. 121–131.

[22] Charles B. Stauffacher, "The Scope of the System," in *Charting the Company's Future,* Financial Management Series no. 108 (New York: American Management Association, Inc., 1954), pp. 9–10. Stauffacher, of the Continental Can Company, contrasts the result with conventional income accounting: "This may suggest a conflict in our approach to profit-planning between what we might call a 'standards' outlook and an 'income estimate' outlook. We try to recognize both these elements in putting costs into a profit plan, yet handle each of them in a way which will make them most useful as both guide to and information on our operations. Simply stated, our method is to make the first calculation on a standards basis and to use management judgment in adjusting these data wherever it appears necessary in the light of historical experience and our operating plans."

[23] G. J. Barry, "Techniques of Control," in *Charting the Company's Future,* pp. 15–22.

facturing departments, which are cumulated to compile a total production budget for the company. A first step therefore is to set up sales forecasts for the part of the company's business to be accounted for by each individual department. As Dodge says, "the sales forecast should really be able to serve as the production schedule—assuming, as we are, that the forecast is accurate." [24]

The budget of production is concerned with materials, labor, and overhead or indirect costs. For materials, past records on the materials absorbed at given levels of production are usually guiding, but may require substantial adjustment if the product mix is expected to change. Also, allowance must be made for the adequacy of material and in-process inventories at the beginning of the period and for the expected change in sales over the period.

Labor cost is budgeted on the basis of past payroll records, making allowance for any expected change in rate or in amount of overtime, etc. Some overhead costs vary with production, and techniques for estimating them are relatively obvious, given the production schedule. A large part of overhead is taken as fixed, regardless of the level of production.[25]

James L. Peirce, of the A. B. Dick Company, provides a good summary of the planning process involved: [26]

> To construct a sales plan, we must predetermine products, markets, prices, outlets, promotion methods, and advertising media. We must integrate volume with anticipated sales costs, because the costs are relied upon to produce the sales. We must plan product development and introduction—and, in turn, research costs. We must preestablish production schedules, inventories, purchase prices for materials. We must set estimates of administrative and financial costs—yes even of taxes. . . . Obviously the process demands of the president himself a high degree of coordination, in order that planning may be done consistently by all divisions of the company. It also demands that the division heads work together with a common purpose and a single definition of operating assumptions.

He also recognizes the necessity of maintaining constant awareness that the actual sales might deviate unduly from the sales forecast on which the budget is based: [27]

> In spite of this background, you sense, in the attitudes surrounding your budget, a suggestion of flexibility. If conditions change suddenly, the budget

---

[24] Dodge, *op. cit.*, pp. 81–87.

[25] Sometimes a variable budget allowance is used to permit variation with the level of production. A least-squares method of doing this is illustrated in Glenn A. Welsch, *op. cit.*, pp. 182–192.

[26] James L. Peirce, "Budgets and People: A Positive Approach," in *Guides to Modern Financial Planning* (New York: American Management Association, Inc., 1953), pp. 3–13.

[27] *Ibid.*, p. 8.

will have to be altered, and this adjustment might be either up or down. You are not uneasy about this prospect. You are simply alert to recognize such a situation if it should develop.

The Bausch and Lomb Optical Company has set up an interesting control system in connection with its sales budget.[28] The company's products and parts are so numerous that they must be reduced to a product classification rather than forecast item by item. A systematic comparison is kept of the relation between budget and actual outturn for each of 22 product classifications. Five charts are set up for each classification to highlight the comparison: (1) the accumulated amount by which sales are over or under the budget is shown month by month from the beginning of the year; (2) the actual sales are plotted against the budgeted sales each month; (3) the accumulated increase or decrease of actual inventory from the budgeted level is shown month by month from the beginning of the year; (4) the actual amount of material is plotted monthly against the budgeted amount; (5) the actual labor is plotted monthly against the budgeted labor.

Controls by product classifications do not provide any indication of the sales of individual items. A relatively small part of the total items accounts for the majority of the sales in the Bausch and Lomb Optical Company, and therefore a selective control is maintained for these items. The control is flexible and depends upon the problems apparent at the moment.

The company finds that some items are bought on a new-order basis several months in advance of sales (shipments). A predictive control is set up for these items, assuming an average lead for new orders, new orders being compared with forecast sales.

THE CASH BUDGET

A cash budget represents a forecast of the cash position and the distributed sources and uses of funds. To attain maximum coordination, the cash budget should be founded on the same sales forecast as used in the sales budget. If the management team is working toward a common goal, the impact of combined efforts can be substantially enhanced. Expenditures in the company are dependent upon funds made available by the treasurer or comptroller, and these officers are vitally dependent upon the sales of the company for funds to disperse.

As classified by Guthmann and Dougall,[29] four classes of cash receipts

---

[28] The system is described in more detail and the controls are illustrated by charts in Walter Rautenstrauch and Raymond Villers, *op. cit.*, pp. 277–285.

[29] Harry G. Guthmann and Herbert E. Dougall, *Corporate Financial Policy*, 3d ed. (Englewood Cliffs, N.J.: Prentice-Hall, Inc., 1955), pp. 396 ff.

and cash disbursements enter into the cash budget, arising from (1) operations, (2) nonoperations, (3) sale and purchase of capital assets, and (4) change in owners' and creditors' investment.

Company operations produce cash sales and receipts from receivables. These usually can be forecast by using ratios to sales in the past, with consideration being given to any special conditions. Particular attention must be given to shifts in product mix and changes in customers or in their financial status.

Nonoperating items include such receipts as rents and interest on bonds owned and a few noncontractual obligations like lunch room receipts. Forecasting them is relatively mechanical. Sale of capital assets is a nonrecurring item, and sometimes the time of payment cannot be forecast effectively. Financing operations are usually planned well in advance, and proceeds are forecast by underwriters on the basis of prevailing market acceptance.

Cash disbursements from operations represent payments for cash purchases, accounts payable, labor, other manufacturing expenses, distribution expense and general and administrative expenses. Given the sales forecast, cash disbursements, except for fixed overhead, are estimated at relatively constant ratios, taking into account known conditions applying to specific items. The company is depending on knowledge of its own internal operations. Various contractual payments, principally royalties, interest, and taxes, are either relatively fixed in amount or bear a predictable relation to sales. Disbursements for plant and equipment represent an important item in growing companies. They are planned well in advance and can be forecast accurately except for unexpected interruptions due to strikes, etc. Cash disbursements to investors include repayment of bank loans, dividend payments, and other items; these too are usually planned well in advance.[30]

Obviously, the planned cash disbursements do not entirely follow past patterns. The management purposively directs flows in a given direction to attain given objectives. These present no problem in forecasting so long as the policies are generally accepted throughout the management of the company, even if they deviate from past relationships.

Fully developed cash budgets are most frequently found in well-established, large companies. In the Johnson and Johnson operation the sales forecast developed in the sales department is accepted without reservation for financial budgeting.[31] The time table of development is the same as in the sales budget. The cash-budget forecast of the com-

---

[30] Further useful discussion of methods of projecting receipts and disbursements will be found in Welsch, *op. cit.*, pp. 203 ff.

[31] The Johnson and Johnson operation is described briefly in *Modern Financial Planning and Control*, Financial Management Series, no. 110 (New York: American Management Association, Inc., 1956).

pany is for funds, including both cash and temporary investments, such as government securities which may be held for the payment of taxes. Note may be made of the company's capital expenditure and inventory control. Capital-expenditure projects are grouped as follows by the engineering department:

1. Appropriations already granted
2. Replacement of worn-out facilities
3. Cost-reduction items
4. Normal growth and accommodation for new products and improvements in existing products
5. Other, e.g., needed for personnel relations or prestige

The management committee must approve specifically any project representing an expenditure of more than $2,500. Control of inventory expenditure is aided by a daily report showing:

1. Unit sales for this day and for the month to date related to the sales forecast for the month
2. Production for this day and the month to date related to the production schedule for the month
3. The unit inventory compared with the planned inventory for the end of the month and also with a minimum inventory

The H. J. Heinz Company experiences a large seasonal variation in cash outgo and income, partly dependent upon vagaries of the weather, especially in the case of pickle and tomato crops.[32] Sales volume is almost twice as much in some months as in others. An orderly listing of receipts and disbursements has led to a workable forecast of the cash budget. Alternate forecasts, based on possible deviations from the plan for such reasons as particularly favorable or unfavorable weather, are kept in readiness to supplement the basic presentation.

The cash-budget figures differ substantially from those employed in the conventional income statement.[33] Sales are not entered at the point of sale but only as cash is received or collected from receivables; other income, such as interest, is recorded when collected rather than on an accrual basis; depreciation and bad-debt allowances are not included since they represent accounting reserves; asset purchases are included when paid for, but omitted from the income statement; and security transactions are recorded as cash is received or paid out, but omitted from the income account, except for the gain or loss on the transaction. The purpose of the cash budget is to serve as a management tool rather than to report on achievement during an accounting period.

The cash budget keeps cash funds in control and in appropriate rela-

[32] A description of the H. J. Heinz operation is given in *How H. J. Heinz Manages Its Financial Planning and Controls,* Financial Management Series, no. 106 (New York: American Management Association, Inc., 1953).

[33] These points are summarized in Guthmann and Dougall, *op. cit.,* p. 397.

tion to the company plan. It may save money by maximizing interest receipts and cash discounts and minimizing interest payments, because the level of needed cash holdings is carefully projected. It aids in preparation for any sort of financing by simplifying arrangements for a line of credit, by better timing, and by clarifying the effect financing arrangements will have on other needs and sources of cash. It establishes the basis for a sound dividend policy and other payment relations. It helps in getting a picture of the coordinated relation of many aspects of the company's operations: working capital, sales, investment, debt, and others.

APPRAISAL OF BUDGET FORECASTING

There can be little doubt that great advances have been made in coordinated planning by use of sales and cash budgets. Quantitative evaluation is impossible. Little can be added to the general impression which develops from a summary such as that presented above. One senses an air of enthusiasm among those who have had experience with these budgets. The author knows of no situation in which there has been an ultimate failure of budgetary plans after a period of trial.

There remains, however, a lurking suspicion that the promise is now being generally overstated. The success or failure of the plans is primarily dependent upon the sales forecast. It is possible that companies with successful budgetary plans have become able to estimate the companies' market penetration much more effectively than past experience would have indicated; it is difficult to be sure. Most of the companies are partially dependent upon the total market situation. Forecasting of the total market is far from perfect. Achievements in sales forecasting in recent years have been made partly because only slight variations have appeared in general-business conditions. There is a definite possibility that some reverses in the use of budgetary planning will appear if total economic activity should deviate somewhat more from halycon prosperity.

At least part of the gains achieved, however, are durable. Many companies have set up controls which provide prompt adjustment to changed conditions. If effectively used, the budgetary plan can do no harm under the most adverse forecast. The explicit estimates made may be very wrong, but there is no reason to believe that implicit assumptions would have been any better. For most of the time the reversal in over-all economic activity will not introduce so disturbing a factor that the sales forecast is entirely misinforming.

Furthermore, the techniques of management cooperation in most companies represent a net gain. The memory of working together and achieving carefully established management goals cannot be readily erased.

FORECASTING CASES

We present here brief statements on the forecasting practices of twelve companies. The cases certainly do not represent a satisfactory sample. They are presented merely to provide the impression of current forecasting work which can be obtained from publicly available sources; an effort has been made to include, in so far as possible, companies which might be considered models for forecasting work.

E. I. Du Pont de Nemours and Company.[34] Forecasts are made autonomously by each of 10 manufacturing departments. They are added together to arrive at an official composite-sales forecast for the company. The forecasts are for one, two, and ten years. The composite-sales forecasts are checked for reasonableness against anticipated changes in the aggregate economic situation in the office of the company's economist.

Each manufacturing department has its own unique problems to face in forecasting. All of the departmental sales forecasts, however, begin with salesmen's estimates of customers' requirements. In many cases the customers' sales are estimated; departmental research organizations are of considerable assistance. It is said that the procedure followed is determined by the fact that sales are largely made to other manufacturers. An appraisal of general-business conditions is provided to each sales department by the economist's office for use in weighing the influence of general business on the sales of the specific products under consideration.

The economist's office includes five professional men, with specialization in commodity prices and interest rates, general economic theory, chemical-market research, and construction. The office is called on to supply forecasts of the general-business outlook for use in the company's financial and other planning as well as for use by the manufacturing departments. A collection of more than five hundred individual statistical series is maintained for ready reference in analytic work and in answering questions about past economic changes which may come up among officials of the company. The forecast of general business is not considered official, and the manufacturing departments can substitute their own forecast if they prefer, but the substitution must be noted in submitting the sales forecast.

Late in July, the economist's office submits to the departments forecasts for the two following calendar years, covering industrial production,

---

[34] This statement is taken from Ira T. Ellis, "Techniques and Uses of Forecasts of General Business Conditions," *Proceedings of the Business and Economic Statistics Section, American Statistical Association,* 1956, pp. 158–161, and from personal correspondence with Mr. Ellis, Economist, E. I. Du Pont de Nemours and Company.

production of chemicals and allied products, price averages, and hourly earnings in manufacturing industries. These are for use in preparing two-year sales forecasts in each department. In early November, for use in preparing an annual sales forecast, the economist's office submits forecasts of industrial production, major expenditure divisions of gross national product, personal income, farm income, and several individual industries—steel, machinery, automobiles, textile-mill products, chemicals, rubber products, and minerals.

From time to time, one or more of the manufacturing departments find it desirable to make spot forecasts. Examples are forecasts of how much of a given food will be packaged in cellophane or polyethylene, and how many nylon hose, "Orlon" sweaters, or "Dacron" shirts may be sold. Although responsibility for such specific forecasts must lie with the manufacturing and sales groups, ordinarily the cooperation of several departments of the company will be sought, including the economist's office.

United States Steel Corporation.[35] A forecast of ingot demand twenty-five years hence is made, and a detailed market forecast for the industry and sales forecast for the company are made for five to ten years ahead and for one year; the industry-market forecasts are made at the central office for general guidance. The long-range forecasts encompass both a normal and a peak expectation. Population and formation of new households are taken to be of central importance.

The central office's industry-market forecast for the year ahead is normally made in August or September of the preceding year. It is chiefly based on demand by consuming industries, although a careful set of general assumptions is laid down. A general economic forecast is made to achieve integration and balance among the various estimates of consuming-industry output. The yearly *market* forecast is provided for the use of line sales managers who are responsible for making yearly *sales* forecasts. These managers are free to make departures from, or specify particular interpretations of, the central-office market forecasts, but the market forecast acts as a general guide in building up the annual sales forecasts. Some adjustments may be made when all of the sales forecasts are put together at the central office.

A short-range sales forecast of three or four months is made by each separate district manager; the forecast is fully detailed by mill unit, product, and month. In practice, the following month's production is almost always determined by this month's orders and the backlog of orders. In times of demand pressure, this applies to a greater or less extent for the next following months. More often, however, direct infor-

---

[35] See James L. Rich, *op. cit.*, pp. 161–166. Also, considerable material was made personally available to the author.

mation from sales offices is most important in the second, third, and fourth month.

Especially at times of critical change in general economic conditions, the central office plays a vital part in the three- to four-months' forecast. General-business indicators are extensively utilized, including employment, trade activity, manufacturing, and the farm economy.[36] Also, consideration is given to a careful analysis of the industry inventory position, estimated by comparing the American Iron and Steel Institute's measurement of monthly steel shipments to each industry with a measurement of the physical output of the industry. Use factors, showing the steel taken by the output of each industry, have to be employed. The use factors applied to production make available an estimate of steel consumption, and the difference between consumption and shipments is indicative of inventories. Shift in steel inventories can be of critical importance in recession periods as noted in Chapter 9. Inventories are thought generally to lie within the range of stocks consumed in seventy-five to ninety days, and when one of these limits is approached a reversal is anticipated.

Corning Glass Works.[37] Four kinds of sales forecast are made: (1) special-project sales forecasts, each of which is a marketing study of a particular situation; (2) five-year sales forecast, the purpose of which is to provide a guide for manufacturing plans so that research and development and requirements for manpower facilities can be approached in an orderly way; (3) an annual sales-budget forecast, discussed more fully below; (4) monthly production and inventory sales forecasts for the next several months, made department by department on the basis of foreseeable sales. These provide means of arriving at what should be done currently in relation to production and inventories.

Annual sales forecasts are made for 22 separate sales departments, both by the sales managers and independently by the market research department. Formerly, only the sales managers made these forecasts, but it was found that since the sales budget was to be used to measure sales performance in the coming year, some managers were overly conservative in order to ensure a favorable measurement of performance; others were overly optimistic in order to stimulate activity by providing a target just beyond reach. For the sales of each department, the market research department takes into consideration the following factors:

1. Any change in prices anticipated
2. Any significant addition of sales manpower

[36] See table of general-business indicators in James L. Rich, *ibid.*, p. 166.
[37] Richard L. Patey, "Preparation and Coordination of Forecasts at Corning Glass Works," in *Sales Forecasting: Uses, Techniques, and Trends*, pp. 111–120, and information personally furnished by Mr. Patey, Manager, Market Research Department.

3. Any addition of new products

4. Any significant changes in user-industry demand

5. Any significant gain or loss in plant capacity

6. Past trends in the various classes of products

7. Order backlogs in the various classes of products

8. Inventories at various stages of distribution

9. Promotional and advertising plans for the coming year

These factors are set against an analysis of general-business conditions, establishing the general economic climate. The forecast often represents a projection of past sales trends, but sometimes, especially for new products, end-use analysis is relied on to a greater extent. In some cases it is very helpful to start with an industry forecast and obtain the sales forecast by estimating the company's market penetration.

The sales forecast made by the sales managers and the market research department are analyzed, the variations are questioned, and a single sales budget is established. The sales budget is matched with a total expense budget, giving a planned pattern of expected sales, cost, and profit. The final sales forecasts are broken down by product lines and items to provide manufacturing schedules for various plants of the company. For instance, the total sales of the Pyrex-ware sales department is broken down by Pyrex-brand ovenware, Flameware, colored Opalware, lamp chimneys, tableware, and the like. Then each product line is broken down product by product. For example, in the ovenware line, estimates are made of the number of utility dishes, custard cups, and pie plates to be scheduled. The product line is scheduled month by month, with allowance for appropriate seasonal variation, and the resulting schedule is used as a measure of performance for the sales department as the year progresses. Revisions may be necessary; for instance, in some lines the sales-promotion plans may be more effective than expected.

The element of educated judgment is considered the most important factor in making adequate forecasts. Judgment, however, is the result of knowledge gained from study and analysis of industry trends, inventory situations, order and backlog trends, and trade-association material; and from contacts with people close to various businesses.

Armstrong Cork Company.[38] Annual forecasts of sales and profits are made by all divisions of the company, but are subject to a system of "checks and balances" in the form of reviews by the company's forecasting committee with the divisions and with the president's office. Moreover, the forecasting committee meets frequently to reappraise the key variables impinging on the projections made. The forecasts are developed against a background of (1) basic assumptions about general economic

[38] Information was personally furnished by Dr. Walter I. Hoadley, Jr., Treasurer.

prospects, provided by the office of economic and commercial research, reflecting its own analysis and the views of informed specialists outside the company; and (2) important sales and market information considered relevant by staff departments and individual divisions. Order indices, maintained by the economist's office for each division, as well as for the company as a whole, are a useful tool in establishing short-term sales forecasts.

Production plans and purchasing programs are set up in accordance with the annual sales forecast. Schedules are usually firm for one to three months and are adjusted thereafter as required. If abnormal seasonal changes or rapid cyclical shifts should occur, prompt revision of the schedules may become desirable.

Dodge Manufacturing Corporation.[39] This is a company making equipment for the mechanical transmission of power, such as V-belt drives, bearings, speed reducers, pulleys, flexible couplings, and clutches. The major need for forecasting is to control production. Production is for stock in anticipation of sales, with lead times of three to five months. Sales have frequently fluctuated more than 15 per cent from one year to the next.

A four-month forecast is made each month and reviewed by the forecasting committee, which includes major operating executives. The forecast includes, for each of the next four months, gross bookings and billings, cancellations, and unfilled orders. Past actual and forecast figures are shown for comparison. Comments are included on the general economic situation and special company and competitive conditions.

The bookings forecast is made on a seasonally corrected working-day basis. Billings depend on forecast bookings, backlogs, and shop capacity. These forecasts are used for over-all inventory control, cash needs, and expense budgeting.

A control on the forecast has been established by plotting seasonally corrected bookings on semilog paper. They tend to move in relatively straight lines between turning points. With the aid of the company's statistical-quality control department, limits have been set for these movements between turns (by the so-called skeptic's method discussed in Chapter 10). Fluctuations outside the control limits, especially if repeated, suggest a significant change in direction or an incorrect estimate of the trend line.

Forecasting turning points is both important and difficult. Outside services are used. One is based on monetary figures; another is based

---

[39] See Donald E. Gates, "Reliable Forecasting in the Smaller Company: Dodge Manufacturing Corporation," in *Sales Forecasting: Uses, Techniques, and Trends,* pp. 121–131. The statement given here rests heavily on information personally provided by Mr. Gates, Director of Market Research.

on leading, coincident, and lagging indicators, as developed by the National Bureau of Economic Research. The Dun and Bradstreet quarterly Survey of Businessmen's Expectations has been helpful. Bookings correlate with the survey data on new plant and equipment expenditures compiled by the SEC and the Department of Commerce, except that Dodge bookings lead by six to nine months, probably because they cover stock merchandise, whereas most capital goods are built to order and are a long time in production.

There has been a tendency for the upward movement of the cycle to last for a year and a half to two years, and for the contraction to last from a year to a year and a half. Inventories of 25 leading dealers are checked quarterly to give a further clue to the timing of turning points.

The 4,000 stock items made by the company are grouped into approximately 100 commodity lines. A pattern of sales, in units, is established for each commodity line, based on three years' experience. Total sales for each commodity line are reviewed monthly, and when deemed desirable, a percentage correction is made to the base sales-pattern figures for individual items.

The annual forecast on which the sales quota is based is made in the fall. The quota may vary from the forecast for sales-policy reasons. The quota is then allocated among the various sales districts, primarily according to results in the last three years, giving most weight to the last year. Presumably because of the complex nature of the industrial market served, reliable relationships have not been found with various regional economic indicators.

Longer-range (five- to ten-year) forecasts are made as required in connection with proposed plant-expansion programs. These have relied heavily on outside projections of producer's durable equipment, with which sales have correlated, and on the projections of the Machinery and Allied Products Institute, as well as on judgments of factors peculiar to the Dodge business.

General Electric Company.[40] Each of more than 100 departments prepares a budget in the fall, showing estimated operations by month for the following year and annually for the succeeding four years, together with a forecast of the tenth and twentieth year ahead. The forecast budgets show all items of regular operating statements from sales to net earnings, with supporting analysis including such data as manufacturing capacity, expenditures for facilities, and number of employees. The sales forecast is made by the functional managers with the assistance of the general manager in each department. By using the sales forecast, the functional managers estimate costs and operating expenses, plant and equipment expenditures, and other investment requirements. The

[40] This material was prepared expressly for the author.

functional managers together with the financial personnel estimate commercial and administrative expenses.

Longer-term sales projections are founded on (1) the anticipated level of the national economy, including such factors as anticipated gross national product, disposable income, military expenditures, construction activity, and electrical energy sales, as provided by a headquarters department; (2) the department's historical share of the market and the possibility of increased participation; (3) expected impact of technological changes; (4) anticipated effect of new-product developments; (5) expected price changes; (6) new uses for the product; and (7) other factors, including managerial judgment.

Shorter-term sales forecasts also take into account the level of unfilled orders, new orders, production schedules, seasonal trends of business, and any anticipated interruption owing to such factors as delays in receipt of material.

The individual departments' budgets are consolidated at the headquarters office, much as regular operating statements are consolidated. The departments similarly prepare estimates of balance-sheet items, and these also are consolidated. From the combined figures taken from these consolidated statements, the source and use of funds can be estimated by months for the ensuing year. The cash position is thus estimated at the end of each month. Similarly, annual cash requirements for each of the forthcoming ten years are estimated.

The detailed budgets of operations and cash flow form the plan for the succeeding year's operations. They are used initially for production scheduling and inventory control. As the year progresses, monthly actual operations are compared with each department's budget at the headquarters' level, and the amount and percentage of deviation are presented to higher levels of management as a basis for reviewing each department's operations.

Union Carbide and Carbon Corporation.[41] Sales forecasts are based on reports submitted monthly by the sales forces in the field. These reports are reviewed by product managers, are approved by operating-division sales executives, and are consolidated by the corporation's estimates division. The resulting short-term sales forecasts cover sales month by month for the next five to seven months, and quarter by quarter for the next six to seven quarters. These forecasts are used to determine production schedules and to make estimates of earnings, cash, net working capital, inventories, etc. Estimates are also used as general-management tools which indicate the corporation's expected performance.

Five-year forecasts, longer-term projections, and special studies are prepared at less frequent intervals.

[41] This material was prepared for the author by Arved Teleki, Economic Analyst.

The economics group of the corporation prepares quarterly forecasts (six to seven quarters) and yearly long-term projections of broad aspects of the national economy. The economic forecasts are available to the sales forecasters who are free to use them as they see fit.

General Public Utilities Corporation.[42] Three major tools are employed in forecasting and planning work: (1) budgets, both operating and construction; (2) load and capacity forecasts; (3) a long-range system-development plan.

The one-year forecasts of operating budgets show, by months, the various primary accounts in income and operating statements. The three-year forecasts of budgets show the totals for each year for condensed income accounts. The construction budgets show anticipated construction expenditures: one-year budgets, by months, for projects and types of plant; three-year budgets, yearly, by project classifications. The budgets are coordinated in the central office of each company from figures submitted by operating divisions in the summer of each year. The company budgets are sent to the parent holding company for review and coordination; this sometimes leads to modifications.

At the operating-division level the basic forecasts of customers, kilowatt-hour sales, and revenues are based primarily on recent trends by major service classification; alterations are sometimes made for special factors. In all cases direct contact is made with the largest industrial customers to ascertain the customer's production schedules and prospects. These also may temper projected trends. General economic data are used in some of the individual company offices in evaluating the operating-division forecasts. Information on general-business prospects is made available by the holding company.

Peak-load and capacity forecasts are prepared for a five-year period by each company and submitted to a joint operating committee, with holding-company participation, for review and coordination. Most of the companies use projection of the trend of annual peaks since 1946, redetermined each year by the least-squares method, with modifications for known load changes. Each company checks with its sales departments and division managers for any known expansions in making the forecast.

The holding company, in cooperation with its operating subsidiaries, has recently completed a long-range system-development plan. The services of outside consultants were used to assist the system's engineers in making the basic study. The plan is considered a general and rather flexible guide in shaping yearly and three-year operating and construction budgets with respect to capital expenditures for generating stations and bulk power-supply transmission systems.

[42] Information personally furnished by Mr. E. W. Morehouse, Vice-President.

New Departure Division, General Motors Corporation.[43] New Departure's major product is ball bearings. Sales forecasts by the month for four months in the future are (1) broken down into units by individual-product sizes and specifications and (2) broken down into summary dollars by end-use–industry purchasers of bearings. The monthly sales forecasts are used primarily for developing cost and profit estimates and production schedules for individual-product sizes and specifications for each of the four months in the basic sales forecast.

Yearly sales forecasts for the next calendar year are broken down into units and dollars by individual-product sizes and specifications. The yearly forecast is used in budget development, determination of plant-facility requirements, and establishment of sales quotas.

Two forecasting techniques are used to check each other. One is the grass-roots approach, which involves asking customers about their requirements. A forecast from customers is considered an informal order because it becomes the basis for developing production schedules. The needed information includes future requirements related to specific needs, orders on hand from the customer, and his past purchases from the company. In so far as possible, this information is obtained from the customer directly and informally when making service calls. At the central office the orders from each customer are compared with the salesman's original sales forecast.

The second technique is general economic analysis. The company's sales are broken down into industry groupings according to the standard industrial classification, and, in those cases where a good relationship is found, forecasts of the related industries are used.

Sears, Roebuck and Co.[44] Disposable income is accepted as the controlling over-all economic variable. Installment credit is considered a modifying factor, adding to or subtracting from disposable income.

From a correlation between retail sales and disposable income, after adjustment for credit changes, estimates of "normal sales for the income level" are obtained. The ratio of actual sales to normal is computed. More stability and less chance of freakish error are found in using ratios rather than dollars; hence, projections are made in terms of ratios, with projected dollar values being derived from them.

The general-merchandise category, the part of the market in which Sears participates, is projected in terms of ratio to total retail sales. General-merchandise sales are broken down into durable and nondurable

---

[43] See Robert E. Randel, "Variations in Forecasting Techniques at New Departure," in *Sales Forecasting: Uses, Techniques, and Trends*, pp. 132–138. Major reliance was placed on information personally furnished by Mr. Randel, General Superintendent of Finish Operations.

[44] This material was furnished by Arthur Rosenbaum, Manager, Economic Research.

divisions, and the ratios to total general-merchandise sales are projected separately, and converted into dollar projections.

Sears sales of durable and nondurable general merchandise are projected as ratios of the country's total sales in each category. To achieve comparability, sales expected from new and expanded facilities are first eliminated. Sales are then put in the form of seasonally corrected annual rates to obtain a projection of basic nonseasonal changes. Forecasts are made separately for mail-order and retail divisions by projecting the ratio accounted for by mail orders. The ratios are adjusted for expected seasonal changes to obtain final monthly projections of sales for existing facilities. In all of these cases, conversion of the ratio projections to dollar amounts is achieved by multiplying by a forecast of the denominator of the ratio.

Additional sales from new, enlarged, and relocated facilities are projected from studies of the market potential in each area and the recent sales experience of stores of similar size in nearby areas. After making the proper adjustments, these sales are added in to obtain estimated total sales of the company. The projections are put on a chart each week to show developments in sales, inventories, and commitments for merchandise. The projection of sales to the end of the year made in late February, 1957, is shown on Chart 11–1.

The projections are made in order to provide guidance to top management in appraising the prospective levels of inventory and the commitments risk they are willing to assume, and to give assistance in planning the detailed budgets which are submitted in advance of each season. Perspective is provided, and the forecasts are eagerly awaited, although no one in the management is compelled to make use of them.

Eastman Kodak Company.[45] Annual sales forecasts were made at Kodak as early as 1904. Roll film, the principal product at that time, had a high seasonal factor which led to considerable irregularity in employment. In that year a stable emulsion was developed, so that films could be manufactured at a constant rate and then stored against peak demand. An estimate of sales for the year ahead was needed in order to set a more stable level of annual production.

Assumptions regarding general economic conditions are found to be important in estimating sales. A series frequently used in the assumptions is disposable income. Information on the economic outlook is obtained from all sources and by all methods which appear promising. Some eight hundred economic time series are regularly tabulated for company use.

---

[45] This material was furnished by Edmund R. King, Chief Statistician. See further Edmund R. King, "Techniques and Uses of Forecasts of General Business Conditions in Eastman Kodak Company," *Proceedings of the Business and Economic Statistics Section, American Statistical Association*, 1956, pp. 167–172.

The general economic assumptions are prepared by the statistical department at the Kodak office. Beginning about August 1 and about February 1, economic forecasts for the coming year and for a total of five years into the future are prepared. After review and approval by

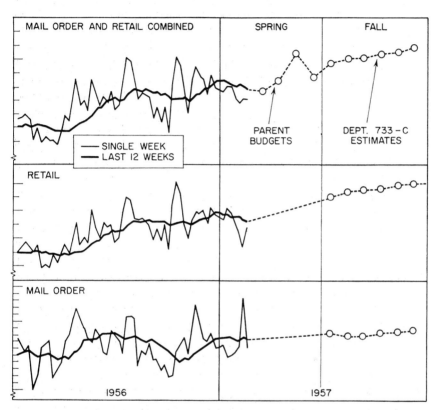

SEARS LISTED SALES—ANNUAL RATES

CHART 11–1. Sears, Roebuck and Co. Sales Forecast. The chart presents the forecast made in February, 1957, for use in evaluating the sales outlook in the fall of 1957. SOURCE: The chart was provided by Arthur Rosenbaum for use in this book.

top management, these become the general-business assumptions and are presented to several groups of divisional and departmental managers. If, for a specific project or purpose, certain executives feel strongly that slightly different assumptions should be used, they may do so if they are explicit about their divergence from the standard assumptions and if the reasons seem justified.

The initial sales estimates are worked out by representatives of various statistical and planning groups in the company, including the control departments in the plants producing the product under discussion; the project is a cooperative one. The forecasting is done by individual-product groups, usually in terms of quantity. The planners take their preliminary estimates through a series of conferences to get them reviewed and approved by those who have the responsibility for company policy and for the production and sales of individual products. Modifying factors particularly are introduced in these review sessions.

Two broad methods are employed in making the sales estimates, although the actual forecasting techniques vary considerably from product to product. (1) A trend-cycle method is used, in which a projection of the past trend of sales of individual-product groups is made and then modified as required by the standard, general economic assumptions. The modification is made by means of a ratio of sales to an appropriate over-all economic indicator, such as disposable income; that ratio is projected into the future. (2) A multiple-correlation method relates the sales of the product to important variables by developing equations of relationships.

Such projections may then have to be modified in accordance with changes in the competitive situation, dealer inventories, or other relevant factors. Numerous other factors, such as sales plans or product changes, also are taken into account.

Final approval is given by the finished products committee, composed of the general manager of the company, the operating vice-presidents, and other major executives, including the treasurer, sales executives, plant production and planning personnel, and the chief statistician. The approved sales forecasts are then utilized by the accounting personnel in preparing numerous budgets and financial statements, after estimates of quantity have been converted to dollar sales by multiplying them by anticipated prices.

The sales forecasts are also employed in scheduling finished-goods production; product-group forecasts are broken down to establish plant quantity figures for each individual finished product according to size, kind, and package. Related to these schedules are planned inventory levels. The whole planning procedure is a process of "gradualization"—a moderate shifting of company affairs to adapt to changing conditions. Monthly meetings with the sales-planning groups and the finished products committee are held in order to review changed conditions which may require revisions in the current year's sales estimates. Shifts in plans can be made promptly and, it is hoped, without necessitating catastrophic changes or involving numerous major critical points.

The quantity sales estimates, for five-year and longer periods, are used in planning future expenditures for plant and equipment. The sales estimates imply that there will be certain prerequisite productive facilities, office space, warehouse space, and customer-service facilities in existence during the future years in question. Once the sales forecasts are available, plans to obtain such facilities can be made. For special projections, as required, economic assumptions for ten to twenty years ahead are prepared, and then a related sales forecast is developed for the same period. Sales estimates for intervals of time ranging from the next month to possibly several decades hence are the basic vehicle for translating economic trends into realistic corporate plans.

Continental Can Company, Inc.[46] For economic background, the commercial research department publishes a summary of the general-business trend anticipated during the following three-year period. For example, in connection with the 1958 budget, an economic forecast for the years 1958, 1959, and 1960 was provided for the operating divisions. Of these, the forecast for 1958 was of principal importance for the budget.

The commercial research department also provides the divisions with more specific and quite detailed reviews and outlooks for their particular markets. The probabilities for each division are anticipated and described as well as is possible on the basis of the current situation and carefully considered projections of the outlook for the industry in which the division operates. The anticipated trends vary somewhat from one division to another. The commercial research department thus provides a reasonably specific, but still preliminary, determination of the sales-volume budget.

Using the preliminary determination, the operating personnel express their specific judgments concerning the expected influence of local factors; they actually prepare the proposed budgets. With detail appropriate to the operating division's product mix, the data on anticipated sales volume is processed through the district sales offices and the manufacturing plants, and is reviewed by division-level management.

The proposed sales budgets are then reviewed and approved by management at the head-office level before any further steps are taken in developing the profit plan. This separate and initial approval of the sales budget serves to emphasize the importance with which it is regarded. The management feels that the development of the budget is so closely associated with the anticipated sales-volume that it would not be sound practice to have operating divisions undertake the extensive detail on expense budgets until they have a firm and agreed-upon sales figure.

The over-all sales forecast has been within about 1 per cent of actual sales in the past few years. As would be expected, greater departures have occurred in specific divisions and plants.

[46] This information was personally furnished by H. T. Heun, Control Officer.

CHAPTER 12

Forecasting Various Economic Processes

We consider briefly in this chapter the forecasting of certain processes of general interest which would have complicated the discussion if presented earlier. They are of three types: (1) processes we would have considered above had we found it expedient to go into supplementary factors, such as short-term changes in the labor force or levels of employment; (2) processes closely related to the forecasts considered above but involving too much detail for a general survey, such as regional population forecasts; (3) processes which are clearly related to those considered above, but the forecast of which presents essentially separate problems, for example, the stock market.

SHORT-TERM CHANGES IN THE LABOR FORCE

Long-term forecasts of the labor force, as developed by the Census Bureau, are presented in Chapter 3. They are developed by applying the forecast of labor-force participation rates to forecasts of the working-age population. For fifteen years into the future the labor force comes largely from the existing population in the country, and therefore a forecast of the birth rate, frequently in error in the past, is not involved. The forecast of the death rate appears to be more reliable. The forecast of participation rates has to depend largely on past trends, since the detail essential for analyzing the reasons for entering or withdrawing from the labor force has not been satisfactorily developed. The trends are considered separately by sex and age groups, the most significant factors accounting for differences in participation rates.

Over the short term, in addition to uncertainties regarding the stability of trends in participation rates and in mortality, temporary variation about the trend line may loom important. As current movements reveal

288

discrepancies, the long-term projection may be revised in time to avoid serious perversion.

Variation about the trend is thus more influential in the short run than error in projecting the trend slope. In 1956, for instance, the labor force increased 1.5 million as against approximately 1 million in 1955 and about 0.8 million in each of the preceding four years. The sharp increase in 1956 was due to a jump in participation rates of teen-age boys and girls and of women 35 to 64 years of age. As shown in Table 3–3, a secular decline is occurring in the participation rates of teen-age workers. However, during the 1953–54 recession, labor-force rates for teen-agers were moving downward at a slower rate than indicated by long-time trends. An increasing tendency for students to take spare-time jobs appeared from 1954 to 1956. Presumably the variations are partly explained by the varying availability of jobs, caused by fluctuation in total demand. Any assumption about the extent of this influence unfortunately is not warranted in the present state of our knowledge. One might argue, in fact, that the higher family income earned by full-time workers in prosperity would discourage the seeking of part-time work by teen-agers. A factor in 1956 might have been the rapid rise occurring in school costs.

The rise in participation rates of women in the 35-to-64 age bracket was in line with a strong upward secular trend, but sharp acceleration occurred in 1956. This must have been partly due to the increased availability of jobs at rising wage rates. Again, the weight to be assigned to that influence at another time is undetermined.

Seasonal influences may be partly responsible for the jump in labor force in 1956. The abnormal expansion during 1955 was limited to the middle half of the year, with approximately normal differences occurring in the first and fourth quarters. The seasonal peak occurs at mid-year. Possibly, there were some unusual factors leading to a low seasonal peak in 1955 or to a high seasonal peak in 1956, but if so, these factors are not obvious. Uncertainties remain in the measurement of seasonal variation in the labor force.

As noted below, labor-force forecasts may be essential in facing public policy questions. The best that can be done is to start with the secular change expected and modify it by any plausible clues to the forces making for temporary variation. Owing to the unsatisfactory state of our understanding of these forces, the temporary variation is likely to be poorly anticipated. The direction of movement may not be in error, for the secular movement will account for at least a minimum change. Because of limitations, the use of short-term labor-force forecasts may be found relatively undesirable except when policy needs make them essential.

EMPLOYMENT AND UNEMPLOYMENT

The level of employment is dependent upon production. Production depends upon demand. The secular level of employment is forecast in Chapter 3 by subtracting labor float from the level of labor force (Table 3–5). Demand is assumed to remain at normal levels in the secular-trend forecasts. Such an assumption cannot be made in the short term. The forecast in the short term is contingent upon the level of production expected.

In addition to the level of production, information on expected changes in productivity is necessary to forecast employment. When productivity is computed by dividing total manhours into deflated gross national product, as it was in Table 3–5, substantial variation arises from year to year. The yearly percentage increases from 1951 to 1956 were as follows:

	Per cent increase in productivity
1950–51	1.6
1951–52	2.5
1952–53	2.3
1953–54	1.2
1954–55	4.0
1955–56	1.5

The percentage changes average out over a period of time, so that secular forecasts are little affected. That fact does not help a great deal in making short-term forecasts.

The variation shown in the year-to-year changes in productivity is no doubt due partly to the crudity in measurement of gross national product, employment, and weekly hours. As revisions are made in these series, percentage changes such as those shown above will be modified to some extent. However, yearly variation is to be expected because several unrelated forces are represented in the measure (see Chapter 3). Unfortunately, the different forces involved cannot be effectively quantified. Probably the most important single influence making for yearly variation is shift in composition of output. As the output of highly mechanized industries increases disproportionately, measures of productivity will rise rapidly, as in 1955. The slower rise in 1956 is partly accounted for by the decline which occurred in automobile production and the leveling off in private construction activity.

Year-to-year changes in productivity can best be forecast by starting with the secular change expected and modifying by the outlook for shifts in composition of output and for other forces, such as change in the marginal quality of employees and effectiveness of new capital introduced, when significant clues are obtainable.

Because of the handicaps faced in forecasting employment, production forecasts are best developed independently, as outlined earlier in the book. Nevertheless, the employment implications of production must be faced in public policy. For this purpose a forecast of employment may have to be derived. The forecast may be used more wisely if its limitations are clearly recognized.

The forecast of unemployment is obtained by subtracting the employment forecast from the labor-force forecast. Since there is no recognized unemployment in the armed forces, civilian employment and civilian labor force are used. Therefore, a forecast of the number in the armed forces is necessary to obtain a forecast of unemployment. Policy of the armed forces is fairly clear over the near future, barring the development of emergencies, so that at most times the forecast of unemployment is not significantly impaired by its dependence on a forecast of the armed forces. Because of the limitations of labor-force and employment forecasts noted above, short-term projections of unemployment are likely to be inaccurate. The forecast may be serviceable in developing perspective on questions of public policy, but close accuracy should not be expected.

Anticipated changes in unemployment in local communities may be more important than in national aggregates, for when policy action is required, measures must be taken at places where unemployment is expected. The basis for local-community forecasts of short-term unemployment is founded largely on expected changes in employment. Some indication of the expected changes in national employment by the industries represented in the community may be derived from production forecasts for these industries. An approximation of employment changes in the local community may possibly be made by applying expected changes in the national percentage to the industries represented in the local community.

Another method is to conduct a survey in the community, asking employers about their anticipated changes in employment. Such surveys are made either monthly or bimonthly by local employment security offices. Employment requirements for two and four months hence are summarized for each important labor-market area and reported bimonthly to the Bureau of Employment Security as an integral item of information in Area Labor Market Reports. These reports are prepared for the 149 largest labor-market areas in the United States. They are used currently as part of the information employed to classify labor-market areas according to the relative adequacy of labor supply. Only limited information is available on the experience which has been developed from the Area Labor Market Reports.[1]

[1] A descriptive statement prepared for the author by the Office of Program Review and Analysis, Bureau of Employment Security, Department of Labor, includes this

POPULATION, NATIONAL AND REGIONAL

Population forecasts are obtained by making assumptions regarding mortality, fertility, and migration, as outlined in Chapter 3. The assumptions made by the Census Bureau in its widely employed projections are as follows.[2] The rates of decline occurring in mortality in the forties are projected to 1960, after which the rates are assumed to remain constant at the projected 1955–60 levels. The rates are projected separately by sex and age groups.[3] A total net immigration of 1.4 million is assumed for 1955 to 1960, approximately the actual number from 1950 to 1955. Thereafter, approximately 1.2 million per quinquennium is assumed. The age-sex distribution of the projected new immigrants is based on the experience of several recent postwar years. Since the fertility experience has been very unstable, four different assumptions are made, leading to as many different population projections; these are labeled *AA, A, B,* and *C. AA* assumes that the fertility rates of 1954–55 will continue;[4] *A,* the fertility rates of 1950–53 will continue; *B,* the fertility rates of 1950–53 will continue to 1965 and decline thereafter to about the prewar level by 1975; *C,* the fertility rates of 1950–53 will decline, beginning in 1953, to about the prewar level by 1975. The highest projection is given by the *AA* series and successively lower projections down to the *C* series. The *AA* projection to 1975 is 228 million, and the *C* projection is 207 million, representing, respectively, increases of 63 and 42 million from 1955, or 38 and 25 per cent. The projections are not intended to represent probable range of movement, as "high" and "low" projections, formerly reported, were often interpreted; they represent merely plausible differences in assumptions regarding fertility. The birth-rate assumptions for the four series are shown in Table 12–1.

By mid-1957 the actual population was slightly above the *AA* projection. This fact of course does not demonstrate that the secular projections are too low, but rather that the projections are not implausible. The mortality rates have been approximately equal to the low projected trend. Net immigration has been slightly higher than the assumed levels

statement: "The employer estimates of future employment requirements have proven their value to local offices in planning their operations to accommodate expected changes in the labor market."

[2] "Revised Projection of the Population of the United States, by Age and Sex: 1960 to 1975," *Current Population Reports,* ser. P–25, no. 123, October, 1955.

[3] The method involved is called "cohort-survival," which requires applying the trend of mortality rates to the population by age and sex for each year to obtain an estimate of the number of deaths each year.

[4] A new projection the Census Bureau is now developing, labeled *AA-A,* assumes 1954–55 fertility rates to 1960, followed by a linear decline to the 1950–53 rates by 1975.

TABLE 12–1

PROJECTED BIRTH RATES BY FOUR ASSUMPTIONS
(Average annual rate per 1,000 population at the mid-period)

Period	Series *AA*	Series *A*	Series *B*	Series *C*
1955–60	24.0	22.3	22.3	20.7
1960–65	23.3	21.8	21.8	19.2
1965–70	24.2	23.0	21.4	19.2
1970–75	25.7	24.3	19.7	19.3

SOURCE: "Revised Projections of the Population of the United States, by Age and Sex: 1960 to 1975," *Current Population Reports*, ser. P-25, no. 123, Oct. 20, 1955, p. 5.

because of temporary measures. Fertility rates have remained high. It is not unreasonable to believe that the fertility rates are abnormally high in the mid-fifties, just as they were abnormally low in the thirties.

The changes in regional population depend upon births, deaths, and net migration in the local area. Projection is illustrated by methods developed by the Census Bureau in forecasting state populations.[5] "Because it is not possible to predict future population changes with confidence, several different series of projections were derived, employing alternative assumptions regarding future changes."[6] The assumptions made in these projections were tested by extrapolating the population of each state from 1930 to 1940 and 1950 by various methods and comparing the results with the Census results in 1940 and 1950. The indications are that plausible projections have been obtained, but that the projections farthest into the future and in smaller states are the least accurate.

Births are projected on the basis of the recent ratios of the state birth rates to the United States rate. Such ratios have been relatively stable, with some tendency toward convergence. The 1950–55 ratio is used as the initial one, and a ratio of 1.00 is assumed for 2000–05. Ratios for years in between are obtained by linear interpolation. The state birth rates are derived by multiplying by the national birth rates projected on the four

[5] "Illustrative Projections of the Population, by States: 1960, 1965, and 1970," *Current Population Reports*, ser. P-25, no. 160, Aug. 9, 1957. Employing the definition of forecasting used in this book, the Census Bureau's projections are properly called forecasts. Note, however, this statement on p. 1 of the report: "The figures are not intended as 'predictions,' but rather as illustrative projections of population under stated assumptions of future changes in the components of population change."
[6] *Ibid.*, p. 3.

fertility assumptions noted above.[7] The products of ratios by national rates, obtained by five-year periods, represent the average annual birth rates for each state in each future period, except that the total number of births implied at each date is adjusted to average to the national births derived from each of the four assumptions.

Initial national mortality rates are used for the full period, as shown in the 1954 United States Abridged Life Tables, published by the National Office of Vital Statistics. A weighted average of white and non-white mortality rates by four broad percentage divisions is developed and applied to each state in accordance with its percentage of nonwhite population. The deaths implied by these mortality rates are adjusted so that their total will match the total derived in the national projection. For the national projection, the extrapolation described above, extending the decline in mortality rates occurring in the forties to 1960, and carrying constant rates at the projected 1955–60 levels thereafter, is accepted as one assumption. Another assumption, developed by the Social Security Administration, involving a continued decline in mortality rates after 1960, is used to derive a second set of projections.[8] Like the projections of births by states, these rates are projected only at five-year intervals.

In view of uncertainties regarding the direction and level of future migration, several alternative assumptions are used. Each series of projections is based on the assumption that the average annual amount of net migration of some previous period will prevail for part or all of the projection period. The periods selected as bases are 1950–55, 1940–55, and 1930–55; these periods appear to offer a varied selection of reasonable alternatives regarding future net migration. The average annual amount of net migration assumed for the states in each period is adjusted to be equal to the level of net immigration from abroad assumed in the national projections (1.4 million for 1955–60 and 1.2 million for 1960–65 and for 1965–70). The age distribution of migrants assumed for the

[7] In addition, they are multiplied by the national birth-rate projections on the new fertility assumption AA-A. This assumption is involved in state projection Series I, as noted below.

[8] The life expectancies at birth (in years) in accordance with this assumption are as follows:

Sex	1954	1956–70	2000
Male..............	66.8	68.4	71.2
Female............	72.8	74.6	76.8

Adjustment to the national level of deaths in this assumption superimposes a downward trend on the state mortality rates, taken as constant over time in the initial computations.

future is based on the age patterns of migrants during the base periods.[9]

Four sets of projections are developed incorporating varied assumptions as to migration, fertility, and mortality. If all combinations of the many projections of births, deaths, and net migration were used they would yield a group of population projections so large as to be unwieldy. Any of the four projections chosen may produce a high projection for one state and a low for another, since changes from the time bases were not entirely similar in the various states. The assumptions involved in the four projections are as follows:

Series 1. Migration for 1955–60 is assumed at the 1950–55 levels; linear changes are assumed after 1960 so that 1940–55 levels are reached by 1970–75; fertility rates of the *AA–A* assumption are used (see footnote 4); mortality assumptions are in accordance with the new Social Security Administration series (see footnote 8).

Series 2. Migration levels of 1940–55 are assumed; fertility assumption *A* is adopted; the mortality assumptions made in the national projections are employed.

Series 3. Migration levels of 1930–55 are assumed; fertility assumption *A* is adopted; mortality assumptions are the same as in *Series 2.*

Series 4. Same assumptions as in *Series 3*, except that fertility assumption *C* is adopted.

As illustrative of the projections obtained, we may note the increases indicated for *Series 1* and *4* on Chart 12–1. *Series 2* and *3* are not in the same range in all cases but the deviations are not large. The projections are about in line with recent population growth. Generally, a somewhat smaller growth is shown if projection is limited to the adult population.

The population definition involved in the state projections is the "resident" population, comprising the civilian population and the armed forces stationed in the area. The results are essentially comparable with those which would be obtained by using *de jure* figures, the civilian population plus persons serving in the armed services whose preservice residence was in the state.

Brief note may be made of the forecast of metropolitan areas.[10] In forecasting the population of an area closely dependent upon one or two predominant industries, attention may be centered on the growth of such industry and the possibilities that shifts may occur in the area's

[9] Age distributions for the period from 1930 to 1950 were developed in "Studies of Population Redistribution and Economic Growth," in *Net Intercensal Migration, 1870–1950*, vol. II, state tables, prepared by E. S. Lee, D. C. Price, and others, unpublished report, University of Pennsylvania, Dec. 1, 1954; age distribution for 1950–55, as developed by the Census Bureau, is shown in *Current Population Reports*, ser. P–25, no. 151.

[10] A condensed summary will be found in Van Beuren Stanbery, *Better Population Forecasting for Areas and Communities*, Domestic Commerce Series, no. 32 (Washington: Department of Commerce, September, 1952), pp. 51 ff.

national share.[11] In older and more diversified metropolitan areas that provide a wide variety of goods and services for national markets, such as the New York, Chicago, and Philadelphia areas, projections are best

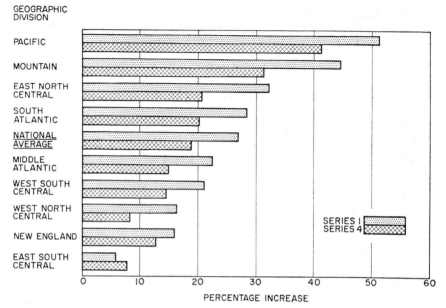

CHART 12–1. Projected Percentage Increase in Population of Geographic Divisions, 1955 to 1970, according to Assumptions 1 and 4 (divisions are ranked by size of increase according to Series 1). SOURCE: Taken from "Illustrative Projections of the Population, by States: 1960, 1965, and 1970," *Current Population Reports*, U.S. Bureau of the Census, ser. P-25, no. 160, Aug. 9, 1957.

made in terms of ratios of the metropolitan population to the population of the broad economic region of which it is a part and to the population of the nation as a whole.[12]

HOUSEHOLDS

The growth in number of households depends on changes in marital and household status and on growth of the population. Projection is illustrated by methods developed in the Census Bureau.[13] Forecasts are

[11] Paul M. Reid, *Population Prospectus for the Detroit Region, 1960 and 1970* (Detroit: Detroit Metropolitan Area Regional Planning Commission, October, 1942).

[12] *Population Estimates, Philadelphia-Camden Area, 1950–2000*, Planning Study, no. 1 (Philadelphia: Philadelphia City Planning Commission, April, 1948), illustrates use of that method.

[13] "Projections of the Number of Households and Families: 1960 to 1975," *Current Population Reports*, ser. P-20, no. 69, August 31, 1956. Employing the definition of forecasting used in this book, the Census Bureau's projections are properly called

derived from assumptions regarding annual rates of change within age groups in terms of the percentage who are single, heads of households, "primary individuals," doubled up with other households, and in other groups (quasi households, such as persons living in hotels, and the

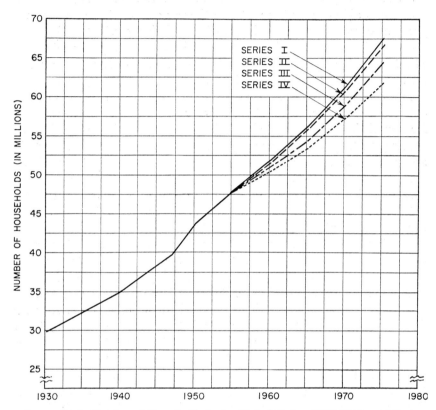

CHART 12–2. Number of Households in the United States, 1930–1955, and Projections, 1960–1975. SOURCE: Taken from data given in "Projections of the Number of Households and Families: 1960 to 1975," *Current Population Reports*, U.S. Bureau of the Census, ser. P-20, no. 69, Aug. 31, 1956.

institutional population).[14] Four series of assumptions are developed on these rates of change, but in all cases certain minimum limits are set; notably, a minimum of one million doubled-up married couples is set, and a 4 per cent minimum of single persons in any age group.

forecasts. Note, however, this statement on p. 1 of the report: "The projections are not intended to represent forecasts or predictions; instead, they show the number of households which would result from the adoption of certain reasonable assumptions about future population changes."

[14] The precise rates of change will become clearer by studying the "steps involved in making household projections." *Ibid.*, p. 7.

The rates of change assumed in the four projections are as follows:
Series I: Equal for each ten-year period to the rates of change in the eight-year period 1947–55

Series II: Equal to the average annual rates of change 1950–55

Series III: Equal to half the average annual rates of change 1950–55

Series IV: No change from 1955 in the per cent of single persons, the per cent of persons who are heads of households, etc.

Chart 12–2 shows the changes implied by the four sets of projections. The increases in households from 1955 to 1975 vary from 29 per cent for *Series IV* to 41 per cent for *Series I.* These are slightly higher than the percentage increases shown for the total population by the methods outlined in the preceding section, because of the rapid growth expected for households formed by individuals independent of families.

The projections are best considered in relation to the plausibility of the assumptions made, and should not be taken to represent a probable range of movement. At mid-1957 the growth in number of households was somewhat in excess of the projection shown in *Series I,* but that is not to be considered clear evidence that any of the projections are too low to represent secular growth.

The implications of the projections with regard to growth in number of families clarifies the picture. In *Series I,* the one which projects the most rapid growth in number of households, the median age of women at first marriage is assumed to decline by a half year from 1955 to 1975; it is assumed to remain at the 1955 level in the other three series. A decline of only a half year occurred between 1890 and 1940, but a decline of a full year, to 20.2 years, occurred in the forties. Little further decline had occurred by 1955.

Some decline in the size of households from 1955 to 1975 is assumed in all cases, dropping from 3.34 persons to as low as 3.14 in *Series III.*[15] The number of children per household shows no decline for *Series I* and *II* since high fertility rates are implicitly assumed in both.[16]

---

[15] The average size of the *family* is larger, 3.6 persons in 1955, and declines less because greater growth is implied for primary individuals than for primary families.

[16] The arithmetic mean of the number of children per *family* rises in these cases because the large increase in primary individuals is eliminated from the denominator of the ratio. The number of households is, by definition, the same as the number of occupied dwelling units. The number of husband-wife families is substantially less, because of other primary families and primary individuals. In 1955 the 47.8 million households were distributed as follows: husband-wife, 76 per cent; other male-head primary families, 3 per cent; female-head primary families, 9 per cent; male primary individuals, 4 per cent; female primary individuals, 8 per cent. "Projections of the Number of Households and Families: 1960 to 1975," p. 4. Making the number of households equal the number of occupied dwelling units forces separate treatment for summer and vacation dwellings. Quasi households, such as institutions, hotels, and large rooming houses, are not counted as households. See further discussion of residential building in Chap. 4.

INTEREST RATES

Interest rates represent the price of money, although market changes reflecting the price may be somewhat involved. For instance, long-term interest rates are derived from the relation between the contractual dollar return and the market price of a bond. Being a price, an interest rate is controlled by demand for, and supply of, funds as well as by institutional factors, which are particularly important in this market.

The principal sources of capital demand are: (1) business plant and equipment; (2) business working capital, especially inventories; (3) building mortgages; (4) government deficits and interim needs; and (5) increase in outstanding installment credit. The principal sources of supply of funds are: (1) gross business savings; (2) personal savings; and (3) government surplus and interim refunding. The demand and supply relationships are prospective; historically the total funds supplied equal the total funds received and the interest-rate adjustment has already taken place. It is the unbalance between demand and supply which indicates a market force tending to change interest rates. Historical figures poorly reflect upward or downward pressures; instead, the amount of funds to be demanded and to be supplied without credit expansion must be visualized.

This is a difficult task which has seldom been performed satisfactorily. The most important available information on demand is derived from plant and equipment surveys and forecasts of government financing. The latter must depend on government budgets and announced financing dates. Demand for mortgage money can best be projected by applying the financed proportion of housing to a forecast of residential housing demand. Inventory investment is most closely related to the general-business outlook. Installment-credit demand is dependent upon the market for principal consumer durable goods and upon disposable income.

The most important clues to personal saving are the Survey of Consumer Finances, the SEC estimates of increase in asset ownership, and a projection of the recent trend of personal savings to disposable income. The business-depreciation allowance included in gross business saving is quite stable over short periods, and the recent trend can be effectively projected into the future. The undistributed-profit portion of total profits is principally dependent on general-business conditions. This summary is quite inadequate, but there is as yet little evidence of effective use of the technique.

One of the difficulties is that varying proportions of total savings are made publicly available and that the same demand may create differing market pressures. Robinson estimates that corporate net saving (with depreciation reserves eliminated) was a much larger proportion of total net saving in 1947–49 than in 1951–52.[17] A large proportion of corporate saving, especially among manufacturing companies is spent internally. Different market effects result when shifts occur in the source of funds, partly because the flow of funds through savings institutions is changed; when personal savings bulk large, the channels employed by savings institutions become important.

With banks amply supplied with reserve funds and with only limited demand pressures, a deficiency in savings flow may produce little or no rise in interest rates. Once it becomes clear that demand will substantially exceed the supply of savings made available without resort to credit extension, interest rates may rise rapidly because of anticipation of what the market will bring in the future.[18] This is to a considerable extent due to fear that the market may become "congested," that new issues will not sell at the rates offered. The influence is, of course, stronger when a large proportion of total savings flows through public markets.

Anticipated declines in interest rates are usually less important, especially in the long-term-interest market. This is true partly because life insurance and other financial institutions often resort to a broadening of market practices to avoid endangering contractual rates of return. The forecaster, therefore, must expect upward demand pressures to produce prompter effects under most circumstances than downward pressures. However, prompt and large inventory liquidation leads to rapid declines in the short-term market.

The amount the Federal Treasury will have to borrow can be the predominant market influence over short periods because of the relatively large amounts which may be involved. Other demands do not flow evenly, but, nevertheless, they are so widely dispersed that there is a tendency toward a fairly continuous flow. In estimating the Federal government influence, there is need for estimates of cash expenditures and cash receipts. These are set approximately for the year ahead at most times by established budgets and existing tax laws. Frequently, Treasury action is not announced far in advance. Leeway is often possible in connection with precise funding dates because of optional call dates on outstanding bonds.

Questioning the business outlook may lead to revision of Federal government expenditures in order to introduce offsetting fiscal controls.

---

[17] Roland I. Robinson, "Forecasting Interest Rates," *Journal of Business*, 27:87–100, January, 1954, p. 94.
[18] *Ibid.*, p. 92.

Therefore, the current forecasts of Washington economists may play an important role in shifting Treasury demand for funds.

Theoretically, the Federal Reserve can be expected to offset technical money-market factors, such as seasonal demand for money (especially the peak fall demand), gold flows, changes in money in circulation, and even large government offerings. Although the Federal Reserve does play a vital role in this respect, often control is exercised by failing to provide a complete offset. For instance, if some hardening of the market appears desirable, the funds made available may be inadequate to take care of the fall seasonal-peak needs. Technical market factors influence interest rates largely as the Federal Reserve permits, if at all.

As often pointed out, the Federal Reserve could, at least temporarily, offset any demand or supply influence. The expectation that the Federal Reserve is going to do so may delay change in interest rates. The action of the Federal Reserve is seldom arbitrary, however, and usually no more than a limited influence is attempted. The Federal Reserve influence may not always be predictable, but with few exceptions policies have followed a consistent pattern, and they can be at least partially anticipated.

Market demand and supply are of central importance in establishing interest rates, although special attention must be given to shifting proportions of savings funds publicly offered, probable effect of anticipated market changes on the current market rate, special effect of Treasury offerings, and the policy followed by the Federal Reserve. Reasonably effective forecasts of interest rates may be expected in the future, although results achieved so far do not warrant detailed illustrations.[19] Experience will play a major role. Particularly, the forecaster must recognize that interest rates typically exhibit a resistance to change, but that they tend to change promptly with the development of critical situations.

THE STOCK MARKET

Brief attention may be given to the forecasting of stock-market averages and individual-stock prices. At the outset it should be noted that stock-market forecasting is significant not only from the point of view of investing but also in adding to perspective in general business and sales forecasting. Forecasting for the guidance of the investor does more than produce gains for some investors at the expense of others. Good

---

[19] *Ibid.*, pp. 95 ff. Robinson suggests a four-stage analysis in forecasting interest rates: (1) preparation of a general-business forecast; (2) comparison of levels of *ex ante* saving and investment implicit in this forecast; (3) a preliminary appraisal of technical money-market factors; and (4) a forecast of the nature of Treasury financing needs and Federal Reserve policy.

stocks may gain in value so that all who invest in them profit. By encouraging more promising ventures and discouraging less promising
ones, the investor may perform an economic service to society in general.

The forecasting of stock-market averages is properly considered separately with regard to the long-term trend, business-cycle movements,
and "technical" variations. The most important single influence in the
long term is commodity prices. Other factors, such as shift in the proportion of total capitalization which is accounted for by equities and
the influence of taxes and social controls on profits, are less clear. At
most times it is reasonably safe to project rising stock-market values
with advancing commodity prices, which are implicit in present secular
trends.

Stock-market prices usually are positively correlated with general-
business expansion and contraction, although they tend to lead general-
business activity. The reason for some consistency of movement with
general business is the pronounced effect of business expansion and
contraction on profits. Any other factor which may be expected to influence profits similarly can be expected to react on stock prices to
about the same extent. This fact largely explains the failure of stock
prices to follow general-business movements as closely since the war
as before. The economy has been disturbed by several dynamic situations since the war, but product demand has remained at a reasonably
high level at all times, so that the effect of general-business movements
has often appeared to be swamped. Other forces have occasionally had
a more powerful impact on profits. For instance, the stock market broke
drastically in September, 1946, a time when general-business activity
was tending to expand rather than decline. The stock-market break was
due to a conviction that uncontrolled inflation would not occur, rather
than to general-business prospects. Uncontrolled inflation, if it had occurred, would have been an extremely important reason for holding
equities. It may be that the postwar period has been unusual with respect to the factors, other than general-business activity, which have
had an important influence on profits. Average stock prices move with
profit prospects whether or not these are dependent upon movements
in general-business activity.

If the major relationship is with general-business activity, the best
stock-market forecast is related to the forecast of general-business activity. If profit prospects are founded principally on other forces, forecasting will have to depend not only on anticipating what these other
forces are but upon predicting the profit prospects involved, not a very
hopeful procedure. If such influences are to predominate, the "business-
cycle movement" type of forecast may be largely ignored. Rather mild

expansions and contractions in general business would be implicitly assumed.

Since the stock market tends to lead general-business activity, the chances are that the forecasts of stock-market turning points will be late. From the standpoint of investors' profits, forecasting the precise turning point is not as important as judging correctly the approximate duration of the bull market which accompanies business expansion and of the bear market which accompanies business contraction. A technique sometimes judged to be helpful in forecasting business-cycle movements is the Dow theory, which is briefly examined below.

Actually, stock buyers have limited interest in business-cycle forecasting of the stock market. The general investor usually buys for the long pull, and therefore he is principally interested in long-term forecasts. The trader is principally interested in buying and selling over the shorter technical movements of the market.

The technical movement involves recurrent spontaneous reactions in a bull market and recurrent spontaneous rallies in a bear market. The rises and falls usually occur within a period of a few months. The market stops rising only when it reaches an "overbought" condition in a bull market; it stops falling only when it reaches an "oversold" condition in a bear market. "Overbought" and "oversold" are terms referring to market prices which come to be accepted by the average trader as high or low, relative to current conditions. A reaction or rally does not, in general, reach the low or high of the preceding reaction or rally unless the bull or bear market is ending.

The trader attempts to forecast how long prices will rise before a reaction in a bull market, and how long the reaction will last; similarly he attempts to forecast how long prices will fall before a rally in a bear market, and how long the rally will last. He thus is interested in the short-term trend of the movement. His effort is to buy early in rising movements and sell before prices turn down, and to sell early in declining movements and buy before prices turn up. Generally, turning points are not anticipated, but transactions are paired along a single rise or fall.

Various methods are used, ranging from intuitive observation to fairly involved mechanical schemes. A few may be noted. A trailing moving average (which spots the moving average at the most recent date of the period averaged) shows the general trend of the movement. Sometimes two moving averages of different lengths are employed, perhaps one of three-months length and the other of six months. When the short moving average falls below the longer one, the end of a rising movement is signaled, and likewise the end of a falling movement is signaled whenever the short moving average rises above the longer moving average. Similar conclusions are sometimes derived from a comparison between an index of widely fluctuating speculative stocks and the general average of the market. Market volume is considered to confirm the price movement. One way of using that idea is to watch the rounding off of a price-times-volume measure. The strength of the market is sometimes measured by the comparable movement of the average rise of rising stocks and of the average fall of declining stocks. A slackening of the increase in rising stocks and a speeding up of the fall in declining stocks is taken to indicate the ending of a rising movement.

Trader speculation is not limited to the technical movement, which usually lasts several months. Stock prices back and fill over various shorter-length periods, although the amplitude of movement is usually less than in the longer technical movement. At the extreme, there are the day traders who follow the practice of getting in and out of the market on the same day. Traders operating on these shorter movements sometimes follow mechanical patterns, perhaps designed by themselves, but more frequently they follow their own intuition with the guidance of close and constant observation.

Any discussion of trading according to the movement of market averages is somewhat artificial, for individual stocks and not market averages are bought and sold. Most traders think primarily in terms of the limited group of stocks in which they are interested and only secondarily of general market movements. Although they typically follow standard security analysis in evaluating stocks, they give some attention to market action. One important kind of work has been most highly developed by the Value Line Investment Survey.[20] The price of an individual stock is compared currently with a figure computed by multiple correlation, employing several controlling variables. The difference in values is measured in standard-deviation units, and thus the actual price is assessed to be about right or significantly high or low (taking into account not only the standard-deviation difference from the computed price but also the extent to which the computed figure is rising or falling).

One school of thought has advanced the idea that stock movements produce certain formations indicative of future patterns.[21] We can do no more than illustrate the formations here. One formation is called a "head-and-shoulders movement." It is composed of three relatively sharp peaks in the price of the stock, occurring in succession and following rapid advance in the stock to the level at which it reacts following the first two peaks. This level is called the "neckline." The first peak is

---

[20] A service sold by Arnold Bernhard and Co., Inc., New York 17.

[21] See particularly Robert D. Edwards and John Magee, Jr., *Technical Analysis of Stock Trends* (Springfield, Mass.: Stock Trend Service, 1954). A more critical statement will be found in George L. Leffler, *The Stock Market* (New York: The Ronald Press Company, 1951).

called the "left shoulder" and is accompanied by a contrasting peaking in volume of sales of the stock. The second peak is higher and is also accompanied by peaking in volume; it is called the "head." The third peak is even with the first shoulder and is not characterized by a rise in volume; it is called the "right shoulder." The stock price falls after that peak to the neckline, and failure of prices to reach the level at the head together with failure of volume to increase with the last rise leads to a "breakout" to lower prices.

Another formation is called a "rectangle." A stock rises and falls to peaks and troughs lying on two approximately parallel lines. The stock will ultimately break through the upper or lower line, usually to substantially higher or lower prices, but the stock-market "chartist" holds that the direction of breakout is uncertain until that occurs. The "symmetrical triangle," or "coil," is a formation with similar connotations. The stock rises to slowly falling peaks and falls to slowly rising troughs, such that lines drawn through the peaks and troughs produce a symmetrical triangle. Sales volume of the stock declines as the apex of the triangle is approached, until suddenly the stock breaks out either in a rise or fall with increasing volume. Although such formations can be illustrated by some stock movements at particular times, no evidence is available on their forecasting dependability.

One idea which has proved generally useful is a "resistance" level. Stock averages or given stocks rise or fall to approximately equal price peaks and price troughs. If repeatedly they fail to break through, they are unlikely to rise or fall to the "resistance" level. If, however, they do break through, the price can be expected to continue to advance or decline for some time. The logic of the idea is fairly clear. The buyer is unlikely to pay higher prices than recent maximums unless prospects are promising, and the seller is unlikely to sell at lower prices than recently paid unless the prospects are unfavorable.

The resistance level is a major concept in the Dow theory. This theory is applied to market averages as well as to the price of individual stocks. In relation to market averages, it is taken as indicative of the continuation of a bull or bear market. The theory as generally stated involves confirmation by another stock-market average of the breakthrough of resistance levels by the industrial average. The rail average was originally employed for confirmation and often is still so employed. Ordinarily, volume is expected to rise when prices rise in a bull market and to fall when prices fall in a bear market. These are some of the major points stressed in the Dow theory.[22]

The Dow theory has been under increasing attack in recent years.

[22] A sympathetic explanation of the Dow theory will be found in Robert Rhea, *The Dow Theory* (New York: Simon and Schuster, Inc., 1938).

The secular growth for rail companies is less than for industrial, and therefore confirmation has not been as effective as in earlier times when railroads were still growing. Some other average, such as for utilities, is sometimes used for confirmation. Since the war, neither expansion nor contraction in general-business activity, as explained above, has led to wide variation in profit prospects, and erratic influences leading to such variation have been unusually important. This has tended to produce less regular bull and bear markets. Erratic influences do not fit the resistance-level pattern too well; they may tend to shift the vertical level of movement rather than to change its slope, a characterization which applies in a limited way to the violent decline in September, 1946.

Recently an effort has been made to forecast the stock market by surveying investors to find out their plans to buy, hold, or sell stocks.[23] It is not necessarily assumed that the investors interviewed are good forecasters or that they can aid in foreseeing the movement of the market for any considerable period of time. The fact is, however, that they may exert a critical influence on the near-future market and thus are in a good position to make their forecasts come true. Their sentiments may be controlling, even some months in advance, if no changes occur in earnings, dividends, interest rates, and other economic factors. Whether their plans would remain firm if such changes should occur is less easy to say. We do know that key traders usually keep an open mind on the outlook, although groups who buy without regard for short-period fluctuations, such as many small investors, are becoming increasingly important.

The *Fortune* survey, described in the preceding paragraph, was planned carefully, and questions were asked to uncover the kind of assumptions on which buying plans are based. If these assumptions are found to be consistent among various groups of investors, market influences may become more apparent. We must wait to see whether surveys of plans of investors have important forecasting value.

OTHER PROCESSES

The forecasts considered in this book fall far short of presenting the complete range of possibilities which might be of interest in economic and social analysis. Many of the possibilities are matters of intensive detail, like individual prices and individual output series or the outlook for various geographical areas. Some social fields, such as health, medical care, education, and religion, have not been touched upon, not because they are unimportant but because they fall outside the main line

[23] Irwin Friend and Sanford Parker, "A New Slant on the Stock Market," *Fortune*, September, 1956.

of development in this book. Although the range has been incomplete, the forecasts covered do throw a limited amount of light on the methods which would be required in other fields.

Brief consideration is given here to a few important processes for which forecasts have been quite unsatisfactory but which are important and germane enough to our framework to warrant some attention.

Wage Rates. Except for short recessions in recent times, average wage rates have moved with average prices, as shown by Chart 12–3. The

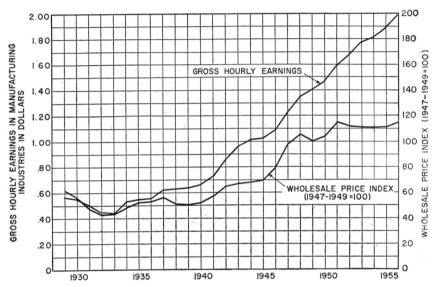

CHART 12–3. Gross Hourly Earnings in Manufacturing Industries and the Wholesale Price Index.

forecast of prices is the most reliable indicator of the direction of movement. Attention should also be given to the level and movement of general-business activity and to changes in unemployment. Wage rates are likely to rise when increases occur in industrial production, even though prices may tend to decline temporarily, as in the buildup phase in 1952, during the Korean engagement. The lower the unemployment level, the more freely wage rates rise, although limited increases in unemployment will not produce wage-rate declines under existing institutional arrangements. No general declines occurred in the recessions of 1937–38, 1948–49, or 1953–54.

To get a clearer picture of likely wage-rate increases in the near future, industry relations must be studied in some detail. They are most likely where prices are advancing more rapidly than costs. Industries with labor-union cases coming up for readjustment represent the most critical areas. Prospects are better understood if these are viewed in relation to recent settlements, which tend to establish something of a "pattern." Compilations made by the Department of Labor aid in summarizing the pattern.[24] The extent to which recent patterns are likely to be followed will be determined partly by the recent profit experience of the companies involved and by unemployment rates in the particular industries. It is true, however, that the outcome will be tempered by the business outlook anticipated by managements negotiating the contracts. Some of the result also is dependent upon continuing contracts, such as cost-of-living and semiautomatic adjustments.

Business Population. Business population—the number of business firms—has moved fairly closely with deflated gross national product in the past. A relation of business population with deflated gross national product and a trend factor fitted to annual data 1929–40 and 1948–52 produces estimates very close to actual in the prewar period and to an approximate trend in the postwar period.[25] Some approximation of the business population can be forecast by use of a gross-national-product projection.

There is a close correlation between the number of firms and deflated income payments by state.[26] The past relation between income and business population in a state might provide a good basis for anticipating future business population, having given a state income projection.

More confidence would be provided by reliable relations between the number of firms in various major groups and satisfactory explanatory variables: also, between a size breakdown and explanatory variables. The Department of Commerce business-population figures are classified by manufacturing, construction, retail trade, wholesale trade, services, and other industries. The forces leading to business births and deaths differ in these various industries, and the numbers required to do a given amount of business vary from one type of business to another. For instance, the expansion of construction firms accounts for an unusually large part of the increase in business population in the postwar

[24] A monthly publication entitled "Current Wage Developments" is issued by the U.S. Department of Labor. It presents a table of important wage changes.

[25] See Betty C. Churchill, "Recent Business Population Movements," *Survey of Current Business,* January, 1954. The equation is $Y_c = 2,264 + 11.20X + 14.74t$, where Y_c is the computed number of firms in thousands; X is gross national product, excluding government and agriculture, in billions of 1939 dollars; and t is time in years in deviations from 1934. The rapid rise in number of firms from 1945–47 may have accounted for a slight wavering of the actual number about the estimates in the following years, or the prewar relations may have changed.

[26] See Betty C. Churchill, "State Distribution of Business Concerns," *Survey of Current Business,* November, 1954, p. 22.

period. Perhaps good relations could be obtained between the number of firms and the amount of business done by line of business.

Consumer Credit. Installment credit to be extended is dependent upon the dollar amount of consumer durable goods which will be sold, the down payments required, and the proportion of buyers who will buy on credit. Projection of sales of consumer durables is made in general-business forecasting. The proportionate amount of down payments will not change much when installment-credit extension is unregulated. No direct method is available for forecasting the proportion of buyers who will buy on credit, but the proportion tends to move with disposable income. Hence the explanatory variables for installment-credit extension are generally taken to be the sales of consumer durables and disposable income. In general, such a relationship assumes that if consumers become overextended in buying durables, the fact will be recognized in the forecast of consumer durables. It would be more logical to estimate the overextension of credit by a direct analysis of credit relationships.

One method employed in analyzing credit relationships is to project the per cent of disposable income which credit extensions in excess of repayments constitute. A figure of 2 to 2.5 per cent is sometimes held to be critical, leading to a self-correcting phase of credit lending.

Noninstallment credit is closely related to disposable income, the total outstanding rising by a somewhat higher rate than disposable income. Irregularities are less than in installment credit, since the movement is tied to a more stable type of purchase and to customary credit-account practices.

Advertising Expenditure. Total advertising expenditure moves closely with the total volume of sales, although it differs substantially for different types of goods and for different markets.[27] A fierce competition has arisen between different media in retail markets, and surveys are commonly made to indicate the effectiveness achieved by various media. On the basis of the indications obtained, expected returns are forecast. Advertising expenditure ordinarily will be distributed among various media on the basis of indicated expected returns.

Fashion Trends. Several fashion-trend services provide forecasts of fashions on a subscription basis. The forecasts are based partly on a "fashion cycle."[28] The length of the cycle varies greatly from one type

[27] To some extent, the relationship between advertising expenditure and volume of sales is dependent upon the practice of budgeting a fixed percentage to advertising expenditure. If each advertising campaign were considered independently on its own merits, a "task" method now emerging in a few large companies, the relationship might come to be less close.

[28] See Delbert J. Duncan and Charles F. Phillips, *Retailing Principles and Methods*, rev. ed. (Homewood, Ill.: Richard D. Irwin, Inc., 1947), pp. 59 ff.

of goods to another and from one time to another. The cycle is difficult to project until it is well under way; fads sometimes arise which follow no preconceived pattern. There is, however, a widespread belief that, once a fashion cycle gets under way, it will run its course and that little can be done to control it. Witness the efforts made by fabric manufacturers to discourage hobble skirts shortly after the end of the first decade of the century. Wide cooperation of fashion leaders in publicizing pannier skirts produced no noticeable effect.[29]

Fashion forecasting is applied to color, styling, and fabrics and to such items as the length of women's dresses. Brown lists three general methods of fashion forecasting.[30] Based on the principle of fashion cycles, counts are made of, say, the frequency of a given color of wearing apparel in successive weeks in a fashionable hotel. If this appears to represent an incipient fashion cycle, projection is made on the basis of the expected shape of the cycle. A second method is based on leader-group analysis. Styles which will be accepted are forecast by watching the styles worn by a "social set." A third method is based on consumer-jury opinions. Proposed styles are shown to a group of "typical" users to obtain an indication of their preferences.

[29] Paul Nystrom, *Economics of Fashion* (New York: The Ronald Press Company, 1928), pp. 11–12.

[30] Lyndon O. Brown, *Marketing and Distribution Research*, 3d ed. (New York: The Ronald Press Company, 1955), pp. 510–511.

CHAPTER 13

Checking the Adequacy of Forecasts

It might seem that this chapter should offer a test for methods of forecasting employed in the past to determine which have been most successful. The problem of evaluation is more complicated than implied by that approach. Seldom can we claim that any historical forecast is solely the product of a single method. Several different methods are almost always used, and the different methods combined shift from time to time.

The checking of individual performance is not much more promising. Many of the best forecasts are not made by individuals as such but by organizations, and the responsibility of any particular individual within the organization changes as time goes on. Some of the most useful forecasts have not become available for public inspection.

The fact that many forecasts are the product of organizational rather than individual effort means that forecasts cannot generally be interpreted as the anticipations of particular individuals. The results are not therefore adequately viewed within an economic-theory framework which contrasts the anticipations of individual decision makers with the realizations later faced. Evaluation in the light of economic theory becomes a complicated process. This fact does not reduce the importance of such an evaluation, but achievements to date are meager and checking results against economic theory will not be attempted in this book.

To some extent our attention must be directed to the improvement of methods of evaluation rather than to actual evaluations. Later in the chapter we trace the effectiveness of forecasting work as revealed by the historical record. The results are put in clearer perspective if attention is first directed to the problem of establishing a satisfactory checking process.

Substantial advances have recently been made in checking weather forecasts.[1] In so far as the procedures are applicable to economic fore-

[1] See especially Irving I. Gringorten, "The Verification and Scoring of Weather Forecasts," *Journal of the American Statistical Association*, 46:279–296, September,

casting, they are procedures for judging a forecast against expected variation and making separate evaluations of the utility of the forecasts and the skill of the forecasters. The improved methods of evaluation recommended here are principally adapted from weather forecasting.

CHECKING AGAINST EXPECTED LEVEL OR VARIATION

If, during the five years 1952–56, forecasts of gross national product had been made on the basis of the actual level in the preceding year, the error never would have equalled 8 per cent, and the average absolute amount of error would have been less than 5 per cent (compared with the average gross-national-product value). Any forecast missing by more than 5 per cent on the average would have performed poorly, as judged by this test. The reason is that the level of activity was relatively stable throughout the period. However, the test assumes that the forecaster should have anticipated this stability, which is not clearly the case. Hence, it is not necessarily true that a 5 per cent error should be rated unsatisfactory.

The change which occurs is a better standard than the level. Economic values are serially correlated; the level of the value in the next time period is partly dependent upon the level in the current time period. Amount of change is a more sensible standard than past levels, but few forecasters would assume that recent changes will continue unmodified into the future. An even better standard is an average rate of secular growth, say 3 per cent per year, instead of maintenance either of recent changes or of last year's level. If 3 per cent growth is assumed for the five years 1952–56, the maximum forecasting error in any year would have been only slightly greater than 4 per cent, and the average absolute amount of error would have been only slightly more than 3 per cent. The fact that recent annual changes in many series have been predominantly influenced by secular growth accounts to a substantial degree for the postwar improvement in forecasts, as explained later in the chapter.

Although a forecast that gross national product would rise 3 per cent from year to year would have come close to the actual turnout, the result would not have been very good judged by the part of the *change* accounted for from year to year. The average absolute amount of deviation of the forecast from the actual for the five years would have come to nearly three-fourths of the total year-to-year differences, thus (in billions of dollars):

1951; Glenn W. Brier and Roger A. Allen, "Verification of Weather Forecasts," in *Compendium of Meteorology* (Boston: American Meteorological Society, 1951), pp. 841–848; and "Panel Discussion on Forecast Verification," *Bulletin of the American Meteorological Society,* 33:274–278, September, 1952.

(1) Year	(2) Actual GNP	(3) 103% of GNP in previous year	(4) (2) − (3)	(5) Actual change in GNP from previous year
1952	345.4	338.1	−7.3	+17.2
1953	363.2	355.8	−7.4	+17.8
1954	361.2	374.1	+12.9	−2.0
1955	391.7	372.1	−19.6	+30.5
1956	414.7	403.5	−11.2	+23.0
Absolute total..	...	...	58.4	80.5
Average........	...	...	11.7	16.1

Projection on the basis of a constant increase of 3 per cent per year gives no weight whatever to the actual variation which occurs from year to year. Judging against actual variation, one would expect the secular-trend method to perform poorly.

It is tempting to conclude at this point that a 3 per cent average error in forecasting the level of gross national product in the early fifties would have represented a poor performance, since one could have done that well by a mechanical projection of a reasonable rate of growth. Certainly the mechanical illustration points to that conclusion. Nevertheless, the deviations shown in column (4) of the above tabulation for the years 1952, 1953, and 1956 do not indicate a particularly poor performance. With a good performance, the recession should have been spotted for 1954, and recovery with more than a secular-growth rise in 1955. The projections in column (3) are off about 2 per cent in the other 3 years. This is less than half of the actual change shown in column (5).

The relatively mild variation occurring in the early fifties sets a high standard for the forecaster. With satisfactory performance, he should be able to locate the times when expansion or contraction will occur. With regard to the amount of variation expected, a minimum error of less than 3 per cent appears unreasonable. Both quantity and price changes are involved in gross-national-product projections. As indicated above, the stability experienced was much greater than in the prewar decade. The minimum performance to be set depends on whether or not the forecaster should have been expected to anticipate this greater stability. There is no objective way of answering that question if the forecasting standard is limited to the naïve model.

Checks against minimum mechanical performance, called "filter technique" in Chapter 10, usually involve comparison either with actual levels or with a recent actual amount of change. The author believes that projecting a plausible growth rate is a better criterion than recent actual amount of change for most short-term forecasts, but the development of a growth indication would be difficult in some cases. If the amount of recent change were used for gross national product from 1952–56, the departure of the projections from actual would approximately equal the actual variation,[2] contrasted with three-fourths of the actual, which is found to be the departure when a growth projection of 3 per cent is employed as the standard. The difficulty with the use of change from the previous year as a basis for checking is that frequently it would be an implausible assumption; the forecaster clearly would not expect the same amount of change to repeat itself exactly in the short period, even if the factors responsible for change were subjected to little analysis. Assuming expected growth to occur is not implausible if nothing is known about short-period variation.

Checking forecasts against a naïve model obviously is desirable. As a general proposition, explicitly developed forecasts should do as well as a mechanical formula which gives no consideration whatever to the actual prospects for short-term changes. The mechanical formula employed may, however, actually set relatively high standards under some circumstances, as illustrated above. What is to be expected in comparison with the mechanical formula needs to be determined separately in each case.

The forecast of events which rarely occur further illustrates this point. Let us assume that a weather forecast is to be made, calling for rain or no rain. Let us further assume that, in the particular area involved, rain actually occurs only 5 per cent of the time. If no rain is forecast every day, the forecaster will be right 95 per cent of the time, possibly a better record than he can attain by taking weather conditions for each day into consideration. The conclusion would not thus be established that his forecasts taking actual conditions into consideration are worthless. The user of weather forecasts may need to bet on the weather every day, not merely on the average day in the year. He may need to know that the chances are very good that it will or will not rain on a *particular* day. The criterion of a 95 per cent average gives no consideration to that chance. Even if the forecaster is wrong more than 5 per cent of the days, his forecasts may be useful.

Similarly, business-cycle turning points occur on the average only about once in 25 months, or roughly 4 per cent of the time. If a general-business forecaster tries to spot the month at which a turning point

---

[2] The only difference from actual is that the change between the series for one year earlier would be used. The actual variation could not be employed, for it would not yet have occurred at the time of the forecast.

will occur, his average error no doubt will be more than 4 per cent. His forecast, however, may be useful. Put on a half-yearly basis, he would be expected to be right 25 per cent of the time by pure chance, and this is a more reasonable criterion. In any case, somewhat like the weather forecaster, the forecaster of general business is asked to state the chances of a turning point in *each* particular period. If he spots the turning point as *near* the actual date, he has achieved a great deal more than by saying for each month that there is a 4 per cent chance of a turning point, or that no turning point will occur since the average chance is slight.

UTILITY OF THE FORECAST

The difficulty in checking a forecast against level or variation indicated by naïve models is that the model does not indicate the forecast needed. In this section we explicitly recognize the problem of weighing the forecast against what may be considered important. If a good accomplishment is achieved against a desirable projection, we may largely ignore how good or bad forecasts are compared to results unrelated to what is desirable. It is true, however, that we cannot ignore the problem of testing the skill of the forecaster, which is considered in the following section.

The principal forecast needed relates to (1) the direction of movement at any time and (2) the time when a major turning point will occur. The amount of change is not unimportant, but at most times and in most situations it is overshadowed by the other two considerations. Major differences in amount of change are likely to be more important than minor ones. Most particularly, a movement which is essentially level should be distinguished from one which rises or falls rapidly. It is useful to recognize a very rapid rise, such as often occurs after a minor recession. Differences in rapidity of movement are most important if the differences relate particularly either to quantity or to price movement, because desirable action is more likely if there is to be a wide change in either.

Average levels or average amount of change, illustrated in the preceding section, provides too blunt a standard. A forecasting record which was continuously correct in stating the direction of change and the approximate turning points might rate very low against average change or level, having performed poorly with respect to the *amount* of change anticipated. A naïve model cannot be readily developed to reflect direction of change and turning points because these do not occur in a mechanical way. We must go much beyond naïve models in evaluating forecasts. It is not difficult to check a forecast which has been carefully and precisely recorded against the actual direction of movement and major turning points when the record of actual change later becomes available. Furthermore, if some standard is set on what is significant with regard to amount of change, perhaps along the lines indicated in the preceding paragraph, a rating scale for evaluating such changes may be developed.

The rating of the forecast against what is indicated to be useful is most important. As has been stated repeatedly in recent years, to omit verification is comparable to conducting an experiment without learning the result. The forecast obviously is not *just* an experiment, but in view of the limitations of forecasting, we cannot afford to disregard the experimental implications. Especially with the showing against naïve forecasts indicated above, ultimate checking of forecasts against the record is important.

What is useful in forecasting cannot be established in any absolute sense. The position we have taken here on the importance of forecasts of direction of movement and of major turning points may be considered merely illustrative if the reader disagrees with the judgment made on their importance. The significant point is that criteria of importance should be set up so that forecasts can be checked against them. The criteria will differ according to the forecasting situation, varying with respect to the kind of forecast undertaken and the use to which it is to be put.

Timing is such a criterion. For many purposes, such as gross-national-product forecasts to provide general guidance or forecasts to guide sales, approximate timing may be satisfactory. Knowing the exact month of the recession trough or of the expansion peak may have only limited advantages over a performance which spots within, say, six months. It may be desirable to have the forecast state both the most probable month and the six-month range within which the turning point is expected to fall. If decisions are to be based on the six-month range, the forecast will be less costly because less straining will be required to develop timing accuracy. The forecast can be made farther in advance because less current information is essential than in precise spotting; current events might have an influence, and the precise way changes are developing can be seen more clearly at a later date. This has been especially true in spotting the expansion peak in recent times. A rounding off has occurred, and the date of the downturn has remained uncertain for a considerable time after it has actually appeared. In fact, the spotting of the exact month of the peak a few months after it has become history is no mean achievement, and can be regarded as a kind of forecast, for it calls for much of the same foresight that forecasts require; the forecaster must continue to look ahead to ascertain whether or not the downturn is yet to occur, since its appearance has not been factually established.

A decision must also be made on how far ahead forecasts should be aimed. A good forecast with exact timing is hard to make far in advance, as indicated in the above paragraph, and should not be rated on the same scale as one made equally far in advance but with only approximate timing. To keep costs down and improve results, the forecast period should be made no longer than necessary in view of the uses to which the forecast is to be put. This applies principally to short-period forecasts. In long-term forecasts, within limits, a few years below some reasonable upper time limit may make little difference in the accuracy of the forecast because of the stable kind of assumptions implied.

Depending on the use to which a sales forecast is to be put, different kinds of forecasts will be found most useful. A forecast statement of a higher level than that which is felt to be most probable or a statement below the most probable may be desired for policy reasons. Such a forecast is best developed by first making a forecast of the most probable level and then adding or subtracting a load factor; the problem of evaluation is unchanged.

If a company finds that either overestimation or underestimation would be far more costly than the other in making company plans, a different kind of forecasting may be needed. This might occur in inventory forecasting, because high inventories might be less costly than low, or vice versa. In studying the various factors which must be projected in making the forecast, it may be desirable to anticipate the highest or lowest likely result rather than the most probable one. Forecasting the probable level might be a completely separate process and one in which the company has no particular interest. The forecaster does not establish company policy. The criteria should be determined by the management itself.

To determine the importance to be given to various types of forecasting, as well as to provide a scale to employ in evaluating forecasts, a weighting scheme should be developed showing the relative importance of each kind of forecast. The weights should relate to whatever scale of importance the management assigns to different kinds of forecasting work. Any kind of forecasting the company considers unessential may be ignored and eliminated from the weighting scheme. The cost of forecasts may not be commensurate with their position in the weighting scale, for the minimum cost of obtaining some forecasts with relatively low weights may be high because of the skill and the data collection they require. Even though such forecasts are given a relatively low weight, they may still be considered essential. If the discrepancy is great, it may be desirable to reexamine the weights or the decision that the low-weighted and expensive forecast is necessary. Some companies, for instance, may rate regional sales forecasts very high but may find it necessary to establish a forecast of the total economy as a background for the regional sales forecasts. Some difficulty may be experienced in rating the importance of a forecast made principally for background purposes. If it is felt that such a forecast is highly important in developing accurate regional sales forecasts, it may have to be assigned a relatively high rating even though its use is subsidiary.

If the weighting scheme is effectively developed, measurement of over-all effectiveness may be estimated by using it. By comparing the forecasts with the actual outcome, achievement scores can be assigned to each forecast. The scores can be weighted by assigned importance to obtain a measure of over-all effectiveness of the forecasting work in the company.

Aside from weights assigned, at least two other factors should be taken into consideration in evaluating the forecasting procedure. Other things being equal, simple forecasting techniques are more desirable than complicated ones, for they will be more readily understood by those who are to use the forecasts, and these individuals will contribute more readily when they have knowledge which bears on the processes considered in making the forecasts. The forecasting procedure should be kept as flexible as possible. In response to new conditions and in making use of new data as they become available, adaptations may have to be made in the procedure used. Furthermore, the checking process may uncover weaknesses in the methods, and replacement of unsatisfactory procedures can be made more expeditiously if the whole framework of forecasting does not have to be changed.

MEASURING FORECASTING SKILL

How well the forecaster does in relation to *special* objectives may differ substantially from how well he would do in relation to *standardized* objectives. It could be that the objectives set by a company present relatively simple problems and that a good record may be expected with limited skill. Cases in point might be total industry sales of a highly stable product or of a new product with large unfilled orders when productive capacity is limited. Such forecasts might be very important for a given company, and the forecasting record might be excellent, but that would not demonstrate more skillful forecasting work than poor forecasts which confront less simple problems.

The effectiveness of different forecasts may vary for many reasons other than skill. Desirable data are much more available for some forecasts than for others. Extensive data are collected in some companies; historical records which provide clues by showing past behavior are lacking in others. The most useful forecasting data, such as inventory levels, can be only roughly estimated in many of our largest industries. Available data are never entirely satisfactory, although they are more satisfactory in some circumstances than in others.

In some industries explanatory variables are particularly effective. Some explanatory variables cannot be readily forecast. Seasonal variations confuse the picture in some industries. The business-cycle variation is far from uniform among industries. Long-period growth is more clearly indicated in some industries than in others and may provide a forecasting advantage.

Type of emphasis may increase the difficulty of forecasting. Some companies require forecasts by quite detailed product lines, the sales of which tend to vary more than total sales. Forecasts by small regional territories are often more difficult to make than forecasts of the company's total market. Some companies emphasize price forecasts. Some find that only a sales forecast is necessary; others also want forecasts of new orders and inventories.

It is readily seen that an indiscriminate comparison of forecast results is likely to be unrewarding. Probably, satisfactory techniques could be developed for comparing forecasts of sales in one industry with those in another or for comparing forecasts of different processes, but little along that line has been accomplished to date, and such comparisons may be of limited value. However that may be, it is useful to recognize that all forecasts are not equally difficult, and we must not evaluate achievement as if they were.

Forecasting skill can be compared by standardizing the objective. All of the forecasts should relate to one process. Gross national product is frequently used. To be comparable, all of the separate forecasts must be made the same length of time before the period forecast, and the length of time forecast must be equal. An error frequently made in comparing postwar forecasts of the forties was to ignore the differences in the times at which the forecasts were made.

SELF-DEFEATING AND SELF-SUBSTANTIATING FORECASTS

In the above analysis the implicit assumption is made that the forecaster is trying to be right. This is not always true in forecasts made by the Department of Agriculture on the basis of intention reports. One of the purposes of these reports is to provide early information on what farmers as a whole intend to do and to encourage them to change their plans if the indicated output would not be in their best interest. As Koffsky says, "Unfortunately perhaps, we are much more often right than wrong." [3] Pig-farrowing intentions are made available in December, and the years when the actual pig crops departed markedly from the intention figures can be explained by unique influences. For example, a fairly substantial departure occurred in the spring pig crop in 1941 because hog prices rose sharply in January and farmers were urged to increase pig crops as a defense measure after the intention reports were made. March intention reports predominate in Department of Agriculture work because of the importance of spring crops, including corn, oats, barley, spring wheat, flaxseed, and potatoes. For all of these, there is a close correlation between intentions and plantings. It is clear that the intention reports do make good forecasts.

Are forecasts self-defeating or self-substantiating in the nonfarm part of the economy? Examples can be cited in which one or the other claim has been made. It is sometimes thought that a forecast of recession at least partially defeats itself by inducing early corrective action. Early 1957 is a case in point because a cutting down on inventory accumulation was at least partially due to anticipated recession. [4] If finished goods stocks are gotten well in hand at an early date, the danger of unplanned accretion of stocks at a later date is reduced. Unplanned accumulation is unlikely to be eliminated entirely, however, because the appropriate level of stocks is set against current sales as a standard. If the level of sales goes down, the need for inventories is less.

On the other hand, it is argued that forecasts are self-substantiating, largely in the tradition of psychological theory. Great fear was expressed by the Council of Economic Advisers in December, 1946, that agreement would be reached among companies that business would begin to decline in 1947, that the companies therefore would make the appropriate curtailment in operations, and thus that the prediction would become "the engine of its own verification." [5] Early curtailments do reduce total spending. If, however, early curtailments are ones which would have been made later if not currently, the prospect for stability will have been improved and not worsened. This will happen particularly if spending is at such a peak level that adding to it can only increase the price paid for goods.

If forecasts are self-substantiating, it should be possible to trace their influence, at least hypothetically, through changes in expenditure. The

---

[3] Nathan M. Koffsky, "Economic Forecasting Methods as Used by the United States Department of Agriculture," *Forecasting Techniques Applied to Business Problems* (Chicago: Monarch Printing and Publishing Corporation, 1954), p. 62.

[4] Early reports (available in May) showed a first-quarter decline in nonfarm inventories of $900 million, at annual rates and after allowance for inventory valuation adjustment. Early reports on inventory investment are based on preliminary extrapolations and may be changed substantially in later revisions.

[5] Council of Economic Advisers, *First Annual Report to the President* (Washington: U.S. Government Printing Office, December, 1946), p. 10.

contention is often made that changes in the stock market induce changes in business activity by a kind of self-hypnosis. It is possible that the pessimism or optimism generated will be a deciding factor in making some businessmen reduce or increase investment expenditure, especially if they had expected to obtain funds from outside sources. One need not rest the case for self-substantiation on vague relationships. The tendency is for businessmen who feel optimistic to increase investment. Any increase in investment will add to demand and bring new converts. Similarly, if some businessmen reduce investment expenditure, demand will be weakened. Investment decisions thus do tend partially to justify themselves for a limited time.

The effect of a sales forecast on an individual business may appear to be fairly clear. If sales are expected to decline, one immediate sequence of effects might be a curtailment of the production schedule, a reduction of inventories, and thus early adjustment. Similarly, the production schedule might be advanced immediately when a sales increase is forecast. The action the company takes may have little to do with the actual sales outcome, but a smoother adjustment may occur if the sales forecast is correct. There is a great deal of variation in the extent to which plans are dependent upon the sales forecast. If sales forecasts are largely ignored in making plans, early adjustment would occur only by accident.

If forecasts are trusted and they turn out wrong, a rapid change in plans may be required; a "surprise" effect is produced. If explicit forecasts are not made or not trusted, with unexpected developments a more cautious and adaptive approach may come to be taken. Moderate changes are less likely to be alarming in such a case because no attempt was made to anticipate them; however, large changes may produce even greater panic than when plans are based on explicit forecasts, because schedules have been set on a simple assumption, such as a horizontal movement or a continuation of recent changes. There is a modern tendency in forecasting to move as far as possible in the direction of the adaptive approach. This is made possible by continuous forecasting and successive adjustment to any changes indicated in the outlook.

Forecasts change greatly from one time to another. The extent to which they are employed in making plans, how far into the future plans are based on them, the methods employed, and effort expended in making them—all of these change. It is not practicable to trace these differences through past history, although we can indicate some of the major forces. The use of forecasts in making plans has advanced rapidly in recent years. The time horizon of plans is much farther away in prosperity than in depression. Forecasting effort expended has varied, shrinking in the thirties and expanding in the fifties.

POPULATION FORECASTS

Repeatedly, a method which for a time has produced correct population forecasts has gained general acceptance. The Pearl-Reed logistic curve, projected to 1920 and to 1930 with an error of less than 1 per cent in each case, came to be generally accepted in the twenties.[6] Long before 1940 the decline occurring in birth rates made obvious the probability of a large error in 1940.

The Scripps Foundation forecasts made on the basis of projections of fertility, mortality, and immigration were gaining wide acceptance in the thirties. High, medium, and low forecasts made in 1935 for 1940 were all within 1 per cent of actual.[7] Projecting basic causes made it possible to go into detailed analysis and to adjust for changes which were occurring in secular growth, contrasting favorably in this respect with the over-all growth projection of the logistic curve. As Dorn states:[8]

Confidence in the reliability of estimates of future population became widespread. O. E. Baker undoubtedly expressed the opinion held by many demographers and non-demographers alike when he said, "the population of the United States ten, twenty, even fifty years hence, can be predicted with a greater degree of assurance than any other economic or social fact, provided the immigration laws are unchanged."

Davis quotes a review published in 1946:[9]

With improved data, new techniques, and the precise measurement of the demographic transition that was occurring, demography tended to become science rather than literature.

Warren S. Thompson, one of the chief founders of the new method, stated in 1948:[10]

Calculations of population growth in the more industrialized nations over the next few decades should not be very far wrong, barring new wars.

Davis quotes Stuart Chase as late as mid-1949 to the effect that population forecasting was an outstanding accomplishment.

It is now well known that population forecasts underwent rapid upward revisions in the forties. With "medium" assumptions on fertility and mortality rates and no net immigration, a Census forecast made in 1947 was 6 million short of actual for 1950 and probably about 25 mil-

[6] Harold F. Dorn, "Pitfalls in Population Forecasts and Projections," *Journal of the American Statistical Association*, 45:311–334, September, 1950, p. 319. The Pearl-Reed logistic missed in 1940 by 3.5 per cent and in 1950 by about 1 per cent.
[7] *Ibid.,* p. 318.
[8] *Ibid.,* p. 312.
[9] Joseph S. Davis, *The Population Upsurge in the United States* (Stanford, Calif.: Food Research Institute, Stanford University, December, 1949), p. 15.
[10] *Ibid.,* pp. 15–16.

lion short for 1960, errors of over 4 per cent and over 13 per cent.[11] Earlier forecasts deviated even further. The principal reasons were that the fertility rates were too low and the mortality rates somewhat too high. The upsurge in births which has followed World War II was not anticipated, and the high birth rates were at first thought to be temporary. The pattern set in the thirties was considered standard. Mortality rates fell below trend projections because of the influence of the new "wonder" drugs, a development not readily anticipated.

By the mid-fifties the postwar fertility rates had remained high so long that they no longer appeared to be temporary. Greater weight therefore has been assigned to them in making population projections. We believe these new forecasts have a better chance of being right than those made in 1947, but we should not forget the assurances expressed earlier about population forecasts which have turned out to be very wrong. Perhaps many students were thinking principally of the potentialities in making separate projections for fertility rates, mortality rates, and immigration when they praised the population forecasts being made. The value of separate projections for these causal factors has come to be widely understood, and they are generally employed in spite of the fact that earlier forecasts using the same set of factors performed poorly.

PLANT AND EQUIPMENT ANTICIPATIONS

Beginning with 1947, anticipations can be compared with actual outturn for plant and equipment expenditures, reported in the joint survey made by the Office of Business Economics of the Department of Commerce and the Securities and Exchange Commission. On an annual basis this comparison is made for all industries combined in Chart 13–1. The discrepancy between anticipated and actual levels in 1947 can be accounted for by the preliminary character of the survey, since it was being set up at that time. Otherwise, the actual levels were closely anticipated except in 1950 and 1955. Only in 1950 was the direction of movement wrongly anticipated, but the discrepancy in that year is partly due to the unexpected Korean engagement in June.[12] Anticipations were far less close in individual industry groups, especially in mining and

[11] The 1947 forecasts are published in P. K. Whelpton, *Forecasts of the Population of the United States, 1945–1975* (Washington: U.S. Bureau of the Census, 1947), p. 39.

[12] Not wholly. On p. 17 of "Ten Years' Experience with Business Investment Anticipations," *Survey of Current Business,* January, 1957, Murray F. Foss and Vito Natrella state: "Actual outlays in the first two quarters had recovered to within a few percent of the 1949 level and in May 1950, in a setting of rapidly increasing overall output, business was scheduling a further rise in plant and equipment outlays for the third quarter."

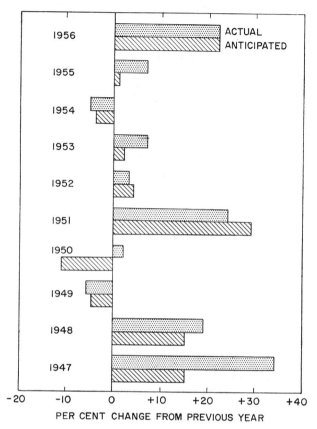

CHART 13–1. Plant and Equipment Expenditures: Anticipated and Actual. As reported in the joint survey made by the Office of Business Economics of the Department of Commerce and the Securities and Exchange Commission. SOURCE: Chart is taken from *Survey of Current Business*, March, 1957.

transportation, including railroads. The anticipations were especially close in public utilities, where long-term forecasting has been used for a longer time and is more fully developed; perhaps the problem is less difficult than in manufacturing, where demand usually appears more variable.

The record is good when comparison is made with actual level of capital expenditure, but the discrepancies appear larger when the change anticipated is compared with the actual change in expenditure (stated in percentages of actual change):

1947	45	1952	135
1948	80	1953	70
1949	85	1954	80
1950	Opposite	1955	15
1951	120	1956	100

In this tabulation a perfect relationship is represented by 100 per cent. The great deviations from that figure show that the changes were not anticipated accurately. However, for several of the years, the standard is unreasonable. In 1949, 1952, and 1954, for instance, the anticipated expenditures differ only about 1 per cent from the actual when the actual level of expenditures is taken as the base. The actual change in ex-

TABLE 13–1

PER CENT DEVIATION OF FIRST AND SECOND ANTICIPATIONS FROM
ACTUAL CAPITAL EXPENDITURES
(By quarters, 1948 to 1956)

Year	First quarter		Second quarter		Third quarter		Fourth quarter	
	1st ant.	2d ant.	1st ant.	2d ant.	1st ant.	2d ant.	1st ant.	2d ant.
1948	−2	+7	−1	−2	−5	+3	−13	−7
1949	−2	+5	+3	+3	+6	+4	−8	−4
1950	+3	+11	−2	+5	−4	+8	−18	−7
1951	−7	+7	−3	+3	+2	+10	−7	−2
1952 *	+3	+9	−2	+2	+7	+11	−3	−2
1953 *	+3	+6	−4	0	0	+5	−8	−5
1954 *	+6	+9	0	+2	+1	+5	−7	−1
1955 *	+5	+8	0	+4	−3	+4	−13	−5
1956 *	−2	+8	+1	+3	+4	+8	+4	+2

* Seasonal corrections are made beginning with 1952. Timing of the anticipations have thereby been materially improved.

SOURCE: Quarterly anticipations of plant and equipment expenditures of the Office of Business Economics of the Department of Commerce and the Securities and Exchange Commission. The table is taken from *Survey of Current Business*, January, 1957.

penditures was so slight in those years that a very small deviation from the actual change amounted to a large percentage. When only a small change occurs, forecasts of actual change are difficult because of the small amount involved. With larger deviations, the standard is more reasonable. Large deviations have been satisfactorily approximated since 1947.

Two quarterly anticipation figures are obtained, the first about four months in advance and the second about one month.[13] The record of these anticipations in relation to the actual level later reported is shown in Table 13–1. Only 6 of the 72 figures reported there are as large as

[13] Actual publication takes place at a considerably later date.

10 per cent. When the discrepancy in amount of *change* anticipated in relation to actual *change* is studied, some wide deviations appear, but serious error is not indicated most of the time. Furthermore, seasonal adjustment of the quarterly anticipations has been made since the third quarter of 1952, and this has produced a substantial improvement.[14]

The survey has performed satisfactorily in the anticipation of turning points. The National Bureau of Economic Research spotted a downturn for the economy as a whole in the fourth quarter of 1948, but plant and equipment expenditures actually increased and were anticipated to do so, although to a lesser extent than actually occurred. A decline was correctly anticipated for the first quarter of 1949. Plant and equipment expenditures rose in the fourth quarter of 1949, and a rise was spotted for the general economy at that time; the survey indicated a continued decline. A substantial decline occurred in plant and equipment expenditures in the first quarter of 1950 and a substantial rise in the second quarter; these changes were correctly anticipated.

Timing relationships have materially improved with the use of seasonal correction since 1952.[15] The direction of change was correctly anticipated at both the downturn and upturn in 1953–54. The survey should be judged against actual plant and equipment expenditures, although these have tended to lag behind general-business movement in most of the period surveyed. The survey thus has not forecast general-business activity.

There is a tendency for the reporters in the survey to overestimate the changes occurring in investment expenditures at cyclical turning points. "For example, in the initial quarter of downturn in both 1949 and the 1953–54 period, seasonally adjusted expenditures were higher than either the first or second anticipations for these quarters. Similarly, the initial quarter of upturn in 1950 and in 1955 is actually lower than either of the corresponding anticipations." [16]

A synthetic correction is now made for the tendency of manufacturers with assets of less than $10 million to understate actual outlays. For 1957 a 10 per cent increase was applied to the anticipations of these small firms, representing the average annual understatement in the previous five years.[17] This is a level correction and does not modify any cyclical bias which may occur.

A great deal of work has now been done in relating anticipations of individual businesses to actual investment made. Unfortunately, extensive

---

[14] Foss and Natrella, *op. cit.*, pp. 18–19.

[15] *Ibid.*, p. 19; and Lawrence Bridge and Vito Natrella, "Capital Expenditures in Nonmanufacturing Industries," *Survey of Current Business*, August, 1952, p. 23.

[16] Foss and Natrella, *op. cit.*, p. 19.

[17] Murray F. Foss and Vito Natrella, "Business Anticipations of Capital Expenditures and Sales, 1957," *Survey of Current Business*, March, 1957, p. 8.

as this work is, it does not entirely clear up the mystery of how a survey with dispersion as wide as that shown in Chart 13–2 can produce results as consistent as summarized above. A plausible explanation might be that some companies always over- or under-anticipate and that the directional bias is taken care of in the process of summarization; indications are that this thesis is wrong. Natrella correlated the discrepancies in anticipations among manufacturing firms in 1954 with those in 1955, and found no significant relationship.[18]

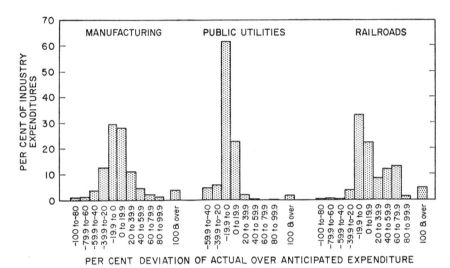

PER CENT DEVIATION OF ACTUAL OVER ANTICIPATED EXPENDITURE

CHART 13–2. Percentage Deviation of Actual from Anticipated Plant and Equipment Expenditures, 1955 (classified by size of deviation of individual companies). From the survey made by the Office of Business Economics of the Department of Commerce and the Securities and Exchange Commission. SOURCE: Chart is taken from *Survey of Current Business*, January, 1957.

However, he found, what is confirmed in other studies, that the anticipations of large companies are better borne out than those of small companies. Also, anticipations for public utilities deviate more moderately from actual than those for manufacturing and railroads, as is also indicated in Chart 13–2. Anticipations are better with large programs than with small, whether the company is large or not.[19]

When we examine in more detail the conditions indicating greater stability, they are found to involve irregularities or unexpected conformity. For instance, approximately the same proportion of large and small

[18] Vito Natrella, "Forecasting Plant and Equipment Expenditures from Businessmen's Expectations," *Proceedings of the Business and Economic Statistics Section, American Statistical Association*, Washington, 1956, pp. 124–125, 132.

[19] Foss and Natrella, "Ten Years' Experience with Business Investment Anticipations," *op. cit.*, pp. 16–20.

manufacturing firms anticipate increases in plant and equipment expenditures when decreases occur—about 15 per cent; and, similarly, about the same per cent of both anticipate decreases when increases occur—about 35 per cent.[20] In 1955 plant expenditures anticipated by manufacturing firms, in spite of the long lead time involved, proved to be no firmer than equipment expenditures.

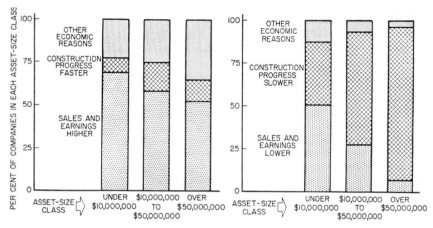

CHART 13–3. Reasons for Deviations from Planned Investment in Plant and Equipment Survey, 1955. I. Manufacturers spending more than anticipated. II. Manufacturers spending less than anticipated. Based on the survey made jointly by the Office of Business Economics of the Department of Commerce and the Securities and Exchange Commission. SOURCE: The chart is taken from *Survey of Current Business*, June, 1957.

Chart 13–3 shows some of the major reasons given by manufacturing firms for spending more or less than anticipated. In addition to the factors listed in this chart, such influences as incomplete anticipations and routine errors in estimating played a lesser part, but were especially important in firms spending more than anticipated.[21] This and other information made available by recent studies helps us understand why investment anticipations have not been borne out in individual cases.

The 1955 study of investment plans and their realization can be usefully contrasted with a similar study made for 1949. Although conditions were quite different in the two years, economic forces tended to produce some degree of stability in the outturn: [22]

[20] *Ibid.*, p. 22.
[21] Murray F. Foss and Vito Natrella, "Investment Plans and Realization: Reasons for Differences in Individual Cases," *Survey of Current Business*, June, 1957, pp. 12–18.
[22] *Ibid.*, pp. 17–18.

As between the 2 years, the differing relative importance of conditions in capital-goods industries is particularly interesting because it is suggestive of a compensatory effect, which serves to limit or modify the investment deviations caused by departures from sales and profits expectations. In the rapid upturn of 1955, forces were set in motion working in the direction of making actual outlays exceed anticipations. With sales exceeding expectations, programs for new capacity and replacements were increased. But the increased demand for new investment goods put a strain on labor and materials supplies in capital-goods supplying industries; delivery schedules were upset and many firms, especially those engaged in large programs, found that earlier anticipations could not be met for these reasons. This factor tended to reduce the excess of actual outlays over anticipated expenditures.

An opposing situation prevailed in 1949. With sales and profits falling below expectations, the incentive to cut programs was increased as indicated by the high proportion of firms which checked this factor in 1949 and also reduced programs. But this decreased demand for capital goods also made possible faster construction progress and equipment deliveries for other programs, as evidenced by the high proportion of supply reasons adduced by firms that exceeded plans in 1949. Undoubtedly the 1949 experience reflected some easing of the early postwar shortages but there can be little doubt that it reflected more than simply the unusual supply situation associated with that period.

The logic of this quotation is that, as long as relatively prosperous conditions are maintained, anticipations of plant and equipment expenditures may be self-substantiating or at least may be influenced by compensating effects, both in expansion and in contraction. If this is the major explanation of the accuracy of plant and equipment anticipations in recent years, a major assumption is relatively stable and prosperous economic conditions.

MANUFACTURERS' SALES ANTICIPATIONS

In connection with the plant and equipment survey, reviewed in the above section, an annual report is obtained from manufacturers showing their sales anticipations for the following year. These anticipations are compared with actual sales in Chart 13–4. It will be seen that the direction of anticipations was correct each year from the first reports in 1948 to 1956. Notably, the declines in sales were anticipated in 1949 and 1954. The significance of this accomplishment can readily be overestimated, however, for cycle peaks had occurred in the fourth quarter in 1948 and at mid-year in 1953. The forecasts recognized a contraction which was already under way. Since the economy was leveling off slowly in both instances, recognition that contraction was occurring and expectation that it would continue was a positive accomplishment.

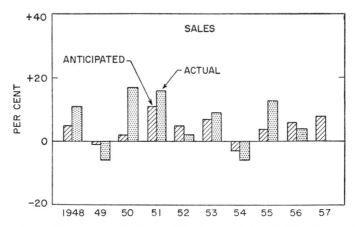

CHART 13–4. Manufacturers' Sales Anticipations and Actual Sales (comparison of deviations from the previous year). Collected by the Office of Business Economics of the Department of Commerce and the Securities and Exchange Commission in connection with the Survey of Plant and Equipment Expenditures. SOURCE: The chart is taken from *Survey of Current Business*, June, 1957.

As shown in the accompanying text table, the degree of contraction was underestimated in both 1949 and 1954 (manufacturers' sales anticipations stated in per cent of actual sales):

1948	95	1953	98
1949	105	1954	103
1950	87	1955	92
1951	96	1956	102
1952	103		

Relatively the worst forecasts were in 1950 and 1955. The errors in those years are in line with other forecasts, as outlined later in the chapter. The substantial underestimate in 1950 is partly due to the unpredictable outbreak of the Korean engagement in June of that year. The underestimate in 1955 shows some failure to anticipate rapid expansion of sales after minor contraction, a state of mind probably partly responsible for the underestimate in 1950.

DUN AND BRADSTREET SURVEYS OF
BUSINESSMEN'S EXPECTATIONS

Surveys begun in 1947 are made quarterly by personal interviews, covering a sample of well over a thousand firms at present but substantially less than a thousand in most of the early period. The sample is not collected on a probability basis, but it may be fairly representative of medium- to large-size business firms. Excluded are the very large firms, for which credit ratings can be obtained from published sources, and small firms, constituting the largest category in the business population, in the credit ratings of which there is limited interest. (The surveys are conducted in connection with the Dun and Bradstreet service in supplying credit ratings.) Reports are obtained on expectations regarding sales, employment, inventories, prices, and profits, as well as new orders for some manufacturers. They are divided into four types of business: durable-goods manufacturers, nondurable-goods manufacturers, wholesalers, and retailers. The firms are asked about their expectations two quarters hence compared with the corresponding quarter a year before. The comparison is put on that basis to avoid confusing the answers with expected seasonal changes. To make the anticipations applicable to the current situation, the comparison must be translated to apply to a change from the current quarter. Although the respondents are also asked about the current quarter compared with a year ago, time translation to compare the forecast with current conditions introduces evaluating difficulties, largely because the early years exhibit an almost universal bias in underestimating the magnitude of change.

Recent survey reports have shown only direction of change. In that form and compared with year-to-year relatives of monthly figures of the Federal Reserve Index of Industrial Production, Dun and Bradstreet sales anticipations reveal a consistent lead, as shown in Chart 6–3. A difficulty in evaluating the Dun and Bradstreet surveys is that figures collected on outturn relate to a different group of firms, and differences due to variations in sampling cannot be measured. Compared with aggregate changes indicated by Department of Commerce series, the sales, inventories, employment, and new orders (when reported) evince predictive value. Hastay correlates the diffusion indices (percentage of firms showing expansion) for these processes, classified by the four types of business listed in the preceding paragraph, with changes in comparable Department of Commerce aggregate series and almost universally finds significant relationships.[23] The anticipations provide a significantly better forecast than naïve projection of current levels at the time the surveys were made, except in retail sales. The correlations use the survey data expressed in expected changes from a year ago, and Hastay recognizes that he has been "unable to separate the purely expectational content of the forecasts from the part that reflects actual change from the initial quarter to the date of the survey."

[23] Millard Hastay, "The Dun and Bradstreet Surveys of Businessmen's Expectations," in *Proceedings of the Business and Economic Statistics Section, American Statistical Association,* 1955, pp. 93–123; *An Appraisal of Data and Research on Businessmen's Expectations about Outlook and Operating Variables* (Washington: Board of Governors of the Federal Reserve System, September, 1955), pp. 25–54.

RAILROAD SHIPPERS' FORECASTS

Railroad shippers, through shippers' advisory boards set up throughout the country under the auspices of the car service division of the
American Association of Railroads, have forecast carloadings for the
coming quarter since 1927. Data are available on 32 commodity groups
(27 in the early years) and for each of 13 regions. The forecasts are
made in terms of expected change from the actual carloadings in the
corresponding quarter a year earlier. The sample of shippers included is
self-selected, in that it depends on voluntary response to requests for
estimated shipments, but the average coverage is about 50 per cent
of shipments and is relatively complete with respect to larger shippers
in any commodity group and with respect to most important commodity
groups in any region. Careful and extensive analyses have been made
of these forecasts, and there is concurrence in finding them of slight
predictive value.[24] The indications, in fact, seem to be that a reversal
of the recent trend is often indicated.

We shall not go into the technicalities of the analyses leading to that
remarkable conclusion. It is worthwhile, however, to consider briefly
its implications. As stated in a recent study: [25]

> Where a systematic tendency exists to underestimate the magnitude of a
> four-quarter change, failure to take account of this bias in assessing the value
> of the expectations may lead to over-pessimistic conclusions. To give a crude
> illustration of the principle, suppose that each shipper's forecast was correct
> as to direction but was numerically only three quarters of the actual change.
> Considered on a quarter-to-quarter basis, such forecasts would seem merely
> to predict a continuation of the previous quarter's level of shipments; yet a
> simple multiplicative adjustment of the four-quarter forecasts would convert
> them into perfect predictors of quarter-to-quarter change. We do not antici-
> pate any such miraculous transformation of the verdict on the forecasting ac-
> curacy of the shippers' estimates. But we do feel that the verdict is open to
> question until an effort has been made to adjust for systematic bias of the
> shippers' estimates by means of some regression of actual changes on the
> forecasted ones. Put in technical language, our impression is that it is still
> not clear that the failure to find the shippers' forecasts of direct predictive
> value is wholly independent of methodological considerations.

Since there are indications that systematic underestimation exists in the
forecasts an interpretation of this kind should not be ruled out.

[24] Robert Ferber, *The Railroad Shippers' Forecasts* (Urbana, Ill.: University of
Illinois Press, 1953); articles by Thor Hultgren, Franco Modigliani and Owen H.
Sauerlender in *Short-term Economic Forecasting*, vol. XVII in National Bureau of
Economic Research, *Studies in Income and Wealth* (Princeton, N.J.: Princeton
University Press, 1955).

[25] *An Appraisal of Data and Research on Businessmen's Expectations about Outlook
and Operating Variables, op. cit.,* p. 70.

Another possibility is that a substantial number of respondents may project a horizontal change from the corresponding quarter of the preceding year, and many others may extrapolate the change which has been occurring. Such forecasts might tend to swamp the forecasts of those shippers who anticipate changes on the basis of specific information. In fact, a situation such as this could account for the indications that, on the average, shippers forecast a reversal of recent trends.[26] To evaluate shippers' forecasts, therefore, we should have information on forecasts by individual shippers or at least some distributions showing the variation in separate forecasts, information not now made publicly available.

There are some indications that shippers' forecasts have been helpful at specific times when dynamic change appeared, although apparently they have been wrong at most cyclical turning points. Furthermore, it is common knowledge that the forecasts are taken seriously by railroads and shippers and that they are periodically reviewed in regional and national meetings of shippers with representatives of the railroads. Possibly more correct forecasting is involved than a direct analysis indicates.[27]

SURVEY-OF-CONSUMER FINANCE AND
CONSUMER-ATTITUDINAL FORECASTS

The surveys of consumer "primary spending units," leading to the forecasts considered in this section, are conducted by the Survey Research Center, of the University of Michigan, at the request of the Board of Governors of the Federal Reserve System. Involved is the most extensive consumer survey made, and it is often used in forecasting, as noted earlier in this book. We may quote summary conclusions reached by a task group asked by the Board of Governors of the Federal Reserve System to evaluate consumer expectations.[28] "Buying intentions properly interpreted, appear to have predictive value." As for consumer attitudinal data, such as evaluation of one's own financial

---

[26] *Ibid.*, pp. 72–73.

[27] Note, however, should be taken of the fact that the forecasts generally move with seasonal changes. Possibly, the shippers and railroad executives are satisfied with a seasonal forecast. See Thor Hultgren, "Forecasts of Railway Traffic," in *Short-term Economic Forecasting*, especially pp. 365, 374–377.

[28] The task group was composed of Arthur Smithies, Guy H. Orcutt, Samuel Stouffer, James Tobin, Hazel Kyrk, Harold C. Passer, Bert Seideman, and Vernon G. Lippitt. See *Consumer Survey Statistics: Report of Consultant Committee on Consumer Survey Statistics* (Washington: Board of Governors of the Federal Reserve System, July, 1955). The quotations in the text are from pp. 37–39. Since 1953 the Survey Research Center has conducted a number of periodic surveys of consumer intentions, in addition to the annual surveys, without Federal Reserve support. These are not reviewed here.

situation, of durable-goods markets, of expected price movements, of expected changes in income, and of expected general-business conditions, "there is so far no convincing evidence that they make an independent contribution to ability to predict." However, "they are highly correlated with buying intentions." We may quote at length a broader evaluation:

> Consumer behavior is necessarily influenced by factors beyond the powers of consumers to foresee or control. These factors, which include unemployment, war, strikes, inflation, recession, provide numerous reasons why plans are not realized and why attitudes are modified. It is asking too much to expect consumer surveys to predict consumer purchases. The level of these purchases will ultimately be determined by the interactions of decisions by consumers, business firms and governments. A survey of consumers can at best provide one piece, albeit a very important one, in a larger puzzle. It is more reasonable to expect surveys of plans and attitudes to predict whether consumer purchases will be high or low relative to the values of factors that households may have difficulty in foreseeing or controlling. One important determinant of consumer purchases is household disposable income; events in other sectors of the economy may cause marked and unexpected changes in income during a year. Consequently, it is often more appropriate to use survey data to predict whether purchases will be high or low in relation to income than whether they will be high or low absolutely.

Furthermore, "a survey may correctly indicate that demand will increase, but the correctness of this prediction will not show up in statistics of quantity purchased unless the businessmen who produce and sell the commodity are able and willing to expand the supply." Supply shortages were particularly important in early postwar years. "For most recent years, the same kind of problem may arise not from shortages but from producers' decisions to operate near capacity even if the prices of their goods must fall in order to clear the market. Weakness in automobile demand may show itself in discounts, high trade-in allowances, and dealer distress rather than exclusively in reduction in the number of new car registrations."

There is room for some disagreement about what consumer surveys show, because the major forecasts are expressed in words rather than in numbers. To some extent qualitative statements are no doubt unavoidable, but they should be as explicit and as unqualified as possible. The task group complains that "the Federal Reserve has tended to couch its interpretations of survey results in guarded language."

The survey can claim major achievements in 1949 and 1951. In 1949, in spite of the recession, strong demand for consumer durables was correctly forecast. In 1951, buying intentions and other attitudes indicated smaller demand than the pre-Korean survey. This was generally correct, and it was timely information, at variance with the general tendency early in 1951 to project the inflationary conditions existing in the second half of 1950. Other successes are less striking, although the survey for 1954 correctly yielded pessimistic findings, but "fears about announcing them in March apparently caused the Board to emphasize the experimental nature of this method of economic research . . . especially in view of limited experience in periods of receding general activity." [29] The first survey, made in 1946, also was entirely correct in predicting an inflationary prospect. Against these four correct forecasts, those made in the other seven years were partially incorrect: 1947–48, 1950, 1952–53, and 1955–56. The 1950 forecast was essentially correct except for the war developments, which the survey could not have been expected to anticipate. The 1952 forecast was also essentially correct, but weakness of consumer demand, growing out of a reaction to scare buying after the Korean engagement in 1950, would have been substantially greater than indicated if the growth of defense production had been ignored. Could consumers have taken that into account? [30]

As stated above, the survey results are best employed in predicting changes in relation to income, in indicating the influence of other explanatory variables on consumer expenditures. The evaluations given here are made from that point of view. The survey can be expected to be helpful when interpreted in this way if past history is a satisfactory guide. Generally, however, past forecasts were made available too late to be of much value in general business forecasting. March is the earliest date at which they have become available. The notable exception on timeliness is 1951, when, on other information, consumer demand was overestimated well into the spring.

The use of consumer surveys would seem sounder if we had a better understanding of the extent to which consumers plan their purchases. Reinterviews of sampled spending units a year later permit a check on the degree of relationship between actual behavior during the year and attitudes and intentions expressed at the beginning of the year. There is a significant relationship, especially in the case of automobiles: the proportion buying among those who say they are going to buy is substantially larger than the proportion buying in the total population. Even in automobiles, however, only about half of the anticipations are fulfilled. Most buyers are persons who did not expect to be in the market.

The facts remain that durable-goods sales generally increase if an increasing proportion of the members of the sample say they plan to buy durable goods. But these are empirical facts. We do not know whether

[29] *Ibid.*, p. 42.
[30] *Ibid.*, pp. 39–46. The yearly summaries given in the reference are pointed and succinct; the partial errors stated in the text are explained.

they reflect the actual plans of those interviewed or a general attitude
with regard to buying among all consumers. If the latter is the case, the
survey may do less well when the stocks of consumer durables are more
satisfactory than in the test period.

Whether the survey reflects specific plans or general attitudes, we
have no alternative source of information on what consumers say they
will do. Some start is being made in relating expressed intentions to non-
attitudinal variables which should play an important part in the decisions
of spending units to buy: age and marital status of the head of the
spending unit, region of the country, income in the previous year and
in the current year, debt and liquid assets at the beginning of the year,
and expenditures on durables in the previous year.[31] Improved information on relations of this type will give us better insight into the dependability of data on consumers' intentions.

AGRICULTURAL FORECASTS

Forecasts by the Department of Agriculture have generally been useful. The evaluation of wheat forecasts by Baker and Paarlberg is the
most extensive work done to date.[32] An accuracy-evaluation score
measures forecasts in accordance with the extent to which decrease,
stability, or increase was properly forecast. Reasonable "ground rules"
are developed to establish the differences between those categories:
"stability" is defined in accordance with actual variation, with a third
of the historical movements closest to zero so classified; to avoid introducing a bias against longer forecasts, change is reduced to a per-month
basis. Agreement in outcome is scored 1.00, stability conditions forecast
as increase or decrease are scored .50, decreases or increases forecast as
stability are scored .25, and increases forecast as decreases or decreases
forecast as increases are scored zero. For the period 1922 to 1951, 558
forecasts relating to wheat production, carryover, and price are evaluated
at an average score of .76, halfway between a pure guessing score of .50
and a perfect score of 1.00. Approximately .80 is assigned on the average
to both production and carryover and .63 to price forecasts. In general,
forecasting accuracy has improved with time. Forecasts at major downturns and in recession have been poorer than at other times. One might
expect that production forecasts would be used in making price forecasts,
but success in price forecasting was poorest, strangely, when production

[31] Lawrence R. Klein and John B. Lansing, "Decisions to Purchase Consumer
Durable Goods," *Journal of Marketing*, 20:109–132, October, 1955.
[32] John D. Baker, Jr., and Don Paarlberg, "Outlook Evaluation—Methods and
Results," *Agricultural Economics Research*, 4:105–114, October, 1952.

forecasting was best. On the average, though, the accuracy-evaluation test indicates a good performance.

Another test employed assigns "error reduction" scores. Measurements are made of the extent to which the forecast error is less than the average

TABLE 13–2

FARMERS' PRICE AND INCOME FORECASTS

(Stated in percentage change from preceding year)

Year	Realized net income of farm operators	Prices received by by farmers
1947 forecast....	−12	−4
1947 actual......	+22	+19
1948 forecast....	−17	−1
1948 actual......	−6	+3
1949 forecast....	−8	−4
1949 actual......	−14	−13
1950 forecast....	−16	−6
1950 actual......	−17	−3
1951 forecast....	+21	+11
1951 actual......	+18	+18
1952 forecast....	+7	−1
1952 actual......	−3	−5
1953 forecast....	−5	−3
1953 actual......	−3	−10
1954 forecast....	−2	−3
1954 actual......	−12	−4
1955 forecast....	−6	−2
1955 actual......	−5	−5
1956 forecast....	+8	−2
1956 actual......	+4	0

SOURCE: James P. Cavin, "Forecasting the Demand for Agricultural Products," *Agricultural Economics Research*, 4:65–76, July, 1952, p. 75, and data from 1952 to 1956 personally furnished by Mr. Cavin.

variation in the series during the test period. The forecast is thus checked to find the part of the actual movement accounted for by the forecast. The naïve forecast, indicating that levels would remain the same from one year to another, would rate zero on this test. In forecasts of wheat production, the error-reduction score is found to be about 50 per cent, although the error varies considerably from forecasts made in December, in which the achievement is very low, to forecasts made in later months, in which the achievement rises successively. In forecasts of wheat acreage, the error reduction is about 25 per cent.

Baker and Paarlberg assign an accuracy evaluation score of .78 to forecasts of farm income and a score of .60 to forecasts of the prices received by farmers for the 1922–1951 period. Cavin finds that the forecast of prices received by farmers is in the right direction each year from 1949 to 1956.[33] There are some substantial discrepancies between forecast and actual prices in these years, although the error reduction is about a third. Cavin finds that in both 1946–47 and 1947–48 slight declines were forecast when rises actually occurred.

The direction of realized net income of farm operators is forecast correctly each year from 1948 to 1956, except for 1952. Error reduction amounts to about half in these years. A decline expected in 1954 was far less than occurred. A large decline expected in 1948 was matched with a much smaller actual decline, and a decline expected in 1949 was matched with a larger actual one. A substantial decline expected for 1947 was matched with a very large actual increase, and an expected increase for 1952 was matched with an actual decline. Table 13–2 shows Cavin's quantitative comparisons.

GENERAL BUSINESS FORECASTS, 1947–56

During this period there was a widespread and increasing use of general-business forecasts. The results shown in Table 13–3 may be representative of the better forecasts during the period, although not necessarily in agreement with the majority in every year. The percentage of years in which these forecasts agreed with the actual direction of movement is as follows:

Total employment	44
Industrial production	78
Disposable income	50
Wholesale prices	70
Retail prices	70

[33] James P. Cavin, "Forecasting the Demand for Agricultural Products," *Agricultural Economics Research*, 4:65–76, July, 1952. Test data for 1952 to 1956 were personally furnished by Mr. Cavin.

Such a test gives no credit for the years when the forecast or actual showed no change and the corresponding figure was very small; some forecasts of that type may be considered as effective as some pointing in the same direction as actual change.

TABLE 13–3

GENERAL BUSINESS FORECASTS, 1947–56

(Stated in percentage change from the preceding year)

Year	Total employment	Industrial production	Disposable income	Whole-sale prices	Retail prices
1947 forecast.....	0	+8	+6	+7	+4
1947 actual......	+2	+10	+9	+26	+16
1948 forecast.....	0	−1	0	+1	+1
1948 actual......	+2	+3	+11	+9	+8
1949 forecast.....	+1	−1	0	−4	0
1949 actual......	−1	−8	−1	−6	−1
1950 forecast.....	−1	−2	−3	−6	−3
1950 actual......	0	+7	+6	−1	−1
1951 forecast.....	+5	+15	+11	+11	+6
1951 actual......	+5	+10	+9	+12	+8
1952 forecast.....	+3	+6	+5	+2	+3
1952 actual......	+1	+3	+5	−2	+2
1953 forecast.....	+1	+4	+3	−1	+2
1953 actual......	+2	+8	+5	−1	+1
1954 forecast.....	−1	−6	−2	−3	−2
1954 actual......	−2	−7	+2	0	0
1955 forecast.....	0	+5	0	−1	−1
1955 actual......	+3	+11	+6	0	0
1956 forecast.....	*	*	+4	+2	+1
1956 actual......	+3	+3	+6	+3	+2

* No forecasts were made for total employment and industrial production in 1956.

SOURCE: James P. Cavin, "Forecasting the Demand for Agricultural Products," *Agricultural Economics Research*, 4:65–76, July, 1952, p. 75, and data from 1952 to 1956 personally furnished by Mr. Cavin.

The error reduction achieved in each of these cases is as follows (stated in percentages):

Total employment......... 22
Industrial production....... 42
Disposable income........ 32
Wholesale prices.......... 27
Retail prices 30

Although the exact levels of error reduction cannot be taken as a clear indication of ability to forecast, the low figure for the employment forecast should not be unexpected in view of the difficulty of forecasting productivity changes from one year to the next. The error reduction shown for industrial production may be taken as indicative of forecasts of gross national product in this period, because of the high correlation between these series.

Although the 1949 recession was underestimated, the 1954 recession was properly gauged, as indicated by the industrial production forecast. Forecast of a slight decline in 1948, when a rise continued for the year as a whole, should not be considered wholly unfavorable since a downturn occurred late in the year.

Failure to forecast the rise in industrial production in 1950 is partially accounted for by the unanticipated demand generated by the Korean engagement in June, but recovery actually was well under way before mid-year. It is worth noting that the forecasts are substantially improved beginning with 1951. Failure to recognize the extent of the expansion in 1955 is widely characteristic of forecasts made for that year.

The Joint Economic Committee prepared forecasts of gross national product for the years 1955 and 1956, and made the following comparisons a year later (in billions of dollars): [34]

Series forecast and adjustment	1955	1956
Gross national product, estimated at first of year .	375.0	400.0
Adjustments for revision of bench-mark data. . . .	+3.4	+3.7
Adjusted gross national product...............	384.0	413.0
Gross national product, preliminary estimate in following year.............................	387.2	412.4
Amount below first of year assumption.........	3.2	0.6
Per cent of forecast deviation.................	0.8	0.2

[34] *Report on the January 1956 Economic Report of the President,* U.S. Senate Report 1606, 84th Cong., 2d Sess., p. 101; *Report on the January 1957 Economic Report of the President,* U.S. House Report 175, 85th Cong., 1st Sess., p. 59. The Joint Economic Committee was called the Joint Committee on the Economic Report in 1956 and earlier.

This example introduces some additional problems. To the extent a level adjustment ("revision of bench-mark data") has been made it should not be charged against the forecast, and adjustment for it is proper in evaluating the forecast. Bench-mark revision represents an important difficulty in evaluating gross-national-product forecasts. A similar difficulty is that successive adjustments are made in the series as time goes on, partly because better data later become available, but usually it is unfair to contrast the forecast with the later revisions of the series.

The adjustment for changes in price involves a different kind of problem. Most gross-national-product forecasts reflect expected value changes, and should be so interpreted unless specifically stated to represent quantity only. As noted in Chapters 7 and 8, an effective value forecast does require a separate estimate of expected price change.

The yearly forecast averages out important short-term changes. The evaluation would be improved if monthly or quarterly forecasts were evaluated. Unfortunately, even for the most recent period, effective data are not available for checking shorter-period forecasts.

THE POSTWAR FORECASTS

During the war, substantial attention was given to postwar reconstruction. Generally, rather pessimistic forecasts were made of the effects of curtailed government expenditures which were certain to follow the end of the war. The forecasts involved problems markedly unlike those usually faced in business forecasting. Nevertheless, they have attracted so much attention that some evaluation is needed.

Forecasting became important to the war effort. Most of the war forecasts were reasonably effective. The forecasting problem seldom involved uncertain demand. With demand known, technological development, supply availability, and rate of output flow had to be anticipated. There is no organized body of information on the forecasts, and they were directed at problems tangential to our main purposes. They will not be reviewed here. It is worth noting, however, that the government gave more attention to forecasting than it had ever done before.

Increased attention and partial success in the war period stimulated postwar forecasts. Although there were forecasts flowing from different governmental agencies, we concentrate our attention on the Hagen-Kirkpatrick projection which is presented in Table 13–4. This forecast was made in the Office of War Mobilization and Reconversion, which had available at the time the forecasting work being done in various other governmental agencies. The forecast shown in Table 13–4 represents the more favorable of two projections made. The less favorable

TABLE 13–4

THE HAGEN-KIRKPATRICK POSTWAR FORECAST AND ACTUAL
DEFLATED EXPENDITURES
(In billions of first half of 1945 dollars; seasonally corrected
and at annual rates)

Gross national product and divisions	1945		1946					1947	
	1st half	4th quart.	1st quart.	2d quart.	3d quart.	4th quart.	Full year	1st quart.	2d quart.
GNP	206.2	182.7	175.5	177.8	173.5	173.0	175.0	174.5	177.5
Forecast		164.6	161.8	165.2	166.3	166.6	165.0	169.0	171.1
		−18.1	−13.7	−12.6	−7.2	−6.4	−10.0	−5.5	−6.4
Priv. cap. form.	4.5	15.0	21.5	28.3	30.9	31.6	28.2	32.2	33.2
Forecast		12.8	13.3	17.1	19.6	22.2	18.1	24.1	25.9
		−2.2	−8.2	−11.2	−11.3	−9.4	−10.1	−8.1	−7.3
Construction	2.0	3.6	6.0	7.0	7.0	7.0	6.8	7.4	7.4
Forecast		2.8	3.3	4.1	5.2	6.2	4.8	7.3	8.1
		−0.8	−2.7	−2.9	−1.8	−0.8	−2.0	−0.1	+0.7
Prod. dur	4.4	8.2	9.3	11.1	12.2	13.0	11.5	14.1	14.5
Forecast		6.0	7.0	8.0	9.0	10.0	8.5	11.0	11.5
		−2.2	−2.3	−3.1	−3.2	−3.0	−3.0	−3.1	−3.0
Inventory	−0.7	+0.8	+3.0	+3.4	+7.9	+8.6	+5.7	+6.4	+6.9
Forecast		+4.0	+2.0	+3.0	+3.0	+3.0	+2.8	+2.5	+2.5
		+3.2	−1.0	−0.4	−4.9	−5.6	−2.9	−3.9	−4.4
Net exports	−1.2	+2.4	+3.2	+6.8	+3.8	+3.0	+4.2	+4.3	+4.4
Forecast		0.0	+1.0	+2.0	+2.5	+3.0	+2.1	+3.5	+4.0
		−2.4	−2.2	−4.8	−1.3	0.0	−2.1	−0.8	−0.4
Government	100.7	56.4	36.9	32.4	26.3	24.6	30.0	25.0	25.5
Forecast		55.5	49.0	43.5	40.2	35.2	41.9	32.7	30.7
		−0.9	+12.1	+11.1	+13.9	+10.6	+11.9	+7.7	+5.2

TABLE 13–4. (*Continued*)

Gross national product and divisions	1945		1946					1947	
	1st half	4th quart.	1st quart.	2d quart.	3d quart.	4th quart.	Full year	1st quart.	2d quart.
Cons. expenditure.......	101.0	111.3	117.1	117.1	116.3	116.8	116.8	117.3	118.8
Forecast.....	......	96.2	99.5	104.6	106.5	109.2	104.9	112.2	114.5
		−15.1	−17.6	−12.5	−9.8	−7.6	−11.9	−5.1	−4.3
Dur. goods.....	7.2	8.9	11.5	12.8	13.4	14.1	13.0	14.8	15.2
Forecast.....	......	9.0	10.5	13.0	14.5	16.0	13.5	17.0	18.0
		+0.1	−1.0	+0.2	+1.1	+1.9	+0.5	+2.2	+2.8
Nondur. goods..	62.0	69.6	72.0	70.2	69.4	69.3	70.2	69.9	70.8
Forecast.....	......	57.7	58.2	58.9	58.5	58.6	58.6	60.0	60.4
		−11.9	−13.8	−11.3	−10.9	−10.7	−11.6	−9.9	−10.4
Services.......	31.8	32.8	33.6	34.1	33.5	33.4	33.7	32.6	32.8
Forecast.....	......	29.5	30.8	32.7	33.5	34.6	32.9	35.2	36.1
		−3.3	−2.8	−1.4	00.0	+1.2	−0.8	+2.6	+3.3

SOURCE: Taken, with permission, from Elmer C. Bratt, "A Reconsideration of Postwar Forecasts," *Journal of Business*, 26:71–83, April, 1953 (Copyright 1953, University of Chicago). The Hagen-Kirkpatrick forecast was published in Conference on Research in Income and Wealth, *Studies in Income and Wealth*, vol. X (New York: National Bureau of Economic Research, Inc., 1947), p. 95.

one assumed secular stagnation which is a complicating preconception held by many economists at the time. On the whole, a fairer evaluation will eventuate if we ignore the philosophical bias involved in the secular-stagnation assumption. The usual post mortems on the postwar forecasts have concentrated attention on the more favorable Hagen-Kirkpatrick projection.

The Hagen-Kirkpatrick gross-national-product forecast shown in Table 13–4 is stated in constant dollars. Although gross-national-product forecasts are no doubt more realistically quoted in current dollars, the price movement was so great in the period that a constant dollar forecast must be judged by constant dollars. Price deflators are specially derived to deflate actual figures for comparison in the table.[35] Using deflated figures, the forecast error reduction is about 25 per cent. Such a result should not be considered wholly unfavorable in any period and, applied to so dynamic a change as was occurring at the time, it must be viewed as quite favorable.

Although the error-reduction method, testing against actual *changes*, makes a reasonable showing, the *level* of the forecast is low. The difference in *level* between the forecast and actual is what gave the forecast its unfavorable publicity. The projected *level* of employment was derived from the forecast of gross national product. Making use of an independent forecast of the civilian labor force, unemployment figures were derived. Unemployment was overestimated from 3 to 5 million throughout the period. This overestimate called for inflationary, instead of deflationary, measures. A highly inflationary situation actually developed.

In deriving employment estimates from gross-national-product projections, change in hours of work and in productivity must be projected. These projections were quite satisfactory. Hours of work were expected to decline about 10 per cent from the first half of 1945 to the last quarter of 1946, and this is approximately what happened. Output per manhour was assumed to decline 6 per cent from the first half of 1945 to the third quarter of 1946, and the actual decline for that time period was about 10 per cent.

The forecasting error was principally in the underestimation of the level of gross national product. Table 13–4 indicates that the level forecast would, in fact, have been much lower if government expenditures had not been greatly overestimated. In the other areas, there tended to be an underestimation, with by far the greatest error occurring in expenditures for consumer nondurable goods. That underestimation was serious, but the situation was so unlike that commonly faced in most current forecasts that generalizations cannot be drawn regarding achievement on the kind of problems with which we are primarily concerned. The error in consumer nondurable goods would not have occurred if the forecasting relationship had been developed in terms of constant prices or in terms of total consumer expenditures, instead of separately for durable goods, nondurable goods, and services.[36] Since the forecasts were made in constant dollars, it would have been natural, in fact, to have developed the forecasting relation in constant dollars.

[35] This is necessary because quarterly figures are employed. Annual data are completely unsatisfactory for the purpose because of important changes within the year and because forecasts were made for only two quarters into 1947.

[36] See the author's "A Reconsideration of Postwar Forecasts," *Journal of Business,* 26:71–83, April, 1953.

Unemployment was far less seriously overestimated in forecasts by Woytinsky, the Econometric Institute, and others.[37] It is not readily possible, however, to trace the methods employed in making these forecasts. Notably, at least in the case of Woytinsky, the level of gross national product was underestimated even more than in the Hagen-Kirkpatrick forecasts. But these forecasters did not rely principally upon gross-national-product models, and they depended on a qualitative evaluation which placed great emphasis on deferred demand and liquid assets. The postwar period was a particularly appropriate time to use such a qualitative forecast.

In the more than a decade which has passed, the use of gross-national-product models has become more and more common. The performance of this model in predicting *change* expected to occur currently was satisfactory even in the postwar period. Its failure to predict the *level* of gross national product accurately is related to the particular characteristics of the postwar forecasting problem and is not a bias likely to occur at most times. Unsatisfactory forecasting of unemployment is generally to be expected, as has been explained in more detail in earlier chapters.

FORECASTS IN THE THIRTIES

Although we have no suitable quantitative record of forecasts in the thirties, clearly they were quite ineffective. Forecasting methods employed in the twenties were ill adapted to anticipate changes in the thirties. Setting favorable and unfavorable factors against each other, a qualitative method, had been widely used. Conclusions derived from it depended principally upon the bias of the analyst, and since optimistic bias was prevalent in the early part of the period of contraction, most forecasts failed to predict any general decline or greatly understated the decline. Timing relationships, a second major method, was not much more helpful. These relationships in the twenties had departed somewhat from their historical patterns, but all regularity seemed to disappear in the early thirties. Nowhere was this more obvious than in the Harvard Index Chart, which is summarized in Chapter 7; the turning points were not effectively forecast by this method after the early twenties, but during the contraction beginning in 1929 unfavorable developments and the violence of the movement led to nonsensical projections. The monetary crisis in Europe in 1931 superimposed a shift in the barometers on the Index Chart which, according to the established method of interpretation, indicated the initiation of a downturn. Deviations in the barometer

[37] See Michael Sapir, "Review of Economic Forecasts of the Transition Period," in *Studies in Income and Wealth*, vol. XI (New York: National Bureau of Economic Research, Inc., 1949), pp. 321–329, 365–367.

measurements reached fantastically large declines in standard deviation units. At best, no available method was helpful in indicating the violence or length of decline, the overshadowing development. Methodological bankruptcy came to be widely accepted.

After the initiation of expansion in 1933, government intervention assumed a prominent position and, in many forecasts, major reliance was placed on expected action by the government. The method did not prove to be very satisfactory in practice. Policy measures during the first part of the decade did not rest primarily on expenditures, and their influence was difficult to predict. For instance, whether the analyst predicted correctly the sidewise movement from 1933 to 1935, partly created by the NRA,[38] depended largely on his ideological bias. Rapid and unpredictable shifts took place in the policies adopted. For instance, President Roosevelt's announcement at a press conference on April 2, 1937, that some prices were too high was so interpreted; it had an unpredictable contractionary influence.

Businessmen became unwilling to look far into the future. Secular-trend and growth forecasts almost disappeared. When economic-growth forecasts did appear, they were unrelated to ability to produce, the essential basis employed in the fifties, when emphasis came to be placed on changes in labor force minus float, productivity, and weekly hours. Expected long-term changes generally relied on demand rather than supply conditions, and long-term demand is undeniably difficult to predict independently of expected supply. Plans were made largely from day to day on the basis of current developments, and when short-term forecasts were explicitly used, the projection usually was for a very short period.

The complete unreliability of productive ability as an indicator of the future marks one important handicap of forecasting in the thirties. To a large, but undetermined, extent the success of forecasts in the fifties rests on expected maintenance of relatively prosperous conditions. Thus, a projection of growth levels provides an approximate base with which expected changes can be effectively compared. No contrasting simplification was available in the thirties.

The disrepute into which methods of forecasting fell, together with reduced use of explicit forecasting, especially beyond a very few months into the future, make a quantitative appraisal difficult. Many organizations discontinued explicit forecasting. Trade magazines and letters which had published forecasts in the twenties discontinued the practice.

---

[38] For evidence that this movement averaged roughly horizontal, see the author's *Business Cycles and Forecasting*, 4th ed. (Homewood, Ill.: Richard D. Irwin, Inc., 1953), p. 316.

The work which persisted was conducted in greater isolation. It is far more difficult to trace a common forecasting pattern than for other decades.

FORECASTS IN THE TWENTIES

A wide interest had arisen in explicit forecasting by the twenties. The activity attained a new standing. Emphasis was placed on general-business forecasting, with work on sales forecasting far more primitive than indicated by the procedures developed in Chapters 10 and 11.

The most famous appraisals of general-business forecasting are those of Cox for business services in the period 1918–29.[39] The services tested include Standard Statistics Company, Babson's Statistical Organization, Brookmire Economic Service, Harvard Economic Society, National City Bank, and Moody's Investors Service. The forecasts were graded on two different scales. The first of these was called adequacy, and represented the product of monthly grades assigned for *definiteness* and *correctness*. The average score for adequacy attained for the full period was +0.33, on a scale ranging from −1 for a wrong forecast to +1 for a right one. Since judgment entered in scoring the forecasts, Cox asked 11 graduate students to assign grades using the same information, and these grades averaged only slightly lower than the ones he assigned. Cox's average adequacy scores by years were as follows:

1919	0.27	1923	0.10	1927	0.18
1920	0.37	1924	0.31	1928	0.43
1921	0.48	1925	0.55	1929	0.11
1922	0.53	1926	0.29		

Relative success in the years 1920 to 1922 may have been a factor in the increasing attention given to forecasting. Low scores in 1923, 1927, and 1929 are related to methodological weakness in forecasting downturns.

A second test relates to success in anticipating (1) the time when downturns and upturns occur, (2) the direction of movement of general business at any time, and (3) the amplitude of the movement. We will consider here only the grading of forecasts of turning points. Forty-six forecasts of turning points could be identified among the 6 services and the 8 turning points in the period studied. Of these, 14 forecasts are graded as helpful and 22 as slightly helpful, or about three-fourths as of some help. By turning points, the scoring of services is as follows:

[39] Garfield V. Cox, *An Appraisal of American Business Forecasts, Studies in Business Administration*, vol. I, no. 2, rev. ed. (Chicago: University of Chicago Press, 1930).

Turning points	Helpful	Slightly helpful	Neutral	Slightly misleading	Mis-leading
1919 upturn.........	...	3	1	1	
1920 downturn......	3	2			
1921 upturn.........	4	2			
1923 downturn......	1	1	1	1	2
1924 upturn.........	1	5			
1927 downturn......	1	3	2		
1927–28 upturn......	3	2	1		
1929 downturn......	1	4	1		

The general inferiority of forecasts of downturns is evident from the table, and is largely due to the leveling which occurred near peaks in this period and to widespread optimistic bias. Poor forecasting does not apply to the 1920 downturn, and the later recessions up to 1929 were so mild that failure to forecast them correctly may not have led to policies which were seriously wrong. The same, of course, cannot be said of incorrect forecasts of the 1929 downturn. As noted in the preceding section, forecasts were relatively inferior during the contraction following 1929. Forecasts guided poorly from the 1929 downturn through the deep depression.

In testing 11 forecasters in their November and December forecasts from 1923 to 1928, Andrew and Flinn obtained results which roughly agree with Cox.[40] The methods employed in evaluating forecasts in the period are more subjective than such a method as scoring error reduction, discussed above, but the tendency for different observers to reach comparable conclusions is reassuring. Most of the forecasts employed were too qualitative to make the use of objective scoring methods possible.

As in the fifties, success achieved is related to the stability of the period. We may conclude that successful general-business forecasting has been principally limited to relatively stable and prosperous times. There are exceptions like successful forecasting in the early years of the twenties. Known improvements in information and methodology should produce moderately successful forecasts even if unstable conditions should return.

[40] Seymour L. Andrew and Harold M. Flinn, "Appraisal of Economic Forecasts," *Journal of the American Statistical Association*, Supplement, March, 1930, pp. 36–41.

Bibliography

Abramovitz, Moses: "Economics of Growth," in B. F. Haley (ed.), *A Survey of Contemporary Economics* (Homewood, Ill.: Richard D. Irwin, Inc., 1952), vol. II, pp. 132–182.

Abramson, A. G., and R. H. Mack (eds.): *Business Forecasting in Practice* (New York: John Wiley & Sons, Inc., 1956).

Agriculture, U.S. Department of: *Agricultural Programs of the United States: Current and Prospective*, November, 1952.

American Management Association: *Company Organization for Economic Forecasting*, Research Report 28, New York, 1957.

American Management Association: *Materials and Methods of Sales Forecasting*, Special Report 27, New York, 1957.

American Management Association: *Sales Forecasting: Uses, Techniques, and Trends*, Special Report 16, New York, 1956.

American Statistical Association, Chicago Chapter, and Chicago Association of Commerce and Industry: *Midwest Conference on Forecasting Techniques Applied to Business Problems* (Chicago: Monarch Printing and Publishing Corporation, 1954).

Andrew, S. L., and H. M. Flinn: "Appraisal of Economic Forecasts," *Journal of the American Statistical Association*, Supplement, March, 1930, pp. 36–41.

Aries, Robert S., and William Copulsky: *Sales and Business Forecasting in Chemical Process Industries* (New York: Chemonomics, Inc., 1950).

Baker, Arthur D., Jr., and G. Clark Thompson: "Executives Find Long-range Planning Pays Off," *Conference Board Business Record*, 13:435–443, 1956.

Baker, John D., Jr., and Don Paarlberg: "Outlook Evaluation: Methods and Results," *Agricultural Economics Research*, 4:105–114, 1952.

Barger, Harold, and Lawrence Klein: "A Quarterly Model for the U.S. Economy," *Journal of the American Statistical Association*, 49:413–437, 1954.

Barnes, Leo: *Handbook of Business Forecasting* (Englewood Cliffs, N.J.: Prentice-Hall, Inc., November, 1949).

Barnett, Harold J.: *Energy Uses and Supplies, 1939, 1947, 1965*, Bureau of Mines Information Circular 7582 (Washington: U.S. Department of the Interior, October, 1950).

Barton, Glen T., and Robert O. Rogers: *Farm Output: Past Changes and Projected Needs*, Agriculture Information Bulletin 162 (Washington: U.S. Department of Agriculture, August, 1956).

Bicking, Charles A.: "The Application of Quality Control to Administrative Problems," *Industrial Quality Control*, May, 1950.

Biggs, Robert M.: *National-income Analysis and Forecasting* (New York: W. W. Norton & Company, Inc., 1956).

Bogue, D. J.: "A Technique for Making Extensive Population Estimates," *Journal of the American Statistical Association*, 45:149–163, 1950.

Bratt, Elmer C.: *Business Cycles and Forecasting*, 4th ed. (Homewood, Ill.: Richard D. Irwin, Inc., 1953).

Bratt, Elmer C.: "A Reconsideration of Postwar Forecasts," *Journal of Business*, 26:71–83, 1953.

Bratt, Elmer C.: "Short- and Long-term Capital Requirements," *Journal of Finance*, 7:128–137, 1952.

Brier, Glenn W., and Roger A. Allen: "Verification of Weather Forecasts," in *Compendium of Meteorology* (Boston: American Meteorological Society, 1951).

Brown, Bonnar, and M. Janet Hansen: *Production Trends in the United States* (Menlo Park, Calif.: Stanford Research Institute, 1957).

Burck, Gilbert: "The Magnificent Decline in U.S. Farming," *Fortune*, June, 1955.

Burck, Gilbert, and Sanford S. Parker: "Another Big Decade for Capital Goods," *Fortune*, December, 1956.

Burck, Gilbert, and Sanford S. Parker: "The Biggest Car Market Yet," *Fortune*, November, 1956.

Burck, Gilbert, and Sanford S. Parker: "What a Country!" *Fortune*, October, 1956.

Burgess, R. W.: "How Many in the Country in 1975?" *Conference Board Business Record*, August, 1956.

Bursk, Edward C., and Dan H. Fenn (eds.): *Planning the Future Strategy of Your Business* (New York: McGraw-Hill Book Company, Inc., 1956).

Business Economics, Office of: *Markets after the Defense Expansion* (Washington: U.S. Department of Commerce, 1952).

Business Economics, Office of: *National Income*, a supplement to *Survey of Current Business* (Washington: U.S. Department of Commerce, 1954).

"Business Forecasting," *Business Week*, Sept. 24, 1955.

Cavin, James P.: "Forecasting the Demand for Agricultural Products," *Agricultural Economics Research*, 4:65–76, 1952.

Census, Bureau of the: "Illustrative Projections of the Population, by States, 1960, 1965, and 1970," *Current Population Reports*, ser. P-25, no. 160, Aug. 9, 1957.

Census, Bureau of the: "Projections of the Labor Force in the United States, 1955 to 1975," *Current Population Reports*, ser. P-50, no. 69, October, 1956.

Census, Bureau of the: "Projections of the Number of Households and Families, 1960 to 1975," *Current Population Reports*, ser. P-20, no. 69, Aug. 31, 1956.

Census, Bureau of the: "Revised Projections of the Population of the United States, by Age and Sex, 1960 to 1975," *Current Population Reports*, ser. P-25, no. 123, Oct. 20, 1955.

Chamber of Commerce of the United States: *Business and Economic Forecasting*, Washington, 1954.

Churchill, Betty C.: "Recent Business Population Movements," *Survey of Current Business*, January, 1954.

Colm, Gerhard: "Economic Barometers and Economic Models," *Review of Economics and Statistics,* 37:55–62, 1955.

Colm, Gerhard: "The Economic Outlook for 1955," *Michigan Business Review,* 7:29–33, 1955.

Colm, Gerhard, and Marilyn Young: *The American Economy in 1960* (Washington: National Planning Association, 1952).

Comer, H. D., and Ralph J. Watkins: "Forecasting a Line by Itself," *Journal of the American Statistical Association,* 22:505–508, 1927.

Compton, J. P.: "How an Index Helps Make Accurate Sales Forecasts—the heart of the budget," *Journal of Accountancy,* 92:473–474, 1951.

Controllership Foundation, Inc.: *Business Forecasting: A Survey of Business Practices and Methods,* New York, 1950.

Cowan, D. R. G.: "Management and Business Forecasting," *Journal of Marketing,* 15:215–218, 1950.

Cox, G. V.: *An Appraisal of American Business Forecasts, Studies in Business Administration,* vol. 1, no. 2, rev. ed. (Chicago: University of Chicago Press, 1930).

Crawford, C. M.: *Sales Forecasting: Methods of Selected Firms* (Urbana, Ill.: University of Illinois Press, 1955).

Crompton, H. E.: "The Long-range Outlook for the Michigan Economy," *Michigan Business Review,* 9:7–14, 1957.

Daly, Rex F.: "The Long-run demand for Farm Products," *Agricultural Economics Research,* 8:1–19, 1956.

Darling, Paul G.: "The Influence of Expectations and Liquidity on Dividend Policy," *Journal of Political Economy,* 65:209–224, 1957.

Dauten, Carl A.: *Business Fluctuations and Forecasting* (Cincinnati: South Western Publishing Company, 1954).

Davis, Joseph S.: *The Population Upsurge in the United States* (Stanford, Calif.: Food Research Institute, Stanford University, December, 1949).

Dean, Joel: *Managerial Economics* (Englewood Cliffs, N.J.: Prentice-Hall, Inc., 1951).

Dewhurst, J. Frederic, and Associates: *America's Needs and Resources: A New Survey* (New York: The Twentieth Century Fund, Inc., 1955).

Dewhurst, J. Frederic, and others: *Statistics of Business Inventories: Report of Consultant Committee on Inventory Statistics* (Washington: Board of Governors of the Federal Reserve System, November, 1955).

Dorn, Harold F.: "Pitfalls in Population Forecasts and Projections," *Journal of the American Statistical Association,* 45:311–334, 1950.

Drucker, Peter F.: *America's Next Twenty Years* (New York: Harper & Brothers, 1957).

Econometric Institute: *The General Outlook for the American Economy, 1949–1960,* New York, June, 1949.

Edmunds, Stahrl: "Plant Capacity: Too Much or Too Little," *Harvard Business Review,* 30:75–85, 1952.

Edwards, Robert D., and John Magee, Jr.: *Technical Analysis of Stock Market Trends* (Springfield, Mass.: Stock Trend Service, 1954).

Ellis, Ira T.: "Techniques and Uses of Forecasts of General Business Conditions," in *Proceedings of the Business and Economic Statistics Section, American Statistical Association,* Washington, 1956, pp. 158–161.

Ethe, Solomon: *Forecasting in Industry,* Studies in Business Policy, no. 77 (New York: National Industrial Conference Board, Inc., 1956).

European Economic Cooperation, Organization for: *Europe Today and in 1960*, 8th Annual Report (Paris: European Economic Organization, April, 1957).

Federal Power Commission: *Estimated Future Power Requirements of the United States by Regions, 1955–1980*, Washington, December, 1956.

Ferber, Robert: "Are Correlations Any Guide to Predictive Value?" *Applied Statistics*, 5:113–121, 1956.

Ferber, Robert: "Measuring the Accuracy and Structure of Businessmen's Expectations," *Journal of the American Statistical Association*, 48:385–413, 1953.

Ferber, Robert: "On the Accuracy of Businessmen's Expectations," *Current Economic Comment*, vol. 16, May, 1954.

Ferber, Robert: "On the Interpretation of the Aggregate Savings Ratio," *American Statistician*, June, 1956.

Ferber, Robert: *The Railroad Shippers' Forecasts* (Urbana, Ill.: University of Illinois Press, 1953).

Ferber, Robert: "Sales Forecasting by Sample Surveys," *Journal of Marketing*, July, 1955.

Foote, Richard J.: "Short-time Price Movements of Farm Products," *Agricultural Economics Research*, January, 1955.

Foss, Murray F., and Vito Natrella: "Investment Plans and Their Realization: Reasons for Differences in Individual Cases," *Survey of Current Business*, June, 1957.

Foss, Murray F., and Vito Natrella: "Ten Years' Experience with Business Investment Anticipations," *Survey of Current Business*, January, 1957.

Friday, Frank A.: "The Problem of Business Forecasting," *Journal of Industrial Economics*, 1:55–71, 1952.

Friend, Irwin, and Sanford S. Parker: "A New Slant on the Stock Market," *Fortune*, September, 1956.

Gainsburgh, Martin R., and others: *An Appraisal of Data and Research on Businessmen's Expectations about Outlook and Operating Variables: Report of Consultant Committee on General Business Expectations* (Washington: Board of Governors of the Federal Reserve System, September, 1955).

Goldsmith, Raymond, and others: *Statistics on Saving: Report of the Consultant Committee on Savings Statistics* (Washington: Board of Governors of the Federal Reserve System, July, 1955).

Graphic Presentation (New York: Francis I. Du Pont and Co., annual).

Grebler, Leo, David M. Blank, and Louis Winnick: *Capital Formation in Residential Real Estate: Trends and Prospects* (Princeton, N.J.: Princeton University Press, 1956).

Gringorten, Irving I.: "The Verification and Scoring of Weather Forecasts," *Journal of the American Statistical Association*, 46:279–296, 1951.

Guthrie, John A.: *Economics of Pulp and Paper*, Bureau of Economic and Business Research Bulletin 12 (Pullman, Wash.: State College of Washington, 1950).

Hastay, Millard: "The Dun and Bradstreet Surveys of Businessmen's Expectations," in *Proceedings of the Business and Economic Statistics Section, American Statistical Association*, Washington, 1955, pp. 93–123.

Hay, W. W.: "Study of the Nature of Demand Would Obviate Many Mistakes of Management," *Annalist*, May 22, 1931.

Heady, Earl O., and Donald R. Kaldor: "Expectations and Errors in Forecasting Agricultural Prices," *Journal of Political Economy*, 62:34–47, 1954.

Hendricks, W. A., and H. F. Huddleston: "A Foundation for Objective Forecasts of Cotton Yields," *Agricultural Economics Research*, October, 1955.

Hill, Kenneth E., Harold D. Hammar, and John G. Winger: *Future Growth of the World Petroleum Industry* (New York: Chase Manhattan Bank, 1957).

Hoadley, Walter E.: "Developing and Utilizing the Sales Forecast," *Management Review*, vol. 40, December, 1951.

Hoadley, Walter E.: "General Business Prospects for Near and Longer Range," *Commercial and Financial Chronicle*, Apr. 12, 1956.

Hoffenberg, Marvin: "Prices, Productivity and Factor Return Assumptions in Long-range Economic Projections," in *Proceedings of the Business and Economic Statistics Section, American Statistical Association*, Washington, 1956, pp. 16–19.

Horner, S. L., and others: *The Dynamics of Automobile Demand* (New York: General Motors Corporation, 1939).

Houthakker, H. S.: "Can Speculators Forecast Prices?" *Review of Economics and Statistics*, 39:143–151, 1957.

Jacobs, Walter W., and Genevieve B. Wimsatt: "An Approach to Orders Analysis," *Survey of Current Business*, December, 1949.

Jacobs, Walter W., and Clement Winston: "The Postwar Furniture Market and the Factors Determining Demand," *Survey of Current Business*, May, 1950.

Jones, A. W.: "Fashions in Forecasting," *Fortune*, March, 1949.

Katona, George, and J. N. Morgan: "The Quantitative Study of Factors Determining Business Decisions," *Quarterly Journal of Economics*, 66:67–90, 1952.

Katona, George, and Eva Mueller: *Consumer Expectations, 1953–56* (Ann Arbor, Mich.: Survey Research Center, Institute for Social Research, University of Michigan, 1956).

King, Edmund R.: "Analysis and Forecasts of Company Sales," *American Statistician*, June–July, 1952.

King, Edmund R.: "Techniques and Uses of Forecasts of General Business Conditions in the Eastman Kodak Company," in *Proceedings of the Business and Economic Statistics Section, American Statistical Association*, Washington, 1956, pp. 167–172.

Klein, Lawrence R., and John B. Lansing: "Decisions to Purchase Consumer Durable Goods," *Journal of Marketing*, 20:109–132, 1955.

Knowles, James W.: "Relation of Structure and Assumptions to Purpose in Making Economic Projections," in *Proceedings of the Business and Economic Statistics Section, American Statistical Association*, Washington, 1956, pp. 7–11.

Kravis, Irving B.: "Expenditure-Income Relationships for Consumer Durable Goods and Problems in Their Derivation," in *Proceedings of the Business and Economic Statistics Section, American Statistical Association*, Washington, 1956, pp. 106–121.

Labor Statistics, Bureau of: *Our Manpower Future, 1955–65* (Washington: U.S. Department of Labor, 1957).

Lewis, John P.: "The Lull That Came to Stay," *Journal of Political Economy*, 63:1–19, 1955.

Lewis, John P.: *Recent Developments in Economic Forecasting*, Business In-

354   *Business Forecasting*

formation Bulletin 22 (Bloomington, Ind.: Bureau of Business Research, School of Business, Indiana University, 1955).

Little, Arthur D., Inc.: *The Technology behind Investment,* nos. 1 and 2, Cambridge, Mass., 1952 and 1954.

Livingston, S. Morris: *Markets after the War: An Approach to Their Analysis* (Washington: U.S. Department of Commerce, 1943).

Lorie, James H.: "Two Important Problems in Sales Forecasting," *Journal of Business,* 30:172–179, 1957.

Lynip, B. F., Jr.: *Factors Affecting the Wholesale Price Level* (San Francisco: California and Hawaiian Sugar Refining Corporation, Ltd., 1950).

MacGowan, T. G.: "Forecasting Sales," *Harvard Business Review,* vol. 27, November, 1949.

Machinery and Allied Products Institute: *Capital Goods Review,* nos. 22 and 24, May, 1955, and November, 1955.

MacNiece, E. H.: *Production Forecasting, Planning and Control* (New York: John Wiley & Sons, Inc., 1957).

Maher, John E.: "Forecasting Industrial Production," *Journal of Political Economy,* 65:158–165, 1957.

Maisel, Sherman J.: *Fluctuations, Growth, and Forecasting: The Principles of Dynamic Business Economics* (New York: John Wiley & Sons, Inc., 1957).

Maryland, University of: "Coal in the Maryland Economy," *Studies in Business and Economics,* vol. 7, no. 3 (College Park, Md.: Bureau of Business and Economic Research, University of Maryland, December, 1953).

Maryland, University of: "Estimating Maryland Government and Business Potentials," *Studies in Business and Economics,* vol. 8, no. 4 (College Park, Md.: Bureau of Business and Economic Research, University of Maryland, March, 1955).

McCracken, Paul W.: "The Role of Business Forecasting in Market Analysis," *Michigan Business Review,* 3:25–30, 1951.

McGraw-Hill Editors: *The Pulsebeat of Industry: Annual Business Forecast* (New York: McGraw-Hill Publishing Company, Inc., Annually).

Melnicoff, David C.: "Long Range Economic Prospects and Marketing Plans," in *The Broadening Perspective of Marketing: Proceedings of the Golden Triangle Conference of the American Marketing Association,* Chicago, 1956.

Mitchell, G. A.: "Mapping Realistic Company Goals: A Tested Approach," *Management Review,* October, 1956.

Modigliani, Franco: "Fluctuations in the Saving-Income Ratio: A Problem in Economic Forecasting," in Conference on Research in Income and Wealth, *Studies in Income and Wealth,* vol. XI (New York: National Bureau of Economic Research, Inc., 1949), pp. 371–443.

Moore, Geoffrey H.: "Analyzing the Economic Cycles," *Dun's Review and Modern Industry,* October, 1953.

Moore, Geoffrey H.: "Diffusion Indexes: A Comment," *American Statistician,* October, 1955.

Moore, Geoffrey H.: "Economic Indicators and the Economic Outlook," *Michigan Business Review,* 7:1–8, 1955.

Moore, Geoffrey H.: *Statistical Indicators of Cyclical Revivals and Recessions,* Occasional Paper 31 (New York: National Bureau of Economic Research, Inc., 1950).

Mossiman, Ary, and Arthur J. Stegeman: "7th Annual Electrical Industry Forecast: Steady Growth," *Electrical World*, vol. 146, Sept. 17, 1956.

National Bureau of Economic Research: *Consumer Installment Credit* (Washington: Board of Governors of the Federal Reserve System, 1957).

National Bureau of Economic Research Conference on Research in Income and Wealth: *Input-Output Analysis: An Appraisal*, vol. XVIII of *Studies in Income and Wealth* (Princeton, N.J.: Princeton University Press, 1955).

National Bureau of Economic Research Conference on Research in Income and Wealth: *Long-range Economic Projection*, vol. XVI of *Studies in Income and Wealth* (Princeton, N.J.: Princeton University Press, 1954).

National Bureau of Economic Research Conference on Research in Income and Wealth: *Short-term Economic Forecasting*, vol. XVII of *Studies in Income and Wealth* (Princeton, N.J.: Princeton University Press, 1955).

Natrella, Vito: "Forecasting Plant and Equipment Expenditures from Businessmen's Expectations," in *Proceedings of the Business and Economic Statistics Section, American Statistical Association*, Washington, 1956, pp. 121–132.

Newhoff, Malcolm C., and G. Clark Thompson: "Industry Plans for the Future," *Conference Board Business Record*, August, 1952.

Newman, F. B.: "Better Production Planning from Controlled Sales Forecasts," *Factory Management and Maintenance*, June, 1952.

Newbury, Frank D.: *Business Forecasting* (New York: McGraw-Hill Book Company, Inc., 1952).

New York Authority, Port of: *Air Traffic Forecast, 1950–1980* (New York: Department of Airport Development, Airport Planning Bureau, June, 1950).

O'Leary, James J.: "An Optimistic Look Ahead: Our National Economy in 1966," *Commercial and Financial Chronicle*, Feb. 23, 1956.

Paradiso, Louis J., and Genevieve B. Wimsatt: "Business Inventories: Recent Trends and Position," *Survey of Current Business*, May, 1953.

Paradiso, Louis J., and Clement Winston: "Consumer Expenditure-Income Patterns," *Survey of Current Business*, September, 1955.

Pearl, Raymond: *The Biology of Population Growth* (New York: Alfred A. Knopf, Inc., 1925).

Picton, Walter L.: *Water Use in the United States*, Business Service Bulletin 136, U.S. Department of Commerce, January, 1956.

Potential Economic Growth of the United States during the Next Decade, Joint Economic Committee, 83rd Cong., 2d Sess., 1954.

President's Materials Policy Commission: *Resources for Freedom*, 5 vols., Washington, June, 1952.

Prochnow, Herbert V. (ed.): *Determining the Business Outlook* (New York: Harper & Brothers, 1954).

Redfield, J. W.: "Elements of Forecasting," *Harvard Business Review*, November, 1951.

Republic Steel Corporation: *U.S.A. Tomorrow*, Cleveland, 1957.

Rich, James L.: "Techniques and Uses of Forecasts of General Business Conditions in U.S. Steel," in *Proceedings of the Business and Economic Statistics Section, American Statistical Association*, Washington, 1956, pp. 161–166.

Roberts, Harry V.: "A Technique for Appraising and Improving Forecasts," *The Broadening Perspective of Marketing: Proceedings of the Golden*

Triangle Conference of the American Marketing Association, Chicago, 1956.

Roos, Charles F.: *Charting the Course of Your Business: Measuring the Effects of External Influences* (New York: Funk & Wagnalls Company, 1948).

Roos, Charles F.: "The Demand for Investment Goods," *American Economic Review,* Supplement, May, 1948, pp. 311–320.

Roos, Charles F.: *Dynamics of Economic Growth: The American Economy, 1957–1975* (New York: Econometric Institute, Inc., 1957).

Roos, Charles F.: "Problems of Business Forecasting and the Outlook for Business," *Journal of Business,* April, 1956.

Roos, Charles F.: "Survey of Economic Forecasting Techniques," *Econometrica,* 23:363–395, 1955.

Sanderson, Fred H.: *Methods of Crop Forecasting* (Cambridge, Mass.: Harvard University Press, 1954).

Sapir, Michael, and others: "Review of Economic Forecasts for the Transition Period," in Conference on Research in Income and Wealth, *Studies in Income and Wealth,* vol. XI (New York: National Bureau of Economic Research, Inc., 1949), pp. 275–367.

Shankleman, Eric: "Economic Forecasting in Great Britain," *Applied Statistics,* June, 1953.

Siegel, Irving H.: "Technological Change and Long-run Forecasting," *Journal of Business,* 26:141–156, 1953.

Silk, Leonard S., and M. Louise Curley: *Forecasting Business Trends: McGraw-Hill Consultant Reports on Current Business Problems* (New York: McGraw-Hill Book Company, Inc., 1956).

Smith, B. B.: "A Forecasting Index for Business," *Journal of the American Statistical Association,* 26:115–127, 1931.

Smithies, Arthur, and others: *Statistics of Saving: Report of Consultant Committee on Savings Statistics* (Washington: Board of Governors of the Federal Reserve System, July, 1955).

Solomon, Ezra, and others: "Forecasting," *Journal of Business,* 27:1–105, 1954.

Stanbery, Van Beuren: *Better Population Forecasting for Areas and Communities,* Domestic Commerce Series, no. 32 (Washington: U.S. Department of Commerce, September, 1952).

Stanford Research Institute: *America's Demand for Wood, 1929–1975* (Tacoma, Wash.: Weyerhaeuser Timber Company, 1954).

Stegeman, Arthur J.: "8th Annual Electrical Industry Forecast, 1957–1970," *Electrical World,* vol. 148, Sept. 2, 1957.

Steinberg, Hyman: "New Highway Program," *Conference Board Business Record,* 13:537–539, 1956.

Stone, Richard, and D. A. Rowe: "The Market Demand for Durable Goods," *Econometrica,* 25:423–443, 1957.

Suits, Daniel B., and Arthur S. Goldberger: "A Statistical Model for 1955," *Michigan Business Review,* 7:25–28, 1955.

Sweiger, Irving: "Forecasting Short-term Consumer Demand from Consumer Anticipations," *Journal of Business,* April, 1956.

Terborgh, George, and others: *Statistics on Business Plant and Equipment: Report of the Consultant Committee on Business Plant and Equipment Expectations* (Washington: Board of Governors of the Federal Reserve System, July, 1955).

Terry, Lyon F., and John G. Winger: *Future Growth of the Natural Gas Industry* (New York: Chase Manhattan Bank, 1957).

Thomas, Margaret E.: "The Predictive Value of Consumer Expenditure Data as a Method of Forecasting Economic Fluctuations," in *Proceedings of the Business and Economic Statistics Section, American Statistical Association*, Washington, 1954, pp. 85–88.

Turner, R. C.: "Problems of Forecasting for Economic Stabilization," *American Economic Review*, Supplement, May, 1955, pp. 329–340.

Universities-National Bureau Committee for Economic Research: *Conference on Business Cycles* (New York: National Bureau of Economic Research, Inc., 1951).

Universities-National Bureau Committee for Economic Research: *Policies to Combat Depressions* (Princeton, N.J.: Princeton University Press, 1956).

Verdoorn, P. J.: "Complimentarity and Long-range Projections," *Econometrica*, October, 1956, pp. 429–450.

Welsch, Glenn A.: *Budgeting: Profit-planning and Control* (Englewood Cliffs, N.J.: Prentice-Hall, Inc., 1957).

Wernette, Philip: *The Future of American Prosperity* (New York: The Macmillan Company, 1955).

Whelpton, P. K.: *Forecasts of the Population of the United States, 1945–1975* (Washington: Government Printing Office, 1947).

White, Helen R.: "Empirical Study of the Accuracy of Selected Methods of Projecting State Populations," *Journal of the American Statistical Association*, 49:480–498, 1954.

Winston, C., and M. A. Smith: "Income Sensitivity of Consumption Expenditures," *Survey of Current Business*, January, 1950.

Wright, Wilson: *Forecasting for Profit* (New York: John Wiley & Sons, Inc., 1947).

Index

Accuracy-evaluation score, 336
Achievement scores, 318, 336–338, 347–348
Adequacy of forecasts, 167–168, 260–261, 274, 311–348
  achievement scores, 318, 336–348
  agriculture, 336–338
  anticipations, 323–336
  checked by level achieved, 312–315, 323–330, 344
  and forecast needed, 315–318
  general business, 338–348
  individual performance, 311, 318–319
  population forecasts, 322–323
  timing, 316
  trend criterion, 312–313
  and variation of activity, 313–315, 324
  weighting of separate forecasts, 317–318
Administered prices, 7, 199–200, 213, 259
Advertising expenditure, 246, 259, 309
Aggregating expenditures, 51–52, 90–91, 94–95, 189–190, 218
  as explanatory variable, 65
Agricultural prices, 216–217
Agricultural products, 123–125, 152, 230–232
  adequacy of forecasts, 336–338
  demand functions, 231
  and foreign trade, 230–231
  intention reports, 232–233, 319–320
  nonfood consumption, 123
  per capita consumption, 124
  price-structure approach, 232
Allen, Roger A., 311–312
Aluminum Company of Canada, 266

American Gas Association, 116–118, 146
American Iron and Steel Institute, 101–102, 219
American Management Association, 252, 256, 259–262
American Standard Sanitary Corporation, 248–249
Analogy, specific, 177
Andrew, Seymour L., 348
Anticipations, 146–150
  consumer, 147, 150, 170, 188, 246
    adequacy of, 333–336
  for *ex ante* model, 192
  general business, 150, 168–169
  housing, 227–228
  instability of plans, 148, 170, 327–328
  inventory, 186
  plant and equipment, 14–15, 146–148, 180–181, 185, 323–329
    adequacy of, 169, 323–329
    financing plans, 147
  and psychological attitudes, 169
  versus rational analysis, 192–193
  sales, 147–150, 280, 329–333
Applebaum, William, 246n.
Area Labor Market Reports, 291
Armstrong Cork Company, 278–279
Audits and Surveys, 244n.
Automobiles, 104–109, 152, 221–225, 258
  acceptance of new models, 223
  and consumer anticipation, 225
  and dealer margins, 223–224
  demand distribution, 106–108
  demand function, 222
  household ownership, 107
  model changes, 108

Automobiles, and other consumer goods, 223
replacement demand, 107–108, 222, 224–225
seasonal variation, 224
used-car prices, 223–225

Babson's Statistical Organization, 347
Bahm, John F., Jr., 246n.
Baker, Arthur D., Jr., 255–257
Baker, John D., Jr., 336–338
Baker, O. E., 322
Barry, G. J., 269
Barton, Glen T., 125n.
Bausch and Lomb Optical Company, 271
Bell and Howell Company, 267
Bethel, L. L., 268n.
Bias in forecasts, 167–168
Birth rates, 44, 292–293
Bland, William F., 235
Blank, David M., 66–71
Blough, Roger M., 104
Bootleg liquor, 13
Boschan, Paul, 100n.
Bridge, Lawrence, 326n.
Brier, Glenn W., 311–312
Brookmire Economic Service, 160, 347
Brown, Bonnar, 52n., 57–59, 130n.
Brown, Lyndon O., 310
Burck, Gilbert, 75–78, 90, 106–108, 132
Burns, A. F., 143
Business-cycle length, 175–176, 192

Capacity measurement, 207–208
Capital appropriations, 147
Capital coefficient (see Capital-output ratio)
Capital-consumption allowance, 9, 19, 21, 73
Capital-output ratio, 22, 68, 71–74, 76
inventory stock to sales, 78–80, 171, 173, 186
Capital replacement, 9, 73, 75, 132
Cash budget, 271–274, 279, 281
Causal relations used in forecasting, 168, 248–249
Cavin, James P., 337–339
Chase, Stuart, 322
Chase Manhattan Bank, 113–116
Churchill, Betty C., 308

Cleveland Electric Illuminating Company, 228–230, 256–257
Coal, bituminous, 119–120, 235
Cohen, Morris, 147n.
Coincident series, 162
(See also Leading series)
Cole, A. H., 135, 151
Colm, Gerhard, 35n., 69, 74–75, 79–80, 87–88
Commitments, timing of, 140, 215
Commodity Credit Corporation, 85
Commodity Yearbook, 216
Compton, J. P., 237
Congested security markets, 300
Construction differentiated from equipment, 72
(See also Investment)
Consumer credit, 139, 152, 191, 309
Continental Can Company, 269, 287
Controllership Foundation, 265
Corning Glass Works, 277–278
Corporations, nonprofit, 24
Costing, direct, 269
Costs, of forecasts, 317
standard, 237
Council of Economic Advisers, 320
Cox, Garfield V., 347–348
Crawford, C. M., 240, 244, 254, 260n., 265
Crisp, Richard D., 263n.
Curran, N. J., Jr., 266
Curtice, Harlow, 224
Cycle, two-year, 234

Daly, Rex F., 60–61, 123–124
Data sources, 150–156
Davis, Joseph S., 322
Deflated expenditure, 18, 344
Demand functions, 249–251
Dewhurst, J. Frederic (see Twentieth Century Fund)
Dick, A. B., Company, 270
Diffusion index, 142–145, 149, 164–167, 331
and duration of run, 144–145, 165
and leading series, 165–167
Disposable income, relation to GNP, 22–24
Dividends, 153, 188–189
Dodge, F. W., Corporation, 162, 248
Dodge, James D., 266, 270

Dodge Manufacturing Company, 251n., 279
Dorn, Harold F., 322
Dougall, Herbert E., 3n., 271–273
Dow theory, 303–305
Dun and Bradstreet survey, 148–150, 330
Duncan, Delbert J., 309n.
Du Pont de Nemours, E. I., and Company, 275–276
Duration-of-run index, 144–145, 155
Dynamic pricing, 203, 237, 259

Eastman Kodak Company, 253, 258, 284–287
Econometric Institute, 345
Econometric models, 193–194
Economist's office, 242, 275
Edwards, Robert D., 304–305
Electric utilities, 109–113, 228–230
  customer-classified, 110, 228–230
  peak loads, 230, 282
Electrical goods survey, 235
Electrical World, 112n.
Electronics, 235
Ellis, Ira T., 275–276
Employment, 27–28, 138–140, 290–291
End-use analysis, 101–103, 119, 243–244, 278, 283
Error-reduction score, 337, 344
Estes, B. E., 260
Evaluation of forecasts (*see* Adequacy of forecasts)
Evans, W. Duane, 96

Farm products (*see* Agricultural products)
Fashion trends, 309–310
Fatigue, 42
Favorable factors, 157–158, 183–184
Federal Power Commission, 109–113, 228
Federal Reserve, 170–171, 195–196, 333–336
Federal Reserve control, 160, 301
Ferber, Robert, 247n., 322–323
Filter technique, 251
Finney, Burnham, 235
Fix-up expenditures, 228
Flinn, Harold M., 348
Flow coefficients, 95–96
Food manufacturing, 235–236

Ford Motor Company, 249
Forecasting committee, 241–242, 278
Foreign investment, 17–18, 187–188
  and foreign aid, 86, 187
  and inventories, 187
  responsible factors, 86–87
  and total loans, 88
Fortune, 57–58, 75–76, 90, 106–108, 186, 227–228, 306
Fortune survey, 148–150, 306
Foss, Murray F., 146–147, 323–329
Fox, Karl F., 231
Friend, Irwin, 146, 306
Full employment, 29–31
Furniture, 126–127

Ganzemuller, George, 235
Gas utilities, 116–119
Gates, Donald E., 279–280
General business expectations, 150
General Electric Company, 280–281
General Foods Corporation, 266
General Motors, 224, 283
General Public Utilities Corporation, 282
Goldberger, Arthur S., 193–194
Government expenditures, 16–17, 52–54, 153, 206–207, 300
  and budgets, 187
  Federal, 81–86
  interest, 82–86
  in relation to GNP, 80–86
  revision of estimates, 181–182, 187
  state and local, 80–82, 86
Grebler, Leo, 66–71
Gringorten, Irving I., 311–312
GNP (gross national product), 10
  relation of, to disposable income, 22–24
    to government expenditures, 80–86
    to industrial production, 26–27
    long-run, to personal consumption expenditures, 89–90, 188
    (*See also* Product expenditures)
GNP model, 177–194, 345
  and control measures, 191
  patterns of relationship, 190
  and price changes, 182n.
  and productivity, 50–58
  recycling, 190–191, 219
  starting with anticipations, 192
  and turning points, 183–185

Growth, law of, 31–35
    underestimation of, 117–118
Guthmann, Harry G., 3n., 271–273

Hagen, Everett E., 341–344
Hammar, Harold D., 113–116
Haney, Lewis H., 215–216
Hansen, M. Janet, 52n., 57–59, 130n.
Harvard Economic Society, 158–161, 347
Harvard Index Chart, 158–161, 185, 345
Hastay, Millard, 331
Hay, W. W., 33n.
"Head-and-shoulders movement," 304–305
Heckert, J. Brooks, 238n.
Heinz, H. J., Company, 273
Heun, H. T., 287
Hieronymus, T. A., 216
Highways, 84–85
Hill, Kenneth E., 113–116
Hitchings, George P., 108n., 221–222
Hoadley, Walter I., Jr., 254, 278–279
Hoffenberg, Marvin, 96
Hours of work (see Working week)
Households, 66–71, 296–298
    classification, 298n.
    compared with families, 66, 298
    declining size of, 70
    quasi, 66, 297
Howard, John A., 261n.
Hubbard, Joseph B., 185
Hultgren, Thor, 143, 332–333

Illegal expenditures, 13
Imputations, 8n., 12–13
Industrial production, 24–27, 140, 148–150, 155, 193, 195–196, 229
    divisional parts, 27
    in relation, to GNP, 26–27
        to investment, 78n.
    as sensitive measure, 133–134
Industry forecasts, 94–132, 218–235
    relation to company, 98
    survey, 233, 243
Industry survey, 14–15, 136–138
    (See also Market situation)
Input-output tables, 51–52, 94–96, 189–190, 193
    and output forecasts, 95–97
Installment credit, 309

Intention reports, 232–233, 319–320
Interest payments, 11, 23, 188–189
Interest rates, 154, 158–162, 299–301
    and investment, 73–74
International Harvester, 240
Inventories, 15–16, 78–80, 140, 148, 154, 191–192, 205, 258, 279–280, 286, 320
    classification, 137, 172, 186, 212
    and foreign investment, 187
    policy, 5–6
    and price changes, 198
    and price decline, 203
    ratio to sales, 78–80, 171, 173, 186
    regression to sales, 171–172
    valuation adjustment, 16, 21
Investment, 10, 13–16, 131, 152, 204–205
    anticipations, 14–15, 146–148, 180–181, 185, 323–329
    capital-consumption allowance, 9, 19, 21, 73
    capital-demand factors, 299
    equipment, 14, 72
        by industry purchasing, 77
    financing plans, 147
    foreign, 17–18, 187–188
    government, 16
    and interest rates, 73–74
    as a per cent of output, 74–78, 90
    per employee, 78n.
    in relation to industrial production, 78n.
    repair and maintenance, 14
    replacement, 9, 73, 75, 132
    and research expenditure, 42–43
    and saving, 20–21
    and self-substantiating forecasts, 198, 320–321, 329
    starting and completion rates, 174–175, 191–192, 199
    (See also Residential building)

Jacobs, Walter, 126–127, 173
Jaffee, A. J., 48n.
Jewel Tea Company, 253
Johnson, N. O., 33n.
Johnson and Johnson, 272
Joint Economic Committee, 57–58, 340–341
"Jury of executive opinion," 241

Keller, I. Wayne, 268–269
Kendrick, John W., 39–41, 53n.
Keynesian theory, 35
King, Edmund R., 284–287
Kirkpatrick, Nora B., 341–344
Kish, Joseph F., 32
Klein, Lawrence R., 336
Koffsky, Nathan M., 188–189, 230–232, 319–320
Korean incident, 323, 335
Kravis, Irving B., 108n., 222n.
Kyrk, Hazel, 333n.

Labor float, 30, 49–51
Labor force, 27–28, 36–38, 43–48, 155
and participation rates, 45–48
short-term changes, 288–289
Lansing, John B., 336n.
"Law of the too heavy anchor," 263
Lawler, Frank K., 235–236
Leading series, 141–142, 161–164
and coincident and lag series, 142, 162
single index, 158
(*See also* Diffusion index)
Lee, E. S., 295n.
Leffler, George L., 304–305
Life Insurance Association of America, 140
Lippitt, Vernon G., 333n.
Little, Arthur D., Inc., 128–129
Lockheed, 256
Logistic curve, 31–33
Lorie, James H., 251–252
Luedicke, Heinz, 215
Lusher, David M., 189n.
Lynip, B. F., Jr., 209–210

MacDonald, W. W., 235
McGill Commodity Service, 216
MacGowan, T. G., 254, 263
McGraw-Hill Department of Economics, 146, 207–208
Machinery and Allied Products Institute, 75
Macy, R. H., and Company, 253
Magee, John, Jr., 304–305
Malthusian law, 34–35
Market Research Corporation of America, 244

Market situation, 171–174, 191, 212–213, 244–245
and disaggregation, 171
and later-stage inventories, 245
(*See also* Industry survey)
Market surveys, 246
using salesmen, 240–241
Methods used in forecasting, 29–35, 189–194, 210, 234–235, 252–253
Metropolitan areas, 294–295
Michigan Research Seminar, 193–194
Mitchell, G. A., 267
Mitchell, W. C., 141–142
Modligiani, Franco, 332
Monetary policy, 160, 301
price effect, 204, 208
Money flows, 140, 258, 271–274, 299
Money gradient, 208
Money supply, 61, 140
Moore, Geoffrey H., 141–142, 144, 161–164
Morehouse, E. W., 282
Mortgage debt, 139–140
Mortgages, commitments to purchase, 140
Mossiman, Ary, 112n., 228

"Naïve" models, 176, 211–212, 245–246, 251–252, 312–315, 333
National Association of Purchasing Agents, 150, 168–169, 215, 221
National Biscuit Company, 267
National Electrical Manufacturers Association, 243
National income (*see* Product expenditures)
National Industrial Conference Board, 85, 145n., 147, 255
National Planning Association (*see* Colm, Gerhard)
Natrella, Vito, 146–147, 323–329
Neilson, A. C., Company, 244n.
New technology, 77
Newbury, Frank D., 247n., 264–265
Newman, F. B., 251n.
NRA, 346
Nystrom, Paul, 310

Orcutt, Guy H., 333n.
Orders, 148, 155, 172–173, 212, 279
and timing of sales, 173–174

Otis Elevator Company, 258
Outlet industries (*see* End-use analysis)
Overestimation in forecasting, 317

Paarlberg, Don, 336–338
Paley report (*see* President's Materials
  Policy Commission)
Paradiso, Louis J., 171–172
Parker, Sanford S., 75–78, 90, 106–108,
  132, 306
Parson, Daniel, 116–118
Participation rates, 45–48, 289
Passer, Harold C., 333*n.*
Patey, Richard L., 277–278
Pattern of wage rates, 307–308
Patterns of relationship, 190
Pearl, Raymond, 31–34, 322
Peirce, James L., 270
Personal consumption expenditures, 10,
  12–13, 89–90
  and disposable income, 188
  long-run relation to GNP, 89–90, 188
  retail trade, 138
Personal income, 18–19
Persons, Warren M., 158, 177*n.*
Petrochemicals, 127–128
Petroleum industry, 113–116, 233–234
  coal competition, 114, 119
  and foreign production, 116
  and gas consumption, 114–115, 117*n.*
  and other energy uses, 114–115
  predictions of paired economists, 233*n.*
  relation to efficiency in energy use,
    113–114
Phillips, Charles F., 309*n.*
Pig-farrowing intentions, 232, 320
Planning and coordination in forecasting,
  242, 266–267
Plans, instability of, 148, 170, 327–328
Polk, R. L., and Co., 108
Population, 155, 292–296, 322–323
  fertility assumptions, 44, 292–293
  and migration, 44–45
  mortality assumptions, 44, 294
Postwar forecasts, 341–345
Prepackaged foods, 235–236
President's Materials Policy Commission,
  2*n.*, 89, 95–97, 119–120, 127–128
Price, D. C., 295*n.*
Price deflation, 18, 344
Price deflators, implicit, 136

"P/V"ratio, 216
Prices, administered, 7, 199–200, 213,
  259
  agricultural, 216–217
  changes in, 6–7, 134–136, 148, 198–
    217
  and capital replacement, 73
  during contraction, 202–205
  critical expenditures, 207
  and debt, 210
  demand and supply factors, 207–211
  effect on incentives, 60
  during expansion, 200
  and financial commitments, 60
  and foreign demand, 207
  and government support, 204
  and GNP model, 182*n.*
  and inventories, 198
  and monetary policy, 208
  and money expansion, 59–60
  and operating rates, 210
  during prosperity, 201–202
  secular, 59–63
  self-justifying, 198
  stabilizing influence in recession, 199
  starting and completion rates, 174–
    175, 199
  and unemployment, 208
  consumer, 135–136, 152
  spot, 135, 156
  wholesale, 135, 156, 159
Product expenditures, 8–24, 140
  as inclusive measures, 133–134
  income assumed, 92–93
  model, 177–194
  percentage distribution, 90
  projection, 50–58, 91
    comparisons, 57–58
  relation to disposable income, 22–24
  statistical discrepancy, 20–21
  trend projection versus causal analysis,
    54–55
Productivity, 36–43
  and capital formation, 42–43, 51
  and composition of output, 30, 40–42,
    290
  factors responsible, 37–38
  and fatigue, 42
  of government, 39*n.*
  and GNP projection, 50–58
  short-period variation, 39–40, 290

Profits, 152, 189
Proprietorship income classification, 189

Quasi households, 66, 297

Railroad shippers' forecasts, 332–333
Railroads, 235, 306
Randel, Robert E., 283
Rate-of-change model, 176, 211–212
Rautenstrauch, Walter, 238n., 268n., 271
Reed, Lowell J., 32, 322
Reforecasting, 263, 321
Regional forecasting, 111, 291, 293–296
Reid, Paul M., 296n.
Repair and maintenance, 14
Replacement, capital, 9, 73, 75, 132
Research expenditure, 42–43
Residential building, 65–71, 225–228
  additions and alterations, 66
  anticipations, 227–228
  capital per unit, 71
  costs, 68, 227
  fix-up, 228
  and household formation, 66, 70, 225–226
  and interest rates, 227
  long cycles, 71
  and migration, 226
  replacement of, 67–68, 71
  seasonal dwellings, 70–71
Resistance level, 305–306
Retail trade, 138
Rhea, Robert, 305n.
Ricardian iron law, 35
Rich, James L., 263, 276–277
Roberts, William E., 267
Robinson, Roland I., 300–301
Rogers, Robert O., 125n.
Roos, Charles F., 208–209, 222, 254
Roosevelt, Franklin D., 346
Rosenbaum, Arthur, 283–285
Ross, Kenneth D., 178–182

Sales, 155
  as barometer, 134
  versus orders, 137
Sales budget, 238, 268–271, 277, 287
Sales-department responsibility, 261–262, 264

Sales forecasting, 237–288
  long-term, 255–256, 280–282, 286
  and related industry, 260
  relation to aggregate industry, 254–255
  top- versus low-level, 265
Sales-force method, 239–241
Sales manager composite, 240
Salesmen call reports, 275, 283
Sapir, Michael, 345
Sauerlander, Owen H., 332
Savings, 20, 155
  and investment, 20–21
  projected balance with investment, 93
  supply of funds, 299
  unincorporated businesses, 24
Savings Banks, Mutual, National Association of, 140n.
  New York State, 140n.
Scripps Foundation, 322
Sears, Roebuck and Company, 283–285
Seasonal variation, 194–197, 224, 247, 258, 278–279, 284, 301
  aggregate, difficulty in forecasting, 196–197
  irregular, 194
  and product mix, 195
  in total manufacturing, 195–196
  and urgent demand, 194
Sebald, W. W., 220
Secular stagnation, 35
Seideman, Bert, 333n.
Self-defeating forecasts, 167, 319–320
Self-substantiating forecasts, 198, 319–321, 329
Serial correlation, 245–246
Skeptic's technique, 251–252, 279
SKF Industries, 267
Smith, A. O., 240
Smith, B. B., 158n.
Smithies, Arthur, 333n.
Snider, J. L., 159
Spears, Richard F., 246n.
Stanberry, Van Beuren, 295n.
Standard costs, 237
Standard Statistics Company, 347
Stanford Research Institute, 52n., 57–59, 128–130
Starting and completion rates, 174–175, 191–192, 199
Statistical discrepancy, 20–21
Statistical-indicator method, 145–146

Statistical Indicators Associates, 145n., 162
Stauffacher, Charles B., 269n.
Steel alloys, 104
Steel industry, 99–104, 219–221, 276–277
  and competitive materials, 103
  and industrial production, 100–101
  inventories, 220–221, 277
  and population growth, 99–100
  unfilled orders, 221
  and use factors, 101, 219–220, 277
Stegeman, Arthur J., 112n., 228
Stein Roe and Farnham, 178–182
Steinberg, Hyman, 85n.
Stewart, C. D., 48n.
Stock market, 156, 158–161, 301–306
  forecasting survey, 306
  and self-substantiating forecasts, 321
  technical variation, 302–304
Stock yields, 154
Stouffer, Samuel, 333n.
Suits, Daniel B., 193–194
Surprise effect, 321
Survey Research Center, 170, 333–336
Swift and Company, 253, 255
Synthetic fibers, 128–129

Teleki, Arved, 281
Telephones, 125–126
Terry, Lyon F., 117n.
Textile industry, 234
Thompson, G. Clark, 255n., 322
Thompson, Warren S., 322
Time horizon of forecast, 63–64, 125–126, 317, 321
  short- versus long-term, 98–99
Timing differences (*see* Leading series)
Tobin, James, 333n.
Towle, Howard C., Jr., 125–126
Transfer payments, 11, 23, 82, 189
Triangle, symmetrical, 305
Twentieth Century Fund, 41, 52–58, 68–69, 74, 83–86, 88–90, 95, 131

Ulin, Robert P., 6n.
Underestimation, in forecasting, 317, 344
  of growth, 117–118

Unemployment, 27–28, 291, 345
Union Carbide and Carbon Corporation, 255, 281–282
United States Steel Corporation, 104, 276–277
Upgren, Arthur R., 5n.
Use of forecasts, 97–98, 238, 256–259, 315–318
  business, 3–7
  compared with making, 261–262
  government, 2–5

Value Line Investment Survey, The, 145n., 304
Villers, Raymond, 238n., 268n., 271

Wage rates, 307–309
Wasson, R. C., 22n.
Water transportation, 85
Water use, 120–122
Weather forecasts, 311–312
Welsch, Glenn A., 268n.
Westinghouse Electric Corporation, 253, 255
Weyerhaeuser Timber Company, 128–130
Whelpton, P. K., 322–323
Wimsatt, Genevieve B., 171–173
Winger, John G., 113–116
Winston, Clement, 126–127
Wood, 128–131
Wooden, D. G., 22n.
Working week, 36–38, 142
  and overtime, 49–50
  and paid vacations, 49
Woytinski, W. S., 345
Wright, C. Ashley, 145–146

Yocum, H. A., 233
Young, Marilyn, 35n., 69, 74–75, 79–80, 87–88

Zeluff, Vin, 235
Zisette, Robert R., 267